Hostilities Only

HOSTILITIES ONLY

Training the Wartime Royal Navy

Brian Lavery

First published in 2004 by the
National Maritime Museum, Greenwich
London SE10 9NF

ISBN 0 948065 48 6

1 2 3 4 5 6 7 8 9

A CIP catalogue record for this book is available
from the British Library.

Design and production by The Book Group

Printed and bound in the UK

CONTENTS

Acknowledgements

This is my first book on the Second World War (though I have published more than a dozen on ships and navies of earlier periods). There are numerous works on the ships and operations of the war, and many personal memoirs and anthologies, but I believe this is the first to tackle the personnel side of the Royal Navy in any detail.

The research was largely done in the National Archive (formerly the Public Record Office) and with the Royal Naval Museum's collection of Admiralty Fleet Orders. I am grateful to Campbell McMurray and Matthew Sheldon of the latter institution for their help. In the National Maritime Museum, Jill Davies, Daphne Knott, Kiri Ross-Jones, Hellen Pethers, Janny Harris and Liza Verity of the Library and Manuscripts Department have been especially helpful. At the Ministry of Defence Naval Library, Jenny Wraight and Iain Mackenzie provided many interesting documents.

I am grateful for comments by Jock Gardiner of the Naval Historical Branch, Vice-Admiral Sir Barry Wilson, formerly of the Royal Naval Museum, Dr Eric Grove of the University of Hull, Commodore Duncan Ellin and Alan Pearsall.

Thanks are also due to Rachel Giles, Fiona Renkin and Eleanor Dryden of the National Maritime Museum Publishing Department.

CHAPTER 1

The Navy in 1939

Just over a million people – 923,000 men and 86,000 women – served in the Royal Navy during the Second World War. At its peak in June 1945 it had 783,000, plus 72,000 women. This was considerably less than the army, with more than 3 million men and women, or even the Royal Air Force with 1,103,000, but it was far greater than any navy that Britain put to sea at any other time. In 1810, at its peak during the great conflicts with France, 142,000 were in the service. During the First World War it rose to 420,000 men.

Naval service is far more detached from 'ordinary' life on shore than the army or the air force. It has a much more distinctive culture, and requires far more induction and training. It is also more likely to leave a lasting impression on those who serve, and the great majority of these million men and women returned to civilian life with broadened horizons and in many cases a permanent attachment to Britain's senior service. Nearly 700,000 men were recruited into the Royal Navy and Royal Marines during the war and 665,000 of these were conscripts or short-term volunteers.[1] The training of these men, and the women of the Women's Royal Naval Service, was a major task in wartime Britain. The country had raised citizen armies before, as had most other countries. This would be the first real citizen navy, the only one in history apart from the Commonwealth navies and the United States Navy in the same conflict.

Early Training

In the days of sail, the Royal Navy did very little to train its men in seamanship. The most important men were recruited by press gangs from the merchant service, where they had learned the trade from an early age. The idea of gangs taking in large quantities of landsmen is a myth, for captains had little use for them. Indeed in 1744, the Admiralty received 'frequent complaints, that when able bodied landmen have voluntarily offered to serve on board His Majesty's Ships, the Captains and other Officers, to whom they have applied, instead of encouraging and inviting them, have threatened and intimidated them, and even refused to receive them …'[2] They were ordered to take them on if medically fit, and to 'take care that they be practiced in going frequently every day up and down the shrouds and employed in all kinds of work which are to be created in purpose for them both to keep them in action and to teach them the duty of seamen.'[3] This was as far as systematic training went. The navy did teach its seamen gunnery, but mainly in the rapid fire of the weapon rather than in accuracy of aim. Smooth-bore guns had a very short range, and Nelson's dictum that 'No captain can do very wrong if he places his ship alongside that of an enemy'[4] remained gunnery policy. The sailor of Nelson's navy was a very unmilitary figure. There was no uniform for ratings and seaman tended to subvert any attempt to drill them in a military fashion, for they despised soldiers and marines as mindless automatons.

The first great revolution in naval training came in the middle of the nineteenth century. Since the repeal of the Navigation Acts in 1849, it was no longer compulsory for merchant ships to carry a proportion of apprentices, or to have mainly British crews, so that source was beginning to dry up. The press gang was no longer acceptable and was not used in the Crimean War which began in 1854. Warships now needed engines, initially as an auxiliary to sail, and engineers had to be fitted into the social strata on board ship. From the mid 1850s, naval ratings were put into a regular uniform, with bell-bottom trousers and the famous three stripes round the square collar. They were now recruited as boys at the age of about fifteen, and trained *ab initio* in hulks, and then in small training ships, before going on to the fleet. For the first time they signed on for a specific period. Since most naval operations of the age involved landing parties of seamen and heavy guns to support armies in the British Empire, the seaman began to take on an increasingly militaristic character.

The second revolution was in gunnery. Guns now fired shells filled with explosives, but the wooden sides of Nelson's day had been replaced by ever-stronger armour. During the late nineteenth century the range of guns increased dramatically and long-range gunnery became an art. By 1914 it was a science, with mechanical computers used to calculate the movements of the enemy.

Officers

At the same time there was some reform in officer training. In Nelson's day they had been started in their careers by the captains of individual ships, often family or political friends. They were trained by a kind of apprenticeship, which produced many good officers but gave the central authorities little control over the process, and seemed corrupt to the different sensibilities of the Victorians. Fewer ships were at sea in the long peace of the nineteenth century so there were few opportunities for new entrants. A new system of centralized training was set up in 1859, based on the old 120-gun *Britannia,* at Dartmouth from 1863. Few issues attracted as much controversy during the early years of the twentieth century as the recruitment and training of naval officers. Apart from the content of the training, there were three main areas of contention: the narrow base from

Dartmouth cadets march past Edward, Prince of Wales (later King Edward VIII) in 1922.

which officers were recruited, promotions from the lower deck and the status of the engineer.

Potential officers entered as cadets at the age of about thirteen after a competitive examination, but private means were needed to support a boy at Dartmouth, so entrance was confined to boys from wealthy upper- or middle-class backgrounds, often the sons of naval officers. The long training process proved too slow during the great expansion before the First World War, and a few merchant service officers were taken in as lieutenants via the Royal Naval Reserve, which did broaden the background somewhat. The Special Entry scheme was set up in 1913, with a much shorter course for boys recruited at about eighteen. They proved successful officers, but since they nearly all came from the public schools the social range was not widened.

The naval officer's education was excellent in places.

> For the most part what emerged was a definite breed of fit, tough, highly trained but sketchily educated professionals, ready for instant duty, for parades or tea parties, for catastrophes, for peace or war; confident leaders, alert seamen, fair administrators, poor delegators; officers of wide interests and narrow vision, strong on tactics, weak on strategy; an able, active, cheerful, monosyllabic elite.[5]

There were two routes from the lower deck to commissioned officer status. One was the very slow path of promotion to warrant officer, after service as a petty officer. This gave the status and responsibilities of a junior officer in a specialized field, but further advancement to lieutenant was slow, and was only achieved when the man was too old to expect any further promotion. As First Lord of the Admiralty in 1911–15, Winston Churchill pushed through a scheme by which young ratings would be selected and trained as 'mates', the equivalent of sub-lieutenant, with good prospects for further promotion. It was less successful than Churchill had hoped, largely because the candidates had to do a good deal of study before selection, never easy in the conditions of the lower deck. The trickle of candidates almost dried up in the 1920s, as budget cuts reduced the number of vacancies. A new scheme was started in 1932, the term 'mate' being replaced with 'acting sub-lieutenant'. Eighteen executive officers, fifteen engineers and two marines were commissioned in the next five years, still very small compared with the Dartmouth entry. From 1937 candidates were allowed several months' study time. Twenty-two lower deck officers were commissioned in the next year.[6]

When the first steam engines were fitted to ships after 1815, they were run by civilian dockyard employees or workers from the engineering firms which supplied them. As their range increased this was no longer practicable and the engineering branch was formed in 1837; senior engineers were warrant officers. In 1847 the most senior were commissioned, and over the next half century steam power came to dominate the navy completely, but the status of the naval engineer improved little. In 1902, inspired largely by Admiral 'Jacky' Fisher, there was an attempt to integrate the engineer officer with the executive officers of the seaman branch. Under the Selborne Scheme all would start together at Dartmouth and engineering would be a sub-specialization, like gunnery, torpedoes or signals. Engineer officers could rejoin the mainstream later in their careers and would be eligible for the top commands. But ambitious officers regarded the engineering specialization as a dead end and avoided it. In 1920 when the executive and engineering branches were again separated, the engineer was still inferior to the executive officer.

Seamen

Throughout the social revolutions of the nineteenth and early twentieth centuries the navy continued to believe that a man had to start at an early age to become an officer, seaman or skilled artisan. As late as 1939, Rear-Admiral Tufton Beamish told the House of Commons, 'Training for the sea ought to begin at an early age if the best results are to be obtained.'[7] Since the 1850s, the standard way to become a seaman in the Royal Navy was to sign up between the ages of fifteen and sixteen-and-a-half for a term of ten and later twelve years, which only started when the boy reached the age of eighteen. After this he could sign on for another ten years, taking him to the age of forty and a pension. Some of the recruits came from naval families, others were young men who were enthusiastic about the sea or the chance to travel. Many were orphans, and others came from families who wanted to get children off their hands. In 1941, one man told John Davies, 'Joined as a boy when I was fifteen. ... Me old man shoved me in. I ain't forgiven the old bastard to this day.'[8] Fifteen years of more or less guaranteed employment seemed attractive to many parents in the hungry 1930s, but was less so in later years. In 1946 a petty officer wrote,

> Is our public aware that its young sailors are kidnapped into its senior serv-
> ice at the tender age of 15, and, to ensure that the sentence is binding, they
> have to sign or have signed for them a document stating that for twelve
> years, from the age of 18, their souls belong to the Admiralty? Imagine: fif-
> teen years signed away by children unaware of life's meaning.[9]

Life was harsh on the Boys' Training Establishments, especially HMS *Ganges*. Tristan Jones joined one of the last boys' courses there in the spring of 1940, and saw much of the pre-war system.

> Since I left *Ganges* I have been in many hellish places, including a couple of
> French Foreign Legion barracks and fifteen prisons in twelve countries.
> None of them were nearly as menacing as HMS *Ganges* as a brain-twisting,
> body-racking ground of mental bullying and physical strain. ...

> Life for a boy trainee at HMS *Ganges* was one long harassment from dawn
> – when the bugler sounded "Charlie" – until lights out at nine-fifteen p.m.
> There was hardly a minute of the waking day when we boys were not on
> our feet and doubling, or sat at attention in a classroom, being yelled at.[10]

Boys were frequently caned on the orders of officers, though apparently not as frequently as the trainee officers at *Britannia* in Dartmouth, for official records had to be
kept at *Ganges* and the other boys' establishments. Less formal was extra drill or the
petty officers' use of the 'stonnachie' or club, which was administered without any kind
of control. This did not bear out the Admiralty's assertion that '... life in a Boys' Training
Establishment compares favourably with that in any good school.'[11]

Seamen were of course the largest group in the Royal Navy, a third the total numbers in the fleet. Stokers were the next largest group, about a fifth of the fleet.[12] They
were recruited between the ages of eighteen and twenty-five, so had usually seen a

Boys drilling in cold weather at HMS *St Vincent*, 1935.

little of life outside the service before they joined. The title was somewhat misleading. Stokers did tend the fires in the boiler rooms, but very few ships were now coal fired; oil fuel took much of the drudgery out of the work. Stokers, too, signed on for twelve years of continuous service. The third major group were the Royal Marines. They also joined as young adults, between seventeen and twenty-three. Unlike the stokers they were highly disciplined in a military sense. The corps' main task was to provide part of the complements of major warships, cruisers and above. On board ship they did some of the duties of the seamen, usually manning parts of the main and secondary armaments. Ashore they completed various tasks, including guarding the naval bases and forming a mobile striking force. The marines were about a tenth of the fleet in 1937.

Branches of the Royal Navy, 1937

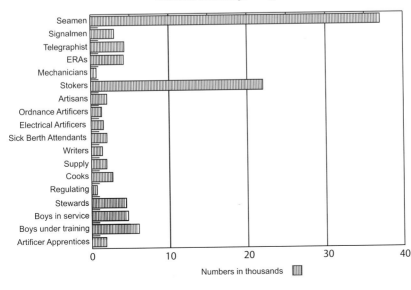

Numbers in thousands

Graph showing intake of men to branches of the Royal Navy, 1937.

The rest of the navy was made up of various specialists. Signalmen were recruited from the better-educated boys in the training establishments. Artificers were skilled workmen who had learned the trade by apprenticeship, inside or outside the navy. The largest body, the Engine Room Artificers, ran the machinery under the supervision of commissioned officers. There were 3452 of them in the fleet in 1937, plus 398 Mechanicians who has risen from the ranks of the stokers. Altogether there were 7360 men of skilled craftsman status in the fleet that year, nearly 7 per cent of the total. Medical officers, of course, trained in medical schools and universities outside the navy, but the ratings of the Sick Berth Branch were trained within the service, in naval hospitals. The ratings of the Accountant Branch handled the administrative and domestic sides of the navy. They included clerical staff (writers), cooks and officers' stewards. All joined as adults, in exceptional cases over the age of thirty.[13] They made up about 7.5 per cent of the fleet.

The Navy and Society

The Royal Navy of the 1930s was as self-contained as any organization could be in the age of wireless and the aeroplane. At its head, the Admiralty still had immense powers, often exercised without the need to refer to any other body. At a lower level, life aboard a ship was always separate from other forms of existence, but it went further than that. Officers, by and large, expected a career for life and hoped to retire as captains or admirals. Most seamen were signed on for twelve years and expected to be in the navy for some time to come. Most seamen's families congregated round the great naval bases at Portsmouth, Devonport (Plymouth) and Chatham and the Admiralty encouraged this by attaching each rating to one of these ports. After retirement, the men probably remained on the lists as members of the Royal Fleet Reserve. They often sent their sons into the navy and the process repeated itself.

The navy had rather ambivalent attitudes to the education system of the country. Only a small proportion of young people went to university in these years. About 10–11,000 men and 3500 to 4000 women matriculated in each year of the late 1930s. This was of little concern to the navy. It had no system of university entry for executive officers, and marine engineers learned their skills at the navy's own college at Keyham. It only recruited graduates for the medical branch, as chaplains and as schoolmaster or instructor officers. The navy demanded basic literacy from boy entrants and nine weeks out of twenty-six of their in-service training were devoted to the continuation of normal education. Likewise, artificer apprentices and the cadets and midshipmen at Dartmouth spent a good deal of time in ordinary school subjects, with a technical bias. For the navy was always sceptical about the ability of the general education system of the country to deliver. In 1942 the Director of Naval Recruiting reported, 'it is curious to relate that in spite of the vast sums spent on education in this Country the percentage of those able to pass a simple and elementary Educational Test is surprisingly low.'[14]

The navy was not completely isolated from trends in society. Unemployment had a positive effect on naval recruiting, making it easier to attract boys to sign on for rather unattractive conditions. Every rating of the early 1930s knew that his chances outside the service were poor with more than 3 million men out of work, and long-service men tended to stay on at all costs. The standard of living ashore was mostly of concern to married ratings, who had to support a family on meagre pay without any official married quarters.

The navy remained rooted in its southern bases and attracted most of its recruits from these areas. Massive unemployment in the shipbuilding areas in Scotland and the north of England did not help naval recruitment; it tended to drive men to the political left, where they rejected the discipline, and the strike-breaking and the imperial roles of the navy. In 1936 the Recruiting Staff Officer for Glasgow, Commander H. T. Strawbridge, told the Admiralty,

> The political views and activities of the "masses" in the Glasgow district is firmly believed to be the principal deterrent to Naval Recruiting in general. The great majority from whom recruits of all branches are taken are rabidly anti-service, so much so, that there have been cases where applicants have stated they dare not mention the fact that they were joining the navy to anyone in their neighborhood for fear of being "roughed".[15]

Naval officers were aware of the political pressures of outside society. On one hand was the pacifism engendered by the slaughter of the First World War. On the other side, the bomber lobby, inside and outside the Royal Air Force, convinced a large proportion of the public that the critical battles of the next war would be fought in the air. For the first time in modern history, the Royal Navy felt the need to justify its existence. From 1929 it staged 'Navy Weeks' in the main ports, learning something from the hugely popular RAF displays at Hendon. *The Wonder Book of the Navy* began with an article on, 'Why do we need a navy?', a question which would not have been asked by a previous generation.

Lean Years

Since its heyday before the First World War, the Royal Navy had suffered a series of traumas. Unlike the Italians and the Russians, it had not been defeated in recent times. Unlike the Germans and the Russians, it had not given rise to mutinies which ended in the overthrow of the state. Yet in view of the great resources given to it in the years before 1914, its performance and its results had been disappointing. In the first place, it had failed to win a great battle against the Germans. Jutland in 1916 was indecisive and was seen as a defeat in some quarters. The supporters of the two British commanders, Jellicoe and Beatty, were still locked in conflict twenty years later. Secondly, the navy had been taken aback by the German submarine campaign of the war and it was the Prime Minister, Lloyd George, who had insisted on the introduction of convoy, which saved the country from disaster.

The naval air arm of the First World War, the Royal Naval Air Service (RNAS), was a very innovative organization, but its duties were not entirely naval, or even aeronautical. It experimented with armoured cars and tanks, and originated the idea of strategic bombing with the Cuxhaven Raid in 1914. Its main duty was to provide shore-based patrols over the sea, a task which was carried out by the Royal Air Force's Coastal Command in the Second World War. Only a small proportion of the force, perhaps 10 per cent, was involved in the purely naval duty of flying aircraft from ships. When the RNAS was transferred to the newly-formed Royal Air Force (RAF) in 1918 the navy lost control of its own air power. By a compromise of 1924 the navy was to provide 70 per cent of pilots and all the observers for shipboard aircraft, but these were still subordinate to the RAF. The two services had very different conceptions of how air power ought to be used.[16]

In the post-war period the navy was cut down to size in ships, officers and resources. Before the First World War it had been built to the 'two-power standard', large enough to fight the two next biggest naval powers in the world. By the Washington Treaty of 1922 it had to accept parity with the United States. Officers had joined expecting a career for life, but the pre-war and wartime boom could not last forever. They were brought to earth when the 'Geddes Axe' of 1922 made a third of officers in certain ranks redundant. The financial and political atmosphere of the time caused further cuts. Exercises had to be carried out at low speed to save fuel, ammunition was rationed, and obsolescent equipment was not replaced.

The Effects of Invergordon

The next shock came from the lower deck. When the crews of several major ships of the Atlantic Fleet refused to sail from Invergordon in September 1931, it was a direct protest against pay cuts imposed by the government, via the Admiralty. These fell hardest on able seamen (ABs) who had signed on before 1925 and qualified for a basic pay of 4 shillings (20 pence) per day. This was to be cut by a quarter. The government made some concessions and the ships sailed immediately to their home ports, but the lower deck expected victimization and indeed a few men were discharged from the navy into the harsh economic climate of depression Britain. The officers were devastated at the ease with which their authority was undermined and suspected a communist plot. It was recognized that the causes went deeper than a mere pay cut, that trust between officers and men needed to be rebuilt.

In his reports on the affair, Admiral Sir John Kelly saw how the behaviour of some officers could antagonise the lower deck.

> Rowdy parties in Officers' Messes which, if imitated on the lower deck, would not fail to be immediately suppressed, and would probably result in disciplinary action.

> Supper parties or "Egg and Spoon Parties" on board ship late at night ... usually following a dance on shore.

Officers who indulged in such 'derelictions', according to Kelly, would never earn the description, 'He's a proper gent, he is.'[17]

The petty officers had done nothing to suppress the mutiny and Kelly believed that most of them were promoted for technical skill or seniority, rather than leadership. 'The proportion of Petty Officers who fall short in their sense of responsibility and power of command' was 'fully 75 per cent of the whole.' Even worse, the leading seamen were often intimidated. 'A young Leading Seaman's authority with a three-badge Able Seaman is practically nonexistent.'

These three-badge men were an important part of the problem. A seaman was awarded a 'badge' or chevron after three years' service with good conduct, and gained 3 pence (1.25 pence) per day. He got his second badge, with another 3 pence, after eight years and his third after thirteen. Many men remained as able seamen because of misconduct or lack of ability or ambition. All, by definition, had joined before 1925 and qualified for the higher rate of pay, so they were the leaders of the Invergordon Mutiny. Kelly proposed to reduce the number of three-badge ABs. He found that a quarter of the men below Leading Seaman in the battleship *Nelson* had three badges and felt this was too many. When men came to the end of their twelve years without promotion beyond Able Seaman, they should not be taken on again without serious consideration. He also proposed a revival of the Short-Service scheme, by which men signed on for seven years with the fleet and five years with the reserves.[18] This was soon adopted, an important reversal of a long-standing policy by which long service had been valued above all.

The Shape of the Fleet

Through all its troubles of the previous twenty-five years, the Admiralty remained faithful to the big-gun battleship as the final arbiter of naval conflict. Of course the admirals had no way of knowing that the next enemy would be Germany, with a relatively small number of capital ships. During this period there were rivalries with the United States and France, not to mention the eventual enemies of Japan and Italy, all of whom had strong battlefleets. Lord Chatfield, First Sea Lord from 1933–38, provided the ultimate defence of the great ships.

HMS *Renown* at the Jubilee Review, 1935.

If we rebuild the battlefleet and spend many millions doing so, and then war comes and the airmen are right, and all our battleships are rapidly destroyed by air attack, our money will have been largely thrown away. But if we do not rebuild it and war comes, and the airman is wrong and *our* airmen cannot destroy the enemy's capital ships, and they are left to range with impunity on the world's oceans and destroy our convoys, then we shall lose the British Empire.[19]

The Admiralty also fought hard for an increased cruiser force because Britain needed large numbers to protect its far-flung empire. By the Treaty of London in 1930 it was allowed fifty instead of the seventy it wanted.

Other parts of the fleet were neglected. Amphibious warfare was hampered by inter-service rivalry or lack of interest. If the Admiralty neglected submarines, it was mainly because they constantly tried to have them banned by the disarmament conferences. This was less crucial to the coming war than the neglect of anti-submarine techniques. Between the wars anti-submarine officers produced optimistic reports of their success in exercises, and officers of the gunnery and torpedo branches were happy to believe them, lest resources be diverted from their own specialties.[20] In 1934 the Admiralty asked for increased sums to spend on various projects, but only £250,000 for anti-submarine warfare, spread over five years.[21]

The Fleet Air Arm was a special case of neglect, mostly hampered by rivalry between the navy and the air force. The standard air historian's charge that the Admiralty of 1918–39 lacked 'air-mindedness' is clearly absurd – if that had been so, it would not have fought so hard to regain control of the air arm. There is, however, a grain of truth that there was no one in the higher ranks with experience of the air, for virtually all naval officers with flying skills had transferred to the RAF on its formation in 1918. In 1937, after nearly two decades of pressure, a new agreement was reached. The Fleet Air Arm would have control of all ship-borne aircraft, providing their aircrews and servicing crews, with shore airfields to support them; the RAF would continue to supply and man the land-based aircraft which operated over the sea. This was no triumph for the navy, just a barely adequate compromise.

The Reserves

The navy had three main reserves of personnel. The Royal Fleet Reserve (RFR), the most favoured by the Admiralty, consisted of men who had served their time in the navy. They were of course fully familiar with naval ways, but many were too old for active service, and as shore instructors they might be out of touch with the latest technological developments. The RFR had 19,000 members in 1937. Retired officers and rating pensioners were also liable to mobilization; in 1939 there were 12,000 officers and 29,000 rating pensioners under the age of fifty-five. There was no way to expand the numbers in the short or medium term, as the RFR and the retired list depended entirely on the number of men who had served in previous years.

The Royal Naval Reserve (RNR) consisted of officers and seamen of the mer-

A Blackburn Shark on a lift on HMS *Courageous* in the mid-1930s. The mixture of RAF and navy personnel is very typical of the times.

chant navy and the fishing fleet. Large shipping companies often encouraged their officers to take part in naval training. Fishing boat skippers formed a distinct part of the
RNR, as warrant officers who were likely to command minesweepers and anti-submarine craft in wartime. But the experience of 1914–18 suggested that the RNR
was not the perfect reserve. Merchant Navy officers tended to regard the safety of
the ship and economic passage-making as their main aims. Furthermore, past experience and future threat of submarine war suggested that the merchant sailors would
be needed in their own service. In 1937 the RNR had 9562 officers and men, about
half the numbers on the outbreak of the last war.

The Royal Naval Volunteer Reserve (RNVR) consisted of amateur seamen who
trained weekly in drill ships and spent a certain amount of time at sea with the fleet.
The idea had been foisted on the Admiralty by public opinion at the beginning of the
century, and at the outbreak of war in 1914 they showed their mistrust of amateurs
by sending many of them to fight as soldiers on the Western Front. Later in the war
the Admiralty began to learn that the RNVR could be useful in the new skills of anti-
submarine warfare. In the inter-war period the Admiralty gave slightly more priority to the RNVR, for it was now desparately short of men. RNVR divisions were re-
established in eight major ports and the members were enthusiastic, but the force
was never large. The RNVR had a ceiling of 5500 officers and men in 1924. In
September 1938 it was decided to add three more divisions, but there was not
much time left. It totalled only 809 officers and 5371 ratings at the outbreak of war.
It was proposed to form RNVR anti-aircraft units, but this was overtaken by
events.[22]

The Royal Naval (Wireless) Reserve began as a group of radio amateurs with limited
Admiralty support. In 1935 they went on board the fleet as civilians, but their status
caused problems, so it was decided to enroll them in a special division of the RNVR.

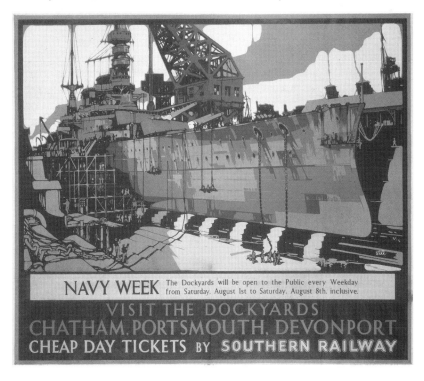

A poster for a Navy Week at
Chatham Dockyard, showing a
battleship in dock.

They numbered 457 in 1937. The Sick Berth Branch consisted of trained medical personnel, mostly from the St John's Ambulance Association. There were 1450 of them in 1937. In all there were 55,583 reservists in 1937, less than half the numbers of the active fleet of 112,000 men.[23]

The Revival

In 1933 the Nazis came to power in Germany, determined to wipe out the losses of the First World War. By 1934 any hope of general disarmament had been given up and the navy was allowed a modest expansion. It began work on its first modern aircraft carrier, the *Ark Royal*. Meanwhile, Nazi Germany, Fascist Italy and Imperial Japan were all showing aggressive, expansionist tendencies. In 1936–37 five new battleships of the *King George V* class were ordered, along with aircraft carriers of the *Illustrious* class. From a low point of £90 million in 1933–34, the Navy Estimates rose to £119 million in 1938–39. This created a favourable atmosphere for naval recruiting. One office had examined 984 volunteers in 1936, rising to 1321 in 1937 and 1838 in the following year. 1729 were examined during the first eight months of 1939, before the war broke out.[24] The pacifist movement engendered by the First World War, while still strong, was no longer dominant in society.

By 1939 the navy had put some of its problems of the last twenty-five years behind it. The Jutland controversy was fading. Jellicoe and Beatty had both died in 1936 and most of their colleagues had retired. The Jutland issue remained of interest, but it had become academic rather than personal. Despite exaggerated faith in Asdic, convoy was adopted as the standard means of protecting merchant shipping in 1937, and this proved a wise decision. With a major war in sight, officers' careers and employment prospects were as good as ever. The lower deck was more contented than in 1931, though not all its problems had been solved. The Fleet Air Arm had been won back, and battleship construction had resumed. Plenty of new problems would come up in the next few years, still undreamed of.

The navy of 1939 was not without its divisions, but it had no great feud to compare with the divisions caused by Fisher's reforms early in the century, or between the supporters of Jellicoe and Beatty in the twenty years after Jutland. Materially it seemed less prepared for war than a quarter of a century ago. Intellectually, it was better prepared. Perhaps its greatest advance, compared with 1914, was its adaptability and resourcefulness, nurtured in the tribulations of the last quarter century.

The Royal Navy was 'probably the most conservative institution in the world' according to Dame Vera Laughton Mathews, the wartime Director of the WRNS, and to David Kirkwood, a 'Red Clydeside' MP, it was 'the most conservative institution in this country.'[25] But despite popular myth, the navy was usually very good at adopting new technology. How would it cope with a vast influx of recruits, women as well as men, mostly with no seagoing experience and not all willing to serve? More immediately, where would it find the means to hold the line against the greatest threat to Britain's existence in the twentieth century, and to train the new navy at the same time?

CHAPTER 2

The Expansion of
the Navy

Mobilization

On 3 September 1939, the first day of the Second World War, Winston Churchill was invited to return to office as First Lord of the Admiralty. He had been forced to resign from the same post in 1915 over the failure of the Dardanelles expedition and had last held government office as Chancellor of the Exchequer in 1929. Since then he had been a political maverick, drawing attention to the dangers of German expansion long before the establishment was ready to face up to it. A famous signal went out to the fleet – 'Winston is back.'

Winston Churchill returns to the Admiralty on the first day of the war, 3 September 1939.

One of his first tasks was to oversee the full mobilization of the navy. It had been practised many times before and went reasonably smoothly. Of 73,000 men in the various reserves, about 62,500 were called up by the end of the year. The older pensioners were given shore-based jobs in recruitment, training and administration, while younger men went to sea. The older ships of the reserve fleet were brought forward, and merchant vessels and fishing boats were taken into service. But many more men would be needed for the five battleships, six large aircraft carriers, nineteen cruisers, thirty-two destroyers, eleven submarines and sixty-eight escort and mine warfare vessels already under construction, not to mention the ships that would soon be ordered under the first War Emergency Programme, and future needs which could not be predicted. The extra officers and seamen would have to be found outside the normal range of naval recruitment.

The Precedents
The navy had only limited precedents on which to base its policy of expansion. During the First World War this issue had been less for several reasons. In the first place, the navy had been expanding steadily in men and materials for twenty-five years, and was at an unprecedented peacetime level of 146,000 men in 1913. Lord Brassey, an enthusiast for naval reserves, claimed as early as 1906. 'The Navy is in fact being maintained in peace time on a war footing.'[1]

Secondly, Britain had by far the largest seafaring population in the world. The country had 12,862 steamships, totalling more than 19 million tons. They ranged from small tramps carrying a few hundred tons of coal each, to the great ocean passenger liners such as the *Mauritania*. They were crewed by more than 200,000 men, with 50,000 more in the fishing fleet. Many of these, it was anticipated, could be brought into naval service, if needed.

Thirdly, the presumption of a short war made planning much easier in the short term. Both instructors and half-educated trainees were withdrawn from the training schools on the outbreak of war. This had the potential for disaster as the war dragged on and there was no supply of freshly-trained men. The situation was mitigated by the fact that the main force, the Grand Fleet, was largely static at Scapa Flow. Training courses and examinations were instituted in the Flow from 1916.

When the First World War broke out in August 1914 the Royal Navy had 139,045 men, plus some Royal Marines and coastguard employed on shore duties making a total of 146,047. At the war's peak in November 1917 it had 420,301 men in service, an expansion of 288 per cent. This was not achieved without some effort, but it was not as difficult as it might have been. 46,000 men were found immediately in 1914 by mobilizing the various reserves. One growth area during the war was the Royal Naval Air Service, which also reached nearly 46,000 officers and men in 1917, compared with 708 in 1914. Most of these never went to sea. The whole force was transferred to the control of the RAF on 1 April 1918.

Other parts of the navy had even less to do with the sea. When war began the Admiralty sent most of the amateur seamen of the Royal Naval Volunteer Reserve, along with surplus marines, to fight on the Western Front as the Royal Naval Division – 20,000 of them were still there in 1917. The seagoing navy had expanded largely through its reserves. Compared with the 46,732 reservists mobilized in 1914, there were more than twice as many in 1917, 116,693. They mainly served on anti-submarine work in the fishing boats, yachts and small vessels of the Auxiliary Patrol. The navy proper, including marines afloat, had also expanded, to 212,690 officers and men.

This was an increase of 18 per cent per year, which was not enormous compared with the peacetime growth rate, between 1889 and 1914, of just under 5 per cent per year.[2]

The Problems in 1939

In 1939, in contrast, there was no assumption of a short war, though few predicted the range and scale of effort that would be necessary. This time the merchant and fishing fleets were much less numerous, and in some respects less suitable than they had been. The merchant navy had suffered hard during the inter-war depressions. In terms of tonnage it had only declined slightly, but its ships tended to be bigger and more efficient, and therefore needed fewer officers. The number of masters in the merchant navy declined by 52 per cent between 1911 and 1936. Other deck officers declined by 33 per cent, and engineer officers by 20 per cent. The number of ratings, mostly in the deck and engine room departments, fell by 47,000. Furthermore, it was obvious that large numbers could not be taken out of the merchant navy in wartime.[3] The submarine campaign of the last war had shown how important merchant shipping was in national defence, and this would prove to be even more so in the next, for the country was far more dependent on imported oil to power its ships, aircraft and tanks. Experience had also shown that merchant navy officers did not adapt well to the command of warships. According to Captain Oram of the Admiralty, the navy had learned 'that it was dangerous to use professional sailors for work outside their normal duties of running merchant ships'.[4]

The expansion of a navy poses very different problems than that of an army or an air force, simply because the recruits will spend most of their time at sea, which is not man's natural environment. Flying is even more unnatural, but the great majority of 'airmen' in the RAF never left the ground except as passengers. Even the aircrews did not have to live in the air, and flights of more than twelve hours were rare. The army, of course, did not leave dry land except as passengers in troopships or landing craft, or as parachutists. Between the withdrawal from Dunkirk in June 1940 and the landings in Normandy four years later, the main body of the army was not in contact with the enemy. Fighting in North Africa and the Italian campaign involved a minority of the army. The great bulk was in Britain. In contrast, the navy was constantly engaged from the start of the war.

Furthermore, the seamen lived a very different life from those on shore. Apart from seasickness, the overcrowding of a warship was one of the most difficult factors. As the Duke of Kent said just before the war, 'The sailor leads an existence the parallel of which cannot be found in any other walk of life. Very often the more active the service, the more restricted his movements. In fact, he then becomes confined to the 24 inches allowed him at his mess table, and the 21 inches allowed for him slinging his hammock at night.'[5] In wartime there was almost constant danger in many operations, such as Atlantic and Arctic convoys. Men needed strong character to withstand these conditions, and they needed good motivation, leadership and training.

The Organization of Naval Personnel

The War Cabinet, as set up in May 1940, had effective power over strategy during the rest of the conflict. The political head of the navy, the First Lord of the Admiralty, was not a member of it, nor was he a very strong character, so the role of the Admiralty was basically administrative, except when it intervened in wide-ranging campaigns, such as the pursuit of the *Bismarck* in 1941.

The sea officers serving in the Admiralty in Whitehall alongside civil servants brought recent naval experience to bear, so they tended to rotate every two or three years. The Second Sea Lord, a senior admiral and member of the Board of Admiralty, was in charge of all matters of naval personnel. Officers were appointed to this job without any particular experience of personnel matters. Sir Charles Little, who held the post from 1938 until June 1941, had served in various administrative posts as Director of the Trade Division at the Admiralty, Captain of the Fleet in the Mediterranean and as Deputy Chief of Naval Staff from 1932–35. He left to become head of the British Admiralty delegation in Washington. He was succeeded by Vice-Admiral W. J. Whitworth, who had led the battleship *Warspite* into action at Narvik in 1940, sinking eight German destroyers and becoming one of the few British officers to emerge from the Norwegian Campaign with credit. In March 1944 he was succeeded by Vice-Admiral Sir Algernon Willis, who had served with most of the outstanding officers of the day, and commanded the covering forces at the landings in Sicily and Italy in 1943. According to his future son-in-law, Roderick Macdonald, he was 'monosyllabic, belonging to the "Never complain, never explain" school. One drawback of this enigmatic style lay in subordinates being faced with trying to surmise the reason for a policy or plan, which in the circumstances, and with the limited information available, might seem unreasonable to the uninitiated.' He had no interest in popularity or public relations and believed that 'if a policy was right it would be seen to be so.'[6]

Under the Second Sea Lord was the Director of Personal Services (DPS), a post set up in the aftermath of the Invergordon Mutiny. According to his instructions as issued in 1932, as head of the Manning Division he was 'responsible to the Board for calculation of the personnel, active service and reserve, required to man the Fleet in peace and war …' He was to 'advise from the manning point of standpoint upon recruiting, training, advancement, Royal Fleet Reserve, entry and disposal of boys, and all matters which affect the manning of the Fleet.'[7] In 1944, under a further reorganization, the DPS's department now had three sections, responsible for manning, welfare and service conditions. The Directorate of Manning was formed;

> The greatly increased complexities of manning problems arising from the expansion of the Navy, the introduction of new specialist branches to man the modern armament and equipment of the Fleet, and the shortage of manpower to meet these requirements, appear fully to justify the formation of a separate Directorate to concentrate on the solution of manning and entry problems. The Department will comprise the Sections at present under the control of the Deputy Director (Manning), the Assistant Director (Air) and the Assistant Director (Entry).[8]

Under the Director of Manning, the Deputy Director (Entry) was responsible for the details of the men's allocation.

> With unlimited manpower allocations apportioning of recruits among the various branches of the Navy is comparatively easy, but with reduced and continually varying numbers of entries, the utmost discrimination is necessary to expand the available allocations to the best advantage. With little to guide him, the Head of the Entry Division has to forecast the requirements of the Fleet and its bases for some months hence, make all the arrange-

ments with the Ministry of Labour, determine the standards and qualifications of the recruits, and decide where and when they are to be posted.[9]

In addition, the Commission and Warrant (CW) Branch was in charge of the appointment and conditions of service of officers, and the Naval (N) Branch was responsible for ratings. Until 1941 the Wrens were under CE, or Civil Establishments, at which time they were transferred to the other two branches.

All these branches had to be consulted about any major changes. The policy on the role of volunteers in recruitment is a case in point. Churchill made a rather general statement to the House of Commons on 4 October 1939, and nine days later the Head of the Naval Branch began to look at some of the details. The DPS agreed with them on the 19th, and next day the Director of Naval Recruiting (DNR) added his comments. The file circulated between these three until the 30th, but it was 13 November before Churchill added his own remarks. The policy was more or less settled by this time, but the file continued to circulate between the Naval Branch and Naval Recruiting until the end of the year, when it ended with the DNR's comment, 'This will be carried out. Should the number of volunteers appreciably increase, the position will be reviewed.' In all it attracted fourteen separate comments over two and a half months.[10]

The officers in charge had no particular training for their roles in dealing with naval personnel, except for the general leadership qualities needed for a naval officer. Captain H. K. Oram, who took over as Director of Training and Staff Duties in the middle of the war, admitted it was 'a job which I knew absolutely nothing about and therefore had to spend the first few weeks ferreting around to find out what it meant'.[11]

The Pace of Recruiting

The main determinant of naval recruiting was the ships that had to be manned. In theory demand was reasonably predictable, especially for the larger ships. Battleships might take four or five years to build, motor torpedo boats or landing craft could be launched within a few weeks, but there were many difficulties in wartime: the shortage of skilled manpower and lack of raw materials; changing strategic needs for example after the Fall of France or the entrance of Japan to the war; bottlenecks caused by the supply of engines or armaments; and developments in technology. Numbers of ships might be increased by getting them from foreign powers, notably the United States, or by using the skills of firms such as yacht-builders or locomotive manufacturers, who had never built warships before. Losses were even less predictable. In 1941, the worst year of the naval war, Britain lost two battleships and two battlecruisers, two aircraft carriers, ten cruisers and twenty-three destroyers. If a ship was lost with nearly all hands, such as HMS *Hood* in 1941, it had no immediate effect on the manning situation; if the majority of the crew was saved, such as the *Ark Royal* in the same year, this might help alleviate the position in the short term.

Every ship had a seaman in command and enough engineers to run and maintain its engines without too much need for outside help. The very smallest vessels, the three-man landing craft, had a seaman in charge and a stoker as engineer. Vessels of the coastal forces were not much bigger but were intended to fight rather than carry troops and equipment. They had crews of up to about thirty men, including signallers, gunners, torpedomen, asdic operators and later radar operators as well as seaman and engineers but they, like submarines, were attached to depot ships or shore bases which carried out much of the maintenance and administration. Corvettes, the smallest surface vessels capable of operating independently, had cooks, officers' stewards and clerks of the miscellaneous branches. Big ships included a full range of all the branches in the service, including airmen, for most battleships and cruisers carried catapult aircraft in the early stages of the war.

Each new ship was given a 'scheme of complement' as part of the design process. Heads of the specialist branches at the Admiralty, such as the Engineer-in-Chief and the Director of Naval Ordnance, were consulted about the men needed for their own particular departments. For example the *Captain* class destroyer escorts, bought from the USA in 1941–44, had eight officers and 146 men. The seaman ratings were headed by a chief and four petty officers and had seventy seamen, including nineteen in various gunnery ratings, ten torpedomen and six submarine detectors. There were six radar specialists, four visual signalmen, and six radio operators and coders. The Engineering Branch was headed by a commissioned or warrant engineer or mechanician who had risen from the ranks. It included five Engine Room Artificers, three Petty Officer Motor Mechanics, two Stoker Petty Officers, nine Leading Stokers and eighteen Stokers. There were ordnance and electrical artificers, sick berth attendants, cooks, stewards and supply assistants. If that was not complicated enough, allowance had to be made for variant conditions and armaments. 'In ships with torpedo tubes and only four Oerlikon guns add 1 P.O. [Petty Officer], 2 A.B. or Ord Smn. and add 1 EA [Electrical Artificer], and (without substantive alteration) reduce 1 A.A.3 [Anti-Aircraft Gunner 3rd class] and add 1 T.G.M. [Torpedo Gunner's Mate], 1 L.To. [Leading Torpedoman] and 4 S.T. [Seamen Torpedomen].'[12]

Nearly all ships ended up carrying more men than they had been designed for. The *King George V* class battleships increased by 23 per cent from 1940–45, *Dido* class cruisers by 19 per cent and *Javelin* class destroyers by 18 per cent. Extra anti-aircraft guns and radar did not diminish the need for visual lookouts. The situation was even worse in aircraft carriers. The *Victorious* had been planned for thirty-three aircraft in 1940; by 1945 she carried sixty. The full ship's company, including the air group, rose from 1236 to 2065, or by 67 per cent. The number of aircrew officers rose from 50 to 111.[13]

The Expansion Programmes
Early in 1940 Winston Churchill presented his first Navy Estimate for a quarter of a century. He asked for a free hand in allocating resources for the navy.

> I regret that it is not expedient to lay precise facts and figures of the proposed strength and cost of the Navy in the coming year before the House as we should naturally desire to do. In the first place, it is physically impossible to make exact estimates for contingencies which are constantly changing; and in the second place, there is no need to tell the enemy more than is good for him about what we are doing.

A. V. Alexander, Labour spokesman on naval affairs and soon to become First Lord of the Admiralty himself in the coalition government, agreed. Though it was still the 'phoney war' before the real conflict, Alexander agreed that 'there has been no occasion in the history of our country when the Navy Estimates have been presented in circumstances of greater danger and of greater urgency.' He cited the precedent of the First World War, though in those years the number of men voted for the fleet,

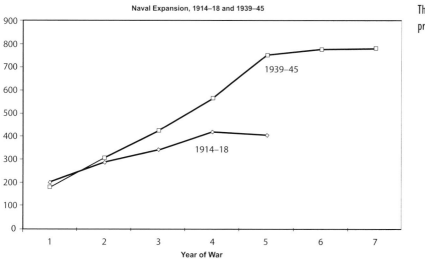

Naval Expansion, 1914–18 and 1939–45

The navy's expansion programmes during the war.

Vote A, had been announced publicly. 'It is obvious to us that it would be unwise to have such detailed information today.' Instead, the House voted for token sums of money, and for 'such numbers of Officers, Seamen, Boys and Royal Marines and of Royal Marine Police, as His Majesty may deem necessary to be borne on the books of His Majesty's Ships and at the Royal Marine Divisions …'. This formula was to be repeated annually for the rest of the war.[14] In the past Vote A had been a serious matter for the government, a total not to be exceeded at any time during the year without going back to ask further permission from Parliament: now, this control was to be removed.

Financial constraints were also removed, and Treasury control was much weakened.

> It has been agreed with the Treasury that forecasts of cash requirements for naval services in the financial year 1940, rendered by Departments and Branches … may be treated as though they had been Navy Estimates approved in the ordinary way. … It will not be necessary to consult the Treasury merely because a proposed service may involve an excess on the Vote or Subhead concerned. But, in order that they may have some idea of the direction in which expenditure is tending to swell or diminish, the Treasury have asked the Admiralty to furnish them with a revised statement of probable expenditure …

This did not pass without protest. 'The proposal is a complete abandonment of any system of financial control as understood by Parliament. It reduces the accounting officer's role to a farce.' But naval manning was subjected to neither financial nor parliamentary control for the rest of the war.[15]

In the first stage, the Admiralty forecast an expansion from 235,000 to 310,000 men, and had no great difficulty in finding them with the aid of conscription; there were still a million men unemployed in April 1940. This programme was soon overtaken by events. The Germans invaded Norway that month, and Churchill replaced Neville Chamberlain as Prime Minister of a coalition government. The enemy attacked the Netherlands, Belgium and France in May, causing British forces to be evacuated from Dunkirk. The war situation was totally changed and new roles were created. The German U-boat campaign was made much more dangerous by bases in France and Norway. The German possession of the Low Countries and the south side of the English Channel made coastal warfare far more likely.

In the short term, more ships were acquired than had been planned for. Some were taken over from the French, while fifty old destroyers came from the neutral United States. Extra merchant ships were converted, while others carried naval gunners for their defence against aircraft. Since it would be necessary to reinvade the continent at a future date, a new Combined Operations organization was set up in June, and needed sailors to develop and man landing craft and ships. The total of 310,000 men was actually reached by the middle of November and the navy was still growing. The Admiralty now proposed to recruit 40,000 more men before April 1941, when the new estimates would be put forward.[16]

The Demand for Men

By the end of 1940 the government was moving towards the idea of a Manpower Budget, which was to prove far more of a constraint than a normal financial budget as the war progressed. As well as an unprecedented expansion in the armed forces, ships and aircraft had to be built, munitions of war supplied, natural resources mined, the transport system kept in operation, and food produced by agriculture. These were the essential industries, but entertainment and culture had to be kept running if morale was not to decline.

The services each put forward their own demands for men, and for the next three years they were usually met in the case of the navy. In September 1940 it wanted to recruit 145,755 men and 13,000 women to the end of 1941, an average rate of nearly 10,000 entrants per month.[17] From mid 1941 it was allocated 110,000 men and 11,000 women recruits until June 1942, substantially the same rate of increase.[18] But by the end of that programme, the manpower resources of the country were approaching exhaustion. Ernest Bevin, the Minster of Labour, wrote in May 1942, 'we have now deployed our main forces and drawn heavily upon the Reserves.' Mobilization of resources had already gone further than it had in 1918, after four years of war.[19]

In November that year the armed forces wanted 1,600,000 more men and women for the following year, including 210,000 for the navy, while industry needed more than a million – but only 1,600,000 were estimated to be available for all the country's needs. Sir John Anderson wrote, 'A gap of this magnitude cannot be closed by the familiar process of trimming the demands and stretching the supply.'[20] Since the immediate danger of invasion had been removed by the German attack on Russia in June 1941, Churchill believed that 'the greatest danger we now face is the U-boat peril', and suggested that priority should go to replacing lost merchant shipping. Alexander persuaded him that it was better to maintain the warship-building programme to protect the merchantmen. The navy was given 85 per cent of the resources it wanted, while the army and RAF demands were cut by half.[21] The Admiralty was pleased. 'The most important event of the year in this connection is the decision of the Cabinet to allow a largely increased number of recruits from the depleted manpower resources of the country. This will involve a record entry, and will impose a severe strain on our resources for training and accommodation.'[22]

In January 1943 an Anglo-American conference at Casablanca agreed plans for a return to the offensive. In the spring the three services, more or less independently, concluded that this would need extra resources. Between them they asked for

373,000 men and women. Again the army and RAF demands were severely pruned, but the navy got practically all the 33,000 men and 10,000 women it wanted, in addition to previous estimates. Its intake was now running at record levels, even by wartime standards. In August that year it took in 18,700 men and 2650 women. In the first years of the war its expansion had been much slower than the army or the RAF, but in the last nine months of 1943 it was allocated 190,000 men and women, compared with 145,000 for the army and 100,000 for the RAF.[23]

The Manpower Crisis

It was expected that 1944 would be the key year of the war, when Europe would be invaded by the allies. Already in May 1943, the projected rise in numbers was causing serious doubts about the training programme, for it seemed impossible to balance the demands of the active fleet with the need for more instructors. The supply of pensioner petty officers and seamen had been exhausted and new resources would need to be found. According to the Second Sea Lord, if 30,000 more men were demanded for the next installment, it would be necessary to pay off four battleships and a cruiser to find the experienced men; if 90,000 were wanted, then the crews would have to be taken out of twelve battleships and three cruisers, or thirty-six cruisers, and 24,000 men would be going through the initial training bases at any one time.

> ... every man in the navy is now earmarked for an immediate job and even then there are not enough to go round, so even if all the instructors were able seamen rated up, some ships would have to be paid off to provide them.[24]

By August the Admiralty was fully aware of the coming crisis and ordered the senior officers of the fleet,

> ... constantly have in mind the seriousness of the manning situation. The man-power and woman-power resources of the country are now reaching their limits and cannot meet all the requirements of the Services. Moreover, the problem is not solely of quantity, but of quality, since the entry of even larger numbers of untrained men from civil life will not provide experienced officers or senior ratings.[25]

Nevertheless in October 1943 the Admiralty put in a huge demand for 247,000 men and 41,500 women. 104,000 men would be needed for new ships coming into service as the naval building programme began to bear fruit. 10,000 more would man landing craft for the invasion, plus 37,000 for the expansion of the Fleet Air Arm, mainly to fight the Japanese. Wastage, anticipated at 53,000 men, had to be replaced and nearly 15,000 new officers were needed.[26]

The standard assumption was that Germany would be defeated by the end of 1944, while British naval effort was to build up in the Far East for use against Japan. Large-scale British participation in the Pacific War began to recede into the distance as full effort would be needed for the invasion of Europe. Also, as Churchill pointed out, the other demands on the navy were less than in the past.

> The question arises, why does the Admiralty require more men in 1944 than in 1943, observing that the new facts are:
> (a) The decisive defeat of the U-boats, largely through the air assistance

(b) The surrender of the Italian Fleet

(c) The accession of the *Richelieu* and many French units to active service

(d) The establishment by the United States of two-to-one strength over the Japanese in the Pacific

(e) The immobilization for a good many months to come of the *Tirpitz,* the only hostile capital ship in the western world (unless the new German carrier is ready)[27]

The navy's allocation was drastically cut to 40,000 men. The Admiralty protested that, on the basis of minimum effort in the Pacific, it would still need 67,200. Even this would involve cuts — half a dozen battleships, one old aircraft carrier, thirteen cruisers and twenty destroyers would have to be reduced to the reserve, or become training ships. Seven light fleet aircraft carriers were expected to complete soon for the war against Japan, but there would be no resources to man them.[28] The manpower situation was reversed. In the early stages of the war the availability of ships had dictated the manning needs; now, ships were laid aside because there were no men to crew them. In the event shipbuilding resources were re-allocated and none of the carriers was finished before 1945. Eventually the figure of 67,200 was agreed, but 17,200 of them would be airmen who would eventually be put in the RAF or the Fleet Air Arm as the situation demanded.

The invasion took place in June 1944 and the naval side was highly successful. Casualties were expected to be 13 per cent, but in fact were much lower. The land side of the operation was less successful. The advance into Germany was far slower than expected and the war was clearly not going to end by December 1944. Far from expanding, the navy lost 6200 of its existing men, who were transferred to the army. Churchill found that there were 80,000 Royal Marines and wanted to know what they were doing. The navy's training programme was questioned.

> Again, let me have precise figures for the intake to the Navy in the next six months, and the numbers employed in all the schools for recruits, both staff and pupils. In my opinion, at least 5,000 recruits who opted for the naval training and who are now in the Navy training schools should be transferred to the Army.[29]

The Admiralty replied that such transfers would be very difficult. More than half the men under training for the navy had volunteered for the service before reaching military age, and it would be a breach of faith to transfer them. Other entrants were mainly specialists — recently there had been few entries for the seaman and stoker branches or the Royal Marines.[30]

The age of naval expansion was over. The British Pacific Fleet arrived on station in March 1945 to revive the national effort in the Far East, two months before the German surrender. It soon found itself a very junior partner to the Americans. In August the first atomic bomb was dropped on Hiroshima and the war ended a month later. At that stage the Royal Navy had 855,000 men and women, little more than the number reached in June 1944. Apart from the mobilization of the reserves, it had quadrupled its size in 58 months since September 1939, an average growth of 65 per cent per year. This was nearly four times the rate of growth in the First World War. Already most sailors were thinking about demobilization, and the Admiralty was making plans to cope with this.

CHAPTER 3

Recruitment

Recruitment

In May 1939 Parliament passed the Military Training Act, introducing peacetime con-scription for the first time in Britain. Men aged twenty and twenty-one were to be called up for six months of military training. Most were to be enrolled in the militia, the part-time reserve of the army, for four years. In the meantime, they were to be 'called out ... for a continuous period of six months for a special course of training at such places as the Army Council might determine.' Men raised in this way were entitled to indicate their preference of the navy or air force, and 'regard was to be had to any pref-erence so expressed.' In the case of the Navy, the men would be enrolled in the newly-created Royal Naval Special Reserve.[1] At first the navy was cautious about the scheme, but the First Lord of the Admiralty decided that 'we should aim at keeping our reserves on the high side, that we should endeavour to provide a course of training which would appeal to the trainees, and generally that our object should be to make the new reserve as useful and popular as possible.'[2] It was planned to call out 12,000 men for the navy in August and September 1939, but this was overtaken by events.

On the first day of war, 3 September, the Military Training Act was superseded by the National Service (Armed Forces) Act. All male British subjects between the ages of eighteen and forty-one were now liable for service. Some were medically unfit or had jobs which were listed in the 107 pages of the *Schedule of Reserved Occupations*. Others could continue in their jobs or education until the armed forces were ready for them. The remainder would be called up by proclamation according to their age groups – men from twenty to twenty-two in December 1939 and from nineteen to twenty-seven in January 1940. The biggest single extension came on 9 May 1940, when men up to the age of thirty-seven were called out. By the spring of 1942, after the act had been amended, men up to forty-six and women up to thirty-one were liable. Women were not eligible for combat roles, and men over forty were posted to 'static and sedentary duties.' Meanwhile, as men reached the age of eighteen they were also conscripted.[3]

Throughout all this, the navy managed to retain a certain voluntary element. The acts still allowed conscripts to express a preference for the navy or the air force. No conscript could be obliged to serve in the Royal Navy or Royal Air Force against his will.[4] A month after the start of the war the Head of the Naval Recruiting Branch wrote,

> The Navy got through the 1914–18 war without any recourse to conscription entries and probably could do the same thing in the present war, but in deference to the government plan for an orderly method of utilizing the manpower of the country was willing to adopt the conscription system. There is, however, no reason why, provided that a controlled system of voluntary entry is maintained, the Admiralty should not equally find part of its manpower requirement from volunteers.

But voluntary recruiting, suggested the Director of Personal Services, would, in practice be confined to 'ratings required for various special services who may be above the age for compulsory military service and need not necessarily be fit for sea service.' This was agreed by Churchill as First Lord of the Admiralty, with the addendum that 'Our policy should be to take all the volunteers who offer themselves, who are not in reserved occupations, etc., and then make up the deficiency by selected men who have been called up and have indicated a preference for the Navy.' This was not announced until the National Service Act was working smoothly.[5] Churchill told the House of Commons,

> The increased wartime requirement for seamen of all ratings will be met by selection from among the men who volunteer for Naval Service when they are called up in the successive age groups. It is hoped that the services of some of the skilled craftsmen we require will be obtained from this source. In the selection of volunteers from these age groups, preference will generally be given to the sea-faring community or those associated with the Naval Service. The Admiralty, however, reserve to themselves the freedom to enter for temporary service from time to time a selected number of volunteers with special qualification outside the age group.[6]

Choosing the Navy
By April 1940 the number of men choosing the navy was embarrassingly high. It could only cope with about 6000 men a month, but already there were 16,000 men who had been medically examined and found suitable; a further 80,000 were awaiting the medical, and this was likely to increase to 100,000 at the next registration of conscripts on 27 April. The navy had only fifty centres for medical examination, the army had 150 and the RAF had sixty, so this was creating a backlog. Men accepted for the army were in the service within two months. The waiting period for the navy was much longer, and the authorities feared this might cause some to volunteer for the navy to delay their call up as long as possible. As a result, many of the men regarded as suitable for naval service were drafted into the army.[7]

The navy competed with the RAF for the best of the recruits. Both services were regarded as more attractive than the army, and needed a large proportion of skilled men. The air force was seen as relatively free from class distinction. Esmond Romilly, Winston Churchill's nephew, volunteered for the air force to avoid 'the interminable drilling, mastery of neatness, submission to all kinds of meaningless routines adminis-tered by a legion of officer class petty tyrants that he anticipated in a war which was basically run by English Tories'.[8] John Davies joined the navy from his job as a school-master and found that his pupils reacted with 'tolerant amusement'. 'All to a man were solidly determined to join the Royal Air Force at the earliest possible moment ...'[9]

In the first registration of conscripts after the start of the war, on 21 October 1939, the figures were 39,000 for the navy and 67,000 for the RAF. After that they ran at about two to one in the RAF's favour. This trend peaked in the aftermath of the Battle of Britain. In November 1940, 52,000 men chose the navy and 155,000 the air force, a margin of nearly three to one. During 1941 the navy seemed the most danger-ous of the services, with the loss of HM ships *Hood, Ark Royal, Prince of Wales, Repulse* and many others. But in September a report showed that its prestige was soaring. The army was still tainted with defeat in France and apparent inactivity since, and more dis-tantly with the Western Front in the last war. The RAF's prestige was declining. People in the south of England felt that its fighters were never in evidence during bombing raids; its men were conceited; it was blamed for recent failures in Crete, and some questioned the morality of men who 'are prepared to shower death from the air on people of any nationality'.

The navy was given almost universal praise. There was a common feeling that officers and men were closer together on board ship, that 'everyone from the admiral downwards shares the danger'. They were 'as always doing their job magnificently'. Each seaman, according to one observer, was 'worth six British soldiers, and three British airmen'. Partly, this was matter of perception. Soldiers and airmen were mostly in bases scattered round Britain, and their grumbles about conditions and leadership could be overheard in pubs and cinemas. The navy was mostly at sea, and sailors were rarely seen outside the naval ports. As one observer said, 'I know no sailors, but I think they are heroic.'[10] These perceptions created a favourable atmosphere for naval recruiting.

At the end of the year the navy still had a very positive image. Five main reasons were found for joining it in preference to other services. The spirit of adventure – 'We have always been a seafaring people'; the prestige of the navy and the individuals who joined it: 'Near the coast, the naval uniform is taken for granted, but in an inland pub a sailor has more glamour than the RAF.' Thirdly, it was believed that the men's welfare was better looked after in the navy. 'While he is afloat, the man has his health and food assured, and is in a settled place.' There was more comradeship and less drilling than in other services. The navy had higher pay and better allowances for family men, and for single men there was 'nothing much to spend it on at sea'. Finally were the negative reasons. The army had its memories of the Western Front. As to the RAF, a typical attitude was 'Don't fancy flying and wouldn't be content with ground duties.'

There were reasons for avoiding the navy, though fear of overcrowding, seasickness and long absences from home came quite low on the list. The RAF appealed to the more adventurous types, and some people complained about the lack of publicity for the navy. But 'by far the most widespread obstacle' was the fear of being rejected. The navy had a long waiting list, and its standards were high. If a man was turned down because of poor eyesight or lack of skills, he would be drafted into the army, for the system made no provision for a second choice. Many recruits preferred to play it safe and volunteer for ground trades in the RAF, which was expanding much faster than the navy at this stage.[11] Arguably this was a defect in the system; if conscripts had been given first, second and third choices, this would have allowed those who failed to make it into the navy to go into the RAF. But the army might have felt that it was getting only the worst recruits. As it was, there was a widespread belief that the army was 'composed of everyone not intelligent enough to gain admittance to the RAF or navy'.[12]

By the beginning of 1942 the difference in preferences was much reduced and in November that year the navy attracted 27,000, the RAF 25,000.[13] The Admiralty put forward reasons for this.

> Possibly due to the Navy being unable to accommodate all those who wished to join it during the early days of the War the rumoured difficulty of getting into the Navy caused the flow of volunteers and Naval Preferences to fall away in the middle of the year [1941], but when later it became generally known that this difficulty had considerably decreased and the possibilities of acceptance were greatly improved the flow ...

It believed that the navy 'with its prospect of world wide service and continuous activity' was more attractive to the younger men who now formed the great bulk of

A 1930s recruiting poster emphasizes the experience of foreign service.

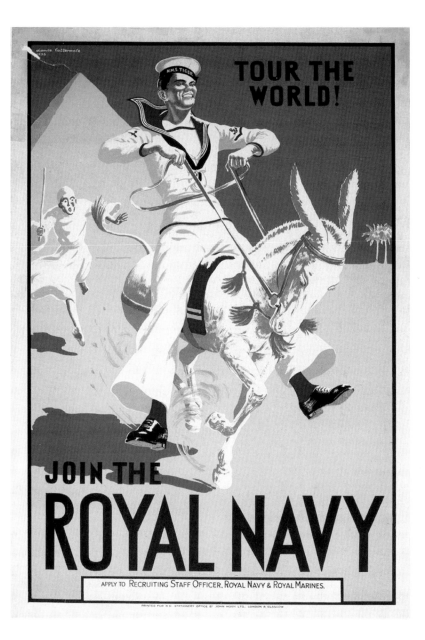

new conscripts.[14] For the rest of the war the navy attracted more preferences than the air force, reaching two to one in the navy's favour in September 1943, and nearly three to one in March 1945. However the overall figures for recruiting were much smaller in these years.

The navy did indeed have attractions for youth, including travel and the uniform. In 1942 Brendan A. Maher visited a recruiting office.

> Peacetime posters, now fading, were still in the windows. One poster portrayed sailors, in crisp white uniforms, smiling and relaxed but ready for anything. Beyond the immaculate decks of their ship rose a background of Malta,

where terraced villas climbed a hill beyond the harbour. … In yet another, still-smiling seamen sat down to dinner, served apparently by white-aproned cooks. This was the life, said the posters. For all these reasons, it seemed inconceivable that anybody would want to serve other than in the Navy. At the age of eighteen, military service would be compulsory. As my own time to serve approached, the decision was obvious; join the Navy.[15]

Volunteering in 1944, George Melly claimed that he was not influenced by his father's commission in the RNVR or his brother's cadetship at Dartmouth. 'It was for no other reason than that I found the uniform "more amusing"'[16] John W. Davies wrote, 'We did not want to be conscripted into any old service. Our minds were made up; we intended to join the Royal Navy, and nothing else would do.'[17]

There was also a negative element in naval recruiting, particularly in the avoidance of the army. J. P. W. Mallalieu recalled his days of military training at public school. 'My memories of the Corps at Cheltenham were still vivid; so I was not going into the army.'[18] Ken Kimberley remembered his school teacher's talks. 'His reminiscences of life in the trenches in the First World War, freezing mud, bayonets, barbed wire and what have you, gave me the creeps. He had seen it all and had first-hand knowledge …'[19]

Unlike the army, the navy did not have to accept all the men who made it their first choice when called up, nor all the volunteers. Much depended on supply and demand at the time. In 1941 the navy accepted just over a third of the men who offered themselves. In 1942, as the great expansion programme got into gear, it accepted three-quarters – almost everyone who came up to medical and craft standards.[20]

During 1939–40, 15,386 men applied to join the navy in the London area. 19.6 per cent were failed for medical reasons and 24.2 per cent for reasons of character, education and so on. Therefore 56.2 per cent went forward to headquarters for the final medical examination, where another 19.4 per cent were rejected. Only 5132, or 32.2 per cent, were finally accepted.[21] This figure of a third was quite common. In 1941 nearly 400,000 men applied to join the navy. Of these, 137,860 were selected by the recruiters. Out of that number, 4449 joined on normal engagements and 40,812 as volunteers for Hostilities Only. The rest, 92,599, were recruited by means of conscription and chose the navy in preference to other services.[22] But soon the volunteer route would begin to narrow. It was only open to those who were not within the current age ranges for conscription. By proclamation of March 1942, men up to forty-six were now to register for National Service, and by the new act of that year men up to fifty were theoretically liable. Volunteering remained a possibility for youths under eighteen who could join in anticipation of their birthdays. Provided the boy came up to minimum medical and other requirements, this guaranteed acceptance into the preferred service, and allowed some choice of branch of service.

Testing

The navy needed to find out whether men were suitable for sea service at all, and what branch of the navy they could best be trained for. It was most concerned about continuous service men, for it did not want to waste money on training men who would later become unfit, and it would be responsible for their health and welfare for some time. The real test was 'a candidate's likelihood to continue efficient and serviceable in any climate, and under all conditions of service, for a period of not less than twelve years.'[23] Only entrants to the artificer, sick berth attendant, writer, steward, cook and supply branches were allowed to wear glasses. Seamen and stokers needed good vision without them. Teeth were important, because only the largest ships carried dentists. Boys for continuous service were rejected if they had five or more missing or irreplaceable. Other candidates were allowed up to ten missing teeth.[24]

Conscripts were examined by doctors employed by the Ministry of Labour which organized the conscription process. Standards for seamen in the navy were still higher than the army or the ground trades of the RAF, but Hostilities Only ratings were allowed a few concessions, as the navy did not have to worry about their long-term future. From 1940 they 'were not rejected for any dental deficiency or condition capable of being remedied, including a gratuitous supply of dentures'.[25] Diseases which might cause problems at sea were still important and J. P.W. Mallalieu was turned down until he had treatment for a hernia.[26] There was concern about mental health, for nervous instability could be a serious problem in a crowded ship – 'all men were questioned with regard to any previous illness of a neurotic or psychological nature, and also concerning a family history of such illness. A note was made as to the mental and nervous condition of each candidate.[27]

Medical standards were measurable, but other methods of selection were primitive in the first two years of war. More than a hundred Combined Recruiting Centres in the major towns dealt with men for all three services. The naval side was manned by recalled chiefs and petty officers, who had no training for the job and little knowledge of modern branches of the navy. Often they had less than a minute to deal with each candidate. 'During that time, the Naval Recruiter concerned made his assessment of the man; obtained answers to standard questions about his willingness to be inoculated, vaccinated and so on; decided whether or not to accept him; and, if he accepted him, allocated him to a branch of the service.'[28] The spelling of a single word was often used as the test of literacy and according to legend one recruiter was overheard to say to a volunteer, 'What, Spell Egypt with a J? You're illegible for the navy.' The recruiter might assess the candidate's educational attainments, though he did not always have knowledge to interpret these.

> "Education?" The rough, deep voice startled me.
> "Oh! I took an honours degree in English at the University of London." ...
> The arbiter of my destiny gestured briefly with impatience.
> "Never mind about that. Have you got the School Leaving Certificate?"
> "Er – yes, of course."[29]

In 1941 the post of Senior Psychologist to the navy was created, with eight industrial psychologists under him, later increased to thirteen. It was decided to appoint Wren recruiting assistants, mostly drawn from civilian life with experience as teachers, employment officers or social workers. They were trained at the London School of Economics, and then promoted to petty officer. Eventually they were to number about 300, including fifty who were commissioned as Personnel Selection Officers, or PSOs. They would gather information on each candidate to pass to the naval recruiter.

> They would collect this information by a three-stage process, in which they would first of all get a group of candidates to fill up a simple form, rather like an extended application form, which would yield facts about the school and work record and leisure activities of each candidate. After 10 minutes or so spent on this, the group would go on to take a paper-and-pencil intelligence test (which, in order to allay apprehensions, was always referred to as an

Candidates being innoculated.

"observation" test) lasting 20 minutes. Then, as the men trickled back one by one from the medical board which saw them on completion of the form and the test, each would be given an interview lasting about 8 minutes.

The interview included questions 'which might help in the detection of men unsuitable for the service' – 'such topics as sickness absence from civilian work, headaches, accidents, dieting, and reaction to air raids.'[30]

Educated women proved to be very suitable for this work. Sir Henry Markham, the Secretary to the Admiralty, was sceptical until interviewed by one of them. 'My fears are completely at rest. I feel that I could tell my whole life story several times a day to Mrs. O'Brien.' The candidates also liked the procedure, and successful ones sometimes gave the women presents.[31] But officials at the Admiralty remained sceptical about the value of psychological testing in choosing men for entry, as distinct from selecting them for particular trades. In the early phase it was questioned, 'whether the considerable additional expense and slowing up of the recruiting procedure has been justified by the production of super sailors...'[32] Of 1942 it was observed:

A recruit is interviewed by a PSO.

214,000 men have been dealt with by R.N. and R.M. Recruiters at Combined Recruiting Centres both as volunteers and under the Armed Forces Act, apart from numerous enquiries both by letter and in person received daily. Of this figure 75 per cent have been selected for the Navy, and of the balance of 25 per cent rejected the majority have been due to medical reasons, classification in a trade not required or on account of insufficient experience in their particular trade. Only 2 per cent have been rejected on the "Selection Test" and it is probable that the majority of these would in any case have been rejected by the Recruiter without the aid of the "Test".[33]

The test was, however, more important in years when the supply of recruits far exceeded the demand.

Terms of Entry

The term 'Hostilities Only' had originated in 1914 to describe men, usually experienced merchant seamen, who joined the Royal Navy until the end of the war. It was revived in 1939, though now it tended to apply to inexperienced landsmen, whether volunteers or conscripts, who would be trained in seamanship and naval ways. It soon became the main method of entry in wartime. In September, the Admiralty was still looking at ways of recruiting men for longer periods. It had no idea what the navy would consist of after the war, so it tended to use the term 'Special Service' rather than 'Continuous Service', as that committed it less to keeping men on for twelve years. Men were to be recruited for seven years, plus five on the reserve. During 1941 this route was closed to adults. Only a limited number of seamen boys, marines and artificer apprentices were recruited for long service, and competitive examinations for the writer and supply branches ceased.[34] For the seaman boys, the waiting list became long and recruiting was suspended for a time in 1942. When it re-opened in November with a slightly higher educational test there were 600 enquiries in a few weeks.[35] Meanwhile the Admiralty was at last beginning to think about the shape of the post-war fleet, which it estimated at 120,000 men, mostly on continuous service engagements of twelve years.[36] About 1800 continuous service boys, apprentices and marines were recruited each year for the rest of the war, compared with an average of about 3500 rejected each year for medical reasons, and 9000 for other reasons.[37]

The Sea Cadets

The Royal Navy was slower than the other services to begin pre-entry training among boys. The army had long supported the Officers Training Corps in the public schools and in 1914 it provided the first generation of officers for the new armies. Since the navy recruited its potential officers at the age of about thirteen, it felt no need for a presence in the public schools. But in 1941 the RAF began to exploit a different form of recruit when it formed the Air Training Corps. This was based in localities rather than schools and so was open to a much wider range of recruits. It soon attracted about a fifth of eligible boys across the country, aged between sixteen and eighteen.

The Sea Cadets had been formed in 1914 by the Navy League, a highly successful pressure group for a larger fleet, but it was privately run and naval support was limited. Its aim was

To teach boys, between the ages of 12 and 18, habits of discipline, duty and self-respect, and to try to remedy the evil effects of street loafing in order that boys may become, by their knowledge, of practical use not only in time of peace but in time of war, and that they may be educated to believe in the British Empire and the British Navy, whereon the Empire primarily depends for its existence.

Boys were not necessarily expected to follow a seagoing career, but were encouraged to enter the Royal or Merchant Navy. They were trained in seamanship, drill, signalling, swimming, boxing, boating, and in rather more obscure subjects such as making field kitchens and dancing the hornpipe.[38]

In February 1942 the Admiralty took over control of the Corps. It had a strength of nearly 10,000 cadets in eighty-nine units, and 500 officers. Boys of twelve and upwards were eligible to join, though the main emphasis was on those between fourteen and seventen, who were likely to be of service in the present war. It offered grants of 12 shillings (60 pence) per annum for older boys, 3 shillings 6 pence (17.5 pence) for younger. A uniform allowance was payable for boys over fourteen. The Corps had increased by a fifth by the end of 1942, though the number of officers declined; the Admiralty set a target of 25,000 boys, far below the strength of the Air Training Corps.[39] Officers were commissioned, unpaid, in the RNVR Special Branch, and recruitment targets were exceeded by 1943, when numbers stood at 41,000.

The navy tended to view the Sea Cadets as a means of publicizing the navy, rather than an effective means of training. Recruiting figures into the fleet were quite small and 2850 ex-Sea Cadets joined the navy or the marines in 1942.[40] Though signalling was an important part of pre-entry training, it was not entirely successful in practice – the personnel selectors found that 'morse is often so badly taught in cadet units as to handicap the early stages of naval morse training.'[41]

The Y Scheme

The 'Y Scheme' of 1941 was another attempt to attract the best recruits. Soon after the start of the war, both the army and the RAF set up schemes by which boys under the age for call-up would be enrolled on unpaid deferred service and given training until they were conscripted.

> These schemes were doubly popular. First, they ensured that a boy whose first choice for National Service lay with the Army or the RAF would be called up for the service of his choice; and, second, that the service in question was drawing from a number of willing volunteers who, knowing into which service they would be enrolled, undertook such pre-entry training as would benefit them for call-up.[42]

The navy's Y Scheme was slightly more ambitious, for it was intended to identify and hold the better-educated young men, to use them eventually as officers, airmen, or in the more technical trades in the fleet. The title caused problems, for it was confused with the Army's pre-war 'Y Cadets' for the Royal Military Academy at Sandhurst. Most people therefore thought that the navy scheme was 'officer-producing'. Brendan A. Maher believed that he was a 'member of the officer candidate program (known as the "Y" scheme).'[43] An official pamphlet of 1944 was ambivalent about this.

> You don't want to be just "one of the crowd"; when the time comes you'd like to take responsibility, to fly your own aeroplane, to captain your own

small vessel. To fit yourself for that, is there anything you can do *now*?' But on the same page it warned, '*This doesn't mean you are certain to get a commission*; you have to earn that through the lower deck, and to prove yourself fit for it by sea service.[44]

Officer selection was only part of the programme, and in 1944 only 38 per cent of entrants went forward as CW candidates, to be assessed for officer training.[45] The main body, it was hoped, would be trained as skilled ratings.

Initially the scheme had some success for the Fleet Air Arm. In the six months up to April 1943, an average of thirty-eight pilot and observer candidates were recruited. After the issue of a Y Scheme pamphlet early that year, this shot up to 677 suitable men in ten weeks, plus 258 who would be suitable after further education at the navy's expense.[46]

An applicant for the scheme would be aged from seventeen to seventeen years eight months. He had to have a secondary education, with a School Certificate and a recommendation from his headmaster or the commander of a pre-entry training unit. He would then be given a short written test and interviewed by a retired captain or admiral and a selection board. Some felt this was too elaborate a procedure for the results attained.

> Such critics asked why there was selection for the "Y" Scheme, and why the production of a school certificate, for example, was necessary, if the idea behind the scheme was not to obtain future officers. Yet, they argued, after selection under the "Y" Scheme and on call-up, and after a few minutes inter-view with a W.R.N.S. Personnel Selection Officer and a C.W. Testing Officer, candidates were relegated to the Lower Deck for the duration of their service.

With hindsight, it was agreed that the standards of the initial selection boards were too low and applicants' hopes were falsely raised. Furthermore, the figures for 1944 sug-gest that not many were trained as skilled ratings. After the 38 per cent had been selected as CW candidates, exactly the same proportion remained as ordinary sea-men. The next largest group, 7.9 per cent, went on to train as supply ratings, while 4.3 per cent became candidates for Radio Mechanician, one of the most skilled grades in the service. In all, less than 10 per cent went on to truly technical jobs that year. They were perhaps unfortunate in that they entered too late, and figures are not available for other years. The Y Scheme had some success in getting some of the best material into the navy against strong competition and in forming a liaison with schools where the recruits might be found.[47]

If a country had to absorb four times its normal population in immigrants over a period of six years, there would be grave fears that its national identity would be swamped. But the Royal Navy's culture was strong enough to prevent this, to instill its own values on the newcomers, and indeed to cause them to spread naval ideas throughout the rest of society. One reason for this success was that an entrant could not stand aloof from the naval life around him. From his first day he was introduced to the dress, language and customs of his new society. The navy's greatest advantage was its confidence in its own history, culture and will to win.

CHAPTER 4

Training Bases

Shore Bases

Potential sailors posted to HMS *Drake* or HMS *St Vincent* were sometimes surprised that they were shore bases. Paul Fussell, in an unsympathetic book on military culture in the Second World War, referred to HMS *Ganges* as, 'actually a mere training camp, cutely named'.[1] In fact it was a development of a tradition which had lasted at least 200 years. The navy had long used obsolete warships as depot ships, in which pressed men were housed from where they could not escape easily. There was no element of training in this, and men often languished in idleness for weeks or were given menial tasks. Nearly a century later, the old ship of the line *Excellent* became the first gunnery training ship in the Royal Navy. Schools for new entrants, torpedomen, signallers, engineers and officer cadets were founded over the rest of the century. Almost all started in old 'wooden walls' left over from the Napoleonic Wars. It was the 1890s before the navy truly 'came ashore', with the building of barracks and schools at the three main dockyards of Chatham, Portsmouth and Plymouth, followed by naval colleges at Dartmouth and Osborne. The tradition of ship names was maintained, partly because the Naval Discipline Act applied only to officers and men actually borne on the books of HM ships.

In 1804 a naval physician claimed that the seamen had a habit of 'applying the language of seamanship to every transaction in life, and sometimes with a pedantic ostentation'.[2] Some of the officers of the 1940s might be accused of the same fault. According to Geoffrey Willans, 'The constant talk of houses as "hookers", the floors as "decks", and upstairs as "up-top" not only depressed me, but had the effect of making me think that my contemporaries were all experts, which was, in fact, very far from the case.' Some even referred to one end of the building as 'the bow'.[3] That was perhaps a little exaggerated, but in all bases the floor was known as 'the deck', rooms as 'cabins', and kitchens as 'galleys'. Sailors did not leave the base but 'went ashore', a certain area was designated as the 'quarterdeck' and had to be saluted by everyone who crossed it. The navy argued that these customs helped to prepare the men for life aboard ship.

Types of Accommodation

The architecture of naval training bases varied from the sublime of Christopher Wren's Royal Naval College at Greenwich ('the most stately procession of building we possess'),[4] to chalets in holiday camps and hastily-constructed Nissen huts. John Davies wrote of HMS *Ganges*, 'To say that the Annexe was utilitarian is to cloak its extreme and depressing ugliness in as kindly a fashion as possible. Low wooden buildings, roofed with corrugated iron, enclosed a small parade-ground within a hollow square.'[5]

George Melly found that HMS *Royal Arthur* at Skegness had 'a certain architectural frivolity completely inappropriate to a Royal Navy Shore Establishment'. He soon discovered that it was a former holiday camp. 'The ceiling of the lobby was painted to represent a summer sky with fluffy white clouds passing over it. In the centre of the room, rooted in the bare plasterboards, was a large and comparatively realistic tree. ... The serving hatch ... was framed by mullioned windows let into the elaborate facade of an Elizabethan inn with a sign reading "Ye Olde Pigge and Whistle" projecting over our heads.'[6]

The navy used the hammock at sea, though less on shore. The chalets of holiday camps already had beds fitted, while most forms of war-built accommodation, such as Nissen huts, were not suitable for slinging them. A base needed lecture rooms, for it was unsatisfactory to combine these with living accommodation. 'In Stamshaw Camp lectures are given in the ratings own sleeping huts ... Nothing more dismal or depressing can be imagined ...'[7] A base needed specialized facilities for the work in question – parade grounds for basic training, workshops for engineers. Some kind of interface with the sea was obviously essential for the later stages of the process, operational training and working up a crew. It was also necessary for some technical training, such as radar and asdic, in which the operators had to learn to react to real conditions under, on or over the sea. The sea interface was less important for basic training. Many of the basic training camps were positioned because of their past or future role as holiday camps, rather than any real need to be beside the sea.

HMS *James Cook* near Tighnabruach, Scotland, used for training landing craft navigators. It shows a typical layout of a Scottish base, with Nissen huts round a Victorian castle.

Much wartime training accommodation had to be hastily erected, with no plans for a long life. The most temporary accommodation of all, and the least satisfactory in the British climate, was the tent. A tented camp was set up in Highnam Court, Gloucestershire in the spring of 1941 to train signallers under the name of Cabbala. It lasted into the winter but was re-sited early in 1942.[8] Next on the list were various types of huts. The most famous was invented by Colonel P. Nissen of the Canadian Army in 1915. It was constructed of semi-circular steel ribs, 6 feet apart, and 16 feet, 24 feet or 30 feet in diameter. They were covered with vertically-laid corrugated steel sheeting on the outside, and horizontally-laid sheeting on the inside. End walls were usually of brick and floors were of concrete. Windows could be set at the ends and the sides, and coal stoves were fitted for heating. The Nissen hut was very common in naval air stations, which were hastily built during the war. Other types of hut used by the navy included the Quonset, similar to the Nissen but built in smaller sections; and the Curved Asbestos, made from different material.[9]

Siting of Bases

The navy had been aware of the danger of air raids since long before the war and planned to move its facilities away from the east coast as far as practicable. The problem intensified when the Fall of France made all south coast bases vulnerable. The air apprentice training base in a former RAF airfield at Lympne on the south coast had to move immediately. On the night of 19–20 May 1940, ten days after the German assault began, more than 100 RAF aircraft retreating from France landed there, with exhausted and hungry crews. The Admiralty was quick to accede to an RAF request to have the base back. It was to be evacuated 'forthwith' to Newcastle-under-Lyme 'where, it is understood suitable accommodation is available.' At six in the evening of the 21st, 140 apprentices boarded a train for Newcastle, with fifteen wagonloads of instructional equipment attached. Fifteen large RAF lorries took more machinery, and on the 22nd another train left, with more than 300 staff and trainees and nineteen wagonloads of gear. There was a third train twenty-four hours later with 120 people and fifteen wagons – in all 250 tons of gear were moved. The captain of the base left by car that afternoon, called at the Admiralty in London and then proceeded to his new command at Newcastle.

His colleagues had set up a new base in the interim. The headquarters was in the Old Bank House near the town centre, and an old nursing home was used for officers' quarters. A 'fair-sized garage' was taken over for technical instruction and Clayton Hall, a large two-storied house, was used as accommodation for 150 apprentices – huts would be built later for a further 200. A modern children's clinic became the sick quarters and the officers considered themselves fortunate in getting hold of Westland School, recently built for 400 girls, as the main place of instruction. Blackboards were already in position, but the navy brought its own desks, from Lympne. The main problem was that the buildings were widely scattered throughout the town.[10]

Portland, on a peninsula on the south coast, was as exposed as Lympne and it was agreed in 1940 that 'exercises with submarines are impracticable; shore instruction is also interfered with by air raids to a highly inconvenient extent.'[11] Though contact with real enemy submarines might have been useful training for anti-submarine personnel, false reports from inexperienced operators would merely have confused the issue. The anti-submarine training operation had moved to Scotland by the end of 1940. Inveraray on Loch Fyne was chosen as the home of the Combined Training Centre and commissioned as HMS *Quebec* in November 1940. According to Rear-Admiral L. E. H. Maund it was 'as far distant as possible from attack but yet within the umbrella of some fighter organization. ... Here the rains might fall almost continuously, but it gave sheltered water and was, as it were, behind the defences of the Clyde.'[12]

A basic training camp in itself was not a particularly valuable target for the Luftwaffe – HMS *Ganges* was raided a few times, but no damage was done. Heavy equipment was clearly the most difficult to move, for example from HMS *Vernon* and *Excellent,* the torpedo and gunnery training schools at Portsmouth. The gunnery schools remained in the south. Luftwaffe activity actually gave some real practice to anti-aircraft gunners and radar controllers. There was a feeling that air raids might test a man's reaction to combat stress, or help build his character. But in 1940 HMS *Vernon* was moved to Roedean girls' school near Brighton.

The Royal Naval Engineering College trained career engineer officers, so it had to be within reasonable distance of a main dockyard, and it had been in Devonport yard since 1879. In 1937 the Admiralty bought 100 acres at Manadon outside Plymouth, to build an expanded college, but it was not complete in 1940, when serious bombing of the dockyard began. Nissen huts were put up so that the trainee officers could get some sleep away from the worst of the raids, and classrooms were erected. The split site was unsatisfactory and Rear-Admiral Ford found 'The R.N.E College therefore now consists of two establishments and a house (Mount View) in Hartley, separated by 3½ miles and the general administration has been complicated by this fact alone. Further, owing to the policy of building a new college at Manadon being deferred much of the equipment now provided at Keyham is out of date and obsolete.'[13]

Training Ships

The navy's static training ship era ended in 1927, when the boys' establishment at Portsmouth, HMS *St Vincent*, moved into a disused marine barracks at Forton, across the harbour mouth from the town of Portsmouth. The concept revived just before the war, when the old liner, *Majestic*, was taken over for training new entrants and artificer apprentices at Rosyth. It was re-named *Caledonia*. By 1937 all east coast ports were considered to be in danger of bombing from Germany and a suitable anchorage was sought on the west coast of Scotland, but eventually it was decided to remove the boys to shore training on the Isle of Man.[14]

Ships of almost any kind were in great demand by 1940, from ocean liners to fishing drifters, from battleships to motor torpedo boats. The navy did as much training as possible ashore, partly to save shipping. Few major warships were devoted entirely to training purposes, except for subjects which had to be completed at sea, such as practical gunnery in the cruiser *Cardiff* of 1917, and deck landing for pilots in the carrier *Argus* of 1918. In the early stages of the war there were very few training ships in the fullest sense of the term, in which the trainees lived and worked on board.

This position began to change in the later stages of the war, as older ships were taken out of service due to manpower shortage. From 1943, candidates for commissions were no longer sent in small groups on board destroyers and cruisers. Two old cruisers and a converted liner were based in the Forth and devoted entirely to the assessment of candidates. In 1944 the battleships *Revenge* and *Resolution*, veterans of the last war, were taken out of service on account of the manning crisis and became training ships for stokers.

HMS *Western Isles* situated at Tobermory on the island of Mull, was the most famous training ship of the war. She was not a training ship in the traditional sense, however, for she served as the headquarters of the training programme, and the men lived and exercised on board their own ships. Submarine depot ships were not strictly training vessels, though the *Cyclops* of the Seventh Submarine Flotilla at Rothesay was mainly used for boats working up in the Clyde and its vicinity. All submarine depot ships had an element of training, however, for they were fitted with Torpedo Attack Trainers to carry out simulated exercises.

Small vessels such as motor torpedo boats and motor launches of the coastal forces, or landing craft for combined operations, were attached to training bases. Coastal forces used relatively cheap and simple vessels and it was quite easy to attach a few to the bases at Fort William and Ardrishaig in Scotland. Landing craft tended to be available, because their use was much less continuous. They were needed for certain large-scale operations such as the invasions of North Africa and Normandy, and in preparation for these it was only natural that the craft should be used to train the crews.

Practical training in submarine detection obviously needed some kind of vessel, and in 1940 the vessels attached to HMS *Nimrod* at Campbeltown were the converted yachts *Shemara*, *Tuscarora* and *Carina* and two former Antarctic whalers, *Bulldog* and *Spaniel*, as well as the submarine *Oberon* as a target. By November 1943 the Training Flotilla, serving both *Osprey* and *Nimrod*, had expanded to fourteen vessels, most of which were of no use for anything else.

Established Bases

Naturally the navy used its own shore bases to the full, despite the danger of bombing. The most important function of Naval College at Greenwich was to impress officer trainees with its architecture. Vera Laughton Mathews of the WRNS wrote,

> The first time of walking up the centre of the Painted Hall produced an emotion which has always remained and which with custom never grew less. Many a one has held her breath at the sight of those vast and perfect proportions, lit by shaded silver candles, with indirect flood-lighting illuminating the early eighteenth-century painted ceiling and walls, yet leaving a mistiness in the lofty spaces which seemed not of this earth. The beauty was awe-inspiring and one talked in whispers, but with head held high for here was the very essence of England.[15]

The boys' training establishments, *St Vincent* at Portsmouth and the new *Caledonia* at Rosyth, were evacuated in 1940 and a new school, *St George*, was set up in Cunningham Camp on the Isle of Man. *St Vincent* became a base for Fleet Air Arm trainees. *Ganges* on the east coast continued a little longer with boys, but was already dominated by adult trainees when Tristan Jones arrived in the middle of 1940.[16] Dartmouth College on the south coast continued with its normal functions until 1942, when an air raid caused serious damage in the area. The cadets were evacuated to Eaton Hall in Cheshire.

Conditions in the established training bases were not always good and one officer wrote in 1945,

> The Factories Act of 1937 provides that "in every workroom … A temperature of not less than 60 degrees shall not be deemed, after the first hour, to be a reasonable temperature". … A trial at H.M.S. EXCELLENT at the beginning of this year gave, during February an average temperature in non-centrally heated lecture spaces of 51 degrees one hour after instruction commenced. At one point during January, instruction had to continue in spaces at 2 degrees below freezing.[17]

The barracks at the three main bases tended to be used for men awaiting drafting to ships and shore stations, though some training was also conducted there. A great deal of expansion was needed in wartime. By 1942 Portsmouth had five new sites, including army barracks at Gosport, a Nissen hut camp for 2000 men at Havant, and another for 1000 at Belmont Park. Plymouth also needed five, four of Nissen huts and one converted school.[18]

Some purpose-built accommodation was completed during the war. Arriving at HMS *Duke* in 1944, George Melly found it depressing, lacking in 'those bizarre touches which helped relieve the austerity of the requisitioned Butlin's camps'.[19]

The Leisure Industry

The Duke of Wellington claimed that the Battle of Waterloo was won on the playing fields of Eton. It is no more far-fetched to suggest that the Battle of the Atlantic was won in converted hotels and holiday camps round the British coast. The navy owed a surprising amount to the leisure business, and in particular the British association between holidays and the seaside. The industry had planned for a major boost in 1938, when paid holidays were made compulsory for the first time. Its facilities were particularly useful in wartime because vessels, buildings and techniques could be mobilized for the navy without loss to the general war effort.

The industry supplied ships for the fleet – paddle steamers of the Thames or Clyde became minesweepers, while motor yachts were numbered among the legendary 'little ships' of Dunkirk. Seaside piers could be taken over for small craft use, and Bognor Pier became part of the anti-aircraft training programme at HMS *Excellent*. Yachtsmen formed the first batch of wartime naval officers. The industry provided many of the buildings that were used to train the wartime navy. Holiday camps, such as Butlin's at Skegness, became training bases for new entrants. Hotels were requisitioned in large numbers for accommodation and for classrooms. Even the municipal swimming pool at Hove, with its associated car park, was converted to become HMS *King Alfred*.

Billy Butlin opened his first holiday camp at Skegness in 1937 with capacity for 2000 people. In the first days of the war it was taken over by the navy and all bookings cancelled.[20] There were problems during the severe winter of 1939–40 and Churchill had to explain to the House of Commons that 'the rigours of this winter have been extreme and have necessarily inflicted severe discomfort on very large numbers serving in camp or billets. Everything possible has been done to improve these conditions.'[21]

Butlin visited *Royal Arthur* in 1940 and found it a sad occasion.

> I stood beside the ship's captain on the "quarter-deck" as he took the salute at the Sunday morning march-past … Where I was standing had been partly the children's playground and partly the skating rink. … You can imagine my feelings as I walked round the camp to find that the dining-rooms, once called York, Gloucester and Kent, were now known as the Forecastle, Foretop and Quarterdeck Divisions. … As a civilian, I was not allowed to walk across the "quarter-deck" where every rating had to salute the flagstaff when passing. All the saluting and standing to attention, and only speaking when spoken to by an officer, was such a contrast to the relaxed, friendly atmosphere I had striven to create.[22]

As a would-be sophisticate, George Melly viewed the camp differently.

Planned for the regimented pleasure of the Fairisle-jerseyed civilians of the late Thirties, they needed no more than a few coats of drab paint and a whaler on the swimming pool to become wartime shore establishments. The redcoats were transformed into petty officers. The intercom system, through which the campers had been hi-de-hied to meals or jollied along to enter the knobbly knees competition, now barked out our orders.[23]

Many recruits liked *Royal Arthur*. John L. Brown found it well equipped – 'two swimming pools with high and low diving boards, a Cinema, Theatre, Gymnasium, Tennis Courts, Playing Fields, Canals etc. Long rows of well-constructed chalets lay behind the halls, and each was divided by a strip of lawn edged by a narrow flower bed.'[24] Derek Hamilton Warner found that 'The accommodation in *Royal Arthur* was very good; two bunk beds to a chalet, with a nice locker.'[25]

The army spent £250 per man in building new accommodation, and Butlin could do it for £175, with the chance to buy it back after the war for three-fifths of the cost. The navy commissioned a camp at Pwhelli in Wales on similar terms. It was opened in three weeks, mainly under canvas to start with. It was commissioned as HMS *Glendower* in October 1940 with a capacity of 8000 men. HMS *Scotia* at Ayr followed in January 1942.[26] It was incomplete when R. A. Greaves was posted there for signal training and he found that sea-boots were essential in the muddy conditions.[27]

At Hove on the south coast, a large municipal swimming pool was under construction in September 1939. It was requisitioned on 11 September, eight days after the war started, and commissioned as HMS *King Alfred*. In the short term it was used for the training of the volunteer yachtsmen of the Royal Naval Volunteer (Supplementary) Reserve.

By early 1942 there were seventeen bases training new Hostilities Only ratings. The holiday camps of *Royal Arthur*, *Scotia* and *Glendower* had a capacity for 9000 men between them. *Valkyrie*, which used hotels on the Isle of Man to train radar operators, had room for 1500, while *King Alfred* held 1000 potential officers. The largest traditional naval site, *Ganges*, could cope with 3000 men after wartime extensions.[28]

Transport facilities were important to all training bases, and before the age of easy road transport, that meant railways. This fitted in well with the leisure industry, for holiday towns and camps were used to large numbers arriving on certain days of the week and then departing a few weeks later.

Sometimes a series of hotels could form a training base, as with *Valkyrie* on the Isle of Man, 'a block of private hotels and boarding houses surrounded by a tall wire fence on the promenade at Douglas'.[29] At Fort William several hotels were taken over as part of *St Christopher*, the coastal forces training base. The Highland Hotel was the administrative headquarters, the Grand accommodated senior officers, while Wrens lived in the Waverley, the Station and an annexe to the Palace. Male ratings lived in Nissen huts or were billeted among families.[30] Normally hotel furniture was put into store and replaced with naval issue. Lieutenant A. H. Cherry was pleasantly surprised at HMS *Osprey*. 'What struck me as unusual was that all decks and stairways were carpeted. Everywhere else carpets and rugs had been removed and stored, where the military had taken over private accommodation.[31] Petty officers were also comfortable.

I doubt whether the navy has any establishment equal to it even at the time of writing [1957]. It boasted putting and bowling greens, and tree-lined walks. I had my own private "cabin", fitted with H. And C., bed, wardrobe and bedside table. The petty officers' mess had been a nursery, and the walls were still covered with coloured silhouettes of animals from popular nursery rhymes. The only creature missing was one that would have been most appropriate: a pink elephant. There were billiards and table tennis, a bar – Ye Olde Seagull's Nest – and deep armchairs in an arch round a large red-brick fireplace.[32]

This base used the Glasgow and West of Scotland Convalescent Homes and the Glenmorag Hotel, on the Clyde near the town of Dunoon. Other buildings included two requisitioned houses near the shore, a parade ground built at a cost of £1000, and a wet (alcohol) canteen for 370 ratings and seventy Wrens. The whole base cost £23,500 to set up. But not all the junior ratings were so comfortable. The sum of £200 was allocated for tubular scaffolding for hanging hammocks.[33]

In many cases, the men had to be billeted out among local guest houses and seaside landladies. At *King Alfred* in 1940, according to Ludovic Kennedy, 'We were all billeted in Hove's numerous genteel hotels where residents were mostly retired service people and old ladies: Rattigan's *Separate Tables* could have sprung from any of them.'[34] Billeting out was also common among the newly-formed commando regiments, some of whom were Royal Marines.

> For training or on an operation everyone came under starter's orders; nobody had to be left in barracks to do the inevitable chores of the spud-bashing variety. The administrative tail therefore consisted of a body of some five hundred landladies, who, whether in Plymouth, Largs, Seaford, Weymouth, Worthing or wherever else our journeyings took us, proved a fine body of women with a fine *esprit de corps*! Some of the soldiers developed the system to such a fine art that they would get the people in their billets to clean their equipment, or would send them round to Troop Headquarters to read Orders![35]

Billeting out depended much on the calibre of the men in question. Rear-Admiral Ford was critical of the civilian-manned training unit for engineers at Pontefract,

> ...they are on lodging and compensation allowance. In the case of men living far from their homes for the first time and having to live in a very unattractive industrial town on a small wage, it is not surprising that they will save their food in order to pay their fares during the week-ends to their homes.[36]

Far superior accommodation might be found in castles and country houses, particularly among operational and amphibious warfare training bases in Scotland. Such sites were usually close to the sheltered waters of sea lochs, but remote from large towns where men might be distracted. At Inveraray on Loch Fyne the admiral selected the house of Rudnha-na-Craig as his headquarters but there was opposition from the Duke of Argyll, whose sister lived there in poor health; compulsory powers were needed to get her out.

In most cases the castle served only as offices and accommodation for senior officers and base staff. It was often surrounded by a Nissen hut camp for the trainees.

At the end of the course for landing-craft officers at Lochailort the classes were assembled in Inverailort House, an 'ungainly shooting lodge which has developed by a process of accretion,'[37] to hear their fate. A pass was followed by 'the long-await-ed tea and cakes with the staff who, to their surprise, turned out to be human beings like themselves, all chummy now.'[38]

The Education Industry

After the leisure business, it was education which supplied the largest number of ready-made training bases. Schools and colleges had natural advantages for naval training – classrooms, gymnasia and laboratories were already provided, and play-grounds and playing fields could easily become parade grounds.

Many civilian colleges simply extended their peacetime functions, training naval officers or ratings in engineering, aircraft maintenance or radio operation and repair. The Naval Estimates of early 1942 listed twenty-seven such establishments, including the Wireless School at Holloway and the London Telegraph Training College whose functions are self-explanatory, the Presbyterian Hall at Brighton which trained 200 telegraphists at a time, and the Gas Light and Coke Company which, surprisingly, trained air fitters. The navy's experience with these schemes was not always satisfac-tory; the standard of training was uneven and not always geared to naval needs, and the navy much preferred to keep training in its own hands as far as possible. Government Training Centres at Wallsend on Tyne and Glasgow were found to be unsuitable for naval engineers, those at Hounslow and Watford in the London area were passable, but the school at Pontefract, according to Rear-Admiral Ford, was 'without doubt the most unsatisfactory establishment which I have visited'.[39] He found much to complain about at Loughborough College, where a course for air engineer officers was set up in October 1942. The authorities regarded it as 'a commercial enterprise from which as much profit as possible should be made'. Facilities were poor, and when it was complained that canteen staff were serving food with their bare hands, the college's response was to erect a screen so that this could not be seen. It was a 'bad show', as someone in the Admiralty noted in the margin of the report.[40]

The public schools of England were more suitable, for they were designed for both accommodation and education. Lancing College in Sussex was taken over in 1940 as part of *King Alfred* for the training of temporary officers. Charles McAra was posted there in 1941. 'I found my new billet most acceptable after the mess-deck of a destroyer. We had bunk-beds in the dormitories, good washing facilities and we ate in the college dining-room, three good meals served by a local catering firm. Round the college were spacious playing-fields for field-training and on Sundays we attended morning service in the splendid soaring neo-Gothic chapel ...'[41] Roedean School for girls, used by the torpedo school HMS *Vernon*, was famous for the sign in the dormitory, 'If you require a mistress in the night, ring the bell.'

The third group comprised non-residential, non-specialist schools taken over for naval purposes. In contrast to *Osprey* further up the Firth of Clyde, HMS *Nimrod* at Campbeltown was one of the least comfortable bases.

> The squalor of H.M.S. *Nimrod*, situated in a commandeered local school, was dreadfully depressing after *Osprey*. ... Appallingly overcrowded, it was devoid of even the pretence of comfort. ... Iron stanchions and strength-ening bars had been fitted from floor to ceiling to take hammocks, and each

matlow [sic] was allowed fourteen inches of sleeping space. There was still insufficient room, and at night men slept on and under tables and stools, and hammocks were slung three deep down the stanchions. Because of the blackout, windows were kept securely closed, and in the mornings the foul air in the hall would have made a goat wince.[42]

A. H. Cherry found the officers' accommodation less than satisfactory. On a single page of his memoirs he manages seven references to the weather, including, 'the terrible coldness of room and bed', 'dreadfully cold in the room' and 'The room remained colder than an ice-box.'[43]

Highgate School in London was taken over in 1941 and commissioned as *President V*, to train ratings for the Accountancy Branch. There was less of a problem in this case, for the city offered much more space to billet men. However, some slept in the main building and John L. Brown records 'We were soon fixed up in our sleeping quarters. These were previously the chemistry laboratories of the school, but now two-tiered bunks lined the bulkheads.'[44]

Commercial premises could also be taken over for training. A school for motor mechanics was sub-contracted from AFN Limited in London. The nearby Pear's Soap Factory was taken over as accommodation for ratings. At the training unit for motor mechanics in Fulham, men lived and were instructed inside the Harrod's carpet warehouse. Rear-Admiral Ford commented; 'The arrangements for housing these ratings is adequate, but there is no service reason why they should ever move outside the building and this in itself is unsatisfactory and the sickness rate gives reason to suppose that many of them are short of fresh air and exercise.' He found the opposite problem in a similar training unit at Isleworth, also on the Thames near London, where most of the men were billeted in private homes. 'Much difficulty has been experienced in providing billets near their instructional centre, and providing adequate feeding arrangements. ... The men will have to walk to and from their billets daily, often a matter of 3 miles each way, and in Winter these early walks before breakfast may have a bad effect on their health ...'[45]

The Accommodation Crisis

By 1943 the accommodation situation was reaching a crisis. No. 41 Royal Marine Commando arrived at Troon station at 4.30 in the morning of 3 April, after a long journey from the Isle of Wight. They were surprised to see small groups of policemen standing around, but soon found out why.

> Voluntary billeting had not been sufficient to accommodate the whole Commando so the boys in blue were there just in case there was any trouble with people who weren't keen to have paying guests. In the event, no problems were experienced, the police remained discreetly in the background and no-one ever learned whether their billet had been 'compulsory' or not.[46]

As demand for sailors reached its peak in the second half of 1943, the naval authorities were at their wits' end for further accommodation. In July, 94,000 new entrants were expected during the rest of the year. Tented camps at *Glendower* and *Duke* and on the on Isle of Man would have to close for the winter, so it was intended to look for further accommodation in the town of Douglas, but

The shortage of accommodation of this type, which has always been difficult to find, is more acute at the present time than it has ever been as all the Service Departments have similar large and urgent outstanding requirements for British as well as Allied personnel who are coming to this country in increasingly large numbers. ... It is considered that there is very little chance of meeting anything but a small part of these requirements unless a claim can be established on a very high level which will give the Admiralty priority over other Departments ...'[47]

A month later, the Admiralty listed 243 sites in use for naval training.[48]

Largs on the Clyde was a centre for both amphibious warfare and aircraft carrier training, and hotel accommodation was in crisis there on the eve of D-Day.

When it was decided to extend [Flag Officer Carrier Training's] duties ... it was obvious that a considerable increase in staff and office accommodation would be necessary. A search was made for all suitable premises ... The only suitable building which could be found to house the enlarged Naval Air Headquarters was Glenblair Hotel. Even this was inadequate and the accommodation had to be supplemented by the building of Huts in the grounds. The existing W.R.N.S accommodation also became inadequate. ... In the face of considerable opposition, two fairly large private houses, Auchencraig and Broomcraig were requisitioned for this purpose. ... It is desired to emphasise that there is no large building such as Netherhall now available in Largs unless one of the very few remaining Hotels is requisitioned, a proposal to which the very strongest opposition may be expected.[49]

As with manpower, the leisure industry was approaching the limit of its resources. There must have been relief in some departments of the Admiralty when the numbers of naval entrants were cut back in 1944.

CHAPTER 5

Basic Training

Entry

Having been accepted for entry to the Royal Navy, a man had to wait until the service was ready for him. John L. Brown wrote, 'We expected to be called within a few days, but nothing was further from the truth; obviously the navy could manage without us at this stage of events. The wait to be called seemed endless and frustrating, but there was nothing that we could do that might speed things up.' After more than six months he was called up early in 1941.[1]

A wartime sailor's career began with the arrival of an official letter from the Admiralty, as John Davies found.

> One morning some six weeks later a small buff envelope lay beside my place at the breakfast table. The superscription ON HIS MAJESTY'S SERVICE, OFFICIAL PAID, left little doubt as to its contents. I opened it gingerly and discovered that the Admiralty expected me to report to His Majesty's Training Ship *Orwell* [actually *Ganges*] on the third day from that date. In the event of failure to comply I would be classed as a deserter. There was also a railway voucher exchangeable at the station for a ticket – a one-way tick-et. There was a postal order for two shillings [10 pence].[2]

Training Bases

In the first few months of the war all Hostilities Only ratings were sent to *Royal Arthur*, while continuous service boys went to HMS *St George* on the Isle of Man. Both

Men arriving at a training base after receiving their kit.

bases were staffed and administered jointly by the three home ports, Plymouth, Portsmouth and Chatham. Early in 1940, *Collingwood* and *Raleigh* were opened near Portsmouth and Plymouth respectively. They had been planned before the war to train the militiamen of the Special Reserves. *Ganges*, near Harwich on the east coast of England, ceased boy training around the same time. It was attached to the Chatham Division and largely catered for men from East Anglia, the Midlands, London and the south-east. *Impregnable* near Plymouth was opened for boys in 1937. During the war it was used for new entrants to the signal branches. *St Vincent* in Gosport, across the harbour from Portsmouth, was for basic training of the Fleet Air Arm from September 1939. HMS *Wellesley* was opened in Liverpool in 1940 for the gunners of Defensively Equipped Merchant Ships (DEMS).

More establishments were added to cope with wartime expansion. HMS *Glendower* in Wales was opened in mid-1940 for seamen and DEMS gunners. HMS *Cabot* started in July 1940 in a converted orphanage in Bristol, to train stokers and miscellaneous ratings for the Plymouth Division. It later moved to a government hostel in Wetherby, Yorkshire. HMS *Duke* at Great Malvern was for potential stokers and miscellaneous ratings. It occupied huts designed for a possible evacuation of the Admiralty from London and was not completed until 1943. Another holiday camp, *Scotia*, opened at Ayr early in 1942 and was mainly used for signallers. In July that year HMS *Gosling* at Risley became the main base for Fleet Air Arm mechanic entrants.

Travel

Each new entrant was ordered to report on a Thursday. The man made his way to the training establishment, a slow journey on overcrowded wartime railways, and a formative experience for those who had never made long journeys before.

> Our journey from Paddington seemed to go on for ever, partly because, as we were about to leave London, an air attack was just beginning. The enemy aircraft were still to the east of London, so we were allowed to leave the station with all the speed we could muster. Once we were away from London it slowed down almost to a crawl, perhaps because if moving slowly there was a possibility that it would not be noticed by enemy aircraft. From then on it was "slow, slow, stop, slow". We could have walked to Plymouth more quickly.[3]

Recruits were met at the station by petty officers and lorries. At *Ganges,* a launch took them across the River Stour. On arrival at the base, new entrants ran the gauntlet of unwanted advice from slightly more experienced men. "Go back home while you have the chance ... You're better off in the Army ... The square bashing will murder you!" "Take no notice, lads," the Chief said. "They've only been here a week themselves!"[4]

Ken Kimberley and his intake were addressed by the captain of the base.

> Welcome to HMS *Glendower*. I am Captain Barker, with me is my Commander and First Lieutenant. The *Glendower* will never sail away, but believe me – myself, and all my fellow officers, Chief and Petty Officers will leave no stone unturned to give you the basic RN training that the life at sea will demand of you. We have experience in peacetime and in war to make sailors of you.[5]

The wartime navy was a melting pot, recruiting men from a greater social and geographical range than ever before. Tristan Jones noted of his draft at Chatham,

> I recall a couple of Scotsmen, one a shepherd from the Highlands, one a hard nut from the mean streets of Glasgow. There were a couple of Geordie coalminers from Newcastle way, and a few East Anglian farmhands, as well as the men from the factories of Birmingham and Manchester, and one or two country boys from Oxfordshire and the Cotswolds. And of course some Londoners, freshly turned up to join us from the local recruiting office.[6]

Once in the base, leave was restricted to the local area, perhaps on weekends and every alternate evening. Most recruits were cut off from home by distance and the expense and difficulty of rail travel in wartime. Telephones were not available. They communicated with their families by letter, sometimes writing very regularly; G.V. Ball apologized when he missed his daily letter from *Ganges* in 1943.[7] Apart from that, the entrants were largely isolated from outside influences to concentrate on becoming sailors.

Uniform

Unlike soldiers and marines, seamen took no oath of allegiance. On the first or second day the men were issued with their uniforms, a defining moment and the first introduction to the strange naval culture. Ken Kimberley writes,

> It was nearly dark as we filed into the long shed. We moved slowly along the counter, taking from the Wrens different items of clothing as we shuffled along. It was all done by guesswork on their part as each Wren eyed us up and down.

> "No. 4 size will do you," said one, whatever No. 4 size was.

> "No. 9s will do you fine." Another Wren handed me a pair of boots.

> When I reached the end of a long counter I had collected two jumpers, two pairs of bell-bottoms to be known as No. 1s and No. 3s, two collars, two shirt fronts, one black ribbon, two pairs of socks, one pair of boots, one cap, one cap band, one oilskin, one overcoat, one pair of overalls, one housewife (pocket sewing outfit), one lanyard and one seaman's manual.

> "That'll do for you, Jack," the cheerful little Wren said. "Move along the counter, find an empty spot and get your name and number marked on everything. I found an empty spot and stamped everything with my name and number: CJX 557233.[8]

According to John Davies, the seaman's shirt was an 'amazing garment'. It had a square-cut neck and short sleeves and many men had difficulty at first in finding which way to put it on. The seaman's trousers were an 'outlandish garment'.

> Six buttons, three vertical and three horizontal. I struggled to find the correct buttonhole for each. The trousers gripped me tightly round the waist, but

below the knees they expanded enormously. I looked down and started momentarily when I saw even the huge boots obscured by blue serge. Cautiously I moved a leg, which led to the realization that this garment was surprisingly comfortable.

New entrants are issued with their uniforms at HMS *Glendower.*

Then came the seaman's jumper, which was separate from the collar.

> Getting into the jumper was an all-in struggle, no holds barred, a wild waving of arms followed finally by a condition of complete helplessness. Breathless and outwitted I at last stood still, my shoulders and upper arms relentlessly caught in blue serge, the extremities dangling helplessly before me.[9]

The sailor would now wear his uniform on almost all occasions, for working, on leave and on parade. When he finally got to sea he might abandon it almost completely, especially on the small ships where most wartime entries were sent; but meanwhile he had to get used to this strange garment.

'Sprogs' soon learned that a 'tiddley sailor' could refine the uniform to his own standards.

> The "little round hat" as far from the central position as authority will permit, with the bow of its ribbon teased into a flat, symmetrical rosette. The spotless "blue jean" collar, with its white borders gleaming ... And your mess-deck masher will affect a white silk scarf (not regulation, this, but allowed) tucked coyly beneath the black. The "bell-bottoms" as wide as canny selection from "Pusser's stores" or instructions to the ship's tailor can achieve ...[10]

By the time they went on their first leave after five or six weeks, the new entrants were trying to ape the experienced men, scrubbing their collars to make them look lighter or even buying bleached ones in the shops around the bases. As James Callaghan wrote,

> We were taught how to tie knots and we discovered how to launder our new, dark-blue collars so that they appeared as faded and washed out as those of any veteran seaman. We risked the wrath of the chief gunner's mate by cutting the tapes of our collars so that they showed a U-front instead of the regulation V-front, and we made sure we had seven horizontal creases (no more, no less) in our bell-bottomed trousers. All these matters were important to us.[11]

This was the Class II uniform of the 'men dressed as seamen', the great bulk of the fleet below the rank of petty officer. It was known as 'square rig' because of the square collar. Men of the Medical, Catering and Accountancy Branches were allocated 'Class III' uniform, a cruder version of that worn by officers and petty officers, with a peaked cap and a collar and tie. John L. Brown hated it, 'a cross between that of a taxi driver and a workhouse inmate'.

Certainly the square rig uniform was popular in many quarters. On the way to join HMS *Ganges*, Tristan Jones met an army veteran of the last war who said, 'Well, matey, at least you'll be all right where crumpet's concerned. They go for the navy blokes a lot more than the army, see? Can't go wrong in your little old navy-blue suit, can you?'[12] But by the end of the war there were many who found the uniform inconvenient and obsolete and one ex-serviceman wrote in 1946,

> Abolish the pantomime uniform known as bell bottoms, and substitute a naval battle-dress or uniform similar to that enjoyed by P.Os and officers – the men are worth it. One has only to watch an A.B dress to have pity on him, with a uniform consisting of tapes and ribbons and bits and pieces, and a blue jean collar to keep the grease from a pigtail soiling his jumper – a blue jean collar that another person has to hold in place while the poor chap puts his overcoat on. Women will object, no doubt, but they do not have to endure the nonsense.[13]

Seaman's Culture

The navy had its own vocabulary, as every comedian knew; but phrases like 'shiver me timbers' and 'yo-ho-ho' were entirely the work of fiction. The navy needed certain specialized terms to do its business – port and starboard seem arcane and useless to the landsmen, but they refer specifically to the left and right sides of the ship when facing forward, and were used to avoid confusion. The *Manual of Seamanship* provided the seaman with definitions of boot-topping, broaching-to, ground tackle, mousing a hook, warping and many other terms that he might (or might not) need in the course of his duties.

As well as the vocabulary of the profession, a seaman had to learn slang terms if he was to have any credibility among his peers. The various officers and petty officers had nicknames attached to their stations, often used by officers as well as the lower deck. The captain was 'the owner', the first lieutenant was 'Jimmy the one' or 'number one', the navigator was 'the pilot' and the chaplain was 'the sky-pilot'.

Many naval terms were of purely lower deck origin. 'Winger' or 'wings', meaning a younger or less experienced friend, 'can, though far from inevitably, imply a homosexual relationship', according to George Melly.[14] 'Oppo' or 'opposite number' implied a more equal kind of friendship. A 'party' was a girlfriend. The navy was known as 'the Andrew'. Ratings with particular surnames had nicknames, according to well established but often obscure custom.

> For instance we have "Shiner" Wright, "Dusty" Miller, "Pincher" Martin, "Nellie" Wallace, "Topsy" Turner, "Pusser" Combe, "Hookey" Walker, "Smouge" Smith, "Paddy" Walsh, "Nobby" Clark, "Bungy" Williams, "Jack" Hilton.[15]

Swearing was almost universal on the lower deck and was something of a shock to middle-class entrants. 'Language deteriorated quickly. An anxiety to appear as street-wise as the next man frequently turned what should have been everyday conversation into obscene nonsense. Sanity slowly regained control over insecurity but the vocabulary of the vast majority underwent a profound change and the few who resisted the trend were regarded with suspicion.'[16] The first words George Melly heard from his chief petty officer were, 'You're a fine specimen of hu-fucking-manity!' In the Royal Marines, Acting-Captain Evelyn Waugh told his men, to no avail, 'The continued use of obscenities in conversation is tedious and undignified. The words punctuate your speech like a hiccup. Instead they should be savoured and reserved for the creative act itself or for moments of the most extreme frustration.'[17]

Petty Officers

Officers were remote figures at this stage. Each of the smaller bases tended to be dominated by a particular chief petty officer, who was remembered by everyone who passed through it – CPO Wilmott at *St Vincent*, CPO Vass at *King Alfred*, for example. In the larger bases no individual stood out, but the petty officer instructors, like all teachers, had characteristics which were soon mimicked by the trainees, and many acquired nicknames which were passed from class to class. John Davies was introduced to his instructors. 'Petty Officer Warples, commonly known as "Morbid", is your seamanship instructor – He's a miserable old bastard, but he'll make you work. Jimmy Parker will take you for gunnery – and Gawd 'elp 'er, although some people do say 'e's human. But it's going to be tough – My bleeding oath it is.'[18] After hearing stories about bullying in the other services, J. P. W. Mallalieu found his CPO surprisingly understanding. When new entrants smoked without permission, he came into the room and said gently, 'By the way, it doesn't matter now, as this is your first day. But in the ordinary way, you mustn't smoke on the mess deck.'[19] Norman Hampson was warned by his father, an army veteran, to expect a harsh regime in the training camps, but in practice 'almost all of those in authority over us were understanding, reasonably patient and unmistakably fellow members of the human race. Even the leading seamen who did their best to bark obscenities at us when they took us for arms drill, were making such an unconvincing attempt to play at sergeants that they were more amusing than intimidating.'[20]

Eric Denton's first three weeks at *Ganges* were 'a dull blur of routine, discomfort and unhappiness.'[21] Fred Kellet found 'It had been the longest six weeks of my life – I had felt terribly alone and been very, very home-sick.'[22] During peacetime national service in the 1950s, anecdotal evidence suggests that the suicide rate was high among immature young men taken away from home for the first time and put into a harsh environment.[23] There is no evidence that this happened in the navy during the Second World War. There were never more than sixty-two suicides in the whole fleet in any year of the war, and it is not clear how many of these were new entrants.[24] There were several reasons for this difference. Wartime entrants tended to be older than the eighteen-year-olds normally conscripted in peacetime. Even the younger men came from a society which was already disrupted by bombing, evacuation, fathers on active service, and general uncertainty about the future. Furthermore, there was less tradition of bullying in the navy than in the army and the air force, which took the great majority of peacetime conscripts.

The Syllabus

The first stage of the seaman's career was his 'Part I' or 'disciplinary' training. In June 1942 the Admiralty regulated who was to undergo this training, largely consolidating previous practice.

> In future all ratings entering the Royal Navy will undergo the full Part I disciplinary course. The only exceptions will be Visual Signals and Wireless Telegraph ratings who receive their technical training in a Naval establishment. The disciplinary courses for these ratings will last two weeks.[25]

All others would have to undergo the full six-week course.

In February 1944 there was a revision of the system, after it was found that selection standards were being applied inconsistently in different recruiting centres and bases. *Royal Arthur* was now to be the centre for all new entrants. They would be sent there for two weeks of assessment and basic training, before completing it there or elsewhere.

A class at HMS *Royal Arthur*, showing a great variety in ages. The leading seaman instructor is in the centre.

At the start of the course the men were divided into classes named after historic admirals such as Collingwood, Frobisher or Rodney, under a petty officer or a leading hand. They soon settled down to a routine of foot drill, knot tying, naval lore and practical demonstrations. Men were barely introduced to the sea, and only in the form of rowing, which might prove essential some day in a lifeboat. Eric Denton describes the experience at *Ganges*.

There were four or five oars on each side of the boat, and one man on the tiller. After a few circles, we had to achieve a straight line, or we would never have got back ashore. Then we went in a sailing boat about twelve feet long. We learnt how to put the sails up and lower them (or did we learn?), and the philosophy of tacking, sailing against the wind – and some how we got back ashore.[26]

The training syllabus included practically no contact with real naval ships. Norman Hampson did not set foot in one until his basic training was over.[27] Men at *Ganges* or *Collingwood* might see them in the distance, those at *Royal Arthur* or *Glendower* rarely saw them at all. In view of the urgent operational needs of the navy it is not surprising that there was no chance to give men short cruises, but day visits might have been possible. Nor did the navy do much to brief men on naval operations. In this respect the navy followed the practices of the boys' training establishments, concentrating on teaching the men obedience and simple skills.

Swimming was essential and teaching methods could be terrifying.

Those unfortunates who couldn't swim got no sympathy from the Clubs, the PTIs (Physical Training Instructors). First we each had to show whether we could swim or not by doing a couple of lengths up and down the pool. … The poor sods who showed they couldn't swim properly or not at all received poolside instruction from the Clubs who would be ready to assist with his boat hook but not always to let them get out when they tried to splash their way to the side. From there on they would be given personal attention until they were able to swim adequately.[28]

Gun drill was common for all seaman entrants. Within a few days of arriving at HMS *Ganges* in April 1943, G. V. Ball found that there were two main elements in the syllabus – 'Seamanship' and 'Gunnery'. In fact more than half of 'gunnery' consisted of foot drill and 'seamanship', in the first instance, consisted of 'advice on what to do and what not to do in the barracks'. But he was soon involved in some lessons in real seamanship, learning how to steer by means of a simulator.[29] In 1942 the Admiralty ordered that training of lookouts should be given more priority, with four hours taken from the gunnery syllabus and six hours from seamanship to allow for this.[30] By 1943 the Torpedo Branch offered several days instruction in its own particular skills, outlining the role of the branch, the torpedo, the mine and high and lower power electricity.[31]

Induction into naval ways was important, as many of the recruits would soon be under the control of another service, or a part of the navy which had very few regular officers. Potential pilots would be under the command of the RAF for most of their flying training; combined operations men were formally outside naval control for two years of the war, and DEMS gunners would work with the Merchant Navy. Many trainee engineers would be sent to civilian colleges for technical instruction. Men in coastal forces or in convoy escort would mostly be under the command of RNR and RNVR officers who were barely part of naval tradition. It was important to instill all new entrants with the rudiments of naval discipline and culture.

Entrants were soon introduced to naval ranks, but often found them confusing. In Mallalieu's *Very Ordinary Seaman*, one man could not get used to the fact that the chevrons on the older men's arms indicated long service, not rank. He was rebuked by a petty officer.

"Sergeant? Their ain't no such things in the Navy. Them three stripes on 'is arm are good conduct badges. …"

"All right, Admiral; he's still a sergeant to me."[32]

At *Raleigh* in 1943 a petty officer

produced a stack of armbands made of canvas painted black. A number of men were called out from the group and told to put these on. Then, O'Shea called on one of us and said: "Go to the lieutenant commander and salute," "Report to the chief bosun's Mate," and so on. It was very reminiscent of the way a dog is trained to "fetch" the newspaper or lie down.[33]

One group of Wrens was undergoing this lesson when the commodore of the barracks entered. He held out his single broad stripe and asked the recruits what it was. 'They gazed speechless at the strange single stripe and then exclaimed 'Sub-Lieutenant.'"[34]

F. S. Holt of the Royal Australian Navy Volunteer Reserve found that, 'The training system at *Collingwood* was geared to cope with brand new recruits and by sheer necessity proceeded at the speed of those with the lowest IQ. With this background our early period in the Training Establishment was frequently boring, depressing and frustrating; in fact I cannot recall learning anything new whatsoever during at least the first six weeks.'[35]

The men left the bases as Ordinary Seamen, or the equivalent in other branches. These ratings had long been recognized as 'Men not fully trained, but generally employed at sea.'[36] As one officer of a training base wrote, 'F[robisher] 88, fashioned and welded together in five weeks, was returning to its individual components, but each man was taking away with him more than he brought in. Each could look after himself and his kit; whatever his category, each could swim, and pull and sail a lifeboat; each knew enough about fighting a ship not to be a nuisance at sea. And, above all, they had a sense of belonging, a rock-bottom foundation for living together, in preparation for the time when they would be locked together for months on end in a steel box far from land.'[37] What they did not learn was 'how to eat a meal in a ship in a howling Atlantic gale, which would be pitching and tossing, and rolling from one side to another like a bath bun.'[38]

CHAPTER 6

The Parts of the Navy

Ranks and Ratings

By the time he had finished his disciplinary training, a seaman would have some idea of the complexity of naval organization. In some respects the Royal Navy was a more cohesive organization than the army, where each regiment had its own badges, uniform details, traditions, and even differences in rank titles, such as the bombardiers of the artillery or the corporal-majors of the Household Cavalry. In peacetime, sailors of the lower deck wore cap-tallies with the name of the ship, but in war that was replaced with the letters HMS, so the navy appeared a unified mass.

Like all armed forces, the Royal Navy was divided into ranks. This was more obvious in the navy than with the wartime army and RAF, which adopted the utilitarian 'battledress' as almost universal garb, while the navy was slow to adopt its own version of battledress, except in the newer branches such as the Fleet Air Arm and Combined Operations. It still had completely different uniforms for officers and ratings.

The Branches

The navy was divided into branches, each specializing in a different skill, and headed by a flag officer or captain based at the Admiralty Building in Whitehall. The Engineer-in-Chief of the Navy was a vice-admiral, the head of the Navigation Branch was a rear-admiral, the Director of the Gunnery and Anti-Aircraft Warfare Division was a captain, as were the Directors of Anti-Submarine Warfare and Torpedoes and Mining. Some branches were self-contained – medical officers were obviously not liable to any other duties and had a career path entirely within their own profession. At the other extreme was the Seaman or Executive Branch, the dominant one from which all fleet and squadron commanders, commanding officers of ships, first lieutenants and watchkeeping officers were selected. Before the war, nearly all its entrants had spent several years training at Dartmouth. There were specialisms within the Seaman Branch of which the Gunnery Branch was also dominant. A regular officer would undergo a 'short course' in gunnery followed by a 'long course' of more than a year at HMS *Excellent* in Portsmouth. After that he would have the capital letter 'G' attached to his name on the Navy List, and would join the elite of the officer corps.

The Torpedo Branch was rather different, for in a sense it was misnamed. Unlike the gun, the torpedo is not difficult to aim, for it needs no calculation of trajectory. It does, however, require a good deal of maintenance. As it developed in the 1880s, the torpedo was the main user of electricity on board ship, so the torpedo officers and men took over responsibility for electrical power. Over the years electricity began to be used increasingly for internal lighting, searchlights, air-conditioning, weapons and for radio, asdic and radio sets. The Engineering Branch took over responsibility for high-power apparatus, but the Torpedo Branch still had much to do with other equipment. It was also responsible for mines, depth charges and other underwater weapons. According to one official in 1932, 'The torpedo side of the service has for many years been a kind of octopus ready to grab any new development and absorb it under the misleading title of torpedo.' This was beginning to back-fire on the officers of the branch, who were in danger of becoming too specialized and restricted. The First Sea Lord wrote in 1933,

> ... the Torpedo Officer appears to be growing less suitable relative to other branches for promotion to the higher ranks ... It is undoubtedly due to the growth of electrical machinery in ships and the ever-increasing need for the Torpedo Officer to spend time between decks rather than on deck ...[1]

Another specialization was Navigation. Since the Navigating Officer generally worked alone, he did not cultivate skills of leadership and this was not a path to the top. Signals was another seaman officer specialization – something of a backwater except for the possibility of serving as flag lieutenant to an admiral.

Seaman officers provided most of the pilots and observers of the Fleet Air Arm. The branch was quite small before its wartime expansion, with only 340 aircraft in 1939. It had poor promotion prospects compared with the Gunnery Branch. When the great expansion programme began in 1937, it was decided to form a separate Air Branch of the RNVR with men recruited directly from civil life and trained as pilots or observers. They wore the letter 'A' in the middle of the curl of the rank stripes. According to Charles Lambe, 'The badge was designed to warn all beholders that the wearer knew nothing about the Navy, or about seamanship and navigation. ... In other words, it was the only badge ever worn by a naval officer to indicate that the wearer was not qualified to do something.' [2]

The Fleet Air Arm created further demand for engineers. Aircraft became far more complex during the course of the war. Even the RAF had done without techni-cal branch officers until 1940, leaving the maintenance of its planes to NCOs and air-craftsmen, and assuming that the pilots would have a vested interest in supervising them. The Fleet Arm lagged behind the RAF in modern aircraft and its most famous aircraft, the Fairey Swordfish, would not have looked out of place in 1918. But it soon began to take on high performance aircraft, including the Seafire adapted from the land-based Spitfire, and American types such as the Wildcat, Avenger and Corsair. Advanced engineering skills were needed to keep them flying. In fact the navy was a little ahead of the RAF in setting up a corps of technical officers. It already had the resources of its own Engineering Branch and from 1939, Lieutenants (E) of more than two years seniority were encouraged to volunteer for two years training, including a full flying course. Others would be taken from the Air Branch and trained as engineers over two years; but this was a long-term plan, soon to be overtaken by events.[3]

Since the abandonment of the Selborne Scheme in 1920 engineer officers were entered and trained entirely separately from the seaman officers. They had no prospect of command of a ship or a fleet, and could only rise within their own branch, as far as vice-admiral. Engineer officers wore a purple band between their gold rank stripes. The other large specialization was the Paymaster Branch, whose members wore white between the stripes. They were responsible for supplies, catering and administration, and the 'pay' mentioned in their title was only a small part of their role.

Substantive and Non-substantive Rates

In the Royal Navy, 'substantive rating', as a chief petty officer, petty officer or leading seaman, was not directly related to skill at a trade, or 'non-substantive rating'. It was a system that had grown up before 1914 but was further developed between the wars, mainly in the Seaman and Communication Branches. Substantive promotion was very slow, and after the apparent failure of the petty officers at Invergordon, the navy was reluctant to give out substantive rank purely for technical skill. According to the King's Regulations of 1938,

> Capacity to command subordinates, powers of organization and knowledge of service routine are important considerations in making recommenda-tions for advancement to higher ratings in every branch: capacity to com-mand subordinates is to be regarded as the primary qualification for Seamen, Signal and Stoker petty officers. Technical skill in a non-substantive rating is not in itself a reason for advancement in substantive rating.[4]

The navy tried to compensate men who might wait for years to become leading sea-men or petty officers, by allowing them to qualify for higher non-substantive rates with extra pay and additions to their branch badges. In 1934 the Signal Branch was reor-ganized on the basis of non-substantive rates. Up till then, a man's pay had depended mainly on eventually reaching a higher substantive rank as leading signalman, yeoman of signals (petty officer) and so on. Four non-substantive grades were introduced for Wireless Telegraphists – Trained Operator, and Wireless Telegraphists 3rd, 2nd and 1st Class, with similar grades for Visual Signallers. The main reasons for the change were:

> 1.   The individual will be encouraged and rewarded for brains, enterprise and effort, the Service reaping the benefit owing to the best men being brought forward for advancement instead of stagnating on a roster.

> 2.   Under existing conditions substantive promotion is necessary to ensure technical progress by V/S and W/T ratings. A slow rate of substan-tive advancement, therefore, imposes a definite handicap on professional advancement. The creation of non-substantive rates for the branch will do much to remove this handicap.[5]

This was very different from the practice of the US Navy, in which advancement through the three grades of petty officer was dominated by training courses and examinations. As an American official publication put it, 'In British naval practice, spe-ciality and rating are generally unrelated. A man may have high status in a speciality without advancing beyond a seaman's rating; or he may be a CPO but still not high-ly qualified in his particular speciality.'[6] In fact substantive and non-substantive rates were more closely related than that suggests. According to the *Gunnery Pocket Book* of 1945, 'Although the Regulations permit advancement to Leading Seaman and Petty Officer without first qualifying for a "non-substantive" rating, such qualification is of great assistance and should in any case be undertaken as soon as possible after "sub-stantive" advancement.' In the Gunnery Branch, certain non-substantive ratings were only open to those with enough leadership skills to become leading seamen and petty officers. '1st class ratings, owing to the duties they have to perform, are reserved for C.P.Os, P.Os and leading seamen passed for P.O., holding a 2nd class rat-ing. 2nd class ratings are reserved for leading seamen, and able seamen passed for leading seaman, holding a 3rd class rating.'[7]

The Royal Navy, unlike the other British services, was meticulous in showing a rating's specialization, and his exact standing within that specialization, by means of a badge on his right arm. According to the American Joint Army and Navy Intelligence publication on uniforms and badges, 136 specialist insignia, or 'non-substantive badges' were in use in 1944, but even that did not reflect the full range of possibilities. There were twenty-five different designs of badges, such as the six-pointed star of the Supply and Secretariat Branch, or the flags of visual signalmen.

The addition of crowns and small six-pointed stars made the position even more complicated. Each branch and sub-branch had evolved separately, so this part of the badge could mean something completely different for each. In some branches they represented skill independent of rank. Among the gunners, a star above meant a second-class qualification, but the man could be any rate from chief petty officer to able seaman. In other branches, such as the Fleet Air Arm and Stoker, the badge showed the rate, and merely repeated the information given by the badges on the other sleeve. Thus a chief petty officer or petty officer had a crown above the badge, a leading rating had a star above it, and a stoker second class or junior air mechanic, equivalent to an able seaman, had no addition.

A badge could mean a good deal to a young seaman. John W. Davies wrote, 'The 'day of days' arrived for me, the course had ended and I was now an anti-aircraft gunner, an AA3 (LC), and as proud as the proverbial peacock. I could not sew my badges on quickly enough. ... Now I wanted some leave to be able to show off my newly acquired glory ...'[8]

Selection

The navy was essentially a collection of specialists working together at their different trades. In wartime, selection for one particular trade was likely to be final, for there was no time for re-training.

> ... it has been the [Director of Personal Services'] policy to avoid transferring ratings from one branch to another where they have been trained and become qualified. There has at all times been such a shortage of the higher ratings that we have not been able to afford transfers of these men to other duties, further, the need for rapid expansion of the Fleet has required that everyone, as far as possible, should be trained quickly for one specific job.[9]

Volunteers outside the age of conscription were allowed to choose their branch, provided they came up to medical and intellectual standards and there were vacancies. Though the navy was always keen to encourage volunteering, the balance was reversed for conscripts; the navy's needs took priority over the man's own wishes. The allocation to branch was done on recruitment, by the Pensioner Petty Officers at the start of the war, and the Personnel Selection Officers after 1941. By the time they were called up, men usually knew whether they were going to be seamen, stokers, signalmen, marines or 'miscellaneous' ratings, and were sent to separate training camps accordingly. By 1944 it was clear that this system was somewhat erratic and it was decided to centralize selection at HMS *Royal Arthur*. From February that year, all new entrants spent two weeks there. The men were kitted out and there was some time for training, but the main purpose was to subject the men to a series of tests.[10]

Before 1944, more detailed selection within the branches was carried out at the basic training camps. Seamen were chosen for training for the non-substantive rates of signaller, wireless telegraphist, radar operator and submarine detector and sent on for specialized training. Others, such as gunners and torpedomen, were usually selected after some time at sea.

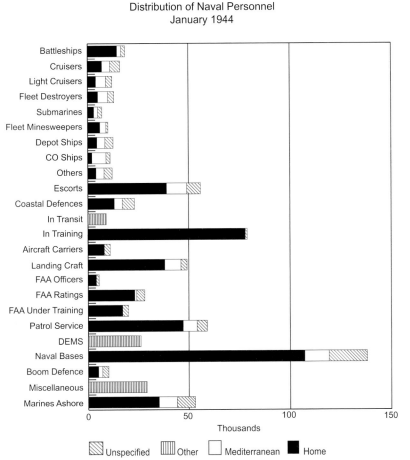

Distribution of Naval Personnel
January 1944

The numbers of men in the different parts of the navy in 1944.

Certain priorities can be identified in the placing of men, and these varied comparatively little during the war. First, men who were fit for, and had volunteered for aircrew duties were pushed forward despite any other uses they might have. Next on the list were potential officers, who were picked out quite early in the training process.

The third priority was to find men who had already had skills which could be useful to the navy – trained medical personnel and engineers, for example. Most members of the Sick Berth Branch were trained within the navy, but dental technicians, dispensers, mental nurses and opticians would usually come into the service fully qualified.[11] The problem of engineering in the armed forces was a broader one, and became a national issue during 1942. Sir William Beveridge was appointed to look into it. He found that the navy did rather well in identifying men with engineering skills, and deploying them effectively. Out of forty-one naval men in the sample, thirty were in responsible or skilled engineering jobs and two more were in semi-skilled jobs. Three more were on aircrew duties, but this was acceptable in view of the primacy of flying. Only six men were not using their engineering skills and all had been naval reservists before the war. They included 'a toolmaker serving as a telegraphist; a horizontal miller serving as a stoker; a chargehand electrician serving as signalman.' Though Beveridge disapproved of this, the navy had gone to some trouble to train two of these men in signalling, where they were performing a valuable function.

Certainly the navy did rather better than the army, which placed more than half the men with engineering skills in non-engineering jobs. According to Beveridge, 'if the Navy were the only Fighting Service our work would be but little indeed.' He attributed this to the Engineering Branch of the navy. Though engineer officers had long complained about their lack of status, the branch was very influential within its own field. Beveridge identified the methods the navy used to find its engineers.

> The trade testing of the navy is centralized, standardized and objective. All the candidates for appointment as Engine Room Artificer or Ordnance Artificer are tested on uniform methods at one of the three home ports by performance against time of a set piece of work; all the candidates for appointment as Electrical Artificer are tested at one of two centres by a similar mechanical test; the test in each case normally lasts several days. Those who pass this test are guaranteed, as possessing a certain minimum of mechanical skill; those who fail it are given the opportunity of training up to it. Those who fail a little more badly are assigned to the appropriate less skilled categories. It is not surprising that even to-day the Navy is able to obtain the skilled engineers that it wants substantially by volunteering. Any skilled engineer volunteering for the Navy knows that he will have a fair test and that, if he passes it, he will be ranked forthwith as petty officer and employed as an engineer.

> … there is an organized search for talent in the Navy. At each of the home ports officers of the engineering branch make a systematic investigation of all men at the general reception centre with a view to discovering men who can be trained for technical work. They find in this general body of seamen and stokers appreciable numbers of men suitable for training for every grade up to Engine Room Artificer, that is to say men possessing qualifications which for one reason or another had escaped notice at an earlier stage and with less expert enquiry. This search for talent is conducted not on paper, by examination of forms, but by interviews making possible a real judgment of personal skill and capacity.[12]

The fourth grade of men was those who could be trained as radar operators, submarine detectors or wireless telegraphists. These fields were relatively new and had little or no application in civil life, so there was no chance of finding men with previous experience. All were rapidly expanding in wartime, and required men of average intelligence or above. The survey showed that a place within the top 30 per cent for intelligence was desirable, but a third of passes came from men within the middle 40 per cent of the range, and one in twenty were lower than that.[13] Such men tended to be selected during basic training as seamen.

Finally, there were the men with no particular, or at least measurable, qualities. Of anti-aircraft gunners it was said, 'There is scope here for men of all levels of intelligence, presumably because success depends to a very large extent on other qualities. But E's [the bottom 10 per cent] stand a poor chance of passing the course.' Quarters ratings, also members of the Gunnery Branch, did not have this problem. One in eight of the passes into this rate were from the bottom 10 per cent.[14]

The navy used certain measurable parameters in selecting men for particular trades. Previous experience was needed for artificers, wiremen and cinema operators. A good education, with school certificates in science and maths, was necessary to be selected as a potential electrical or radio mechanic, or a visual signaller, or to train as a chiropodist or neurological assistant in the Sick Berth Branch. Air Artificers, Mechanics and Fitters needed a high degree of intelligence. Signal ratings – coders, visual signallers, wireless telegraphists, automatic morse operators and teleprinter operators – had to be of high integrity in view of the confidential material they would handle. But some trades could be selected for more negative reasons. A coder did not have the high standards of eyesight required by a signaller. A convoy signalman was less well educated than one who worked with the main fleet.[15]

Medical standards were also used in the selection for different branches. Signalmen and airmen required the very highest standard of eyesight. Seamen, stokers and marines needed slightly lower standards. Artificers, shipwrights, air fitters and mechanics, sick berth attendants, writers and marine bandsmen were allowed to wear glasses. The navy was reluctant to let go of men whose eyesight deteriorated, fearing that their skills would be lost. In February 1942 they ordered that they should be transferred to jobs where good eyesight was not required, such as submarine detector or air mechanic; failing that they were to be considered for shore-based jobs in the boom defence service.[16] From 1943, candidates for the non-flying parts of the Fleet Air Arm were allowed poorer vision. Standards of hearing were high for signalmen, seamen, marines, airmen and telegraphists.[17]

Until the end of 1942 there was no special procedure for testing the aural abilities of submarine detectors. Surgeon Lieutenant-Commander Ransome-Wallis was appointed to look into the issue. He eliminated candidates who had had certain diseases of the ear, and took care to test the hearing of the others. He used an audiometer to test the men's reactions to changes of pitch, he found that men with a musical background were better at this. In June 1943 he claimed considerable success.

> The aural tests described above have done much to eliminate poor operating at sea. It is interesting to note that these "pure tone" tests agree very closely with the results reported by Commanding Officers at sea. Every single rating who has been returned to H.M.S. "OSPREY" as a bad operator has been found to be below our aural standards. … "Aural intelligence" plays probably the greatest part in the success or otherwise of an operator.[18]

Good technical training was important, for the safety of the ship or the success of the operation might hinge on a single man, often a junior rating. Mistakes or negligence by lookouts, engine-room watchkeepers, leadsmen finding the depth of water, asdic and radar operators or anti-aircraft gunners could have serious and immediate consequences. Conversely, well-applied skills could have very important results. In May 1945 Ordinary Seaman Norman Poole was convinced that he saw a ship among many confused radar echoes of rain squalls. His superiors failed to confirm this but Poole persisted 'almost to the point of insubordination' and eventually the echo was identified as the Japanese cruiser *Haguro*, which was surrounded and sunk. Poole was awarded the Distinguished Service Medal.[19]

The selection process could cause problems by its very efficiency. Before the war, stokers were distinguished from other branches by their joining after the age of eighteen, with no particular experience. They included men of all types, and the best of them might eventually become highly skilled ratings as Mechanicians. In wartime stokers, unless they were volunteers for the branch, tended to be men who were not fit for anything else. Rear-Admiral Ford complained of 'the drafting away of the rather thin cream to become Engine Room Mechanics and Motor Mechanics.'[20] The need for one type of man could also impinge on the supply of another. By late 1943, increased demands for landing craft officers and for the Fleet Air Arm led to a shortage of suitable men to train as radio mechanics.[21]

The Manning Divisions

The men of the lower deck were attached to home ports, the great depots at Chatham, Portsmouth and Plymouth. In peacetime, each division had a roughly equal number of men, with an equal distribution of ships of each type allocated to it. Men might travel round the world, but they could be sure that their ship would return to the same home port. If the ship was in British waters, it would return to the home port for maintenance. On shore duties or a training course, the men would be kept within their home port area. Married men could safely settle their families in the district. These divisions were the closest things the navy had to the regimental system of the army, but they were much bigger. Unlike army regiments the port divisions were not marked by any badges. In peacetime an insider might know that HMS *Rodney* belonged to Plymouth or her sister-ship, *Nelson*, to Portsmouth, but wartime cap tallies did not give this information. Anyone might notice the preponderance of west-country accents from a Plymouth ship, or Cockneys in one from Chatham.

In 1940, men who signed on for long service were allowed the choice of home port, as far as vacancies allowed. For those who had no preferences, men from the

Portsmouth Naval Barracks after an air raid, *c.* 1941.

London area were allocated to Chatham. Those from the Birmingham, Newcastle and Southampton areas were sent to Portsmouth, and those from Bristol went to Devonport. From the inland area around Derby, half went to Portsmouth, half to Chatham. From Scotland, one third were sent to each of the depots.[22] Hostilities Only men were allocated at the navy's convenience, except that men who had a father or brother already serving in one of the port divisions were invited to apply for transfer to that division.[23] The home ports each had their nicknames, which were more or less affectionate – Chatham was 'Chats', Portsmouth was 'Pompey' and Devonport was 'Guz'.

With the vast expansion of the navy, there were always thousands of men in the barracks at the home ports – nearly 140,000 in February 1944 [24] – and many passing through – an average of 500 in and out per day at Chatham.[25] New facilities were built, but this did not prevent gross overcrowding. As one rating complained, 'in Portsmouth Naval Barracks in 1942 there were 120 men in messes meant for 30, and 16 knives and forks in the mess. Every other night ratings slept down cold, damp air-raid shelters. It could escape no intelligent person that the real reason why half the men slept down the shelters was that there was no room for them in the buildings. As a result of this many died of pneumonia.'[26] The barracks were hated by the Hostilities Only men. The three-badge recalled pensioners, on the other hand, pre-ferred permanent postings there in order to avoid sea-going drafts.

Each of the divisions was headed by a commodore. Under him, the commander was responsible for the actual drafting, under the control of the Director of Personal Services. As John Munday was told during his officer training in 1943, 'The comman-der's main duty is to see that at all times the barracks can supply men for immediate draft from Admiralty requirements.[27] In peacetime, drafting was carefully regulated to give each man a due proportion of home and foreign service, sea and shore time; in war this was rarely possible.

A fourth division was formed in 1939, for the Fleet Air Arm. Ratings of the branch could not be employed in their normal duties at Chatham and Devonport, for there were no suitable airfields, so they were all attached to Lee-on-Solent near Portsmouth.[28] More new drafting pools were added during the war, all functional rather than geographical – the Royal Naval Patrol Service at Lowestoft, with 62,000 men in January 1944, was one of the largest; Portsmouth for Coastal Forces, with 23,900; and Liverpool for merchant ship gunners. Combined Operations had more than 50,000 men in January 1944.[29] There were small drafting depots, mostly with men unfit for sea service – the Boom Defence Service (9000 men), harbour defence (1320 men) and controlled minefields (1368 men).[30] Admiral Ford commented,

> This diversity of drafting arrangements has some advantages and some dis-advantages. The great advantage is the case of access which the individual rating has to the drafting authority, the great disadvantage that many differ-ent authorities have to be dealt with if the true picture is to be obtained. Further co-ordination between the various authorities is difficult to obtain and the mere existence of a number of pools possibly involves some waste of manpower. ... There appears to be no easy road along which drafting effi-ciency can be reached. The present system has grown up during the course of years during peace when the tempo was slow. In war a hand to mouth existence is led by the drafting offices ...[31]

Navies Within the Navy

As well as the division into ranks and branches, the officers and men of the wartime navy were in practice divided by the type of ship they served in. In the peacetime navy, the drafting authorities would attempt to give each man a balanced career, with time in large ships, destroyers, escort vessels and in shore bases (though even then the submarine service was a separate entity). In wartime none of this was possible. A temporary officer, or a Hostilities Only rating, would usually be trained to serve in one type of vessel only. Nicholas Monsarrat, for example, wrote of his own career as he took over a frigate, 'Together with ocean convoy escort, it was in point of fact the only sort of Navy I knew anything about; the ship I was going to command would be the biggest one I had ever boarded, and her job, convoy escort, had been my life for as long as I could remember.'[32] This division was little recognized by regulation, though it was at least as important as most of the others.

In a traditional fleet, including the Grand Fleet of 1914–18, different types of ship would serve together. In modern war different vessels, such as submarines, coastal forces or escorts, would serve either on their own or with others of a similar function. There were six or seven different navies in wartime, each with its own mix of officers from regular navy, RNR and RNVR, with a parallel mix of long-service ratings and HOs. At the beginning of the war, the Admiralty favoured something akin to the First World War, with regular officers and crews in the battleships, cruisers and destroyers of the main fleet, and reservists in the much smaller vessels which conducted the anti-submarine campaign. At first a large part of the anti-submarine war was indeed conducted by converted trawlers, manned by reservists. They were soon replaced by bigger ships, corvettes, then frigates which were almost as big as destroyers. They were mostly captained by RNR officers, with RNVRs in the junior officer ranks, and occasionally in command later on. They had regular senior petty officers, and Hostilities Only crews. Of forty-six *River* class frigates in commission in mid-1944, ten were commanded by regular RN officers and four of these were escort group leaders. Thirty-two were commanded by the RNR, and four by the RNVR. Out of more than 400 other commissioned officers in these ships, only six were regular RN all first lieutenants, half of them in escort group leaders.[33] In February 1944 anti-submarine vessels employed 52,500 officers and men, the largest single group in the navy.[34]

Minesweeping was also left to reservists, initially of the Trawler Division of the RNR. The mainstay of the service at the beginning of the war was the Skippers RNR, former fishermen appointed warrant officers in the Royal Navy. 'The trawler skippers could be a problem. They were nearly all professional fishermen and great seamen, but they were not easily amenable to naval discipline, nor did they take kindly to too much flag signalling.' The old class of skipper was gradually replaced.

Meanwhile new branches began to emerge. The fast, light craft of coastal forces were dominated by the RNVR from the beginning, as one officer wrote.

> The crews of M.T.Bs and M.G.Bs vary from 8 or 9 in the smaller boats to nearly 30 in the larger ones and, in a few, even more. They consist mainly of "Hostilities Only" ratings, men who have come straight from civilian life with a short training period when they entered the Navy and a further short period of special training for Coastal Forces duties. Their officers nearly all wear the wavy stripes of the R.N.V.R. and have served their time as Ordinary Seamen before obtaining their commissions.[35]

In Combined Operations, the crews of landing craft did much of their training in co-operation with the army. They were encouraged to think amphibiously, rising above their loyalties to their individual service. RNVR officers and HO ratings and marines made up practically all the crews of smaller landing craft, while the larger landing ships were run by the merchant navy or RNR officers. Officers and men wore naval uniform and had naval ranks and ratings, but technically they were not even part of the navy between 1941 and 1943.

Initially destroyers were officered by the regular navy. In August 1941 it was decided to withdraw one RN officer from each destroyer and replace him with a reserve officer, who would be specially trained in torpedo and anti-submarine work and in watchkeeping. Increasing numbers of RNVRs joined destroyers over the next few years. In April 1945 six destroyers of the O class, for example, had two or three regular officers each, including the captain and first lieutenant in each case, with three to five RNVRs.[36] By February 1944, destroyers on fleet service employed 9500 men, in addition to those on anti-submarine work.[37]

The submarine service was another preserve of the regular navy in the First World War, but at the beginning of the second war Edward Young was one of two midshipmen under training at *King Alfred* who were persuaded to volunteer for the service. He became the first executive RNVR officer to serve in a submarine, late in 1940.[38] By the end of the war more than half of submarine officers were RNVR. Twelve submarines were commanded by them, with seven more under dominion Volunteer Reserve officers.[39] The service remained quite small throughout the war – 7817 ratings in September 1944.[40]

The big-ship navy of battleships and cruisers was the last to be affected. Its officers and men were mostly regular Royal Navy, with few RNRs or RNVRs. Even this began to change as the war went on. Early in 1942 the Admiralty decreed that it was 'essential to extend the existing arrangements for the replacement of R.N. Officers by Reserve officers to all major war vessels not already affected.' The principles had changed. 'With the expansion of the Naval forces that has taken place within the last two years, the Fleet must be manned with Reserve officers with a leavening of Active Service officers, and not manned by R.N. Officers diluted with Reserve officers.' On each capital ship, a RNVR officer was to be appointed to shadow a regular officer for one to three months, before the latter was withdrawn, and this process was to continue until no more than three regular officers were left, with the exception of the captain, executive officer and specialist officers. The same procedure was to be adopted in cruisers and aircraft carriers, until only two regular officers were left.[41] In fact it never went this far with the big ships. In April 1945 the battleship *Duke of York* had seven regular RN officers including the captain, commander and first lieutenant. At the other end of the scale, twelve out of fourteen seaman midshipmen were regulars, plus two RNR. There were three regular specialist officers of the Gunnery, Torpedo and Navigation Branches plus two from the reserves. All ten engineers were regular RN and there were 23 RNVR officers in various ranks up to lieutenant-commander.[42]

The HO rating began to make inroads. Applying pre-war standards to the cruiser *Hawkins* in 1942, Captain Oram concluded that two thirds of his men were 'immature sailors' who had been at sea for less than two years.[43] In 1944 the cruiser *Newfoundland* had 30 per cent long-service ratings, 66 per cent Hostilities Only, 2 per cent Royal Fleet Reserve and 2 per cent recalled pensioners.[44] As Captain Oram put it of *Hawkins*,

> ... the ship was steamed and defended by a cross-section of British provincial life with a handful of South Africans thrown in as leaven. The Jolly Jack of peacetime was a rare bird indeed, so rare that one was tempted to pipe a tear of affection for the breed, now a practically extinct prototype. The wartime sailor, faithfully modelling himself upon his glamorous predecessor, was conscious of the ready-made aura which attached to his own interpretation of the part. He was often dismayed to find that the dazzling mythology surrounding this sea business did not quite come up to expectation. There was much to be said for the 'new boys', though. The model set for them to follow was good and by his exacting standards we were able to run our complicated machines on a very weak mixture of RN spirit! [45]

CHAPTER 7

Traditional Training Methods

Training Organization

There was little centralized organization of training in the navy, even within individual branches. In theory the Admiralty was all-powerful, the only service ministry which was both an administrative centre and an operational headquarters. It practice, it never had the means to exercise these powers in full. In the age of wireless, captains complained about being bombarded with trivial signals. Yet the central administration remained quite small and there was no naval staff for planning future campaigns, until Winston Churchill imposed it in 1912. The navy was a collection of ships, sailors and fleets, rather than a set of officers in Whitehall. Much power remained with the commanders-in-chief, including those of the home ports.

Each training base was formally under the control of one of the area commanders-in-chief; Chatham (known as Nore Command), Portsmouth, Devonport, Rosyth for eastern Scotland and north-east England, Orkney and Shetland for the extreme north, and Western Approaches for most of the west coast for the United Kingdom. This was perfectly rational in the case of basic training, for the camps were closely related to the home port divisions and it was reported in 1943, 'The output of HMS *Collingwood* goes to Portsmouth, the output of HMS *Raleigh* to Devonport and the output of HMS *Ganges* to Chatham.'[1] It was also logical for some kinds of practical training. The home port commands each maintained their own gunnery, torpedo and signal schools, dealing mainly with ratings from these commands. DEMS gunners for merchant ships were trained at bases in the Western Approaches command, and most of the merchant ships they would serve in took part in Atlantic convoys.

The position was rather more complex for other forms of specialized and operational training. Some schools, especially for engineers and wireless operators, were in civilian colleges. Many of them were in the London area so a disproportionate number were under the Nore Command. Many schools had to be situated away from enemy aircraft and submarine attack. This was quite convenient in the case of anti-submarine training, for the schools on the Clyde were in Western Approaches Command, which dealt with the bulk of the anti-submarine war. Radar training on the Isle of Man was also in the area, and this was not inconvenient, though the ratings might go to all kinds of ships. Less suitably, Western Approaches also included many of the Combined Operations training bases, which had little or nothing to do with the main functions of the command. Even more awkwardly, the main Coastal Forces Training base at Fort William was under Western Approaches, though coastal warfare was confined to the east and south of the country.

Admiral Sir William James, as Commander-in-Chief at Portsmouth, took his duties seriously and visited the schools under his command regularly.

> Then on the 23rd I did a good round of the ratings. First the Grammar School, where I found a good-looking lot of youngsters who will mostly be writers, and then to two Holiday Camps at Hayling Island. I do not suppose you have ever seen a Holiday Camp. ... – scores of little sleeping huts, communal dining and play rooms, and the better ones had tennis courts and swimming baths. ... They serve our purpose admirably.

Commander-in-Chief Western Approaches, on the other hand, was heavily involved in directing the Battle of the Atlantic. His command was widely dispersed, and a trip to an isolated Scottish base might take several days of travel.

Though they did not formally command the bases, the heads of the various branches at the Admiralty naturally had a good deal of say in how the training schools were run. Sometimes they appointed officers to inspect and report on the schools; Admiral Sir Frederick Dreyer on DEMS gunners in 1941, Rear-Admiral Ford on engineers' training in 1943, for example. The senior officers of each branch tended to have a good idea of what was wanted of a trainee, and since the officers themselves had undergone a common training, there was some kind of consensus.

Control was light and often erratic. Methods and standards could differ considerably between schools teaching the same subject. In 1943 Dr Vernon noticed significant differences between HMS *Nimrod* at Campbeltown and HMS *Osprey* at Dunoon, 50 miles further up the Firth of Clyde. At *Nimrod* the men had thiry-eight hours of lectures during the course; at *Osprey* they had nine. At *Nimrod* they moved from one instructor to another during the day, at *Osprey* a section of ten to twelve men stayed with the same instructor for all their shore-based tuition.[2] More co-ordination between the different courses, and perhaps a more centralized command such as the United States Navy's Bureau of Personnel (BuPers), might have led to greater efficiency. Summarising the wartime experience of the gunnery schools, one officer commented,

> Although there is quite a lot to be said for Schools developing along individual lines and thus enhancing efficiency by a sense of competition, it is considered that in the long run this method defeats its own ends. The raising of different requirements by the authorities teaching the same subject clouds the issue for the Admiralty and this, combined with constantly changing ideas, sometimes results in little progress being made.[3]

Instructors

The navy tended to separate education from instruction, though its terminology was confusing. The Instructor Officers were at the top of the educational hierarchy. They all had honours degrees in mathematics, science or engineering. They were recruited as lieutenants, and trained midshipmen, mainly in the larger ships of the fleet. They had prospects of promotion to Instructor Captain. There were 152 of these officers in the navy in 1937.

Below these were the Schoolmasters, of whom there were 108 in 1937. They needed teaching experience and a certificate but not a degree, though many had them in 1939. They started with the warrant rank of schoolmaster and their promotion prospects were little better than other warrant officers. They might be commissioned after ten years and eventually reach the rank of Headmaster Lieutenant, though only 1 per cent could serve in the highest rank of Headmaster Commander.[4]

They worked mainly with the boys in the training establishments and afloat. At *St George*, the boys' establishment on the Isle of Man, it was noted, 'Thanks to enlightened civilian schoolmasters, drafted into the navy with the meager "thin ring" rank of Warrant Schoolmaster', standards of teaching were matched to the educational background of the individual.' Captain H. K. Oram noted that extra schoolmasters were needed at HMS *King Alfred*, to teach simple mathematics to officer candidates.[5] Apart from that, the navy did not systematically recruit trained schoolteachers. It had no room on the training curriculum for anything but the most practical training of Hostilities Only ratings and temporary officers.

Instructors in the training schools were far removed from the well-educated officers of the Instructor Branch, for they were usually petty officers or seamen. In 1943, according to the Second Sea Lord, there were three main sources for instructors in basic training establishments. The 'old men', or petty officer pensioners, were suitable for initial training, but were out of touch with modern methods in craft and technical training. In any case their numbers could not be expanded. Others were leading seamen of 'the "failed C.W. type"', men of good education who had failed the officer training course. Thirdly, there were able seamen given acting rate. The Admiralty had recently instituted the rate of Leading Seamen (Not Qualified) for this purpose. Ideally each instructor should have a class of not more than twenty-five men, but in practice they ranged from thirty to forty. The standard of instruction was poor.[6]

Rear-Admiral Ford found faults with the teaching of stokers. 'The instructors are almost invariably old pensioner Chief Stokers. They have not been taught how to teach and there is no doubt that the standard of instruction is very low. At Stamshaw Camp instruction consisted almost entirely of dictating notes.'[7] F. S. Holt of the RANVR was dissatisfied at HMS *Collingwood*.

> Rather impatiently we listened daily to formerly retired "Gunners' Mates" (recalled to be instructors) continuously reciting naval gunnery drill like gramophone records. So "parrot fashion" were they that if interrupted with a question, a dazed look would come over their faces and they would proceed to start from the beginning again.[8]

John Davies found that the standard varied among the aged petty officers and chiefs at *Ganges*. One 'would have made an excellent schoolmaster. His explanations were economical and lucid, delivered quietly but with effect.' Training as a radio mechanic at Robert Gordon's College in Aberdeen in 1941, Roy Fuller had a 'splendid technical instructor, to whose lucidity and patience we owed much.' Later at Lee-on-Solent he had 'Some talks on theory ... of low quality compared with Aberdeen.'[9]

CPO Hayward describes his first experience of teaching at HMS *President V* in 1941. 'Standing in front of a class for the first time, expected to utter words of wisdom, is a mighty lonely experience. To start with, we had no syllabus, and just a sketchy outline of what we were supposed to impart. Nor was there much time in which to do it. Yet I found myself enjoying it after a time.'[10]

Eventually there was some effort to improve standards, as each branch activated its own programme with little co-ordination. In the Gunnery Branch J. P. W. Mallalieu, author of *Very Ordinary Seaman* and a lieutenant-commander, was put in charge of a School of Instructional Technique at *Excellent* in 1943. In the Anti-Submarine Branch, Petty Officer John Whelan went on a course in HMS *Nimrod*.

The final hurdle during examination week was the delivering of a lecture. Every would-be instructor had to prove his ability to make a lucid, cogent, intelligent and gripping speech before an audience comprised of qualified instructor officers, warrant officers, chiefs and petty officers. Experts sat in various parts of the hall assessing the candidate's ability.

Candidates from the dominions spoke at length on 'life back home' until satirised by one of their number. Several candidates got drunk, and Whelan himself got carried away with his account of Napoleon's Russian Campaign of 1812, but passed, along with three others. 'There was a shortage of instructors but (and I say this with some pride) the Navy did not lower its standards.'[11]

Standards were quite high at *Nimrod* in October 1943, as reported by Lieutenant-Commander D. M. Carmichael. 'Teaching in "school" is of a very high standard, and all relevant to A/S. While all the Staff are no doubt painfully aware of the ignorance of the average rating, schoolmasters alone appear able constantly to keep it in mind and adjust their teaching to it ...'[12]

A new wartime edition of the *Torpedo Training Manual* gave hints for instructors. They were to breathe properly and stand upright, for sitting was 'entirely out of keeping with the relations that should exist between the lecturer and his audience.' They were to look the audience in the eye, avoid 'ugly gestures, mannerisms and theatrical tricks', and to deliver the lecture, not recite it, ideally at a rate of about 110 words per minute. They should 'Rejoice in the possession of nerves, because this shows that you care whether your lecture is a success or not.'[13]

Class Organization

In the basic training camps one man from each class was chosen as class leader. Roy Fuller asked his chief petty officer why he had been selected and found that he usually chose solicitors, if available – 'one of the few laymen with a good opinion of the profession.'[14]

In most cases, men were classed together without any regard to individual ability, and Dr P. E. Vernon considered the value of this.

> While psychologists generally advocate the grading of classes of children on the basis of natural aptitude, so that the bright are all taught together, and the average and the dull, it is by no means certain that this principle should apply to S.D. candidates. The main reason, namely, that quick learners will not be held up by waiting for slow ones, nor slow ones discouraged by seeing how inferior they are to quick ones, still holds good. And as each class has to be divided into three sections anyhow, it would seem better to do so on the basis of some principle, instead of haphazardly.

However there were important objections to this.

> In a section containing bright and dull members, the former can assist the latter to some extent in their work at sets and tables; this will be impossible if all members of a section are about equally bright ...[15]

It was a debate which was to dominate British education for more than fifty years.

Dr Vernon suggested that a six-hour learning day was long enough during an intensive course. Lectures were in forty-five-minute periods in many schools, though the instructors of the Patrol Service objected that it took a third of that to get the men warmed up and that going to six or more classrooms in a day was unsettling; Vernon countered that 'men whose schooldays are not long past cannot concentrate effectively for more than $^3/_4$ hour'.[16] John L. Brown describes the day at HMS *President V*, training accountancy ratings.

> The course consisted of lectures in Naval Stores, Victualling, Clothing, Mess Traps, Typing and Recreational Training. A general session was generally included once a week. There were two lectures each morning divided by a stand-easy from 10.45–11.05. Morning lectures finished at 12.30. Afternoon work commenced at 14.30 and finished at 16.15 …[17]

At *Mercury*, the Signal School in Portsmouth, each instructor was expected to keep a register of his class. He was 'responsible for the conduct and dress of the ratings under his charge for instruction, and is responsible that they understand all Signal School orders, routines, etc.' A 'Backward Practical Reading Register' was to be maintained by the Regulating Office in the school, and each instructor was to report men who failed to come up to standard, so that they could be given extra instruction after normal working hours.[18]

Lectures

Psychological studies suggested that the training schools sometimes made too much use of lectures, especially with the majority of men who were not intellectually inclined. Of anti-submarine training in 1943, Dr Vernon reported,

> I am certainly not suggesting that lectures are valueless. A/S instruction must cater for the "verbally-minded" minority as well as the "practically-minded" majority. But I do consider that most of the lectures would be of much more use to the majority if non-verbal techniques of imparting information were adopted to a greater extent. Some lecturers scarcely even employ the blackboard, relying wholly on the spoken word. At least they should write up an outline of the main topics, and illustrate as much as possible by simple pictures and diagrams.[19]

At *King Alfred*, potential officers were sometimes discouraged from taking notes during lectures, as it 'interferes seriously with the value of the instruction.' Instead they were expected to see the importance of 'using their own brains to flog out problems.'[20]

Comparing the three main stoker training establishments, Rear-Admiral Ford wrote, 'There is a general lack of equipment and drawings. H.M.S. CABOT was the best off in this respect since they had collected a number of exhibits and had a Chief Stoker who was somewhat of a genius in making technical drawings.'[21] By 1945, after stoker training had moved afloat to two old battleships in Plymouth Harbour, the situation had improved somewhat. 'Visual aid models, made from plywood by the ship's staff, are used to assist in explaining the operation of various components [including] the closed feed controller, the boiler automatic feed regulator and the oil relay dynamo governor gear.'[22]

Large scale models were used to point out the different parts of a ship, or to demonstrate procedures such as anchoring.

Trainee cooks at a lecture.

The highlight of the lesson was the act of anchoring itself. The anchor was eased out of the hawse-pipe and lowered till it was a few feet above the water and then its whole weight taken by a quick-release device called a Blake slip. When the order came from the bridge "Let go!" the seaman who was standing by with a heavy hammer knocked off the slip and away the anchor plunged and the cable rattled out. It was a splendid moment and the squad cheered reverently like an orchestra at a successful rehearsal applauding a conductor they admired.[23]

Small-scale models were produced in large numbers for help with ship recognition. They had the great advantage that the ship could be viewed from all angles, including from above for the benefit of aircrew.

It was generally recognized that some form of practical instruction was needed, in which the trainees themselves participated. As P. E. Vernon wrote, 'Even if a man has written down in full what he is supposed to do in a certain situation, and revised it, it does not follow that he will apply this knowledge in the given situation, unless he has actually practised doing so.'[24] This was relatively easy in teaching the basic elements of the seaman's craft, such as knot tying.

Morbid's method of instruction was the acme of simplicity. He would ignore us sulkily for a minute or two after the class had assembled, and then contemptuously take a rope's end in his enormous hands. "Clove 'itch", he would mutter, or "Carrick bend" or "Rolling 'itch", after which he would make the hitch in slow time. His huge hands were deft and sure. Then he would hold up the finished hitch for us to see, staring at us moodily, and finally throwing it down in disgust. A pause, and then he repeated the process, this time growling words of explanation – "Up 'ere, over 'ere, down 'ere, and up the middle. Now do it yourself" – and after that it was a matter of making the hitch ourselves, until it was difficult to make a mistake.[25]

Foot drill

Foot drill, or 'Gravel grinding' as it was often known in the navy, was a strong element of basic training. It was also common in the naval barracks where men spent some time between appointments to sea-going ships, and in the gunnery schools such as HMS *Excellent*. Tristan Jones's first impression of Chatham Naval Barracks was of a 'strange and overwhelming' place, full of 'power, male and menacing' where 'squads and battalions of blue-uniformed men drilled and doubled to the loud, harsh shouts and bawls of drill instructors.'[26]

As usual the navy fondly believed that it was continuing in the tradition of Nelson, but this militarization of the seaman was another Victorian innovation. In 1824, Captain Anslem Griffiths was expressing a common opinion when he wrote,

> The character of seamen is one which is inimical to form or parade, while in the soldier precision of movement and an approach to mechanism form the very essence of his utility. ... all attempts to drill the seaman into unnecessary military parade will tend to break down the whole of his natural character.[27]

Boys with a model of the bows of a battleship at HMS *St Vincent*, 1937–38. The same model was used to train naval airmen.

The machine-age navy of the later nineteenth century had different attitudes. In the new sail-less battleships, drill provided a vital function. On such a ship the men worked in small groups in turrets, magazines, galleys or engine rooms and messed in equally small compartments. Foot drill allowed the whole ship's company to operate together as a visible unit and this was an important factor in morale. Foot drill became common at HMS *Excellent* from the 1880s onwards, as the training ship moved on to the progressively-reclaimed Whale Island, where a 'summer parade ground' formed the centre of the complex, with a smaller 'winter parade ground' in a slightly less exposed position. Lord Chatfield, a student at HMS *Excellent* in the 1890s and its commander in 1906–09, describes the situation. '... Rifle drill and battalion drill dominated gunnery training; the object of the qualifier was to command a battalion of seamen, drilling on the parade ground with martial voice under the critical eye of a Staff officer.'[28]

As the 1920 edition of the *Royal Naval Handbook of Field Training* put it, 'The chief prop of discipline is drill, for although of itself of little fighting value, its utility as a means of exercising officers and men in instant obedience cannot be overestimated.'[29] There was a further expansion of foot drill in the aftermath of Invergordon, when it was felt that more formal discipline would help prevent a recurrence.

In the working-up base at Tobermory during the war, Commodore Stephenson convinced a reluctant crew of merchant seamen of the values of foot drill.

"The great thing as I see it," I continued, "is to have one man giving the orders, but, of course, that's difficult for you. You've always been accustomed to going your own way, and I hope you'll always be independent minded. We don't want to change the Briton; but just now independence has to be forgotten for a bit and people have to learn to obey instantly. But, of course, it's not easy to learn new habits like this. Habit makes everything easy – for instance, on Friday nights your legs take you automatically into the 'Pig and Whistle' without you telling them. That's pure habit."

"Well, how do we get this habit you're talking about?"

"Well, sometimes we take about eighteen people ashore and we form them up and say 'Quick March' 'Halt' 'Right Turn' 'Left Turn' 'On Caps' 'Off Caps' 'About Turn' 'Sit Down' 'Stand Up' 'Stand on your heads'. It doesn't matter what the order is – it's just practice in obeying orders. That's what we do in the navy."

There was rather a pause and then someone said: "Can we do it, sir?"[30]

Foot drill had several obvious advantages for the organizers of training programmes. It was well known to the recalled pensioner petty officers who made up the bulk of the instructional staffs. It had a relatively low staff–student ratio. It needed no particular equipment. The wide roads of the converted holiday camps were useful; training facilities at HMS *Glendower* in 1941 included 'a parade ground of approximately 70 x 100 yards and a complete system of wide concrete roads which are used for squad drill instruction.'[31]

Not everyone in the navy agreed that foot drill was valuable. One officer, writing in 1954 but apparently with wartime experience, regarded it is 'a poisonous growth' which had crept in gradually under the influence of HMS *Excellent*.

Apart from mere voice production – which I think can be more cheerfully achieved off the parade ground – taking charge of a squad at rifle drill has always seemed to me a very stupid occupation. The man "in charge" can utter only the approved form of words laid down in the drill book. Woe to the individual who improvises a movement or departs from "The Drill." It is unforgivable to be original.

Nor was it any more effective in inducting new recruits. 'They are smacked onto a Parade Ground, shouted at, given a rifle and taught the funeral exercises. I can hardly think of anything more calculated to destroy a boy's affection for the Navy.'[32]

This was hotly disputed by a class of petty officers, also with wartime experience.

> To say that there are never any smiles of laughter during rifle training is absolute nonsense, I cannot remember one session of rifle drill passing without some amusing situation arising that is talked about for a long time afterwards.

> The crux of the matter is that taking a bunch of raw men as new entries one must first ensure that each and every man is capable of carrying out the simplest of orders without question. It is the easiest, simplest and cheapest method to give them parade training.[33]

Commodore Stephenson at Tobermory had an answer to the point that 'the man "in charge" can utter only the approved form of words laid down in the drill book.' 'Officers are made to give orders in detail, in their own words – not in the words of the drill book – and are made to rap out new orders every few seconds so as to keep their brains and the men alert.'[34]

Certainly some wartime recruits, such as Ken Kimberley and John L. Brown, found foot drill quite enjoyable after the initial shock. John L. Davies wrote, 'Most servicemen appear to dislike parade ground drilling, and I can understand, but I actually enjoyed it; it installed in me a feeling of pride and patriotism, a feeling that I belonged.' The poet, Roy Fuller, found that 'We came to enjoy squad-drill.'[35]

Private Study

Official manuals were issued for most trades, beginning with Part I of the *Admiralty Manual of Seamanship*, as issued to all new entrants in the Seaman Branch. It was less well organized than the contemporary *American Bluejacket's Manual*. In 1941 Rear-Admiral Macnamara at Scapa Flow was given a copy of the American book and commented, 'It is the best [such] book I have ever seen, and from what I can remember, this edition – 1940 – is even better than its predecessor.'[36]

The Royal Navy's *Seamanship Manual* had no introduction and launched straight into matters of practical importance: 'Naval Routine', beginning with 'Bag and Hammock Instruction'. This chapter went on to describe saluting, the ranks and badges of the three services, and the system of organization and watch-keeping on board ship. The second chapter dealt with flags and signals, the third with knots and ropework, and then there were four chapters on elementary navigation, from the point of view of the rating who would be expected to help record the speed or find the depth, to steer the ship by compass, or to avoid other craft in charge of a ship's boat. This led into two chapters on the construction of boats and how to handle them under oars, sail and power. There were chapters on anchor work, rigging and life-saving. The section on 'Messing, Provisions and Stores' was one of the most useful to a disorientated entrant as it described the standard rations and the archaic methods of issuing them to a mess. The final chapters were on watertight doors and valves, and on sea terms.[37] John Davies thought it was 'fascinating but formidable, a book full of strange, cosmopolitan terms gleaned from the seven seas of the world.'[38] In places it was opaque, and Roy Fuller used this as an excuse for failing to learn the point of the compass. 'As the four cardinal points are predominant to the four half-way cardinals,

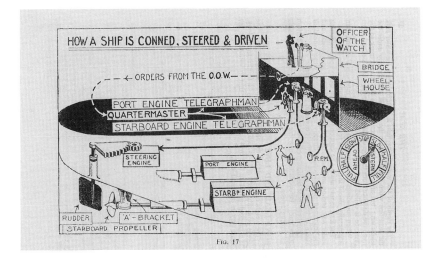

FIG. 17

Illustrations from the *Seaman's Manual* of 1943, showing techniques of steering and anchoring.

so the eight cardinals and half-cardinals are predominant to the intermediates.'[39]

In April 1943 Captain Oram noted that the *Seamanship Manual* Part I 'contains too much detail and too much advanced seamanship for training the hostilities-only seamen ...' A reprint was due, and in view of wartime paper shortages, was it worthwhile to produce thousands more of the 460-page hardback volume? Lieutenant-Commander Crick of the Commission and Warrant Branch was given the job of producing a much-abbreviated *Seaman's Handbook*, and it was ready by June. It was

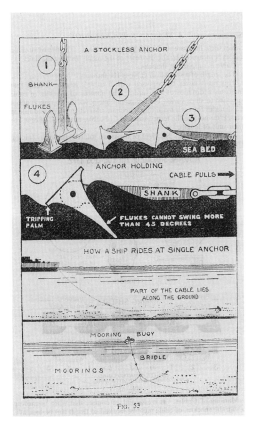

FIG. 53

reduced to 120 pages, with paper covers. It was arranged more systematically, starting with the seaman's role.

> Seamanship is the art of ship management and maintenance, and the capac-
> ity to use foresight and common sense, to make fullest use of the seaman's
> experience.

> No warship has room for "passengers" who stand about indifferent to what
> is going on around them. The seaman must develop sea sense …

There were some line drawings, for example, on anchoring, steering the ship and the
care of a hammock, but they did not appear as clearly as hoped, because of thin
wartime paper. The passage which had caused Fuller concern appeared in a simplified
form, reflecting more modern practice.

> The "points of the compass" are no longer engraved on the magnetic com-
> pass card, but are still used to indicate the general direction of the wind,
> and the bearing of an object. It will be seen from the accompanying sketch
> that each quadrant is divided into eight parts, the division marks being called
> "points," each having a distinctive name given to it.

More than 100,000 copies were printed for the training establishments and delivered
at the end of 1943. The author was commended by the Admiralty 'for the zeal dis-
played'. [40]

Manuals were obviously important in craft and technical training. None were
available, however, for the newest trades such as radar in the early stages, and even
the operational manuals for new pieces of equipment were rather sketchy. In the
Engineering Branch the bible was the *Engineering Manual for His Majesty's Fleet*, as
reprinted in 1939. Two years later it was replaced by the much shorter *Machinery
Handbook*, issued to all artificers, apprentices and stokers on joining.

The provision of manuals depended on the inclinations and abilities within the
different branches of the service, and the results were patchy. The *Gunnery Pocket
Book* of 1945 was clear and concise. The *Torpedo Training Manual* of 1943 was intended mainly for instructors and gave little guidance to students. The Anti-Submarine
Branch had no real training manual during the war. Yet again this contrasts with the
situation in the US Navy. By 1945 it was stated,

> There is no lack of material for advancement in rating … Available also are
> manuals for study for advancement in every rating; basic manuals on vari-
> ous subjects such as Diesel Engines, Gyroscopic Compasses, etc.; and gen-
> eral training courses for nonrated men, petty officers, and chief petty offi-
> cers. There is a special series of manuals on aviation subjects and a manual
> for each of the 17 aviation ratings. [41]

In contrast, one officer of the Royal Navy's Anti-Submarine Branch lamented the use
of 'Out of date Handbooks, or lack of Handbooks, not on sufficiently generous and
explicit lines (vide American Handbooks). [42]

Study was not easy in the cramped accommodation of a ship's messdeck, and the
culture there did not always encourage reading. John Davies's petty officer at *Ganges*

said, 'You can't learn nothin' from a bleeding book' as he issued the *Seamanship Manuals*.[43] Some men had no inclination for study and John L. Davies wrote, 'The others managed to do it fine, they would simply settle on their beds and get down to it, whereas I would make an attempt, but give it up, so I had to rely on a quick browse through my notes before a particular lesson. Fortunately this always proved sufficient to get me through.[44]

CHAPTER 8

Modern Training Methods

The Royal Navy and Film

Films were useful to the Royal Navy in several ways. First, they could entertain the men aboard ship, especially in ports and anchorages where there was little else to do. Secondly, film would be used to put the navy's message across to the general public. The most famous example of this was *In Which We Serve*, made by Noel Coward and based very directly on the exploits of Lord Louis Mountbatten in HMS *Kelly*.

As early as 1925 the Admiralty had supported a publicity film on *Life in the Royal Navy*. In the following year a film on the Fleet Air Arm was commissioned, and in 1935 films were made of deck-landing on the aircraft carrier *Courageous* – not without temperamental differences between the film crew and the naval officers.[1] In 1941 the Admiralty drew up its own outline for a recruiting film to be shown in cinemas. Two friends, unimaginatively named Smith and Jones, join up and volunteer for Submarine Detector (SD) duties after listening to Churchill's broadcasts.

> Anti-submarine school (Nimrod). A group of seamen arriving, among them Smith and Jones.
>
> Series of shots showing the training at Nimrod.
>
> Smith and Jones are drafted to a destroyer.

Naturally the film ends with the sinking of a U-boat.[2]

Training Films

Thirdly, film could be used in training. The capital cost of a film was quite high and some, on the use of particular asdic or radar sets, for example, would go out of date very quickly. Against this they had many advantages. Cinema was regarded as entertainment, and showing films improved morale. They could relieve hard-pressed instructors, compensate for some of their shortcomings in instructional technique, and help impose uniform standards of procedure throughout the fleet.

The navy was a slow starter at this, as one officer recognized in the autumn of 1940.

> It has been recognized by the Army and R.A.F., particularly the latter, that the Sound Film is a most valuable medium of instruction owing to its interest value and its scope. The Navy has fallen far behind the other two services in developing this medium of instruction. ... Now that personnel have to be mass-produced under poor and unrealistic training facilities ... it is more essential than ever that the potentialities of the film should be available to the maximum degree possible.[3]

There was a naval film unit at Tipner in Portsmouth, attached to the Naval School of Photography, but procedures were complicated and bureaucratic. Each script needed constant supervision by the department commissioning it, financial controls were strict and there was not much co-operation with the film industry. There was little interest in film production at the top, and the Admiralty Building did not even have a film projector. In August 1940 the Captain of HMS *Excellent* wrote,

> I am convinced that a very great deal could be done in a short space of time to improve A.A. training, both ashore and afloat, if the full resources of the civilian Film Industry, with all its technical and psychological knowledge and drive, were mobilized to help.[4]

In November the commanders of some of the training schools were asked what kind of films they would find useful. Most were interested in traditional subjects such as gun drill, anchor work, the duties of a lookout and rowing. Several suggested a film on the day's routine on board ship, useful for new entrants who had little conception of sea life. Most of the captains suggested something on anti-submarine work, with ideas spelled out in detail by the Flag Officer at Great Yarmouth.

> Anti-submarine – Technical aspects of A/S operations with sound track, including Screening with an Attack and counter-attack, showing the tactics required to obtain the best value from the Asdic installation and the best use to be obtained by high speed manoeuvring, etc. – Tactics to be adopted by Escorts of Convoys and Searching Force. Procedure and operations of the system of A/S underwater defences and Asdic beacons.[5]

One of the first successes of the Film Unit was the *Eyeshooting Film*, produced by HMS *Excellent*. Since air attacks on ships were far heavier than expected, and the British method of directing the fire of anti-aircraft guns proved inadequate, it was essential to train many more gunners in the use of visual sights.

The film was ready by April 1941. It tackled the subject progressively in eight parts, beginning with first principles. It dealt in turn with the approach angle of the aircraft, the amount to aim off, the use of the sight and ended with the effect of the wind. It was recommended that all eight parts should not be shown at a sitting, but the men should have time between showings for questions and practical demonstrations. A hundred copies were produced and sent to the squadrons of the fleet, depot ships and training establishments around the world. It was a success as a film as well as a training aid. The Ministry of Information wanted to show it at the London Scientific Film Society.[6]

Further productions followed. A First Aid film began with a casualty during a boxing match.

> Shot of Audience – Oh! Ow! Biff! Watch his left.
> Percy – I'm sorry Sir, I didn't mean to 'it him so 'ard, Sir.[7]

The introductory anti-submarine film, when it came, was less successful than *Eyeshooting*. At HMS *Nimrod* in 1943, *Meeting the U-boat Menace* was scorned. 'The forced heartiness of its acting and its attempt to "boost" Campbeltown moved even the dullest rating in Class P to derisive laughter. The showing of it at HMS *Nimrod* and elsewhere should be discontinued forthwith.' *Current of Electricity* was incomprehensible to most ratings, but the advanced anti-submarine training films *Attack by Asdic* and *The Hedgehog*, were very successful.[8]

There were often security problems in dealing with the latest technological apparatus. When a ten-part naval radar film was issued in 1943, the Admiralty ordered,

> They are to be handled in accordance with the instructions for the treatment of confidential matter given in C.B. U.2D. Suitable precautions must be taken to ensure that they are not show to unauthorized persons.[9]

Films might be more dramatic or more comical than intended in the cinema of a converted holiday camp. George Melly describes his experiences at *Royal Arthur*.

> We ... were shown a film about the effects of VD – "You're off to the pictures now to learn how to whip it in, whip it out and wipe it!" Due to the size of a screen designed for a full holiday-camp at the height of the season this proved a rather unnerving experience and several ratings fainted. I wasn't among them, but I did become hysterical with suppressed laughter while watching a silent documentary on the correct way to brush your teeth. The enormous lips opened to reveal teeth the size of important Victorian tombstones while a huge brush moved up and down them, and a little later a King Kong-sized finger with a surprisingly dirty nail massaged the gigantic gums.[10]

Filmstrips were also prepared for training purposes, sometimes as a synopsis of a moving film for use where a projector was not available. The increased use of film created a new trade group in the navy – Cinema Operator. Some were civilian men who had worked as projectionists in civil life. Most were Wrens who were trained in a school at Chatham, set up in November 1942.[11]

Simulators

Fourthly, films could be used as part of a simulator, a process which became increasingly common over the years. Despite its advantages, the cinema film was a very passive form of training, and there was nothing to stop trainees from falling asleep. A particular film could not be used too often with the same class. Simulators, on the other hand, involved the trainees in active operation, and could be used almost infinitely to improve the men's skills.

The navy had used simulators much longer than it had used foot drill. In 1812 Captain Phillip Broke improved the gunnery of his ship *Shannon*, by having two seamen elevate and depress a gun barrel, teaching the gun captain how to fire with the roll of the ship. This was later improved by Lieutenant George Smith, who saved labour by moving a target rather than the gun. The gunnery revolution in the early twentieth century brought many simulators, including Captain Percy Scott's 'dotter', which was again used to cope with the problems of rolling. Much more elaborate was the 'splasher' in which an officer under training looked through a slit to observe the 'splashes' of cotton wool round a model ship, allowing him to control the fall of shot. It required a crew of sixteen men, including the officer in command and four Royal Marines whose rifles would simulate gunfire.[12]

Simulators had many advantages. Naval seamen lived constantly a few minutes away from an emergency situation and they had to be trained in experiences that they had never encountered before. Many of these, such as aircraft attack, would only occur at unpredictable intervals, and it was vital that men were trained before the real attack happened. Training with real aircraft or ships was expensive and always had a certain element of unreality. Naval exercises, in general, were more expensive to mount than army manoeuvres, and could not simulate all the conditions of wind, weather and visibility that were likely in action. For all these reasons simulators, or 'synthetic training devices', were essential in the training of seamen.

In 1943 the Admiralty defined a Synthetic Training Device as

> A piece of instructional apparatus by which the semblance of operational or functional considerations is artificially created by scientific means, so as to provide realistic training or exercise of individuals or teams in their operational or functional duties, each individual being an active participant, and by which the requisite assessment and correction of performance are sometimes aided.

It found that there were 186 different devices in use, including ninety-nine for gunnery, twenty-two for radar training, nineteen for anti-submarine warfare, fourteen for air training, twelve for torpedo and electrics and ten for navigation, including air navigation.[13]

Some devices were quite simple, and were intended to prepare men for their first experience of the sea. G. V. Bell describes a machine at HMS *Ganges* during his basic training. 'This morning we had Compass and Wheel lesson first. You have a small replica of a ship's wheel in front of you and the instructor shouts orders which you repeat and then obey and then you have to read the compass. It's quite easy really.'[14] The Look-out Teacher could be improvised at a shore base or on board ship. Its object was 'to train lookouts in scanning routine. Lookout searches through binoculars at ordinary lookout seat, and aircraft is projected through series of mirrors, speed, bearing and angle of sight altering realistically.[15]

The Dome Teacher

An anti-aircraft simulator was first proposed by Sub-Lieutenant H. C. Stephens of the Royal Naval College at Greenwich in 1940. Range facilities for anti-aircraft training were very limited, few training aircraft were available, and the problem of aircraft attack on shipping was increasing.

In January 1941 the Captain of HMS *Excellent* saw a demonstration of the Advanced Spotlight Aiming Teacher at a Fleet Air Arm base.

> Attacks of all types, it is claimed, can be represented exactly as seen by the naked eye in practice and the full sound effects of own and enemy action, with a suitable commentary, can readily be added. The control apparatus on which personnel are to be trained is mounted in the centre of the teacher ...[16]

He was convinced that 'the method employed for reproducing aircraft attacks by photographing models might be of assistance to H.M.S. EXCELLENT in connection with the production of Anti-Aircraft Instructional films, and also for use in a similar type of Aiming Teacher which is under consideration for Close Range A.A. training in the Navy.'[17] Stephens developed

an optical arrangement by which a sound film could be used to project on the inside surface of a dome the image of an aircraft making a close range attack. The rate and change of elevation and bearing and the apparent growth in size of the aircraft, as it approached, were all correctly shown. This dome was in a huge inverted thrush's nest, 40 ft in diameter, except that instead of mud it was lined with plaster painted blue to represent the celestial concave.[18]

The prototype, known as the Dome Teacher, was built at *Excellent* during 1941 and was a great success. More than 200 were built for the navy, plus 200 more for the army and air force, and *Excellent*'s own example was a star exhibit to VIPs visiting Portsmouth. A portable version was also in use by 1943, the 'dome' being 'an inflated hemisphere of balloon fabric with suitable air-lock corridor for entry'.[19] A more sophisticated simulator was the Waller Trainer, which needed five cinema projectors and contributed to the development of Cinerama after the war.[20]

Visiting HMS *Glendower* in 1941, Admiral Dreyer regretted that there was no Dome Teacher for training DEMS gunners, but he recognized that other parts of the service must have priority. However, he noted that several other simple but ingenious devices were in use.

The Training of Lookouts is extremely well carried out by means of an apparatus resembling a spotting table in a completely darkened room and fitted with realistic lighting effects. ... Six or eight men with binoculars can be under instruction at any one time. The method is to darken the room and focus the binoculars on a pin point light on the lookout table. ...

The "spotter" box is for instruction in quickly recognizing the types of aircraft exhibited in it. The panorama is a moving sky background with cloud effects which can be illuminated to give various light conditions and also the effect of aircraft flying through haze, cloud and mist. ...

The approach angle teacher consists of a model aeroplane of the type under discussion mounted so as to move at any angle on a pivot set into a white background.[21]

A later device was the Cinema Laying and Training Teacher, introduced in 1945. This was built round a gun of up to 4.7-inch calibre, as a larger gun could not be accommodated in a reasonably sized building. A curved cinema screen was placed at a 20-foot radius from it, covering an arc of 160 degrees. It required an instructor and a cinema operator to work it, and members of the class of trainees might help to operate the training handwheel of the projector. The instructor would begin with a lecture, then operate the gun himself as layer and trainer. Then the class would try one by one. Films were carefully graded, beginning with an attack on a surfaced submarine in a calm sea. Pitch and roll were introduced in later films, then zig-zagging. The climax was a mass attack by up to sixteen fast-moving E-boats. There were several films for shore attack, shot on sites around the Solent and the Isle of Wight.

The Gunnery Branch's ninety-nine devices in 1943 included five for close-range anti-aircraft aiming, including some for training fighter pilots; twenty-four for close-range surface and air gunnery, including the Dome Teacher and its variants, as well as the much simpler devices noted by Dreyer, and the 'Punch and Judy Show' to teach tracer observation; six for long range surface gunnery; fourteen loading teachers, simulating the breech mechanisms of various guns from 4 to 7.5 inches; night vision trainers, rangefinder simulators, recognition devices, and the RYPA Platform to 'Impart a roll, yaw and pitch motion to a director sight, rangefinder, gun etc.' For a slightly more difficult exercise, the 'Peaty' Rolling Platform was used 'To give "rough weather" experience to guns' crews in firing a gun mounted on a hydraulically-operated platform.'[22]

Anti-Submarine Simulators

In the anti-submarine field, the Attack Teacher had first been used in HMS *Osprey* at Portland in 1925, and developed ever since.[23] In the latest version of 1939, the A/S 22, the object was 'the Training of Officers and Ratings in the tactical use and the operation of Asdic Installations in Trawlers.' It was housed in four rooms, one with a generator to power the operation. Another had a mock-up of a bridge, including compass and part of the asdic installation. A third was the wheelhouse, containing the wheel and the engine room telegraph. The fourth room had a plotting table with a glass top covered with thin plotting paper. The submarine was projected on to the underside of this in the form of a cross of light, and the attacking vessel by an arrow representing its course. The asdic signal of the trawler was represented by a beam of light; when that impinged on the submarine signal it operated a photo-electric cell which produced an echo. The device was operated by an instructor officer in overall charge, a plotter who was a qualified anti-submarine instructor and who controlled the movements of the submarine (taking care not to let the exercise drift off the confines of the table) and a helmsman who controlled the course and speed of the ship. The trainees included potential commanding officers, anti-submarine control officers and asdic operator ratings.[24] The Attack Teacher was found to be very useful, and in 1945 there were twenty-eight in use in the Scottish bases alone.[25] A mobile version was fitted in a double-decker bus to travel round the minor bases; thirty of these were in service by 1943.

The Mass-Procedure Teacher was designed 'for simultaneous teaching of up to twelve S.D. ratings in Asdic operating procedure. Battery of control training units are connected to a master control panel. Each operator hears transmissions and echoes.

The exterior and interior of the Attack Teacher Bus, 1941.

Plate 6A.

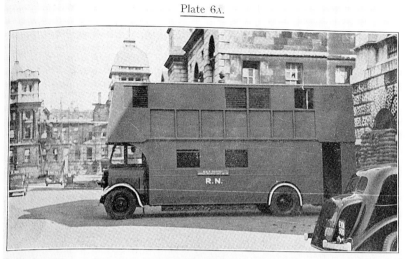

Attack Teacher Bus.

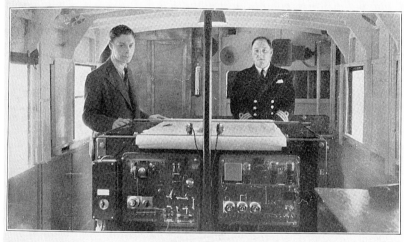

Upper Deck.

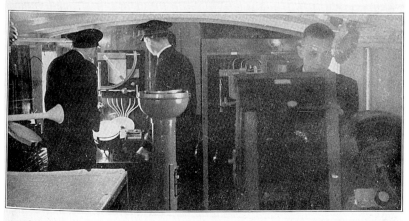

Lower Deck.

Submarine movement can be simulated, and all situations reproduced.'[26] Not everyone was happy with it. In 1944 one officer suggested some improvements, noting, 'Instructors and officers [are] concerned with Mass Procedure Teachers, that the Teacher itself requires so much of the Instructor's time and attention operating the master controls, that far too many mistakes on the part of the student pass unnoticed.'[27]

A new device, the Tactical Projector, was designed by the Admiralty Research Laboratory at Teddington and constructed at Liverpool in 1943. It was based on a screen representing an area of sea 7 miles square. Projectors were used to put images of escort vessels, convoy ships and submarines on the screen. Each escort vessel was operated by a trainee who had a control panel with steering, speed, radar and asdic controls. A radar beam of 5000 yards range and an asdic beam of 2500 yards range were also projected on the screen for each escort. Coloured filters were used to prevent the escort operators from seeing the submarines. The instructor would send out a ping when the escort vessel detected the submarine, or an echo in the case of a radar contact. The new device claimed several advantages over the older Tactical Table, which was,

> not only slow and laborious, but lacks realism, especially in the speed of the operation itself. In addition there is no permanent record as to what has taken place.

> In the projector system the whole tactical situation is presented pictorially and continuously throughout the whole phase of the problem. There is an additional advantage in that a class can obtain instruction from merely looking on, although they themselves may not be taking an active part in the problem.[28]

The Depth Charge Driller at Liverpool.

The radar training ship HMS *Isle of Sark.*

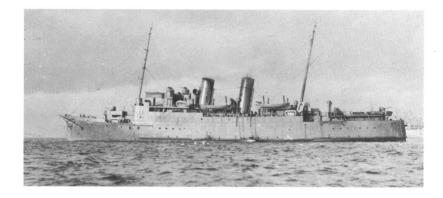

Gramophone records were useful in the training of asdic operators, as Dr Vernon commented.

> Discrimination between different types of echoes and between the various hydrophone effects, are obviously difficult for the inexperienced and the reporting of Doppler is particularly inaccurate. ...

> The introduction of gramophone records into training is a considerable help in practising these discriminations, and they would be still more useful if they could be marked, with a full key prepared, so that the officer or the instructor could reproduce just the sound he wants. Practice in the distinction between pitch intensity, and quality changes could easily be given with gongs or tuning forks. But the main defect in instruction at present seems to me that most of the men only listen passively while the lecturer tells them which noise is which.[29]

However Lieutenant-Commander Carmichael observed a few months later that 'disappointingly little use' was made of records. 'Those which were played to Class P were badly reproduced, and no advantage was taken of the opportunities they offer to set the class a problem.'[30]

Use of the Real Equipment on Land

It was clearly necessary to give radar trainees some practice on sets which operated over the sea, in order to give them some idea of the conditions they were likely to encounter in service. This was a great advantage of the site at the Isle of Man. A 'Type 271 set was installed at Douglas Head ... , with an interrupted view across the Irish Sea, safe from enemy interference.'It was not in the least bit impressive and consisted of two light grey steel boxes, one above the other and an aerial housed in a turret on the roof.'[31]

The Anti-Submarine Branch was even closer to the sea, as it was interested in what happened under it. To help with this, asdic sets were installed near *Nimrod* at Campbeltown. Obviously shore training had its limitations, as Dr Vernon observed of the Asdic School.

> In spite of the ingenuity of the designers of shore apparatus, conditions are considerably easier on shore than at sea. There are fewer distracting noises, no quenching or fading out such as occurs in hot weather, no rolling or

tossing, and the quality of the echoes is not really identical.[32]

Training Afloat

Again the three seaman branches of gunnery, anti-submarine and radar had the most need for training in the use of equipment in real sea conditions, though this had to be used very sparingly in view of the crying need for all kinds of ships for active service. Gunnery training in the old cruiser *Cardiff* in the Clyde was largely confined to officers and the more advanced non-substantive ratings. The Radar Training Flotilla in the Irish Sea consisted of three ships including the *Isle of Sark*. A. H. Cherry's first experience in anti-submarine sea exercises was not a fruitful one.

> The submarine had submerged, but the waters were too rough for the yacht on the surface, and her submerged oscillator, from which the sound emissions emanated, was bobbing out of the water most of the time … resulting in loud quenching noises which sounded like someone gargling in the depths below. There were many echoes from tide ripples, reefs, fish and whatnot, but the submarine was perfectly safe. Not one officer who took a turn in the hunt could locate our quarry. By noon a couple of the students were spending their time between stretching out and leaning over the side; they weren't exactly happy.[33]

Dr Vernon found that it was difficult to give men enough sea training in these vessels, and most of them spent unduly long periods waiting around for a chance on an asdic set. 'It seems unfortunate … that there is so little instruction during the ten or eleven days of sea training, when each man only gets about only thirty minutes' operating, and an hour or so of watching the operator or look-out, per day.'[34]

Testing

The navy needed testing procedures both during and at the end of practical courses, to ensure that men were really learning what was required of them. In peace and in war it was very reluctant to let go of men who had signed on for twelve years, including artificer apprentices. Admiral Ford commented, 'There appears to be a reluctance to discharge an apprentice once accepted for training. Under any form of recruitment there must be some round pegs in square holes and it is both to the advantage of the Navy and to the individual that such misfits should leave at the earliest date to take up a more congenial career.'[35]

In wartime, the main issue was to check how men were progressing with craft and technical courses. This was usually done by a combination of written examination and practical test though, as always, the individual branches or training bases usually set their own standards. Very few men failed the disciplinary courses, but the craft and technical schools in the various trades tended to require higher standards and tested men quite often to measure their progress; failures were sent back to the depot for re-allocation in other duties, for there was no question of anyone being discharged unnecessarily from the navy at this stage. In the Signal School, for example, regular tests were laid down in the syllabus and, in addition, instructors were expected to fill in weekly forms showing the progress of individual members of the class. Sometimes severe testing could be used to control the standard of a course. Admiral Ford hinted that a failure rate of 20 per cent among motor mechanics would help in 'the elimination of the weaker members of the class'.[36] But most officers would have considered this wasteful, and discouraging to the failures.

The navy used a great variety of methods in its training, finding uses for the most advanced simulators alongside the more traditional drills and lectures. As usual there was no central plan and each branch produced its own ideas and methods. One of the most successful was the Gunnery Branch. The combination of the Eyeshooting Film, the Manual and the Dome Teacher showed an innovative and integrated approach to the problem.

CHAPTER 9

Seamen and Signalmen

The Seaman Branch

The second stage of naval training was to teach each man a craft or skill which would be useful to the navy, for which, the entrants were divided into various specialist branches.

The Seaman Branch was naturally the largest. Some of its members were non-specialists, with no badge on the right arm. Most eventually qualified for one or other of the sub-branches – gunnery, torpedo, and anti-submarine at the start of the war. In peacetime men would serve some time in the fleet before selection. In wartime that was not always possible and in 1943 the basic training schools were expected to find their quota of men every month to send straight on to further training – 240 submarine detectors, 250 seamen torpedomen, and 650 for the various grades of seaman gunner.[1]

If he did not go on to further training, a man would be sent to a seagoing ship as an ordinary seaman, where he would be expected to qualify for the next grade, able seaman. As the rules stood in 1943, regular seamen needed to serve six to nine months, conscripts nine to twelve months, with a minimum of four months' sea service.[2] The man would be tested in arithmetic and dictation, and in professional subjects — he had to be 'fairly efficient in steering, heaving the lead, rowing, knotting and splicing both hemp and wire rope, and in the general duties of a Seaman.' Sometimes courses were held on board ship to help the candidates. Promotion to able seaman brought a pay increase from 2 to 3 shillings per day for a continuous service man in 1943, and it confirmed him as a fully-fledged seaman but, oddly enough, it was not marked by any kind of badge.

The able seaman was no longer the man who made the ship go, as he had been in the age of sail. It was no longer his skills in running up a mast, taking in sail, handling ropes, operating capstans and manually loading and training guns which made the British navy superior to its rivals. The able seaman who did not acquire some measurable skills, in gunnery or torpedo work for example, was likely to be left behind for promotion. He was needed to steer the ship, as a lookout, in raising anchor, rowing boats at sea and in harbour, and in tending lines when the ship came alongside. But these activities either required few men, like steering, or were only needed intermittently. The able seaman was likely to spend a good deal of time in unskilled and menial tasks, such as cleaning the decks or looking after a petty officers' mess.

Gunnery

In peacetime seaman gunners were selected from the ranks of the able seamen after they had spent some time at sea. A recommendation from the captain was necessary, after which the man was put on a roster for the gunnery school in his home port; a high recommendation could advance him up the roster. In larger ships it was possible to be trained at sea for 3rd class and most 2nd class ratings.

Lookouts.

The branch was reorganized just before the war, into three classes and four sections. First class ratings in each section had to take considerable responsibilities; they were chiefs or petty officers, or at least leading seamen passed for petty officer. Second class ratings were leading seamen or able seamen. Third class ratings were able seamen; they might retain the rating if they became leading seaman but if promoted to petty officer before qualifying for a 2nd class rating, they would relinquish their non-substantive rate and pay.

Quarters Ratings, who wore the letter Q under their non-substantive badge, operated the guns and their mountings and handled ammunition. The more senior rates served as captains of guns and turrets. Members of the Layer section wore the letter L. They were responsible for training the larger guns, that is pointing them in the right direction, and for laying them, giving the appropriate elevation for the range of the target. Some of the senior ratings worked in director towers of the larger ships, assisting the Gunnery Control Officer in tracking the target through gyro-stabilized binoculars.

> On the Director Layer, more than any other individual, except perhaps the Control Officer, depends the success of a gunnery action. He works alone and unobserved and he must make himself worthy of the responsibility imposed on him. ... If his opponent in the enemy ship is quicker and steadier than he, by virtue of drills and practice, his ship will be sunk instead of the enemy's.[3]

Others layers worked in the turrets and with the guns, following the instructions from the director tower through the transmitting station. If necessary they could lay and train the individual guns themselves.

The third section, the Control Ratings (C), were trained to work optical range-finders. They operated inclinometers which measured the distance between an enemy ship's masts, and hence her relative angle to one's own ship. The 1st class ratings were qualified to serve in the director tower, where they advised the Control Officer on the fall of shot and changes in the enemy's course. By the end of the war, part of their function was being taken over by radar.[4]

The quarters, layer and control ratings had to work very closely together in guns and turrets, often directing less qualified men. A destroyer's 4.7-inch gun, for example, had a Quarters Rating 2nd Class in command, probably a leading seaman or petty officer. The gunlayer and the trainer, who pointed the gun in the vertical and horizontal directions, were both Layer Ratings 3rd Class. The other four members, with no gunnery qualifications, were employed in loading and communication. The 1945 manual stressed the importance of teamwork; 'the crew does not consist of seven men doing seven jobs but is a team doing one job.'[5]

Excellent at Portsmouth remained the leading gunnery school. Just before the war it processed 300 officers and 2000 men per year. It had batteries to the north and west of the island, equipped with different types of guns for loading and aiming, though not of course firing. A tower was fitted with a rangefinder, and trainees discovered that the Nelson Monument in Portsmouth was exactly 5270 yards away. For anti-aircraft gunnery, a High Angle Control Building was opened in 1941. The Gunnery Branch was still regarded as the custodian of naval discipline, and foot drill was interspersed with lectures and gunnery drills. Leading Seaman Syme noted that 'The regime was essentially harsh ... the idea being to keep us on our toes all the time.' In 1941 one officer found he was there 'to learn a bit about gunnery, a lot about discipline and a good deal about the comfortable side of naval life.'[6]

Since it was impossible to fire long-range guns near Chatham, Portsmouth and Plymouth, sea training was essential. During the war officers and senior ratings were sent to HMS *Cardiff*, an old cruiser based on the Clyde. There were several types of practice, each with its own advantages and disadvantages. 'Towed Target Battle Practice' was 'very slow and spotting the fall of shot is very inaccurate. It is impossible to simulate a quick alteration of course.' A target towed by a motor boat was faster, but not very manoeuvrable. A radio-controlled target ship had 'the great advantage that both ships have complete mobility but is restricted by the fact that only shells below a certain calibre may be used.' In 'throw-off firing', one ship fired her guns at another, but they were offset by 6 degrees from the true aim so that they should hit the water a fixed distance away. The accurate measuring of the fall of shot was very difficult. A variation of this was 'throw-short firing', in which the fire control system was adjusted so that all shots would fall well short of the target.[7] Besides firing with their main armament, cruisers and battleships were equipped for 'sub-calibre' firing. Guns of a smaller calibre could be fixed in line with the big guns in the main turrets and fired in exercises. Practice of this kind conserved the barrels of the main guns, saved on ammunition, and gave good practice for the control system and the trainers and layers over a relatively short range.

Anti-Aircraft Gunners
The anti-aircraft (AA) gunnery section saw the greatest expansion during the war, because dive-bombing attacks on ships proved far more dangerous than anticipated. The numbers were made up mainly by Hostilities Only ratings. The senior ratings were trained to work director towers for close range armament or to assist the Air Defence Officer of the ship, but much of the time AA ratings depended on 'eye-shooting', aiming the guns themselves. They used sights with two or three rings, each representing 100 knots of an aircraft's speed.

> The method of using the sight is very simple. Look at the aircraft, note its direction of flight and estimate its aim-off speed. Point the gun so that the

The principles of eyeshooting.

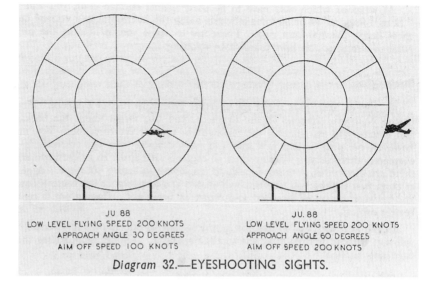

JU 88
LOW LEVEL FLYING SPEED 200 KNOTS
APPROACH ANGLE 30 DEGREES
AIM OFF SPEED 100 KNOTS

JU. 88
LOW LEVEL FLYING SPEED 200 KNOTS
APPROACH ANGLE 60 DEGREES
AIM OFF SPEED 200 KNOTS

Diagram 32.—EYESHOOTING SIGHTS.

aircraft is flying towards the centre of the sight, with its nose the distance from the centre corresponding to your estimate of its aim-off speed. As the attack develops and the aim-off speed increases, bring the nose of the aircraft further and further out from the centre, always adjusting direction of aim-off to keep the aircraft flying towards the center of the sight.[8]

AA gunners were trained using the *Eyeshooting Manual* and film, the Dome Teacher and numerous other simulators. Each of the three main gunnery schools had an anti-aircraft range, with a good prospect over the sea – *Excellent* had one at Bognor Pier, the Plymouth gunnery school in the fort in the breakwater of Plymouth Sound and Chatham had one looking over the Thames at Sheerness. There was another near Southport in Lancashire, convenient for Liverpool and attached to Western Approaches Command, while the Patrol Service had one at Covehithe just south of its depot in Lowestoft. There were ranges near the main naval bases at home and abroad, at Scapa Flow, Alexandria, Malta, Colombo, Trincomalee, Karachi, Halifax and several other places.

Trainee gunners could carry out non-firing practices against aircraft to understand the general principles of aiming, but there was no ideal way of giving them realistic live practice. They could fire at radio-controlled targets, but this was expensive and the aircraft was slow. Sleeves towed by aircraft slowed the plane down. Flares could be towed by aircraft at a greater speed, but there were safety problems. In 'throw-off firings' the gunners would deliberately aim a certain distance from the aircraft, but it was difficult to measure accuracy.[9]

Several new grades were introduced during the war, either to 'dilute' the skills of the older sections or to take account of new technology. Gunners for the Patrol Service had to deal only with lighter weapons and did not need the full course; from 1941 they wore the letter P under the badge. Light Craft gunners were trained as anti-aircraft gunners for coastal forces and landing craft. Gunners for Defensively Equipped Merchant Ships (DEMS) were trained in considerable numbers at HMS *Glendower* in Wales and HMS *Wellesley* at Liverpool; there were 33,000 of them in the fleet in 1944. They learned how to shoot the lighter guns fitted in merchant ships.

Boom Defence was added during 1941, for the men who operated the light guns on the craft which maintained the harbour defences.

Aircraft Recognition

Anti-aircraft gunners had to be familiar with aircraft recognition, not only to avoid firing at friendly aircraft but to estimate the speed and bearing of a target. The navy used every possible technique – models, puzzles, cartoons, films, silhouettes and photographs, but a poster of 1943 still showed one Oerlikon gunner looking up a handbook, while the other urged, "Urry up, 'Bert. Is it one of ours or theirs?' Gunners were instructed to 'Fire on any plane approaching your ship in a hostile manner that is not recognized as friendly.'[10] The RAF suspected that the navy did not take aircraft recognition very seriously, and instructed its pilots to keep well clear. The Admiralty issued its first *Manual of Aircraft Recognition* in 1942, and it continued to believe that the safety of the ship was paramount.

> Since at most close-range weapons the gunner must act on his own initiative, the ability to distinguish friend from foe is vital to him, and he must attain complete efficiency and reliance in this respect. ... But, if there is any doubt as to the identity of an aircraft which is heading at the ship on an attacking course, he should have no hesitation in opening fire.

The *Manual* offered many hints in training gunners and lookouts, including co-operation with the RAF and Royal Observer Corps, who were 'usually keen to help and full of ideas.' It offered some priority in teaching. 'Enemy aircraft, the targets of our guns, should first be taught; and of the enemy, at first only those in common use. Concentrate on the head-on view of these.' It used silhouettes, and photographs and described the 'outstanding characteristics' of each type, followed by a 'general description'. The Fleet Air Arm's own Fairey Barracuda, for example, had a 'large tailunit with abnormally high tailplane. Thick wings with extensive flaps. Deep, narrow fuselage with side windows.'[11] But opinion was beginning to move away from memorising detailed descriptions, in favour of training in immediate recognition by studying photographs taken from every angle. The *Joint Services Aircraft Recognition Journal*, founded in September 1942, provided means to do this and was widely distributed in the fleet.

Torpedo

The Torpedo Branch had non-substantive organization rather like the Gunnery Branch, with three classes of seaman torpedoman. The need to train the men in two separate skills, torpedo and electrical, caused difficulties. Four days after the start of the war, the Admiralty ordered that ratings would be trained in either torpedo (known as Whitehead after its original inventor) or electricity. Since much training was now to be carried on at sea, this was the only practical solution for men in the larger ships. Battleships and cruisers carried torpedo officers who could supervise the process, though some of them had no torpedoes.

> In view of the fact that torpedoes are not now carried in certain battleships and cruisers, the training of S.T.s [Seamen Torpedomen] in Whitehead subjects in such ships cannot be expected to reach the normal standard. It is not desired to restrict the qualification of S.T.s in such ships; but ratings so

AVENGER

Aircraft recognition notes on the American torpedo bomber, Grumman Avenger.

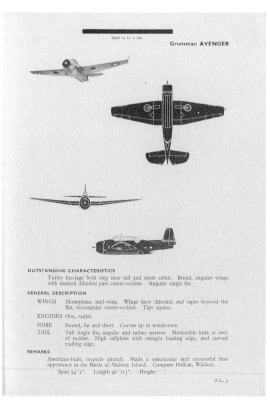

qualified are not to be considered as available for draft from such ships as Seamen Torpedomen and will be required to remain for duty as S.T.s in the ships in which they qualify.[12]

In effect, these men would become electricians. It was intended that this procedure should be self-sustaining. 'Should the present emergency … prove of long duration the expansion of the Fleet will call for a very great increase in the numbers of torpedo non-substantive ratings required. Ships will be required to provide periodical quotas and it is essential that men trained on board as acting ratings should be available to replace a proportion of the confirmed ratings called in.'[13]

This might have signalled a perfectly rational division between the electrician and the torpedoman proper, but by 1943 the old system had begun to reassert itself. Most men were now trained in both and those who had still only mastered one aspect were to be sent to the training schools as soon as practicable.

By that time there were several shore courses for the basic seaman torpedoman, conducted in three schools. Chatham ratings went to HMS *Marlborough*, Portsmouth men to HMS *Vernon* (mostly re-sited to Roedean School) and Devonport ratings to HMS *Defiance*. The main Seaman Torpedoman qualifying course consisted of seven days on high power electrical, eight on low power, four days on the study of mines, three days' school work and fifteen days on the torpedo. A torpedoman would learn how to charge the weapon with air and electricity, to transport it and its warhead, to carry out various maintenance tasks including oiling, to operate torpedo tubes and deal with misfires, to fit and maintain the gyroscope and to make final adjustments before firing. He had an 'All round knowledge of torpedo, inside and out.'[14] Unlike his colleague in the Gunnery Branch, he had little role in the aiming of the weapon.

Meanwhile, other types of electrician were introduced. Wiremen had worked as electricians in civil life. They had a two-week course in ships' electrical systems and were then promoted to leading rate within the Torpedo Branch. The Electrical Artificer was one of the most skilled men in the fleet; a survey showed that his standard of intelligence and ability was as high as most officers.[15] The Electrical Mechanic was a 'diluted' version of the Electrical Artificer, a Hostilities Only man selected for training by his good education, without necessarily having any previous technical experience.

The Torpedo Branch was highly complex. By 1943, no less than 131 different courses were offered in the torpedo schools, sixty for officers and seventy-one for ratings. The latter included long courses leading to non-substantive rates, as well as much shorter courses for men appointed to particular types of ship, or introductory courses for RAF personnel working with torpedoes.[16]

Asdic

Submarine Detectors were in particularly short supply. On 7 September 1939 the Admiralty ordered that, 'Every endeavour is to be made to fill vacancies which may occur by men trained at sea. They could be confirmed in the rate after two months' service and then sent ashore for courses at training schools. After further time at sea they would be eligible for promotion to Higher Submarine Detector and Submarine Detector Instructor.[17]

The branch consisted of Submarine Detector ratings, trained principally to operate asdic, which found submerged submarines by means of echoes. It had to expand rapidly on the outbreak of war, as crews were needed for newly-commissioned anti-submarine trawlers, corvettes and later frigates. There were just 1205 Submarine Detector ratings in the fleet at the outbreak of war, including recalled reservists and pensioners. By July 1941 3064 were available and in July 1943 there were 5767. A total of 390 new entrants were under training at that time, with 190 more training for higher ratings.[18]

After 1940, *Osprey* at Dunoon and *Nimrod* at Campbeltown were the main anti-submarine training bases. At *Nimrod* the course lasted six weeks and consisted of 163 periods of shore instruction, of forty-five minutes each. There were thirty-eight periods of school work, on 'arithmetic, elementary sound, electricity and magnetism' under class officers or qualified schoolmasters; fourteen periods of background, including an introductory lecture, films on HMS *Nimrod* and the asdic set, and lectures on the theory and operating of the sets. There were seven periods of demonstrations, including gramophone records of asdic noises, and five more on extra-curricular work such as air raid precautions. Routine naval discipline included ten periods of rifle drill, physical training and route marches. Candidates spent two periods on compass reading and had nine lectures on the asdic sets, with twenty-four periods of practical training on them. They had fourteen lectures on asdic procedure, with seventeen periods operating on the Attack Teacher, plus twenty periods on the Mass Procedure Teacher.[19]

There were sixty-three hours of sea training, though each man spent only about a twelfth of that time actually operating a set. A. H. Cherry, an American volunteer, describes it.

> This primarily consisted of training periodic sound transmissions through a compass arc, sweeping this arc for contact or target, which might be a U-boat. Immediately the sound-wave came in contact with a body, an echo would be set up, and it was this echo which was the basis of study. This echo could be a school of fish, a whale, tides, the wake of a passing ship, a submarine, or the track of a torpedo being shot at your ship.[20]

The Submarine Detector had to be able to operate a set for long periods without losing concentration. He had to know how to report a contact and then keep track of it during an attack; it was noted that 'The outstanding defect of inexperienced operators is their inability to report to the C.O. or the A/S Control Officer, during attacks. They are so intent on keeping the echo and making the correct movements that they cannot, like the skilled man, maintain a continual flow of advice such as the navigator must have.' To counteract this, instructors made a habit of asking men questions during shore training.[21] During an attack, operators learned to move the asdic beam across the immediate area of the submarine to follow its movements.

Like radar operators, submarine detectors were key men in destroyers and escort vessels. According to Roderick MacDonald, 'Our Anti-Submarine expertise depended entirely on the skill of the H.S.D., sensible, careful Leading Seaman Clark.[22]

The Communications Branch
The Communications Branch was never quite sure whether it ought to be a subdivision of the seamen, or a separate group. Visual signallers operated with flags, flashing lights and semaphore and were often to be found on the bridge with the officers.

Along with the seamen, they were the only group of ratings with the authority to assume military command – 'The general authority vested in Executive Officers, and in the ratings shown in Roman type in appendix XVI, part I, to command one or more ships or boats or to direct any work or undertaking which requires the co-operation of different branches of the service'.[23]

In 1939 the Admiralty found that the educational standards of newly recruited boy seamen were falling, and introduced a scheme for direct entry to the Communications Branch. It was abolished in 1941 as too many of the boys were coming out as signallers and there were plenty of young conscripts who could be sent to sea much quicker.[24]

Visual Signallers

Visual signalmen were selected at various stages for good education, 'good handwriting, spelling, memory and, in view of the confidential nature of the work, for integrity and reliability'. At the recruiting office, John Davies was told that the Telegraphy Branch was the 'brains of the Navy'.[25] From *Ganges* in 1943, G. V. Ball wrote to his family,

> Did Dad mention that signaling was good? Our instructor says that it's the cleanest job in the navy (other than officers). Anyway, the Instructor asked if anyone knew Morse but no-one did, or if anyone had a good education. He is putting my name down. In fact I'm the first on the list. He hasn't been able to find anyone else who is suitable.[26]

But the Signal Branch had to compete with other needs; both these men became CW candidates, and eventually officers.

Training required little equipment. Buzzers were needed for training in morse, as were signal lamps. Flag signals demanded some kind of flagpole, while a certain amount of space was needed for semaphore. Training took place on a wide variety of sites. The central school at Portsmouth, HMS *Mercury*, did most of the higher-grade courses, while the schools at Chatham and Portsmouth were rather smaller. By 1942 signaller candidates were doing their initial training at *Royal Arthur* alongside seaman

Visual signallers exercising in semaphore at a training establishment.

trainees, and in more specialized schools in *Collingwood* near Portsmouth, *Scotia* at Ayr and *Impregnable* near Plymouth.

At the central school, Hostilities Only men did a fourteen-week course in signalling, compared with twenty-five weeks for regular seamen. They practiced semaphore around the edges of the football field, but were not allowed to stand on the pitch itself. They were taught the correct posture, as well as the letters themselves. 'Ratings ... should also be taught to place their arms a little forward from the shoulder line, so that they can see that their arms are in the correct position, without the necessity of moving the head or body to the right or left.' At *Royal Arthur* in 1941 they practiced to records of *The Whistler and his Dog* and *Teddy Bears' Picnic.* At *Mercury* the trainees used flashing lamps, and were told 'that it is not necessary to bang the shutters to make good morse.' They also learned morse by buzzer. They had to learn the flags of the signal code, and how to make simple combinations without referring to the signal book. They learned the techniques of hoisting the flags and the importance of stowing them away correctly afterwards. They carried out marching manoeuvres on the parade ground, with each man representing a ship, useful for the 'Teaching of Fleet movements and movements of precision generally.'[27] Signals procedure was just as important as the learning of the different codes.

Wireless Telegraphists

The training of wireless telegraphists was even more dispersed than that of visual signallers. By 1942 they too started in the basic training schools at *Royal Arthur*, *Collingwood*, *Scotia* and *Impregnable*, but the often went on to privately-run radio colleges for their more advanced training. When Ordinary Seaman Greaves was sent to the London Telegraph Training College at Earls Court, he found it very liberating after the discipline of *Royal Arthur*. 'To be in the uniform of the senior service, as a young man, in civvy billets – a hotel no less – with little in the way of naval routine and discipline, represented only by a petty officer who honoured us with an occasional visit, was little short of wondrous.'[28] In 1942 there were eight such establishments in use by the navy, five of them in Scotland.

A Wireless Telegraphist had to be proficient at morse code, for voice transmission was still restricted to specific uses (e.g., over short distances). Training did not lend itself well to simulators, and only four types were noted in the Communications Branch in 1943, mainly for training radio telephonists. The R/T Trainer Type 25 was used for 'training in correct speech and procedure on R/T sets. Several trainees' cubicles with standard equipment are connected to an instructor's central control station, which shows by certain lights how each trainee's controls are set. Interference, variable in pitch and volume, can be introduced.[29] The telegraphist, on the other hand, practised regularly with a buzzer, and orders were issued that men travelling as passengers by ship were to continue their buzzer practices daily.

The *Handbook of Wireless Telegraphy* of 1932 had nearly a thousand pages of highly technical text on the theory of radio, though the junior ratings were not expected to know it all. In addition there was the *Book of Reference BR 222*, known as 'the green dragon', giving the characteristics of every set in use. If these volumes were not daunting enough, the telegraphist also had to learn a great deal about wireless procedure, including enemy reports, world-wide routing of signals, distress calls, radio direction finding and commercial traffic.[30]

Radio telegraphists could be rated as 'trained operators' after six months' service. They then went on to a non-substantive rate. In 1939 the course for Wireless

Telegraphists 3rd Class was cut to four weeks, with a seven-week course for promotion to 2nd Class. These were increased to five and eight weeks respectively in 1942. Throughout the war the Admiralty advertised courses through Fleet Orders, but it was often impossible to provide reliefs for men on course, owing to the acute shortage of communications ratings, so gaps had to be filled. 'Commanding Officers of ships refitting in home waters are to take full advantage of the time available to send all ratings who are eligible and are recommended to H.M.S "Mercury" or the nearest signal school for these courses.'[31]

Radar

When the first radar sets were introduced to ships just before the war, they were operated by existing members of the Signal Branch. A separate branch was set up in 1940, and most of them were taken straight from the training camps without a full course of seamanship training. They were regarded as equal in intelligence to signallers, but needed less technical ability, so they were given no extra pay. In February 1940 it was anticipated that about 150 ratings, nearly all Hostilities Only men, would be needed for the time being.

By March 1941 operators were being trained at Holyhead and Glasgow, in old patrol boats and yachts based in the Clyde and the Irish Sea. Classes of eighteen men were undergoing a fourteen-day course, and standards were low. 'The instruction is designed to accustom ratings to take ranges and bearings, to make intelligible reports to the bridge, and to make good small defects at sea.' It was only after they joined their ships that operators were 'trained to detect a submarine with confidence'. Only two trained operators were borne in escort vessels equipped with radar, although no one could maintain concentration for more than an hour; other men, mostly telegraphists, were trained on board to keep watch and to call the operator if any unexpected echo was seen.[32]

In 1942–43 it was policy to fit all ships with radar as they came in for refit. Battleships might have fourteen sets, carriers nine, corvettes one or two. Different types were used for long- and short-range anti-aircraft warning, fighter-direction, and anti-aircraft and surface-fire-control at long and short ranges. As the Admiralty knew, 'Operators cannot be employed actually watching the scan for periods of more than half an hour at a stretch without serious risk of eyestrain. For this reason in some cases, although the set can be operated by one man, two must be on watch in the office when it is being used for warning purposes to allow for watching the scan in alternate half-hour tricks.'[33] A typical set needed six men to operate it over three watches. Some, such as the Type 281 used for anti-aircraft detection and gunnery control in battleships and cruisers, needed twelve to fifteen men. Battleships had forty-five men in their full radar complement in 1942, cruisers had twenty-one and destroyers had six.

By the middle of 1942, the greatly increased demand left the new RDF (Radio Direction Finding) Branch in some confusion. Ratings were now part of the Seaman Branch, though it was 'impracticable at present to afford them a seaman's training owing to the large demands for R.D.F operators', and they wore the same badge as Ordinary Telegraphists. All were attached to the Portsmouth Division. It was proposed to expand the branch mainly by taking men from the basic training establishments, and high standards of eyesight were not needed. A few men could be transferred from other branches, if their eyesight was declining or they had failed courses.

The Admiralty was concerned about 'irregular' training and transfer of ratings to radar duties, especially in the Mediterranean Fleet. In May 1942 it was reported that 'courses for R.D.F. operators have been carried out in H.M.S. "Canopus", the ratings thus trained being qualified without proper arrangements being made to transfer them to the R.D.F. Branch, and to the Portsmouth Division.' Only acting RDF operators were to be created in this way.[34]

In September it was accepted that for the moment operators would learn one type of set only, and would have no knowledge of plotting. To assist the manning situation on board ship, captains were allowed to appoint some of their men as acting RDF operators, with no shore training. Ships with a full complement of operators could expect many of them to be drafted out for promotion or to man other ships, and their complements would be diluted with inexperienced men.[35]

HMS *Valkyrie* on the Isle of Man was now the main radar training base, with a small base at Sherbrooke House in Glasgow for refresher training of officers and ratings attached to Clyde-based ships. *Valkyrie* had room for 1500 ratings in 1942 and they tended to enjoy the posting to the island, as rationing was lighter than on the mainland.

Radar was still officially secret when Fred Kellet arrived at HMS *Valkyrie* in 1941. The instructor, 'an enthusiastic but rather untidy-looking officer', told the class,

> You are about to be introduced to the latest development in detection equipment, using ultra-frequency waves which the enemy is incapable of detecting as far as we know. You may know of existing radio equipment known as HF/DF or "huff-duff", that is high-frequency direction-finding which enables us to determine the direction from which radio signals are being transmitted. This is altogether different — we transmit a very accurate directional signal which is reflected back by any solid object it encounters and from the time it takes to get back we can establish how far that object is from us. It is a range and direction finder – hence the name – RDF.

A Type 271 radar set, c. 1942.

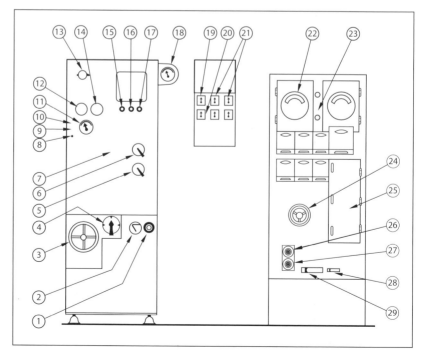

1 Heater lamp
2 Blumer + transmitter switch
3 HT control
4 Mains + filament switch
5 Pulse switch
6 Band width switch
7 Gain
8 Crystal
9 Meter
10 Oscillator current
11 Radiation meter
12 Tuning control for height
13 Coupling bar
14 HT control
15 Brilliance
16 Focus
17 Range control
18 Radiation meter
19 Range control
20 Spare Ac output
21 Blower and transmitter
22 Voltage
23 Pilot Lamp
24 Ring main switch
25 Voltage control (behind door)
26 Stop button
27 Hand auto switch
28 Main switch

The most advanced set was the Type 271, which could detect a surfaced U-boat. For training purposes, one was erected on Douglas Head giving an interrupted view across the Irish Sea. Earliest versions used the A-scope, in which a target appeared as a blip on a single horizontal line, giving the range; the operator had to read off the direction in which the aerial was pointing at the time. One of the first tasks to be learned was switching the set on and off; this involved twenty-one separate operations when the set was cold, and they had to be done in the right order. The operator had to turn the aerial by hand, and when he got a contact he read its position by means of a periscope. Ordinary Seaman Lindop describes his initiation.

> First impressions were that it appeared to be of bewildering complexity with a mass of coloured knobs, dials, meters, switches, co-axial cables, handles and cathode ray tubes. It was the size of a bulky wardrobe and the transmitter, buried in the basement, the size of a small room. The Instructor gave details of how the instrument was switched on and gave a practical demonstration with the CRT [cathode ray tube] light up with a vivid emerald green tinge, on the left side a large blip caused by the ground returns and the top of the trace, an "A" trace, looking like grass, which was the term for it, this was the equivalent of noise in a radio set plus odd returns from mountains and the like. Turning a large wheel in the front of the set rotated the aerial so that it was pointing at the mountains of the Lake District some sixty miles away and on the CRT appeared a large blip on the sixty mile range; our first echoes.[36]

From 1942 the A-scope was replaced by the Plan Position Indicator, in which the cathode ray tube gave an overall view of the area. 'In this, own ship is in the centre of the C.R.O. and the beam sweeps round like the hand of the clock, showing blips which fade at relatively low speed.'[37]

One of the most difficult tasks, as Lindop suggests, was to eliminate interference from the set. In the old-style A-scope set, a spot indicated the movement of the beam. If the spot was stationary the operator had to carry out a six-stage procedure, including;

> 1. With the Brilliance Control adjusted to give a spot on the C.R.T. remove the Sync connection and note if spot disappears.

> 2. If spot disappears time base is not working and the trouble will probably be due to failure of the 400 volts supply, or to a defective V3.

> 3. If 3 fails to achieve results, check components and diodes in grid and anode circuits of V3.

By 1942 the supply of suitable men was becoming critical. Ideally they would have a high standard of intelligence, but this had already been diluted. Nevertheless, as the captain of *Valkyrie* complained, 'there has been no corresponding increase in the number of entries.' The basic training were supposed to send a hundred men a week, plus twenty more from the fleet, but only 63 per cent of this demand was met. Even so, the targets were now being raised to 150 men a month.[38]

Ken Kimberley was trained afloat in the *Isle of Sark* in the Firth of Clyde.

> When it was my turn in the cabin I donned the earphones and sat perched in front of the PPI. ... in the gloom of the tiny cabin I watched the scan. A thin green line swept around a full 360 degrees. We were now out in the Firth of Clyde and there were lots of ships around us. That meant lots of 'echoes' as the thin line picked up each one with a bright green 'blip'. ...

> I was nervous, as it was my first go. "Bridge – radar," snapped the Officer of the Watch in my ears. "Give me the range and bearing of the ship dead ahead." ... Requests for range and bearing came into my earphones thick and fast, but I coped. At last my watch came to an end.

The failure rate during the course was about 10 per cent, though this could be halved if the failures were allowed two weeks' extra instruction.[39] When qualified, radar operators were key men in most ships. John Davies records an incident when a captain sent a car to recall a man named Barker. The boatswain's mate thought this meant him, but the captain replied 'Oh, I didn't want you. I meant Barker the radar man.' Able Seaman (Radar) E. P. Miles of HMS *Royal Eagle* commented, 'They always did want us.'[40]

By 1943 officers in aircraft carriers were advocating a new branch, of aircraft plotters. The interception of attacking aircraft and the guidance of friendly ones was done by officers using their navigational skills, but the captain of HMS *Indomitable* suggested that ratings might be trained to take on some of the duties. They would help man the Action Information Office, the predecessor of the Operations Room which became the nerve centre of post-war ships. RDF ratings were recommended for this, but for the moment the idea was not adopted.[41]

In March 1944 the Radar Branch was reorganized and given its first badges. One type of radar operated over a broad area, searching the sea and air and providing data for plotting the movements of enemy and friendly forces. The other type was used to direct the weapons of the ship onto a target. Radar Plotters fulfilled the first task, operating search radars with a wide beam; they were now part of the Seaman Branch. As well as being competent to operate the sets, they were sent on courses on plotting. When qualified some of them would form part of the team in the ship's Action Information Office. A new gunnery rating of Radar Control was created for the rest, with three classes like the other gunnery ratings. Their main job at this stage was to replace the visual rangefinders operated by the old Control Rating section, for radar could provide a far more accurate range than any visual method.

Photographers

The Photography Branch was formed in 1921, and by 1930 it had the badge of a bellows camera. F. R. King began his training at Tipner, part of HMS *Excellent*, in 1940. Progress was erratic, and too basic for one who already had experience. 'We started our photography course by learning how to fit film in a pin frame. It was at least uninspiring.' On another day, 'we did a little camera work but the camera wouldn't work.' He was sent on to the Royal Naval Air Station at Ford to complete his training.

Standards improved later in the war. A photographer was expected to have an elementary knowledge of photo-optics, to process still and cine films, print photographs, maintain stores and records and service cameras. If sent to a Fleet Requirements Unit of the Fleet Air Arm he was to undertake flying duties (with extra pay) and to operate cine cameras.[42] Some worked in photo reconnaissance, some helped with the production of naval films.

Radio Mechanics

In 1942, partly because of the need to service delicate radar installations, the Radio Mechanic Branch was established, with responsibility for maintenance of radio, RDF and radar equipment in ships and aircraft. This left the Wireless Telegraphists and radar operators free to concentrate on operation.[43] It took over existing Air Fitters (Radio) from the Fleet Air Arm, as well as Wireless Mechanics in the rest of the fleet.

Radio Mechanics were selected from new entrants with School Certificates, and men already in the fleet were accepted after an aptitude test. Failed officer candidates, were also taken on. Roy Fuller happened to have School Certificate credits in maths and physics and volunteered because 'a spell in a civilian technical college ... greatly appealed.'[44] Trainees were given a course in radio theory and workshop practice at one of a dozen civilian colleges around the country, ranging from seventeen weeks for general service candidates, to twenty-four weeks for Fleet Air Arm duties. After that they did a further eighteen weeks practical work on radio and radar sets. Every man who completed the course spent one day as a Radio Mechanic, equivalent to an able seaman, and was then promoted to Leading Radio Mechanic. He was promoted to Petty Officer after a year's service, provided he had the relevant recommendation and certificate.[45] Radio mechanics wore the same 'fore and aft' uniform as artificers and had equal status with them.

The new branch took the cream of new entries but at first it could not afford to give an all-round training.

> It is the intention that the Radio Mechanics shall eventually be capable of maintaining all W/T and R.D.F equipment, but in order to meet immediate needs training must be specialized in certain directions until circumstances admit of complete training. Advancement will not be prejudiced meanwhile, though ability to maintain all types of equipment will be a qualification for advancement to Chief Petty Officer.[46]

It is not surprising to find in 1944, 'The war has unfortunately given the branch a rushed start and poor training.'

By that time there were nine groups within the Communications Branch as a whole – besides Radio Mechanics, Visual Signal Operators and Wireless Telegraphist Operators, the branch included Coders, who were 'experienced in naval and mercantile marine codes and ciphers'; Radio Telephone Operators; Special Operators, who worked with foreign equipment; Direction Finding Operators, Teleprinter Operators and Automatic Morse Operators.

CHAPTER 10

Engineers and Others

The Engineering Branch

The Engineering Branch of the navy did not have to face any major technological changes during the war, for the jet engine did not arrive in the Fleet Air Arm until late in 1945. Its biggest problem was the much greater number and variety of engines in use. Since the early years of the century, new warships (apart from submarines) were nearly all powered by steam turbines driven by oil-fired boilers, but the war brought back one old type, and introduced several which had been common outside the navy. The old type was the reciprocating steam engine, used on corvettes and frigates because it could be made easily by a great variety of engine builders. The diesel engine had been common in submarines, but now it became the main propellant of thousands of landing craft. In itself it was relatively free of maintenance, but each craft needed its own stoker (an anachronistic title in the circumstances) to carry out simple maintenance if the vessel was to be self-sufficient in action. Petrol engines were used in certain types of landing craft, and also in hundreds of coastal motor boats, launches and torpedo boats, designed for high speed.

The Engine Room Artificers

The most highly-trained ratings of the fleet, the Artificers, were fully skilled men who had learned the trade by apprenticeship, either outside or inside the navy. These included the middle-ranking group among the engineers, the Engine Room Artificers (ERA). If trained inside the navy, they joined at the age of fifteen or sixteen as Artificer Apprentices, after a stiff competitive examination. They trained for four-and-a-half years and could expect to be promoted to Petty Officer soon after qualifying, with a fast track to Chief Petty Officer. Many would become warrant officers and perhaps commissioned officers. Fully qualified ERAs were equivalent to junior engineer officers in the merchant navy, and were recognized as such by the Board of Trade, but merchant navy engineers did not have to go through so many hoops to reach the senior ranks of their profession.

The navy expected high standards of its artificers.

> The training and education of Artificer Apprentices is intended not only to make them good Workmen, but to give them a real understanding of the tools, materials and machines they will have to handle, and also to make them self-reliant, ready and resourceful.

> Accordingly, their knowledge should not be gained simply from books or taken on trust from their teacher; they should be trained to approach subjects from the standpoint of observation, and to reason out their own conclusions.[1]

By 1940 there were three establishments training artificer apprentices. The

Mechanical Training Establishment at Rosyth had been completed just before the start of the war. The Apprentice Training Establishment at Torpoint near Plymouth had been evacuated from Chatham. According to Rear-Admiral Ford, 'The buildings are adequate but lack a covered in space for divisions, a gym and swimming bath.' The Royal Naval Apprentice Training Establishment at Newcastle-under-Lyme was also improvised and consisted of 'a number of requisitioned properties spread over a considerable distance.'[2]

About 600 apprentices started every year by 1944, half of them air artificers who began with three weeks at the Fleet Air Arm depot at Lee-on-Solent where they were kitted up and given some basic training. Then they joined the others at either Rosyth or Torpoint. For the first four months they all worked at a bench, drilling holes and learning to ship, file and scrape. Then the apprentices (apart from the air apprentices) were tested and allocated to the different branches. The majority would become Engine Room Artificers, eventually able to keep watch in an engine room and carry out repairs on boilers and main and auxiliary machinery. Eighty per cent of the potential ERAs would train as fitters and turners, the others would become boilermakers, engine smiths, coppersmiths and moulders. Each apprentice had to turn out a major piece of work a year to show his progress. In his fourth year a boy might spend up to ninety hours making a claw coupling with clearance of up to .002 inches in the sleeve, with 5 marks deducted for every thousandth of an inch beyond that.[3]

The bench work followed a system which had been set up at the beginning of the century, when much of the navy was in small ships spread around the British Empire. It was arguably less relevant in the days when most ships sailed in flotillas, or returned regularly to their bases. However Rear-Admiral Ford agreed that the training was based on 'unalterable principles' and produced 'a body of pure craftsmen which probably cannot be surpassed in the world and which has no counterpart in the Engineering Industry of the country.'[4]

In their third and fourth years apprentices had a good deal of theoretical training in marine engineering, engineering drawing, mechanics and electricity. As Ford pointed out, this did not include the erection of steam engines.

> ... no time is available under the present syllabus for teaching such important matters as "lining up" of high speed machinery, I.C. [internal combustion] engines and their components, stripping, fault finding and testing, allowable tolerance for wear for high speed machinery, and the preservation and adjustment of ball and roller bearings, and such like vital matters for men who subsequently have to maintain and repair the machinery of H.M. Ships.[5]

Ford pointed out the instruction was 'that required to convert the boy into a craftsman, who has in addition theoretical knowledge of Engineering. It is a fallacy (although one believed by the bulk of Engineer Officers), that the aim of the instruction is to turn out a fully qualified E.R.A., O.A. or E.A.'[6] They would go to sea as Artificers 5th Class, equivalent of leading seamen. They spent time in engine room watchkeeping and with the various types of machinery, including boilers and auxiliary motors. After a year, and passing another examination, they were rated 4th Class, equivalent to petty officers.[7]

The apprentices, like continuous service boys, signed on for twelve years, and the navy did not take in men who were not going to be needed after the war. The training course was little altered by wartime requirements. However, it was possible to expand the ranks of the artificers by taking on men who had already had some training in civilian industry. Men who had completed at least two-and-a-half years of an apprenticeship in engineering trades could take a stiff trade test. If successful they might be given four to six months' training at the London Polytechnic before going to sea as Artificers 4th Class, where they were given a year to eighteen months' training as engine room watchkeepers. The quality of their civilian training varied widely, and they were considered inferior to the navy's own products.

Mechanicians

Mechanicians were recruited from intelligent Leading Stokers to help make up the numbers of highly-skilled engineers. After an eighteen-month course in the Mechanical Training Establishment at Devonport he would become the equivalent of a fully-trained Artificer, with the rank of Chief Petty Officer. There were only 398 of them in the navy in 1937 and the numbers did not expand fast – eighty were under training in 1943. Admiral Ford deplored this. They were 'the elite of the Stoker entry … men of considerable intelligence', and he recommended that 'owing to the comparatively short time it takes to train a Mechanician as compared with the training of an Artificer Apprentice it is considered that an increase in complement of Mechanicians is not only expedient but would add to the efficiency of the Fleet.'

Since the men were already familiar with the working of engines, most of their training was in craft work. Part A, lasting four-and-a-half months, was in bench work as a fitter, during which three major exercises were done. Ford commented, 'Mechanician candidates from the nature of their previous work are inclined to be clumsy and unaware of their strength … it is considered better results would be obtained if lighter jobs were given and the men made to control their strength.' In Part B, also lasting four-and-a-half months, half the men trained in boilermaking and machining then went on to shaping, slotting and milling. The other half worked the whole time on machine tools. For Part C, lasting the remaining nine months, the men did two weeks on boat engines, two on internal combustion engines and spent the rest of the time on turning, fitting and general repair work. Ford commented that 'The course appears to want some imagination brought to bear to make it more interesting and more in line with modern requirements.'[8]

Stokers

The Engine Room Branch proper consisted mainly of stokers. Since few ships were now coal-fired, they mostly worked in running and simple maintenance of boilers and steam engines. As Rear-Admiral Ford wrote in 1943, 'The stoker under modern conditions has a difficult job to carry out. He requires intelligence, mental alertness and a reasonably high standard of education, if he is to watchkeep on machinery with understanding.'[9]

Culturally the stokers were very different from the seamen, because they had been recruited as young adults and were never broken into naval ways as much as the seamen. Wartime entrants were nearly all adults in both branches, but traditions lingered, as Tristan Jones noted.

> The Stoker POs were usually humane and friendly, with very little disciplinary bullshit about them. Often, if things were steady and quiet, the PO would be reading a cheap paperback under the forced draft fans, and his

mate, the stoker, would be making cocoa or tea. They appeared to be completely isolated from the world we knew topsides, and the most comfortable ratings in the ship, with no officers to oversee them directly.[10]

Stoker training was divided into two parts. Part I, lasting five weeks in 1943 and four weeks in 1945, was the basic disciplinary course. Part II lasted six or seven weeks and introduced the trainees to their work in the boiler and engine rooms. HMS *Cabot* was set up in July 1940 for Part I training of men under the command of the Plymouth Division, and moved to Yorkshire two years later. HMS *Duke* was commissioned at Great Malvern in 1941 to take a thousand stokers as well as miscellaneous ratings. Rear-Admiral Ford visited both establishments in 1943 and was 'much impressed by the good state of discipline, smartness and keenness shown by recruits'. Portsmouth men were trained at Stamshaw Camp near the city, where conditions were less than comfortable.

A stoker at work in the boiler room of HMS *Norfolk*, 1943. A drawing by Stephen Bone.

Part II of the training began at the same base (often many miles from the nearest ship), and consisted of four weeks of theoretical lectures. After that the men went to Plymouth, Portsmouth or Chatham, where they had some practical instruction in the Mechanical Training Establishment attached to the division. Admiral Ford found that facilities were not satisfactory. 'The final two weeks of instruction ... consists mainly in the duties of a Stoker in a boiler room and the duties of a Stoker entering a Double Bottom [a ship with a second "skin" of steel plates]. At Chatham the boiler room work was taught adequately but there were no facilities for Double Bottom work. At Portsmouth the exact opposite was the case.'[11]

Two old battleships, the *Revenge* and *Resolution* of 1915, were taken out of service in 1944 on account of the manpower crisis and sailed to the Clyde, where they were commissioned as HMS *Imperieuse*, the new stokers' training establishment, carrying out both Part I and Part II training afloat. By the end of the year the liberation of northern France reduced the danger of bombing and the ships were towed south to Plymouth. Part II of the syllabus was now given a more practical emphasis. The men were issued with the *Machinery Handbook* and grouped into classes. During the next two weeks they were instructed about boilers, with at least one day's practical work. Stoker Bracegirdle describes this phase.

> ... I was sent down to A Boiler Room. It was strange at first. I had never been in one before ... It was very warm and dirty. My job was to change the sprayers every ten minutes or so. It was quite simple really. Once you had taken the dirty sprayer out, you cleaned it in shale oil, it was very repetitive work but one got used to it.[12]

During the seventh week they had lectures each day followed by practical instruction in the boiler room, then in the eighth and ninth weeks they learned about auxiliary machinery. In the tenth week they studied the main machinery, following the path of the steam through the engine room, and in the final two weeks they learned about safety and damage control.[13]

Engine Room Mechanics

By late 1940 it was obvious that a far greater number of skilled engine room personnel would be needed than could be supplied from within the navy or industry. Such men were also in great demand for the army and air force and in particular for a vast expansion of the aircraft industry. The Ministry of Labour was unable to supply more than half the men the navy needed. At a high-level meeting between the Admiralty and the Ministry of Labour, it was decided to form new categories within the Engine Room, Electrical and Ordnance Branches, to be known as 'Mechanics'.

Engine Room Mechanics were introduced early in 1941 as an alternative means of recruiting men to artificer standard without undergoing a four-and-a-half year training course or working up through the ranks of the stokers. They were frankly regarded as 'dilutee' ERAs. Recruits were to be selected from among Hostilities Only ratings 'either having some previous experience or a sufficient standard of intelligence to enable them to be trained.' They would only be employed on repair staffs in shore bases. It was estimated that 2200 men per year would be needed for the three grades of Engine Room, Electrical and Ordnance Mechanic.[14]

The course lasted twenty-four weeks and the men learned how to do quite heavy work, specializing in the trades of fitter, turner, machinist or welder. Even so it was not fully successful, having been set up when there was 'a degree of urgency about the matter which did not allow the implications to be considered in great detail.' There were about a thousand men under training in the summer of 1943, but it was planned to stop recruitment and let the scheme run dry by early 1944.[15]

Men who had learned shore-based trades before entering the navy were known as artisans; they included shipwrights, coopers, blacksmiths, painters, joiners and plumbers. They had to be between the ages of nineteen and twenty-eight on entry, and 'good workmen at their trade'.[16] They wore a badge depicting a crossed sledgehammer and axe on a fore-and-aft rig uniform, and had a similar promotion structure to the artificers, except that there was no route to warrant and commissioned rank for some grades. When Winston Churchill found out about this in 1939, he commented tartly, 'Apparently there is no difficulty about painters rising in Germany!'[17]

Navies Within the Navy

The three main specialized manning divisions — the Patrol Service, Combined Operations and Coastal Forces — each had their own ways of using engineers, and their own training schemes. Between them these three services took up about 40 per cent of naval ratings, and their need for engineers was even greater, for they had to be thinly spread among a large number of small craft.

At the beginning of the war the Royal Naval Patrol Service was mainly made up of experienced fishermen and the engines of the boats were run by 2000 engine room ratings, 60 per cent of whom were stokers. All the original craft were steam-powered, but in May 1940 motor minesweepers began to join the service. Six hundred new engine room ratings were enrolled, mostly men who had experience in petrol engines up to 100 horsepower. They were re-trained in diesel. The service continued to expand and had 3000 vessels by 1943, including fishing boats and yachts of different types, purpose-built naval vessels and foreign vessels, both naval and merchant. They were manned by 60,000 men, of whom 17,000 were engine room ratings. A training school was set up in St Luke's School, Lowestoft, near the headquarters of the Patrol Service. About 600 steam enginemen were trained in diesels.

More than 1700 motor torpedo boats, launches and gunboats of coastal forces were built to fight in the English Channel and North Sea. Very few British-built engines were available, so most boats used petrol engines of Italian or American origin, with consequent problems of supply. Coastal Forces engines had to run at relatively low speed of most of the time, but be ready for a sudden boost in action. They had to move at high speed in all weathers and 'the motion of a corvette in a seaway is positively stately in comparison with the motion of a coastal force craft in the same seaway.'[18] This placed great strain on the engines, for in bad weather one propeller or another was often out of the water, causing the engine to race. The crews had to work in extremely cramped conditions in rough seas.

The Engine Room Branch trained many motor mechanics to work on the small ships of coastal forces and combined operations. At first they were generally recruited from experienced men in the motor industry, but again the Ministry of Labour was unable to meet the full needs. The first specialized school was set up at Andrews Garage in Bournemouth at the end of 1941. A factory in London belonging to AFN Limited was taken over from the army, with a capacity for 300 men, and the Automobile Engineering Training College at Fulham in London had capacity for 200. These became Royal Naval Training Units (RNTU). Demand continued to increase during 1942 and the Harrods factory was taken over to increase the capacity of the Fulham college to 600, while factories adjacent to the AFN works were taken over to increase its numbers to 780. It was now possible to train about 3000 men a year, but there was still need for expansion. The Pear's Soap factory was acquired, along with the other premises of the Automobile Engineering Training College at Wimbledon, so that 6000 could be trained per year. In fact only 2300 men were being trained in July 1943, because of cuts in the supply of men to the navy.

It was found that those who had been joiners, bricklayers, plumbers and policemen did best in the course. They enrolled for a six-month course, and were chosen rather arbitrarily for either petrol or diesel work; by September 1943 the course was being lengthened so that men could learn both types of engine. Rear-Admiral Ford commented that there was a general lack of equipment for training in diesel engines in all the establishments. Instruction in fault-finding was good but wiring instruction at Hounslow was 'unrelated to marine work'. On passing out, Motor Mechanics were the equivalent of leading rates.

Electrical Artificers and Mechanics

Electrical Artificers trained in exactly the same way as the Engine Room Artificers for the first two-and-a-half years, but in the six months after that they spent almost all their workshop time in the electrical shop. In their fourth year they spent twenty weeks in the electrical shop of the training establishment, along with eleven weeks of electrical work in the dockyard, with almost all of their last six months, except for trade tests and disciplinary training, on electrical work. They had advanced lectures on electrical practice, including magnetism, current electricity, instruments and electrical machines.[19] When qualified, the Electrical Artificer was able to carry out a wide range of duties;

> Maintains and effects major repairs to ship's electrical equipment including gyro compasses and torpedoes. Undertakes armature winding, etc., and repairs involving use of machine tools together with maintenance work which torpedo ratings are not qualified to do. Has working knowledge of electronics and servicing valve amplifiers.[20]

These artificers had their dilutees in the form of the Electrical Mechanics. They were recruited from Hostilities Only men with at least fourth-form secondary education, not necessarily with experience in technical work. They were given one month's preparatory course at a torpedo school and then went on to do five months' intensive work in a government training centre at Southampton. When qualified they could do all the tasks of an artificer, except that 'skill of hand as fitter, turner or instrument maker may be less'.[21]

Ordnance Artificers and Mechanics

The Ordnance Artificers also began their careers alongside the Engine Room Artificers. They, too, began to diverge in the second half of the third year, when they spent a good deal of time in the blacksmith's shop. They studied the *Gunnery Pocket Book* in some detail, 'amended where necessary to suit Ordnance as opposed to Seaman ratings'. They spent considerable time learning about hydraulics, which powered most major gun turrets. During eight weeks at the Gunnery School at Chatham they concentrated on the working and maintenance of the 15-inch turrets, the largest in use apart from the 16-inch. They also learned about the 8-inch turret, common on heavy cruisers, and studied rangefinders, fire-control instruments and directors.

The Able Seaman 'Qualified in Ordnance' (ABQO) had completed the Quarters Rating 3rd Class course at a gunnery school. He worked as an assistant to an Ordnance Artificer and picked up some of his skills. He had to relinquish the status on promotion to Leading Seaman. The Ordnance Mechanic was selected from among the ABQOs and sent to the Government Training Centre at Southampton for an eighteen-week course in precision fitting and turning, followed by six months' practical training in ships and dockyards. He still worked directly with an artificer and did not handle the more difficult work on fire-control gear.[22]

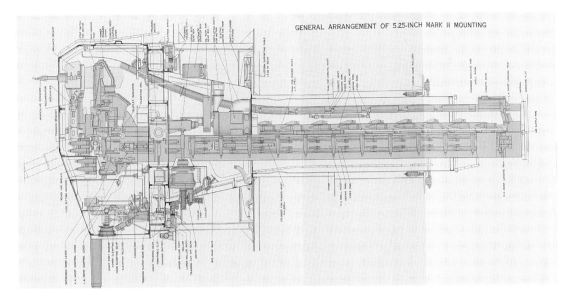

GENERAL ARRANGEMENT OF 5.25-INCH MARK II MOUNTING

The Fleet Air Arm

Maintenance of naval aircraft required particularly high standards, and had peculiar problems. Nearly all of the aircraft were single engined, and they were often expected to operate singly for long periods over large areas of sea, so reliability was especially important. They needed strong airframes to stand the stresses of deck landing on a moving hull, brought suddenly to a halt by an arrester hook. Radio failure at a crucial moment, for example when sighting an enemy force, could have enormous consequences. Their folding wings made them more complex than land-based machines. Each aircraft often had to carry out a variety of roles, such as torpedo-spotting-reconnaissance in the case of the Fairey Swordfish. This required rapid conversion by the crew in the carrier. Maintenance work had to be done on a mobile platform, often on days when flying was impossible because of heavy seas. Space was very confined in the hangar deck of a carrier. There was no possibility of bringing in spare parts or expertise during a voyage, so each carrier relied on its own resources to keep its planes flying. A large fleet carrier might have a full range of skilled men, but escort carriers had servicing crews of three air fitters airframe, three engine, one ordnance and two electrical, plus five air mechanics ordnance, two electrical and three radio mechanics – a total of nineteen skilled men.[23]

The Fleet Air Arm had two main badges for non-flying ratings. Skilled air fitters had a four-bladed propeller and semi-skilled air mechanics had a two-bladed propeller. The branch tended to follow the engineers in structure, though had no time to train a pool of highly-skilled ratings and had to rely on civilian recruits. Like the engineers, there were three main levels of skill – fully-skilled artificers, 'dilutee' air fitters and semi-skilled air mechanics.

The Fleet Air Arm was the last branch of the navy to expand to full strength, and the last to begin to wind down, because it had been planned to use it in the war against Japan until the atom bomb intervened. By September 1944 it had 42,264 ratings, plus 10,405 under training.[24]

Air Artificers

At the top of the Fleet Air Arm's ratings were the Air Artificers. The first three-year

Work for the Ordnance Artificer – a 5.25-inch gun turret.

course for airframe and engine apprentices started at RAF Halton in August 1938. In January the following year the course for electrical apprentices started at Rosyth and for ordnance specialists at RAF Cosford. In August 1939 the Air Ministry reduced the training period for its own apprentices to two years. The Admiralty, always anxious to keep up the high standards of its artificers, disagreed with this and in November it set up its own scheme in a Royal Naval Air Station at Lympne on the south coast of England. This moved far inland to Newcastle-under-Lyme in Staffordshire in 1940, though airframe and engine specialists were still at RAF Halton until January 1941. After that all air apprentices were given one year's instruction in the artificer schools at Rosyth and Torpoint, then went to Newcastle for a further two years. In May 1943 the course was increased to three-and-a-half years.[25]

Compared with ERAs, Air Artificers spent more time in theoretical instruction and less at bench work. In 1943, they were organized in two groups; Airframe and Engine, and Ordnance and Electrical, perhaps because it was difficult to provide a full range of skills on tiny aircraft carriers.

The training scheme only started a year before the war, it took at least three years to complete and about 300 were taken on every year, so only small numbers of navy-trained craftsmen became available. It was difficult to recruit experienced men from civilian life, so the navy relied on volunteers from the RAF for the whole of the war, and the Fleet Air Arm, more than any other branch, had to find ways of producing 'dilutees' and semi-skilled men.

Air Fitters and Air Mechanics

Below the artificers were the 'dilute' grades, mostly confined to intelligent Hostilities Only ratings, perhaps with a little civilian experience, who spent twenty-five weeks in training. These were the Air Fitters, divided into four main groups – Airframe, Engine, Electrical and Ordnance. Airframe and engine fitters were trained in quite large numbers – more than 3000 of each had started the course by the autumn of 1943. The course for ordnance began in April 1943 and by August, 310 had begun, and 273 had qualified. The course for Air Fitters (Electrical) only started in August 1943, with 361 men.[26] They were in great demand by this time.[27]

Qualified Air Fitters wore the fore-and-aft rig of artificers, with four-bladed propeller badges on their arms, with the letters A, E, L (for electrical) or O under it. They could expect to be promoted to leading rate within six months of qualifying. After some service they were entitled to apply for a twenty-five-week conversion course to Air Artificer, followed by a stiff trade test.

The lowest grade was the Air Mechanic, defined as a 'Semi-skilled maintenance rating employed on minor inspection and repair by replacement. Few had previous trade experience.' They were divided into the same specializations as the fitters.[28] For airframe mechanics the course consisted of 'Maintenance and minor routine inspection of airframes and minor repairs in accordance with approved repair scheme.' Engine mechanics learned 'Maintenance, minor routine inspections, starting, running up and testing power plant installed in aircraft. Simple adjustments and repairs by replacement.' They were trained in an eighteen-week course and wore a two-bladed propeller badge with the appropriate letter, on the square-rig uniform.

Air Fitters and Air Mechanics were trained under the auspices of the RAF. Airframe and Engine Fitters went to RAF Hednesford just north of Wolverhampton, where courses started in April 1939. Air Mechanics (A) and (E) started at RAF Henlow in Buckinghamshire in September 1938, then moved to St Athan in South

Wales in the following month. In February 1939 they went to RAF Locking just across the Bristol Channel near Weston-super-Mare, then to Hednesford in August 1942. Air Mechanics of the Electrical Branch remained at Henlow all this time, to be joined by air fitters (L) when the course started in 1943. Air mechanics of the Ordnance Branch remained at RAF Kirkham in Lancashire after the course started in March 1940.

Sailors who had just competed their disciplinary training at HMS *Gosling* near Warrington had 'an almost excessive regard for the navy' but were then transferred to the control of another service, with very different ways. Admiral Ford complained that they were 'imbued with RAF terms, methods and drills', and they resented being under the control of the air force. The navy appointed officers to look after them in the RAF stations, but only at the rate of one per 500 trainees. In the early stages of the war these officers were commissioned from warrant rank, with long service and steeped in naval ways. They 'gave most devoted service and by their tact and common sense maintained relations with the RAF on very good terms.' By 1943, as Ford complained, they were now junior RNVR officers 'whose knowledge of the Navy and Naval custom and procedure is very slight.'

All the same, Rear-Admiral Ford found much that was good in the RAF training. Hednesford, despite its 'almost forbidding aspect', had a 'general air of good discipline'. Training was generally good at all the bases, and standards of equipment were 'almost lavish', though the failure rate among naval personnel seemed somewhat high.

Just before the war the Admiralty reached agreement with the Gas Light and Coke Company of Fulham, London, to train apprentices as air fitters. This programme was completed by June 1940, but it was decided to train 450 more unskilled men. The first batch of fifty started in May 1941. The programme was boosted late in 1942 when it was estimated that another 5000 men would need to be trained during the next year, and the company set up a dormitory for 100 men in its works.

In 1941 it was found that suitable men were not coming forward for air fitter courses in sufficient numbers, and it was decided to upgrade selected air mechanics by giving them basic education and training in engineering skills. A course was started in the Government Training Centre at Watford in December 1941. It was decided to convert the centre to be run on naval lines and barracks were prepared by June 1942. There was capacity for 650 men on the course.

The Fleet Air Arm had many air bases in isolated sites, and the local population was too small to provide labour. This led to the creation of extra trades. Motor Mechanics (Motor Vehicle) were trained to service the cars and lorries which kept these bases supplied. Fifteen hundred Royal Marines were also in the service in December 1944 at home and abroad, mostly as drivers.[29]

Accountancy and Domestic

The Accountancy Branch included writers (clerks) and stores ratings, all with a six-pointed star as the main badge. The domestic staff included cooks, officers' cooks and officers' stewards, with a similar star. They had a letter inside the badge itself – W for writers, OC for officers' cooks, for example.

The navy used the term 'writer' for an office worker. When fully trained, he was able to work in pay and cash offices ashore and afloat, working with the ship's pay ledger and dealing with all kinds of pay and allowances, including income tax, allotments to relatives, and saving schemes. If employed in a captain's or an admiral's office, he carried out general secretarial and administrative work, and kept personnel and disciplinary records. He was able to type and perhaps had some shorthand; he had 'detailed knowledge of complex regulations'[30]

The Stores Rating had similar qualifications. He was responsible for issuing and accounting for all kinds of naval stores, including tools, hardware, cordage and wireless instruments. He might specialize in victualling, including the issue of food to messes aboard ship and the preparation of menus. A sub-group of the branch specialized in naval air stores.

In the early stages of the war, writers and stores assistants were trained at HMS *President V*, in Highgate School in London. This was used for 200 trainees, most of whom were billeted out. In 1943 it was expanded to take 250 male supply ratings and writers as well as 250 Wrens. Meanwhile HMS *Demetrius* was set up at Wetherby in Yorkshire as the main training base for the newly-renamed Supply and Secretariat Branch. George Melly was posted there in 1944, much against his will.

> My mathematical sense has always been shaky. I can't add up rows of figures twice and reach the same answer. … [I] did my best, given a persistent inability to concentrate on something which doesn't interest me, to work out how much pay less tax would be earned by a 1st Lieutenant, acting-captain of a motor torpedo boat, with a wife, two children and a dependent mother.[31]

Alan Brundrett found HMS *Demetrius* quite relaxed in 1944, more like a college than the navy, and he was able to order a daily newspaper. The course had been reduced from ten to eight weeks. It consisted of two parts of four weeks each – 'Captain's office' including naval administration, and 'Ledger'. He learned typing, but only at the rate of twenty-five words per minute, and the different types of correspondence as defined by the navy – routine, formal, demi-official and memorandum. He took notes on the advancement paths within different branches, the pay structure and on naval law.[32]

Cooks were divided into two classes, for officers and 'ship's company'. After their disciplinary training it had been normal to send them to the barracks at their home port, where they spent eight weeks working under the supervision of the cooks there and learned the trade. In 1940 it was decided to hold back twenty-five ratings who had completed their disciplinary course at *Royal Arthur* each month, to give them eight weeks' training in the base as cooks, and this became normal policy in the other bases.[33] The cooks studied the *Manual of Naval Cookery,* with chapters on cooking for a general mess as used in most ships, spices and condiments, invalid cookery, field cookery for landing parties, bread and cake making, cleanliness, serving of meals and the dietary values of various foods. Cooking was regarded as a menial trade rather than a high art in Britain at that time, and the status of naval cooks was low.

Stewards specialized in looking after the officers' needs in cabins and wardrooms. Derek Hamilton Warner was trained at HMS *Drake* in 1943. He learned how to wake up an officer. 'A cheerful "Good morning, Sir", tell him the time and what the weather was like, then ask him as to what uniform he would be requiring.' He had to learn much naval protocol including the different types of uniform – number 1 for parades, number 3 as working uniform, full mess dress and undress and tropical. According to the *Manual for Officers' Stewards*, 'The duties of a valet may be described as those of personal attendance on an officer, care of his clothing and personal effects, and tidiness and cleanliness of his cabin, furniture &c.'[34] The steward learned how to clean cabins, lay out a table, prepare a menu and serve wines. He was taught something of 'marketing', which in those days meant going to a local market to buy suitable provisions – all in a relatively short course of one month.[35]

Sick Berth Attendants (SBAs)

The oldest non-substantive badge, introduced in 1885, was the red cross inside a ring of the Medical Branch. The duties of a sick berth rating might vary considerably. He might work in a shore hospital as a nurse, in a large ship (frigate or above) under a medical officer, or in a smaller ship, such as a corvette, as the only medically-trained member of the crew. He was 'Normally capable of routine nursing, changing dressings, elementary dispensing, first aid, cookery for the sick, sterilization of instruments, and dressings, and elementary diagnosis of injury and sickness; administrative and clerical duties'.[36]

SBAs learned the trade in the three main naval hospitals at Chatham, Portsmouth (Haslar) and Plymouth (Stonehouse). At the start of the war the nine- to twelve-month course was reduced to ten weeks, largely by eliminating theoretical study. It was changed to twenty, and later to ten yet again when there was pressure to send men to the fleet. Hostilities Only ratings arrived in batches of about forty. In the hospitals the Sister Tutors were in charge of SBA training, under the Medical Officers. They were as domineering and memorable as the CPOs of the training establishments. At Haslar in 1942, Eric Alleston's was known as 'Rectum Rosie' because of her constant references to the alimentary canal. A. J. E. McCreedy's at Stonehouse a year later was 'the fastest bed-maker I have ever seen.'[37]

The Sick Berth Branch grew from 1187 officers, warrant officers and ratings in 1937 to 12,000 at the end of the war. The great majority were basic sick berth attendants, who wore the plain red cross. More specialized ratings had letters above the badge. There were nearly 400 dental assistants in 1943. Other groups, mostly selected from men with previous civilian experience, included dental mechanics who made dentures, dispensers, laboratory assistants, masseurs, mental nurses, operating room assistants, optical dispensers, radiographers and sanitary inspectors in shore establishments.[38]

HMS *Standard*

Finally, the navy had to deal with the men who could not be fitted in anywhere, but who could not be discharged without a good reason – frequent deserters and men with low morale or temperamental instability, though not clinically insane. In peacetime the navy would not have recruited them, in wartime it had to make the best of them, for discharge would serve as a poor example to others.

HMS *Standard* opened in January 1942, in an unlikely site. It was a former Ministry of Labour training camp at Keilder in Northumberland, in a valley with hills on three sides and a river on the other. It was extremely isolated to keep the men away from outside influences and to prevent desertion. Only 100 men were taken on at one time, under the supervision of a medical officer, chaplain, schoolmaster and disciplinary petty officers. The men worked at a strict regime, cutting down trees until these were exhausted, then carrying out the un-naval tasks of land drainage, farm labouring and building a reservoir. Leave was denied for the first month, then allowed on an increasing scale as long as the man behaved well. After three months their position was reassessed, and most stayed there for three-and-a-half to four months. Out of 842 trainees, 680 went on to naval employment, including shore service in boom defence or depot ships, and 271 became eligible for seagoing ships. [39]

CHAPTER 11

Promotion and Advanced Training

The Need for Petty Officers

Though recruiting and training of sailors and junior officers was not without its problems, there was even greater difficulty with the supply of men for the higher 'substantive' and 'non-substantive' ratings. Such men needed years of practical experience and a mature attitude, and these could not be improvised. The leading seamen, the lowest ratings with any formal authority over their juniors, were 'Men qualified and selected as capable of taking charge of others, or specially qualified technically.' They wore the badge of a single anchor on the left arm, above good-conduct stripes. They were known as 'hookey' or 'killick', after a type of small anchor. Petty officers were above the leading seamen – 'Men with responsible duties generally employed in taking charge of lower ratings: they mess separately from the latter and have many privileges as regards leave, etc.' They wore a badge of crossed anchors, and after a year in the rate they changed uniform to the collar and tie and peaked cap of the fore-and-aft rig. Above them, the highest men on the lower deck, were the chief petty officers – 'Men who hold particularly responsible positions, mess separately from the petty officers, and have further privileges.'[1]

The Evolution of the Petty Officer

The term 'petty officer' was an ancient one. Originally it used the word 'officer' in the sense of the holder of a particular office, and included, for example, the yeoman of the sheets, whose job was to ensure that certain ropes ran freely during manouevres. In Nelson's day it did not necessarily imply leadership or command; petty officers included technicians. A petty officer had no formal qualifications, and if he transferred to another ship he would probably lose his rate. By 1853 the rates had evolved into chief petty officers and petty officers 1st and 2nd class. In order to retain long-service men, the petty officer rating was increasingly guaranteed against reduction in rank, and regulated by examination.

By the beginning of the twentieth century it had evolved yet further. Admiral Fisher wanted something much closer to a sergeant in the army or the marines. 'Petty officers are required primarily to command those junior to them; therefore, the chief attribute of a petty officer should be "power to command". It is not unfair to say that in a large number of our present petty officers this attribute is conspicuous by its absence ...'[2] One reaction was to abolish the rating or petty officer 2nd class in 1907. Even so, by 1931, as Admiral Kelly found, the petty officers still did not have enough authority over the men.

The Leading Seaman

The rating of leading seaman, or leading hand to use a term which covered all the branches of the navy, was another case where something turned out very different from what was intended. It had originally been planned as a superior kind of able seamen. In 1853 a Committee on Manning proposed a group 'To be designated "Leading Seaman" to consist of Men who are thorough Helm and Leads Men, and Practical Riggers, capable of doing Duty as such in any Part of a Ship.'[3] This was approved, and in 1862 the Queen's Regulations regulated their examinations and gave them certain privileges and 2 pence extra per day.[4] Equivalent grades were soon created in other branches, such as leading cook, leading stoker and leading writer. The term was used in the sense of 'men of deserved influence', but it had unintended implications of leadership in another sense. There was tendency for the leading hand to be given more responsibility over the years, especially after the rating of petty officer 2nd class was abolished. He was not recognized as a superior officer within the meaning of the Naval Discipline Act; and striking one was treated as 'an act to the prejudice of good order and Naval discipline' rather than an assault on a superior officer.[5] Captain Pelly of HMS *King Alfred* was well aware of the lack of authority of some leading hands and petty officers in 1943, and encouraged junior officers to support them. 'You must also bear in mind that the young higher ratings, and particularly the Leading Seamen, have a difficult job. They find themselves in charge of men older than themselves, some of whom endeavour to trip them up.'[6]

The System of Promotion

The system assumed a slow and steady progress for each man. It was designed to prevent unsuitable men from rising, rather than to make them suitable. Again, the shadow of the First World War hung over the navy. On the eve of the Second, the Head of the Naval Branch at the Admiralty wrote of the 'risk of saddling the Navy for many years with immature and inferior leading seaman which position arose out of the last war.'[7]

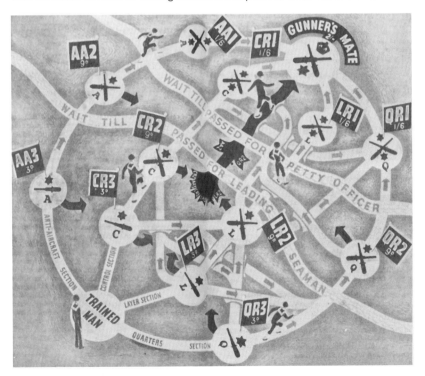

The promotion path in the Gunnery Branch. Typically, the highest degree of specialization is in the middle of a career; gunner's mates have to know something of the work of all the sub-branches.

There were six requirements for advancement in the Seaman Branch – total length of service; sea service; educational tests; health (no man with venereal disease was to be promoted); skill in seamanship or in a non-substantive rate; and the recommendation of one's captain after the prescribed period of sea service, intended to identify leadership qualities. The educational test for advancement to leading seaman, ET1, was held three times a year in peacetime. It involved knowledge of simple and arithmetic and vulgar and decimal fractions, and of English; 'Writing an ordinary passage of English to Dictation. Writing a simple essay. Meanings of words, technical and otherwise. Explanations in the candidate's own words of passages taken from the King's Regulations and Admiralty Instructions, the daily press, etc.'[8]

Seniority was also an important factor. The numbers of permanent leading seaman and petty officer were strictly controlled in peacetime – 400 chief petty officers, 800 petty officers and 1200 leading seaman in the Seaman Branch. In wartime this was increased to 1000, 4000 and 8000,[9] and the rest of the posts were filled by acting and temporary promotion. Accelerated advancement was available even in peacetime; men with special recommendations from their captains could be pushed forward by up to four months. Apart from that, everything depended on rising up the divisional rosters at the three home ports. These were maintained for each different rate within each branch, but essentially fell into two types. The highly skilled ratings, such as artificers, mechanicians and artisans, would be advanced when they fulfilled the conditions of service, education and recommendation, irrespective of vacancies. This was also true of the promotion of an ordinary seaman to able; but otherwise in the Seaman Branch, as with stokers, signalmen, and 'miscellaneous' ratings, the man had to rise to the top of the roster by seniority or accelerated advancement before he was promoted to fill a vacancy. Six or seven years might elapse in peacetime between passing for a rate and actually achieving it. In the circumstances, many men became disillusioned.

'Stripey' and the Promotion Problem

Pre-war recruiting pamphlets claimed that 'the rating of Petty Officer, at least, ought to be reached during his service by any man of reasonable ability who has personality and ambition.'[10] But this was not the whole story. Naturally 'Stripey' the long-service, unpromoted able seaman, formed a much smaller proportion of the navy in war than in peace, but his influence was still felt. To Nicholas Monsarrat he was a 'legendary character'.

> ... either he hasn't the brain and energy to pass for Leading Seaman, or he doesn't welcome responsibility, or he "likes it where he is", or for any other reason ... He may sound dull and stupid but he is rarely that; more often than not he knows it all ... Give him a job and he will work his way through it; not with any flash display of energy, like one of those jumped-up young Petty Officers, but at a careful and steady pace ...[11]

On the lower deck, seniority respected more than rating. A man's stripes were more prominent than the anchor badges of his rate, and were determined by his own choice about when to join the navy and his ability to keep out of trouble. His substantive rate depended on the will of his officers. This had unfortunate effects and probably deterred men from seeking promotion. It tended to undermine the authority of inexperienced leading seamen. When John L. Davies was promoted to leading seaman and gunnery instructor just before attaining the three years which would have qualified him for his first good-conduct stripe, his officer was concerned that 'it could provoke the senior ratings.' He allowed him to wear a stripe unpaid until he was qualified for it.[12] In a similar vein, Roy Fuller and his fellow radio mechanics were told by a petty officer that they were not 'proper' leading hands.

"How long have you been in the Navy, Percival?"
"Fourteen months."
"There you are. How can you be a proper leading hand in that time? In peacetime a bloke waited seven years or more for his hook."[13]

One of the problems was to be found in King's Regulations and Admiralty Instructions;

When a rating requests and is granted permission to refuse advancement or to revert to a lower rating, his name is to be removed from the port division advancement roster. He is not to be re-instated, except by Admiralty approval in special cases, and he is to be warned to this effect.[14]

A man who turned down promotion due to a youthful lack of confidence had to stay with the decision for the rest of his career.

Another problem was in the pay of different rates. An Ordinary Seaman's first promotion would be to Able Seaman, recognizing skill and experience but giving no executive responsibilities. It brought a substantial pay rise, in the 1940 scales, from £1.18.6 (£1.93) to £2.18.11 (£2.95) per week, or 53 per cent. On promotion to Leading Seaman the wage would rise to £3.7.8 (£3.38), or only 15 per cent.[15] A leading seaman was expected to exercise his authority in working hours, but also to live and keep order in the same mess as the ordinary and able seamen, so he could never fully relax. It would not be surprising if many seamen thought the promotion was not worthwhile. The next step, to Petty Officer, was more desirable, for it brought the right to live in the Petty Officers' Mess. This was an incentive to the long-service able seaman, but few Hostilities Only men could see a career stretching that far ahead.

The Duties of Petty Officers
As early as 1941, an American observer noted that traditional practice, combined with the inexperience of wartime officers, caused extra responsibility to be placed on the petty officers on British ships.

The officers rely on the petty officers much more than do the officers in our Navy. For example, the signalmen not only read but interpret the signals. They always tell the OOD [officer of the deck] the meaning of the signal and not the signal itself. The officers were not concerned with such matters, except the captain who knew the meaning of all the signals. Other petty officers perform their duties in the same manner as the signalmen. There is no officer assigned to the plotting room during action. With the exception of the engineer officer and the two gunners, the officers (in observer's opinion) did not have even a working knowledge of the equipment they worked. They did not seem interested in such matters. This is no doubt due to the great reliance placed on their petty officers.[16]

In 1943 Captain Pelly advised newly-commissioned officers;

> ... you should bear in mind that the responsibilities of the higher rating are more important now than they have ever been. They should be made to feel that they are in your confidence, and they should be made to feel that they really are the men that matter. Bring them into any discussion of a job of work, drill, improvement or amenity. Not nearly enough is done by officers to encourage the status of Higher Ratings.

He warned junior officers to be aware of the problems of fast promotion. 'On the other hand, do not expect too much of your higher ratings. You cannot expect their standard to be a high level one, as large numbers are at present being made and many of them are of very limited experience.'[17]

Petty officers had certain privileges in return for their responsibilities. They messed and slept separately from the seamen. They were free from menial duties and had messmen – often three-badge able seamen – to clean their accommodation and fetch meals. After one year's satisfactory service they changed into the fore-and-aft rig.

Petty officers in the adult training camps or at sea were rarely as fierce as those in the boys' training establishments, and most were positively fatherly and genial. George Melly commented,

A chief petty officer impresses his authority on a seaman on board a destroyer, c. 1941. A drawing by John Worsley.

'Not like that,' roared the Chief...

I found that, in general, Petty Officers and Chief Petty Officers, if not religious maniacs or just nasty by nature, tended to be reasonable men. Long association with the sea and its ports had given them a certain tolerant sophistication, part cynical but certainly affectionately so. They had learnt to mistrust the moral imperatives of any one place because they had seen them replaced by others, often equally rigid and ridiculous, elsewhere. The [sic] made allowances too for us temporary sailors. We were there because we had to be. One day the war would be over and the Navy its old self; a machine for sailing in.[18]

The Master at Arms and the Coxswain

In battleships, fleet aircraft carriers and cruisers, the Master at Arms was the senior rating. He was essentially the head of the ship's police, with a number of regulating petty officers under him. He tended to be a remote and unpopular figure on most ships.

A small ship, a destroyer or below, had a coxswain instead, known as 'swain' to the lower deck. Not to be confused with the other type of coxswain who took charge of a ship's boat, these petty officers combined the duties of master at arms and chief supply petty officer. To D. A. Rayner he was 'the third most important man, as far as the happiness of the ships is concerned', after the captain and first lieutenant.[19] Nicholas Monsarrat recognized his importance.

A good coxswain is a jewel; … The coxswain can make all the difference on board. As the senior rating in the ship, responsible for much of its discipline and administration, he has a profound effect on producing a happy and efficient ship's company. Usually he is a "character", to use an overworked but explicit word: that is, a strong personality who would make himself felt in any surroundings, and who is, in his present world, a man of exceptional weight and influence. He keeps his eye on everything, from the rum issue to the cleanliness of hammocks, from the chocolate ration to the length of the side-whiskers of the second-class stokers …

He is the friend of everyone on board, and a good friend too – if they want him to be, and if they deserve it: failing that, he makes a very bad enemy.[20]

With several thousand ships in commission in November 1943, it is not surprising that the supply of such 'characters' was running short. A. H. Cherry attributes a mutiny in HMS *Braithwaite* to the failings of the coxswain. Rather than 'a key man below-decks, a man to lean on, the very pivot on which good discipline depends', a 'strong faithful arm that should have been a tower of strength, pointing the way for a ship's company', he was in fact 'a man of weak personality, having little or no control over the lower deck ratings at all …'[21]

The Growing Crisis

Even before the war started, there were shortages of suitable men for leading hands and petty officers, due to rapid expansion in the last few years. In April 1939 it was noted that the promotion rosters at Devonport and Chatham had almost dried up, and the position was even worse at Portsmouth, where hardly anyone met all the requisites for promotion to leading seaman. There were 165 men who had passed the test, but had not enough sea time; 141 who were not yet recommended by their captains; seventy-seven more who were not recommended from their sea service, and twenty who had not passed Educational Test No. 1. The response was to reduce the sea time required from one year to six months, though the man still had to serve one year in the rating of able seaman. The requirement for Educational Test no.1 was waived, though it had to be passed within two years of advancement, or for confirmation within the rate.[22] This policy was extended to other branches during the course of 1940.[23]

In the Home Fleet in December 1939, orders were issued for each ship to be ready to train its own men for both substantive and non-substantive rates, so that it would not feel the loss when those already trained were transferred to other ships. In the case of petty officers, 'Every Ship is in addition to train understudies for all higher ratings holding key positions in order that the release of a proportion of these ratings could, if required, be effected without undue dislocation.' This could work in the battleships and cruisers which spent relatively little time at sea and which had facilities and men to carry out training; it would not work in destroyers and smaller ships. 'In the case of small ships, where the few key ratings borne are relatively of greater importance and where facilities for the training of understudies are strictly limited, it is realized that this requirement cannot be met fully and the release of such ratings will, therefore, not be called for unless absolutely unavoidable.'[24]

Early in 1940 the Admiralty issued its policy on 'Advancement of Ratings During the War'. It was regarded as essential that all ratings, including Hostilities Only men, should have equal prospects of advancement; but at the same time all should 'attain the same standard' before it was awarded. The numbers of higher ratings would be frozen at the figures in the Navy Estimates of 1939–40 and any promotions beyond that would be temporary – the man concerned would have the letters (Ty) after his title. Continuous service ordinary seamen could now be rated able after six months service including four at sea, and Hostilities Only men needed nine months (including training). To take the next step to leading seaman, a man needed only six more months at sea; for the moment petty officer rates remained unchanged.[25]

In 1941 another order diluted the skills of the Stoker Branch. Leading Stokers could be replaced by Temporary Leading Stokers in certain circumstances. These were men who had not undergone the appropriate training course and had the letters NQ (not qualified) after their names on the muster book. They would be sent on courses as soon as circumstances permitted. In every ship with four or more leading stokers, 25 per cent were to be withdrawn for other duties, and the captain was given authority to promote NQ men where necessary. It was realized that this would create problems lower down the scale, with the loss of stokers 1st class through promotion. It was accepted that up to half of the stokers in any ship might be inexperienced men of the second class.[26]

Other branches tackled the problem in slightly different ways. Combined Operations was an entirely new service made up mostly of HOs in all ranks. It needed a large number of leading seamen as coxswains of small landing craft. In July 1941 it proposed that 'Men recommended for Leading Seamen to be advanced, on your authority [ie Rear-Admiral Hughes Hallet, Combined Operations] to acting temporary leading rate irrespective of the professional and time qualifications laid down in A.F.O. 341/40. Such advancement would be effective only while men are serving in Combined Operations organization.' Recommendations for further promotion to petty officer were to be sent on to the Admiralty and the commodores of depots 'with a view to special consideration being given to their advancement.' [27]

The submarine service was made up of a high proportion of junior ratings by 1943, most of whom had 'had little time to work up in seamanship, and have not had opportunities to undergo Seamanship Courses due to the low state of the Drafting Margin, and have consequently lacked the confidence to face Fleet Examination Boards.' It was agreed to create ratings of Leading Seaman (Submarines) and Petty Officer (Submarines) for the duration of the war. Their advancement would be within the submarine service and they would revert after the war or on leaving submarines. Because of their temporary status petty officers, who would normally be entitled to a different uniform after a year in the rate, would have to pay for it themselves or wear their old square rig.[28]

By early 1943, as the naval expansion programme moved into top gear, the Director of Personal Services was becoming seriously concerned about the situation.

> From the latest statistics we are 18 per cent short of Leading Seamen and 8 per cent short of P.O.s. ... The existing shortage of P.O.s seems likely to be reduced by the end of March 1943, but there is not the slightest prospect of any improvement in the Leading Seaman situation and in fact it may deteriorate as the number of P.O.s grows. With next year's expansion to face, this situation cannot be allowed to go on. Ships commissioning when the shortage of higher ratings is most acute obviously suffer more than ships abroad who cannot be got at and naturally retain men advanced in the ship to the full numbers allowed. Owing to the slower rate at which men are advanced to Leading Seaman there is a further inclination to retain P.Os in lieu of Leading Seamen and thus the P.O. situation becomes more acute than the numbers borne reflect.

Captain Oram of the Training and Staff Duties Division was concerned that 'the standard of Petty Officers should not be lowered.' He proposed the revival of the petty officer 2nd class, but this was quickly rejected by the Naval Branch. Eventually a new Admiralty Fleet Order was issued on 'the acute shortage of Leading Seamen.' A 'drastic cut' was to be made in their numbers. A third of existing leading seamen were to be withdrawn from seagoing ships, and half from shore bases (except for instructors). Their places, according to a custom which was now becoming established, were to be taken by NQ men rated up. It was hoped that 'Under this scheme Commanding Officers will have the opportunity of testing and forcing men for higher rating and they will always be in a position to revert those who prove unsuitable after trial.'[29]

By now the crisis had attracted the notice of the First Lord of the Admiralty.

> There is increasing evidence that the number of higher and trained technical ratings is not keeping up with the rate at which the navy has expanded and that a large proportion of men entered for 'Hostilities Only' lack the normal incentive for advancement. This may be partly due to the fact that the wages of many are being 'made up' by their civilian employers, and in any case they do not contemplate a career in the navy with its attendant responsibilities.

> The shortages in the ratings concerned are chiefly in Seamen Petty Officers and Leading Seamen, Petty Officer and Leading Telegraphists, Yeomen and Leading Signalmen, Senior Artificers (Electrical and Engine Room, the latter

with certificates qualifying them to take charge of watches) and in Supply and Writer Petty Officers.

All these rates are, normally, only attained after some years of experience except in the case of exceptional men.

In the Seaman Branch there are also shortages of men with high electrical and gunnery non-substantive ratings.

It is evident that casualties to men in sunk or damaged ships is affecting the number of higher Engine Room ratings available, as the proportion of casualties is usually highest in the Engine and Boiler Rooms.[30]

In August that year the navy was short of 2050 leading seamen and 940 petty officers. There were also numerous vacancies in the non-substantive rates. Commanding officers were ordered to make 'the most economic use' of existing personnel. They were to reduce demands to an absolute minimum and to ensure that 'not a single officer or rating is retained in a ship or establishment if his services can be dispensed with or replaced by a less highly trained man even though his going may cause inconvenience.'[31]

As was also the case with accommodation, the navy was reaching the ends of its resources for future higher rates. It would take many months for the best of the new entrants to become leading seaman, and in the meantime the expansion programme went on. It was perhaps fortunate that the extra 247,000 men demanded for 1944 were not allowed. Instructors could now be drawn from the training schools, more men of three or four years' experience were available, and the crisis eased.

Higher Non-Substantive Rates

The 1st and 2nd class gunnery ratings, seamen torpedomen and submarine detectors were usually chiefs, petty officers and leading seamen, and these grades, too, were affected by wartime shortages. From the first month of the war, the Admiralty realized that some kind of 'dilution' was necessary in the more skilled parts of the seaman branch. There was less time for formal training in schools, more training on the job on board ship. In the case of torpedomen, it was ordered in September 1939 that 'Men selected at sea for higher Torpedo rating … should be instructed on the lines of courses shown in the Torpedo Training Manual, in so far as they are applicable. … the instructions … that the paid acting rating of Torpedo Gunner's Mate [i.e. petty officer] may be granted only in ships abroad, is suspended.'[32]

The Home Fleet orders of December 1939 demanded that

Every ship is to be prepared to surrender a number of higher non-substantive rates (mainly 2nd class), depending on the authorized complement, and to replace them with acting ratings trained in the ship. The number required to be withdrawn at any one time would be very small.

At sea, ships had to make do with less qualified men. There were three main grades in the Anti-Submarine Branch. The Submarine Detector (SD) was an able or leading seaman, the Higher Submarine Detector (HSD) had taken an advanced course which qualified him for promotion up to petty officer and the Submarine Detector Instructor was a leading seaman or above. By 1940, ratings on board ship were already being diluted. Large destroyers of the Tribal Class had carried three HSDs and three SDs; they were now to have one HSD and three SDs. Old destroyers of the V and W classes had originally had two HSDs and two SDs; now they were to have one HSD and four SDs.[33]

The rapid expansion of the Radar Branch, opened wide the path to promotion in 1942. All examinations for leading seaman and petty officer were waived and captains were allowed to promote any number of men after six months' service – 'the only requirement is the Commanding Officer's recommendation as being a reliable and safe operator on such set (or sets) that he is required to operate in his own ship, and able to take charge within his own department.' Maintenance ability was not a requirement, as it was in the Signal Branch at the time. After a further year they were eligible for promotion to petty officer, having passed a ten-week course at Portsmouth.[34]

Despite the efforts of the training schools, the situation continued to get worse. By August 1943, only 76 per cent of the required gunnery ratings were passing through the schools, and 63 per cent of torpedomen.[35]

The Engineering Branch

The paths of advancement in the Engineering Branch are described in the *Machinery Handbook* of 1941.

> On first going to sea, a junior engine-room rating will generally be employed in a boiler room, and his first step will be to prove himself an efficient and reliable boiler-room watchkeeper. ... As opportunity offers junior engine-room ratings who have qualified as boiler-room watchkeepers, and have shown that they are capable and zealous in the performance of their duties, will be selected for training as watchkeepers in the engine room. ... Stokers who are selected by the Engineer Officer as likely to make good leading stokers will be given a course as watchkeepers on the auxiliary machinery, and will, if they show themselves worthy, be recommended for the Leading Stokers Course at the Mechanical Training Establishment at their home port. Attention to the instruction given at this course will enable a leading stoker or stoker to acquire the professional knowledge necessary for advancement to stoker petty officer, if recommended in due course.[36]

There was a ten-week course for leading stokers at each of the home ports during the war, intended to produce candidates for stoker petty officer. This was causing problems by the end of 1942, when it was noted that many men serving overseas could not get home to do the course, and were not eligible for consideration as stoker petty officer until they had, so they lost seniority. It was decided, somewhat grudgingly, that when they finished the course they should have backdated seniority equal to that of the average acting leading stoker of similar seniority who had served at home.[37]

Rear-Admiral Ford considered that the course was very unsatisfactory. There was a certain amount of training in tools, but that would turn the man into 'an efficient E.R.A.'s mate', work a leading stoker was hardly ever asked to do. Even worse was the instruction in bricklaying, intended to be useful in the repair of boilers. It was 'largely a waste of time. No Leading Stoker, except possibly one per ship, can be spared under modern conditions for repair of brickwork, since nearly all Leading Stokers are employed in practice in watchkeeping on the more important auxiliary machinery'. Lectures had some value, and the course was of some use in selecting mechanicians, who were only 5 per cent of those who passed; but overall Ford was 'at a loss to understand the policy which led to the introduction of this course', presumably at the turn of the century, and recommended that it be dropped for the rest of the war, until there was time to think of something more relevant.[38]

The 'Miscellaneous' Branches

The conditions for promotion of writers, supply ratings and cooks were laid down by Admiralty Fleet Order of April 1940. For advancement to leading writer or supply assistant, applicants with at least nine months' service were given a short oral examination in their work by the accountant officer, or by the administrative authorities ashore in the case of a small ship where none was borne. Petty officer candidates were examined by boards including an accountant officer and a warrant officer. The peacetime arithmetic, shorthand and typing tests were waived. In view of this, the Admiralty was determined not to lower the standards for chief petty officers, and they were still to take tests. In the case of cooks, it was not practicable to send them ashore for further training as in peacetime. They were to learn the finer points of the trade afloat, and be examined by a board including an accountant officer and a warrant cook.[39]

In the Sick Berth Branch, the promotion crisis came in September 1943. It was noted that 'Owing to the continued expansion programme, the number of ratings qualified for promotion in the Sick Berth Branch has not kept pace with requirements except in the Portsmouth Division.' There were sixty-four SBAs there qualified for promotion to leading rate, and seventy-four leading SBAs qualified for petty officer, but none in either category at Plymouth or Chatham. This was a problem likely to arise in a small branch under the stress of war, and it was decided to waive advancement by roster for the rest of the war.[40]

Wartime Promotion

Naturally the manning situation led relatively easy promotion for regular sailors. Sidney Greenwood writes,

> Promotion was rapid. I progressed through these rates: temporary acting leading stoker; acting leading stoker; leading stoker and petty officer within two years. Escapades of mine during that period would, had they happened in peacetime, surely have deprived me of any one of these tentative steps. How I escaped the delicate hold on the first is an indication of the scarcity of senior ratings.[41]

In wartime the procedure was brief. A Luftwaffe bomb at Devonport Barracks had created many vacancies for chiefs and petty officers in that division, and the quota had to be filled.

> "Recommended for advancement," said the Divisional Officer, an R.N.V.R sub-lieutenant hardly qualified to know or judge my ability.
> "Recommended for advancement," said the First Lieutenant, who was eminently qualified.
> "Request granted," said the Captain.

"Request granted," repeated the Cox'sn.

Thus John Whelan gained the crossed anchors of a petty officer with seniority back-dated to the day of the bomb a month earlier.[42]

For some Hostilities Only candidates, promotion could be quite swift and men could make leading seaman within a year or so in some areas. Ex-schoolteacher John Davies found one of his former pupils, who had left a year previously, serving as a leading hand in *Ganges*.[43] Telegraphist air gunners of the Fleet Air Arm became leading hands on qualification, while potential pilots and observers gained the rating as soon as they began flying training. Beyond that, promotion to petty officer was rather slower, and the rate was mostly filled by regular naval men. This was especially true of instructors and John Whelan noted, 'It was not until 1944 that the first H.O. Petty officers qualified as S.D.I.s [Submarine Detector Instructors]. It was possible to become a junior R.N.V.R. Officer within six months of joining, but it took far longer to make an asdic instructor.'[44]

In general the Admiralty remained protective of the highest rating, chief petty officer. In most branches three years' service as a petty officer was required, which meant that few Hostilities Only ratings would rise so high; indeed the rate was not open to non-regular seamen in the Communications Branch, for example.[45] In October 1942 the chief petty officers' mess on some ships, planned 'on the basis of numbers borne in normal circumstances' were now 'comparatively empty'. Captains were invited to move in other suitable ratings, such as shipwrights, electrical and ordnance artificers.[46] In the frigate *Ettrick* in 1943, the engine room artificers outnumbered the chief petty officers by three to one.[47]

The United States Navy

There were many strong contrasts between the United States and British navies in this period, as well as many similarities. The US Navy had begun on the British model but developed differently. By 1900 the US Navy had chief petty officers, and petty officers 1st, 2nd and 3rd class. This was not radically different from the British system of the time, with chiefs, two grades of petty officer and leading seamen. The Americans, however, never adopted any equivalent of the 'non-substantive' system. A man's skill and authority was represented by his rating as seaman or petty officer. The two navies reacted differently to hard times around 1930, when money and therefore promotion prospects dried up. The British tried to develop an alternative system which recognized skills, partly independent of rank. The Americans froze all men in their existing grades for a time. In the short term this caused considerable hardship for those at the bottom end of the scale.[48]

Non-commissioned ranks are notoriously difficult to equate between the services of different nations. The American Joint Army and Navy Publications, *Uniforms and Insignia* (JANI) of 1943 gave only a general guide. 'British CPO is slightly higher in responsibility and authority than USN CPO, while the British rating Boy – made up of youngsters of fifteen to eighteen years old – is definitely lower than USN Apprentice Seaman; the ratings between these extremes would have to be adjusted correspondingly to conform to this greater coverage in the British ratings compared with USN.'[49] A petty officer 1st class in the USN was equivalent to a technical sergeant in the army, the second-in-command of an infantry platoon, the equivalent of a British sergeant. This would make the American petty officer 1st class equal to a British petty officer, though the latter had certain privileges; a separate mess and a

The path to promotion in the US Navy.

ENLISTED ADVANCEMENT

A The division training officer discusses plans with the man for completing the rate requirements when the training course is checked out.

B The training course must be read and re-read. Regular periods of study and good reading habits make for more rapid progress in advancement.

C Training in practical work with ship's gear is necessary for advancement in rating. This training is given the men by petty officers.

D In regularly scheduled classes, conducted by division training officers, trainees gain information and skills necessary for advancement.

E The men learn from each other in small study groups. These study groups are voluntary and are in addition to class meetings with instructors.

F Satisfactory application of practical factors is required knowledge for advancement in rate. Training employs actual practice with ship's gear.

G The candidate is called before the Examining Board consisting of three officers and is graded on requirements. Records are kept on results.

H The Board reports its findings to the Commanding Officer. The man is rated in accordance with the standing policy of the Bureau of Naval Personnel.

peaked cap after a year of service. An American petty officer 2nd class was equivalent to a leading seaman. There was no real equivalent of a petty officer 3rd class in the Royal Navy, but in view of the technical skill involved, he might be considered similar to an able seaman with a non-substantive rating in gunnery, torpedo, etc.

The American system was better for introducing a man gently to responsibility. A petty officer 3rd class continued to live with the seamen, but unlike the British leading seaman he was not the senior man in a mess, for the petty officers 1st and 2nd class would also be there. He did not have the same problem in controlling hostile and resentful juniors at all hours of the day and night. By the time he became a petty officer 1st class, he would probably have had several years of responsibility. On the other hand, supporters of the British system might argue that the US system diluted authority too much, and that American petty officers were lacking in authority.

There was no real equivalent of the three-badge AB in the US Navy. Service stripes or 'hash-marks' were worn less prominently on the lower sleeve. Seamen came from a society with far higher expectations than Britain in the 1930s and 1940s and assumed they would advance during their careers. The American system laid much greater stress on the officers' role in selecting petty officers. *Naval Orientation*, published in 1945 to aid the training of midshipmen, outlined an eight-stage process.[50] Though individual British officers no doubt did their best to advance suitable men, there was far less guidance and encouragement. Publications such as *King's Regulations and Admiralty Instructions* presented the promotion path as a series of hurdles rather than a golden opportunity, with innumerable conditions.

> No rating is to be placed on, or remain on, the port division advancement roster unless he was qualified to be recommended and was recommended on the last return S. 507 either for advancement or for accelerated advancement, but ratings removed and subsequently replaced will resume their position on the roster according to their seniority or date of passing.[51]

British divisional officers were given much less positive encouragement to identify and train suitable men – peremptory instructions from the Admiralty on 'forcing men for higher rating' were not as helpful as they might have been.[52] Since good petty officers could only be created by long experience, the problem was ultimately insoluble, but a closer study of modern methods, and less adherence to traditional practices, might have helped.

CHAPTER 12

Permanent Officers

Selection for Dartmouth

The great majority of regular naval officers entered through the Royal Naval College at Dartmouth. It took on boys aged around thirteen to complete their general education and train them to become naval officers. It cost parents or guardians about £200 a year to support a boy, more than the income of a typical worker. With some extra expenses, it cost about £850 to put a boy through the course in the 1930s. There were concessions for the sons of naval officers, and from 1941 one place was reserved for the son of a rating.[1] But in general a Dartmouth education was for the rich and the privileged.

It was an age of 'people's war', in which all classes had to feel that they had equal opportunities. The Labour Party was a principal member of the coalition government and could not be seen to encourage class distinction, while Churchill had a long record of trying to open commissioned rank to all classes. A scholarship scheme was started in 1941 to make it possible for sons of families of moderate means to enter Dartmouth. This involved 'assistance towards the expenses of training and maintenance. The poorest parent will be relieved of all expenses arising from the boy's training including the cost of travelling to and from the place of training.' Parents whose income exceeded £700 a year would pay the full fees of £65 per term. Those earning under £300 would pay nothing towards the fees, though there were many incidental expenses including £37 a year for the sports and library funds, stationery, tailoring and bootmaking.[2]

The Admiralty was keen to show that Dartmouth was neither exclusive nor expensive. A leaflet distributed to schools pointed out that 'the fact has been established that with care [a cadet] can live on his pay of 5 shillings a day and thus reduce the expenses of parents and guardians.' 'Expensive tastes' were not encouraged.[3] Academic qualifications were not enough on their own and headmasters were asked searching questions about the boy's other qualities. Was he keen to enter the navy or had he been persuaded by others? Was he good at games? Did he show leadership qualities? Did he have common sense and initiative? They were invited to point out any 'marked selfishness, lack of physical or moral courage and any other deficiency which makes it improbable that he will develop into a leader of men.'[4]

Four hundred and ten candidates sat the entrance examination in June 1941, the first time that scholarships were offered. Of these, 297 boys competed for the ten scholarships for boys from state-supported schools, and sixty-five for scholarships for boys from public schools. This was regarded as a success, but the number of state-school applicants declined steadily after the initial enthusiasm. Only 123 applied for the September 1944 entry – more than enough to fill the places, but the Admiralty worried that they were not attracting the very best candidates.[5]

In September 1943,

> There were forty-six of us in the Term, a mixed bunch from different back-
> grounds as ten were Grammar School scholars, ten open scholars and
> twenty more of us whose parents had to pay, on a generous means related
> basis, taking part in an experiment in equality of opportunity which was
> ahead of its time.[6]

Sometimes a boy first heard of his acceptance by means of a letter from Gieves, the
naval tailors, who had been informed by the Admiralty.

> Dear Madam,
> Will you please note that your son's number at the Royal Naval College,
> Dartmouth, is 442. His name, together with number, should be marked on
> all articles of the outfit.

The official letter, signed the Secretary to the Admiralty, followed a few days
later.[7]

Training at Dartmouth and Eaton Hall

Dartmouth College was completed in 1905, replacing two wooden training ships. It
retained some of its pre-war dignity in 1941; there were still thirty-five 'Cadet personal attendants' and a large staff of cooks and cleaners to maintain a level of com-
parative comfort. In all the college had a staff of forty-five naval officers, nineteen ratings, twenty-seven Wrens and 323 civilians, including twenty engineer and carpentry
instructors.[8] This was interrupted on 18 September 1942 when two bombs hit the
college. The cadets were on leave at the time, but one Wren was killed and the workshop was seriously damaged. It was decided to move to Eaton Hall in Cheshire. One
of the September 1943 term described it.

Cadets at Eaton Hall are
inspected by the King, 1945.

The house itself was an immense Victorian pile, pinnacled like St Pancras Station, designed to enable princes and house parties of more than a hundred guests to be entertained. The main entrance, which we were not allowed to use, led through the Marble Hall and on to the main staircase which still had vast wall paintings by Reubens on either side of it.

All had changed. Classrooms filled the main bedrooms, stripped of their finery, science laboratories had taken over the kitchens in the cellars, which had produced meals for a king to eat.[9]

Younger cadets in a classroom at Eaton Hall, 1945.

The content of the education was summarized by the headmaster in 1941.

In the main, the course at Dartmouth College follows that of Secondary School education ... Seamanship is taught throughout the training. In the last year there is a small amount of navigation and there is a thorough Physical Training course. Engineering, which is a practical workshop course, starts at the beginning of the course and goes on right through. This is an important and most valuable feature.[10]

There were doubts about the age of cadets, and the range of subjects. The Engineer-in-Chief, though generally favourable, pointed out that 'during the age of puberty many boys are resistant to education, and do not allow their natural intelligence to control their lives until such times as it becomes evident to them that they have to make their way in the world.'[11] According to a report of 1945:

There is undoubtedly a danger that the Dartmouth Education by being directed towards the production only of Naval officers will be regarded in the educational world in general as being worth very little for wider purposes. We note for instance that passing our examination carried no exemption from Matriculation [for university] and that the placing of a boy who does not pass into the Navy due perhaps to unsuitability for a Naval career presents a great difficulty. ... in recent years art has been introduced to the College and that a much enhanced place has been given to music. The lack of cultural education in any school must cause it to be regarded as narrow and inferior.[12]

Scholarship boys had some good effects.

The entry of the scholars from the grant-aided schools appears to have introduced a greater desire for thoroughness — more sense of responsibility — in work, games and hobbies. It is tending to show up the rather dilettante attitude of some Preparatory school boys.

However most of them had never been to boarding school before and were introduced to a new experience at the age of thirteen.

The boys who have spent some years at a boarding school before entering the college are mostly much quicker to co-operate in doing things large and small for the benefit of their House and others generally. Some of the grant-aided school scholars are quick to learn co-operation, others are proving very slow. The point is important, as it very much affects the question of leadership (others do not easily follow one who is patently out for himself, unless indeed he is leading them into trouble) and it becomes more important the higher they get in the college.[13]

The Special Entry Scheme

The 'Special Entry' scheme was started in 1913 as a faster way of providing officers during the great expansion. It was aimed mainly at public school boys between the ages of seventeen and eighteen years. They had eight months' training as cadets in a cruiser, then became midshipmen and were the equal of the Dartmouth cadets in most respects. Clearly it had great advantages for boys who had failed to enter Dartmouth at thirteen, or who had been uncertain about their choice of career. The examination was held every six months and this gave a candidate three chances; it was unusual to pass first time. The examination, conducted by the Civil Service Commission, was also used for entry to other services, and naval candidates might be offered a cadetship in the Executive, Engineering or Paymaster Branches of the navy.[14]

In 1936 the Admiralty announced some reforms in the Special Entry scheme, regarding it as a major factor in future expansion programmes. Whereas about forty-five cadets were taken on for Dartmouth each term, a hundred would be selected for special entry to the Executive Branch, with thirty-six engineers, thirty-two for the accountants and forty Royal Marines. The age limit would be raised to eighteen years and eight months, allowing boys to serve as prefects and house captains at their public schools and gain leadership experience. Candidates would now have four chances at the exam.[15]

The Special Entry examination seemed to generate more passion than any other, perhaps because the boys who failed were old enough to know their own minds and protest; perhaps because it was the last chance of entry as a regular naval officer. An army officer quoted the questions asked of his son. He was asked to confirm the name of his school whether he had a new headmaster and whether he was a prefect, requiring only 'monosyllabic answers'. When asked his brother's rank he replied, 'He is First Lieutenant in the "Wolfhound"' and was rebuked. 'There's no such rank. I presume you mean he is the Senior Lieutenant?' Then, 'To the very sensible question "Why are the Russians not helping the Chinese?" my boy gave a very good answer indeed, but he was completely non-plussed by the next question, "What is the name of the Russian [sic] general in the Far East?"'

A headmaster was confused about standards. One candidate got 684 marks for educational subjects at his first attempt in March 1938, but only 130 in the interview. He went to a naval crammer for a few months and as a result his educational marks rose slightly, but his interview mark sank even lower to 90. At a third attempt his educational score actually fell, but his interview mark rose dramatically to 250, making him just eligible for an engineering cadetship. Such variations left the schools 'utterly at a loss to explain the fact either to themselves or the Parents'.[16]

In May 1940 Churchill discovered that three candidates had been failed, though they finished fifth, eighth and seventeenth in a competitive exam involving 400 people. One, it transpired, had 'a slight cockney accent'. Another was the son of a chief petty officer, the third of a merchant navy engineer. Churchill was incensed that they took the written examination *after* the interview, which they had already failed. 'I am sure that if the Committee, when they had these boys before them, had known that they were among the cleverest in the whole list they would not have taken so severe a view and ruled them out altogether on the personal interview.' He ordered reform of the system, and that 'Cadetships are to be given in the three cases I have mentioned.'[17]

As always, the navy preferred to take on the relatives of naval officers, even if this looked like nepotism in the spirit of the times. With the Special Entry scheme, three places were reserved for the sons of naval officers to prevent those 'who from heredity and from their interview marks appear to have the makings of first class Naval Officers and who have achieved the necessary qualifying standard, having to be refused entry because they have been unsuccessful in the competitive scholastic examination'. The Second Sea Lord believed that '"Naval blood" does count' and wanted these numbers doubled.

Just before the war Special Entry courses were held on board the old monitor *Erebus*, carrying two 15-inch guns on the minimum size of hull. She was fitted with a gymnasium on deck and moored in Portsmouth Harbour. Peter La Niece served on board her in 1937.

The monitor *Erebus*.

Our day started by scrubbing decks, then a morning assembly, which in the Navy is called Divisions. One group of Cadets provided a Guard for Morning Colours; the ceremony included short Morning Prayers. Thereafter our time was spent between classroom instruction in Navigation, Gunnery, Engineering, Torpedoes and Electrics and Seamanship – Theory and Practice, much of the latter was either pulling (rowing) or sailing in boats. Every time a class completed boatwork all cadets had to be mustered to hoist the boats by hand. The balance of our time was spent "square bashing" on Whale Island Parade Ground.[18]

The Training Cruiser

After promotion to midshipman, Dartmouth and Special Entry boys were united in the training cruiser. In the years immediately before the war this was the old cruiser *Vindictive*. Her captain during 1938 described the training and its effects.

The Cadets now acquire a good grounding and preparation for their first ship as midshipmen.

They have carried out all the duties that a seaman performs in a ship, viz:- quartermaster, boatswain's mate, sideboy, L.T.O. and S.T. of the watch, helmsman, leadsman, crew of all types of boats, sailmaker's mate, boatswain's party, gunner's party, signalman of the watch, seaboat's crew, lookouts etc. For a short period they have lived on the messdeck under the same conditions as a seaman.

They have acquired a certain amount of "Power of Command" and can drill a class at P.T. and elementary Field Training; they can cox a 25-ft power boat, and have a good practical knowledge of sailing a skiff, whaler and cutter.

They have acquired a measure of self-confidence and enough knowledge, practical and theoretical, on which to build real officer-like qualities. They go to sea keen to learn more. But this is and can only be a beginning and, unless this training is continued during their time as Midshipmen, it will be to a great extent wasted. Practical pilotage, practical navigation and seamanship, whenever their ships are at sea, is essential to consolidate their knowledge.

Only the general principles of Gunnery, Torpedo and Electrics are taught in VINDICTIVE and subsequent technical training in these subjects as Midshipmen is essential. Realistic preliminary instruction is difficult to carry out owing to the complete lack of modern equipment in VINDICTIVE.[19]

Dartmouth and Special Entry cadets sat a stiff examination. In December 1939 the Pilotage section included questions such as 'Explain briefly the causes of Spring and Neap tides.' In Navigation Part 1 they were given practical exercises in deviation of the compass, plotting fixes and calculating tides. In Part 2 they answered theoretical points such as 'the principles on which a Mercator's chart is constructed'. In the 'General and Gas' section they were asked about how to deal with gas attacks, as well as miscellaneous questions about naval practice and culture – the definition of a crusher (regulating petty officer), leatherneck (marine) or an Irish pendant (a loose rope. They were tested thoroughly in the Rules of the Road at sea, for these were essential to any bridge watchkeeper. Under 'Seamanship' they had to know 'What preparations have to be made before a ship comes to a buoy. A cutter is to be used.' They were asked some very technical questions on interpreting signals, and under 'Torpedo' they had to know such things as 'Why do we have low power [electric] supply in all ships?' The engineering section was different for Dartmouth and Special Entry candidates, but included questions like 'What duties are carried on by the Engine Room Department at action stations?'[20]

Commander P. B. Caruana in the engine room of HMS *Mauritius*, 1944. A drawing by Stephen Bone.

Many felt that Special Entry cadets were better than the Dartmouth boys. In 1934 Vice-Admiral Gordon Campbell told the House of Commons, 'My own experience, having commanded both Dartmouth and public-school cadets, leaves me no hesitation in saying that public-school cadets make better officers than Dartmouth cadets. The initial training is far superior.'[21] Roderick Macdonald was a cadet on one of the 1939 cruises, and he wrote later, 'While the mixture of different entries to the Navy seemed to work, a public school like Fettes, tough yet philosophically versatile, may ironically have been better than Dartmouth as preparation for the W.W.II Navy, if only because contemporaries were not committed to the Navy.'[22]

When war started the training cruiser was withdrawn to go on active service, and the Special Entry boys went to Dartmouth instead, creating accommodation problems.

Officer-Like Qualities

'Officer-like qualities' were essential in any cadet, just as their opposite, 'lower deck attitudes', were fatal to the prospects of a commission. 'OLQs' were mentioned many times in King's Regulations and in training programmes, though they were ill defined and it was never clear how far they were considered to be innate, and how much could be taught. In theory they formed the third element in the syllabus in the training cruisers before the war, after general education and professional and technical knowledge, but this was not borne out by the allocation of marks; 500 out of 5300 for Dartmouth cadets and 5500 for Special Entry. Nevertheless they were regarded as important in the training of midshipmen as well as cadets when they went to their first post as the fleet.

> The Executive Officer will be responsible for the development of officer-like qualities in the midshipmen, and is to arrange that every opportunity is taken to train them in seamanlike work. For this purpose the Midshipmen are to be regarded as an integral part of the ship's organization and they

should be given posts of definite responsibility according to their experience and seniority. In particular, they should be given the greatest possible amount of experience in charge of boats; and this and other duties which develop initiative, and a sense of responsibility, should take precedence over the more formal methods of instruction.[23]

Despite such work, Roderick Macdonald did not feel that any real leadership training was given during his Special Entry course. 'Officer-like Qualities were somewhat vaguely stipulated as the aim pre W.W. II rather than Leadership. Public school boys were for some reason assumed to have absorbed Leadership at school since it was not taught or alluded to in the training cruiser.'[24]

Ranks

Midshipman was one of the oldest ranks in the navy and the badge, a white collar patch, was also the oldest in any of the armed services. It was adopted with the first naval uniforms in 1748 and remained essentially unchanged. A midshipman was an officer, not yet commissioned and junior to warrant officers, but senior to all chief petty officers. The young men of Dartmouth and Special Entries, would spend two years and four months as midshipmen learning their trade.

Sub-Lieutenant was rather newer, revived in 1861, for junior officers on the way to becoming lieutenants. Though he was commissioned, the peacetime sub-lieutenant was still not regarded as fully-fledged. At sea he lived in the gunroom of a big ship with the midshipmen, rather than the wardroom. He spent much of his time under training at the Royal Naval College in Greenwich, and was promoted to full lieutenant after sixteen to twenty-eight months, depending on his examination results.

Permanent Engineer Officers

Complaints about the status of engineer officers were still voiced in Parliament during the war, though overshadowed by comments about the selection of executive officers. In March 1942, for example, Sir Percy Harris told the House of Commons of 'a grievance among engineering officers to the effect that they are regarded somehow as an inferior grade. … I think that far greater use should be made of the skill, knowledge and expert training of the engineering officers. … I have heard that parents are saying to their boys, "Do not become trained for an engineer officer, because all the higher posts will be denied to you."'[25]

The main training centres for professional naval engineers were at Keyham and Manadon. The colleges had capacity for up to 360 cadets, though numbers of entrants actually fell during the war. In September 1943 there were 240 cadets, including some from the Commonwealth. The course lasted eleven terms, or three and two-thirds years, reduced to ten terms for part of the war. Around twenty cadets entered each term – about fifteen of these were from the Special Entry and the rest from Dartmouth, from the merchant training ships *Conway* and *Worcester* and from selected artificer apprentices.

During the first half of the course the cadets learned scientific subjects such as mathematics and thermodynamics, with a small amount of history and English (only 25 marks out of 2000 in the exams). They also learned about workshop appliances and electrical engineering, with 200 marks allocated to their main task of marine engines and boilers, and 100 to ship construction. The second half of the course was closer to their practical work, with 300 marks out of 3000 for workshop practice,

Engineer sub-lieutenants under instruction in the Royal Naval College at Keyham.

400 on marine engines and boilers and 650 more on marine engineering and design. Other subjects included electrical engineering, chemistry and metallurgy and the economics of engineering.[26]

The course had to resolve the perpetual problem between the technical skills of an engineer and officer-like qualities. Rear-Admiral Ford attempted to define what was required.

> ... Naval Engineer Officers must first be leaders and secondly engineers. This definition does not by any means imply that all officers are required to be cast in the same mould, but it does imply that leadership and decision and officerlike qualities is one of the primary requirements for a Naval Engineer Officer. It is doubtful whether these qualities are in any way tested by a competitive examination even when tempered by selection.[27]

But he found that 'the staff at the college are required by the syllabus to turn out fully-qualified engineer officers who had only to learn Engine driving to enable them to carry out with competence the duties of a junior engineer officer. To this end about 20 per cent of the time is spent in purely functional instruction.' They learned a great deal about the theory of engineering, but rather less about the details of the types of engine they would have to operate at sea.

Another issue concerned theoretical and practical engineering. At the most basic level, an engineer officer might find himself doing repair work among oil and grease, or reprimanding a drunken stoker. At a much higher level, he was potentially a scientist and an innovator. Admiral Ford commented on the training in 1943,

> It is by no means clear at present what will be the position and scope of the Naval Engineer Officer after this War. If by any chance it is intended that he should be a scientific engineer capable of absorbing the technicalities of Mechanical, Electrical and Radio engineering some very large alterations in the instructional syllabus will be necessary ...[28]

There was no sea time during the course. In the engineering industry, it was common for undergraduate trainees to alternate between college and industry, but the navy had no real equivalent of this. At the end of the course, officers left the college with the rank of acting-lieutenant. This was intended to keep them in line with their contemporaries from Dartmouth and the executive Special Entry, who would have been at sea for some time by that age. But it caused difficulties at sea and Ford suggested that the rank of sub-lieutenant might be more appropriate until they had gained some experience and an engine-room watch-keeping certificate.

Accountant Officers

In 1937 there were 533 officers of the Accountant Branch in the fleet, compared with 3490 executive officers and 974 engineers. There were also 117 Accountant Branch warrant officers, a higher proportion than in with the executives, but lower than among the engineers, where technical skill was rewarded at these levels.[29] Accountant officers supervised the writers, stores ratings and cooks and acted as secretaries to senior officers. They were mainly posted to large ships, shore bases and headquarters. They were mostly recruited through the Special Entry scheme.

The Admiralty did not envisage a large expansion of the Accountant Branch in 1940; temporary officers could be selected from among Hostilities Only ratings in the same way as CW candidates for the Executive Branch, but only men who already had qualifications as accountants, or those with defective eyesight.[30] Under the revised orders of 1943, only men already in the Accountant Branch as ratings were to be considered for commissions in the branch. They would serve three months as a CW candidate like the others, then go before a selection board, then to an eight-week course at *King Alfred* if they passed.

Meanwhile the training of regular accountant officers continued. After a twelve-month course they were examined in ship's office work, captain's secretary's work, the Naval Discipline Act and court martial procedure, typing, coding and ciphering and a foreign language (including an oral exam). This comprised a total of 1200 marks. They might also have 100 more for the report on their professional competence, and another 100 for an optional subject, such as naval history, economics or a second foreign language.[31]

Promotion from the Lower Deck

The Admiralty had a problem in dealing with the long-service men of the lower deck, many of whom might be thought to have a better claim to a commission than Hostilities Only men with very short service and little experience. The difficulty was that the Admiralty did not want to promote too many of these to permanent commissions and then have to discharge them after the war; nor did it want to give temporary commissions to permanent members of the navy.

> It is necessary to man the large additions made to the Fleet in war by personnel serving for the period of hostilities only; many of the officers must accordingly be on a temporary basis. While Their Lordships' policy is to obtain a high proportion of such officers by promotion from the Lower Deck ... the grant of such commissions on these lines to continuous service ratings would normally result in their having to leave the service at the termination of hostilities instead of continuing the career in the Navy on which they have embarked. ...

The training given to such selected ratings is thus designed to qualify them to undertake any of the duties of their future rank as required by the exigencies of the service, and to enable them to achieve a complete mastery of their profession. The period of such training must therefore be considerably longer than that for the temporary R.N.V.R. Officer who is only expected to carry out the limited duties of one special type of appointment for the duration of the war.

Continuous-service ratings were to be encouraged to seek promotion through a much slower route as warrant officers, after which accelerated advancement to commissioned officer was available in suitable cases.[32] Underlying all this, perhaps, was a belief that a man who had enlisted in a training school at the age of fifteen was unlikely to have the background and education to make a good officer, except by long training in the navy.

Owing to the lack of appeal made by the Boy/Apprentice entry to the average secondary school, it is by no means representative of the pick of the secondary school boys. All experience to date suggests that secondary school headmasters do not encourage their boys to make use of this type of entry to the service. This may be partly due to the lack of prospects of earning a commission, and partly to the fact that such boys often leave school before obtaining School Certificate, an important point to the headmaster and important also to the boy himself as regards his subsequent prospects of obtaining employment ...[33]

It was possible to open CW papers on a long-service rating to consider him for a commision, but captains had to be circumspect about it.

It is not generally desirable that a long-service rating should be informed of the commencement of a C.W. Form No. 1 concerning him, although he will no doubt acquire knowledge of his prospects in the course of time without this information being definitely disclosed to him. It is difficult to lay down hard-and-fast rules on the subject, however, since in some cases selection involves transfer from the communications to the seaman branch which would disclose to the rating his position, while the special interest taken in a selected rating by his divisional officer must also give some indication to the rating that he is under observation for promotion. For permanent long-service ratings, therefore, who are candidates for permanent commissions, a suitable reticence should be maintained on the subject ...[34]

Warrant Officers

The main route from the lower deck to officer status, then, was via the rank of warrant officer. In the age of sail, warrant officers had been numerous and disparate, for the term included all non-commissioned men appointed by the Admiralty or the Navy Board, rather than the captain of the ship. Throughout the nineteenth century the higher grades of warrant officer were made into commissioned officers, while the lower ones became ratings as artisans. This left the middle category, consisting initially of carpenters, boatswains and gunners. New types of warrant officer were added in the late nineteenth century, reflecting the changing needs of technology –

warrant engineers, usually promoted from engine room artificers, arrived in 1897 and there were 326 warrant officers in the Engineering Branch in 1937.[35] Signal boatswains were created in 1890 and were later joined by warrant telegraphists in the Communications Branch. The warrant master at arms was a kind of ship's police chief, promoted from one of the other branches. In all there were 536 warrant officers in the executive branches in 1937.

Warrant Officer John Webster from County Cork, serving as Boatswain of the Royal Naval Barracks, Devonport, at the age of 73 in 1945. A drawing by Stephen Bone.

The warrant shipwright replaced the carpenter in the days of iron and steel hulls, and there were sixty-six of these in 1937. There were fourteen warrant ordnance officers. Warrant writers, supply officers, cooks and stewards were appointed in the Accountant Branch from 1909, reaching a total of 117 in 1937, and there were fourteen wardmasters in the Medical Branch. All wore a single stripe on each arm, thinner than that worn by a sub-lieutenant, with the same uniform and cap badge as a commissioned officer. Although they were all highly specialized in the duties of their own branch, there was no distinguishing badge to tell one kind of warrant officer from another, except for shipwrights, electricians, wardmasters and ordnance officers. In all there were 1232 warrant officers in the navy in 1937, a fifth of the number of commissioned officers.

Schoolmasters were recruited by direct entry, but other warrant officers had all spent some time as ratings in the appropriate branch. They were usually selected in their twenties, and had to pass an educational test, be recommended by their captains, have an excellent record and pass various professional examinations as necessary. By an order of 1932 seaman warrant officers, including boatswains, gunners and torpedo gunners, had to learn enough navigation and pilotage during their period in acting rank to earn a certificate stating that they could keep watch at sea and in harbour under the supervision of a commissioned officer.

There was some difference of opinion about the qualities of warrant officers among those who served with them. To Dunstan Hadley they were 'those pearls of great price that the Navy produces'.[36] George Melly constantly found himself in trouble with them. They were

> ... Martinets, sticklers for the letter of the law, hard resentful men who realized they had risen from the ranks on merit but been blocked for a commission on class grounds. Caught uneasily between the relaxed bonhomie of the PO's mess and the easy formality of the wardroom they were punctilious in their insistence on outer form, correctitude, the marks of respect as laid down by King's Regulations.[37]

The Admiralty was aware of the strengths and limitations of the warrant officer. 'The type of officer obtained from this source may be very much "set in his ways" and unsuitable for staff appointments, but within his limits he is an extremely valuable officer.'[38]

The naval warrant officer was rather a different figure from his namesake in the army, who usually served as a regimental or company sergeant major and lived in the sergeant's mess. The army warrant officer was known for his military propriety and his parade ground discipline, rather than his technical skill. The naval warrant officers had their own mess in a large ship, and lived in the wardroom with the commissioned officers in a medium-sized ship such as a destroyer or a frigate. They were junior officers rather than senior NCOs.

The status of the warrant officer was changing in the long term. Captain Pelly of HMS *King Alfred* could remember the days when

> ... the Warrant Officer was described as the link between the Wardroom and the Lower Deck. In those days a Warrant Officer, in addition to his specialist duties, was a store-keeping officer, and as such, the importance of his department carried much more weight than it does in these days of general messing and centralized store-keeping. In consequence the modern Warrant Officer, by reason of his status as a junior officer who, apart from his specialist duties, plays a much larger part in the internal economy of the ship, has handed the title "link" to the higher rating.[39]

Warrant officers were mostly found in the larger ships, and in shore bases. They often served as the chief engineers of frigates and vessels of similar size, but apart from that their role was mainly at flotilla level in destroyers and escort vessels. The system of having specialized officers in the leading ship of a flotilla tended to break down in the Second World War and Roderick Macdonald rarely saw his flotilla officers as the ships were detached all round the world. The system was 'too inflexible to allow for deployment and losses in a World War'.[40] Captain Wellings of the US Navy observed the two warrant officers of the destroyer HMS *Eskimo*, 'half-leader' of a destroyer flotilla in 1940. Edward George Mason, the gunner, was twenty-eight years old. He 'was theoretically the flotilla (eight ships) fire control gunner. Actually his ship duties came first and in his spare time he visited the other ships of the flotilla when in port.' His colleague Lancelot Orry Stollery, the torpedo gunner, was thirty-three. He was, in Wellings' opinion, the best watch-keeping officer in the ship – 'Reason: A qualified top watch stander for seven years in addition to being a good seaman.'[41]

It is difficult to see why such officers should not be commissioned and have an equal career structure to the others. They clearly had the combination of leadership qualities and technical skill required by all officers. Only tradition, and class distinction, as Melly implies, kept them separate.

The further promotion path for a warrant officer was very slow. After ten years' service he would advance to Commissioned Warrant Officer, and replace the narrow stripe with the broader one of a sub-lieutenant. Subject to vacancies, he might become a full lieutenant. After a further eight years, if he was not too old, he was eligible for promotion to lieutenant-commander. In wartime this was accelerated, and in 1941, for example, thirty-nine seaman warrant officers were commissioned; but still the numbers were not large compared with the size of the fleet.[42]

Not long after the war, the navy began to recognize the anomalous status of warrant officers and in 1948 their title was changed to branch officer. Nine years later they were replaced with Special Duty officers, who enjoyed the full status and rank of the commissioned officers, with promotion prospects up to commander.

Direct Promotion from the Lower Deck

Since the beginning of the century it had been recognized that paths for promotion from the lower deck were far too slow to allow a man to reach senior rank before retirement. It was Winston Churchill, during his first spell as First Lord of the Admiralty, who introduced the first accelerated scheme in 1912. A modified scheme was announced in 1931, in the aftermath of the Invergordon Mutiny. In a typical career, a boy would be picked out by the time he went to sea after basic training. He would be sent to a capital ship or a large cruiser where training facilities were available, and given accelerated promotion to able seaman after a year. He would pass for leading seaman at nineteen-and-a-half, and a year' later he would go before a fleet selection board. If he passed he would go to Devonport barracks for a modified version of the petty officers' course, then go before another selection board. If he passed he would be given the rank of acting sub-lieutenant, if he failed he would remain a petty officer.[43] The Admiralty ordered that boys should be selected for 'character, service, self-reliance, physical fitness and capacity to hold their own among the ship's company' in addition to their ability to pass examinations. The first six officers were appointed in September 1933. Twelve more had started the next course, but only six were commissioned.[44] After that the scheme began to falter. Plenty of candidates put themselves forward, but few were able to pass the examinations, on account of the lack of study time and facilities on the lower deck. The Admiralty was accused of paying lip-service to the idea of lower deck promotion, but in practice making the ladder from the lower deck to the quarterdeck almost impossible to climb.[45]

In 1937 the Admiralty announced the Upper Yardman scheme by which candidates would be allowed time for study. This, and the increased size of the navy owing to the threat of war, caused some rise in the numbers of commissions. In 1938 thirty-one ratings began training in the battleship *Ramillies* and seventeen of them were eventually commissioned in the Seaman Branch. Seven engineers were also commissioned that year. Meanwhile forty-two seamen were selected for the 1939 course. One was discharged as unsuitable, and one had already taken the seamanship examination. Of forty who sat, three failed and three obtained first-class certificates, and the bulk of them, twenty-six men, obtained second-class certificates. All forty-one came before the selection board who recommended twenty-four of them for com-

missions; eleven should be rated acting petty officer and promoted to warrant officer when vacancies arose, and the remaining six should remain as acting petty officer, at least until they had further experience. The matter was mentioned in
Parliament in July 1939 and MPs were given the impression that the scheme was a
failure, which was denied by the Admiralty.[46] But it was not a high rate of success, in
view of the great demand for officers soon to be created by the war.

The lack of promotion continued during the war, but the rate did not acceler-
ate very much. In May 1941, thirty-eight men were selected for the course, but ten
of these were at sea and were put on to the next course. Of the twenty-eight who
started in May, sixteen were commissioned, four were sent for technical training to
become warrant officers, and the rest failed. The Commission and Warrant Branch
informed the First Lord that 'out of the fifty-five ratings who underwent these courses eleven failed to be selected as officers.' But of the forty-four passes, eight went
into the inferior grade of warrant officer. By the end of the war there were serious
doubts about whether the scheme was working. '... the Upper Yardman, at the age
of selection, has already spent too long on the lower deck. He has been influenced
by the lower deck outlook during his impressionable years at sea, and he is too old
to acquire rapidly that breadth of outlook and spirit of service necessary in an officer.' It was proposed to institute another scheme, by which a few boys would be chosen on entry to the training school and given an advanced course of training to bring
them up to Dartmouth standards.[47]

The lack of promotion for long-service members of the lower deck was often
mentioned in Parliament, particularly as it affected the older men of the reserves.
Walter 'Stoker' Edwards had served on the lower deck himself before being elected
as member for Stepney in 1942, and he described the problems.

> ... the granting of commissions ... is a very sore point with the lower deck.
> Having served on a ship where many of the candidates get their sea train-
> ing, to me there seems to be something wrong. People have been selected
> as candidates for commissions and put through their course of sea training,
> and have never been able to conduct themselves in a sailor-like way, yet they
> have been passed as fit to take charge of ships and men. There have been
> extreme cases where chief petty officers, with 20 or 30 years experience,
> have not been thought worth considering for commissions, yet people with
> no sea experience are selected on the experience they have had outside,
> which has usually been that of a bank clerk or some office worker.[48]

There can be little doubt that the Admiralty, by placing too much stress on the obsolescent rank of warrant officer, by refusing to grant temporary commissions to permanent men, by regarding time on the lower deck as a difficulty rather than an advantage, gave cause for discontent on the lower deck, and failed to use some of its tal-
ent to the best advantage. After the war it would rectify the situation; up to a third
of officers would have served on the lower deck, and they would be promoted to
ranks indistinguishable from those of Dartmouth entrants.

CHAPTER 13

Selection of Temporary Officers

The Problems of Expansion

By 1936 all three services were looking at the problems which might be created by rapid wartime expansion, and in particular the need for large numbers of officers. The navy was much more anxious to offer a permanent career than the other services, and it needed longer training in specialized skills, so it anticipated more problems. On the other hand, its growth was dependent on ships becoming available, so it did not plan to expand so rapidly. One solution for the army was to create a new class of Warrant Officer Class III or Platoon Sergeant Major. The navy did not see this as an acceptable solution, as junior executive officers had to be able to stand watch, and therefore needed enough education to learn navigation. In any case, the army's scheme did not last the war.

By 1936 the army was beginning to accept that the greatest part of expansion in the officer corps would come from men commissioned from the ranks. It already had some tradition of promotions of long-service regulars in wartime, especially to administrative grades such as quartermaster. But the army would have to go beyond this to make up the numbers and it planned to select suitable conscripts as early in their career as possible. At the beginning of the war it was decided that all new officers would have served for a period in the ranks.

As late as March 1939, the navy was not anticipating a large-scale problem and the head of the Commission and Warrant Branch stated, 'the increase of requirements of officers in the Navy is nothing like so big as that in the Army.' It was not proposed to increase the permanent officer corps to any great extent, in view of what had happened in the last war.

> Owing to the fact that naval cadets enter the Navy before the usual school-leaving age and to the length of time required to train naval officers, it will be desirable to continue entries at the normal level in order to avoid dislocation after the war. ... During the last war entries were maintained at the high level which had prevailed just before the war or even higher. It is difficult to see what the purpose of this was; it substantially increased the difficulty of reducing after the war.[1]

Some naval expansion was anticipated in 1939. The head of the CW Branch accepted that some promotions from lower deck regulars were inevitable and 'It will hardly be possible to keep these down to the peacetime level. There will therefore be a risk that there might be a surplus of this type of officer after the war.'[2]

In practice the navy was to expand the officer corps through the reserves, though not in the sense originally intended, for the traditional reserves, the RNR and the

RNVR, were not nearly large enough to cope with the demand. The Royal Naval Supplementary Reserve, comprised of yachtsmen volunteers, provided a further 2000 who were quite quickly available. After that, completely new sources had to be tapped.

Officers' ranks, showing the distinction between Royal Navy, Royal Naval Reserve and Royal Naval Volunteer Reserve.

In 1939, therefore, the Admiralty decided to revive the temporary officers of the RNVR, by selecting men, mostly recent conscripts, from the lower deck. After completing training the men would be appointed as temporary midshipmen, sub-lieutenants or lieutenants in the RNVR. This caused resentment on two counts. For the officers who had served in the RNVR in peacetime, it tended to degrade their status, for the new officers had never served in any reserve, and most were not volunteers. The temporary officers themselves could not understand why they had to be segregated from the regular navy by their wavy stripes, making them instantly recognizable as amateurs; it was not necessary in the army or air force, and everyone shared the same dangers in wartime.

Churchill had been an advocate of opening up the officer corps ever since his days as First Lord of the Admiralty before the First World War, but there were limits to his tolerance.

> There must be no discrimination on grounds of race or colour [in the employment of Indians or Colonial natives in the Royal Navy]. In practice much inconvenience would arise if this theoretical equality had many examples ... I cannot see any objection to Indians serving in HM ships where they are qualified and needed, or, if their virtues so deserve, rising to be Admirals of the Fleet. But not too many of them, please.[3]

Even this was more liberal than official Admiralty policy. Commissions were normally only open to 'British subjects of pure European descent and the sons of persons who are British subjects at the time of the boy's entry'.[4]

The Supplementaries

The Royal Naval Volunteer Supplementary Reserve was formed in 1937, essentially for yachtsmen. In peacetime it was simply a list of men who would be called up for naval training in the event of war.

The Royal Naval Volunteer Reserve was often thought of as a force of yachts-men, but in fact it attracted very few. As one member of the inter-war period wrote, 'To join the RNVR meant giving up so much leisure that it was almost impossible to combine the two.'[5] The Supplementary Reserve scheme would solve this problem. Its object, it was announced, was

> to maintain in time of peace a list of gentlemen who are interested in yacht-ing and similar pursuits and, though ineligible through age, place of residence or lack of time to join the R.N.V.R., are desirous of being earmarked for train-ing for commissions as Executive Officers in the R.N.V.R. in the event of war.[6]

In contrast to the Admiralty's grudging acceptance, the yachting community reacted enthusiastically. Thousands applied and the lists soon had to be closed. It was attrac-tive, for example, to Ewen Montagu. 'There were no drills or periods of annual train-ing, a factor of importance to me with a busy junior practice at the Bar.'[7]

Each applicant filled in a form with two lines on his educational qualifications, but with three-and-a-half lines for 'Special Qualifications (Knowledge of Navigation, Practical Seamanship, etc.)' He agreed

> That in the event of my enrollment in the Royal Naval Supplementary Reserve I undertake to serve subject to the provisions of the "Naval Forces Act 1903," and the acts incorporated therein and of the Admiralty Regulations made in pursuance thereof, and to the Rules of the Division for the time being, and to the customs and usages of His Majesty's Naval Service should my services be required on mobilization.[8]

At the start of the war in 1939, about 2000 yachtsmen were taken into the navy in batches to train as officers of the Royal Naval Volunteer (Supplementary) Reserve. But in fact the first batch included men who were selected for other reasons, most-ly the sons of naval officers of some distinction. Ludovic Kennedy was one; his father was captain of the armed merchant cruiser *Rawalpindi,* killed while Ludovic was on the course. His colleagues included Bill Richmond, son of a rear-admiral who became Master of Downing College, Cambridge, and Peter Beatty, son of the most famous admiral of the First World War.[9] By early 1942 only experienced yachtsmen over the age of thirty-five were still considered eligible for entry in this way, and the numbers were very small, since the great majority had already volunteered.[10]

CW Candidates

For most of the war, the standard method of selecting officers was to find men on the lower deck who had the necessary qualities. Most of these would be Hostilities Only ratings with a good education, sometimes men who had joined with the specif-ic expectation of becoming an officer. The standard procedure, as outlined in December 1939, was for the man's commanding officer to open a 'Form CW 1' on the man – so called because it was issued by the Commission and Warrant Branch of the Admiralty, which dealt with officer appointments. The form was also known as the 'White Paper' and the candidates became know as 'CWs'. The form could be started on any man at any time, but the scheme was particularly directed at new entrants in the initial training bases.[11]

The initial selection of CW candidates was based largely on formal education, which in those days usually meant a middle-class background. This indeed was implicit in the scheme, for the original Admiralty Fleet Order of January 1940 demanded 'Candidates must be of a superior standard of education in view of the shortness of the course it is possible to give in wartime.'[12] A group of young officers wrote to Mr C. G. Ammon MP in 1942:

> Every trainee fills in a questionnaire which is examined. Men with suitable qualifications are noted and watched. The snag is that no one who has not at least had a secondary school education is even considered, no matter what brilliance he may show while at the training establishment, thus many who might make very brilliant officers are overlooked. The official excuse for this is that without a secondary school education men cannot master the officers' training course. This, speaking from personal experience, is not true. Any intelligent man can easily master the course, while no matter how high his educational qualifications, unless they are linked with intelligence a good officer does not result. Particularly important is the understanding which an officer has of his men, and the present insistence on education results in a gap between officers and ratings. There is no doubt that the system as at present worked definitely prevents the average rating from ever being considered for a commission.[13]

It is not clear if this had any immediate effect, but in any case the standards had to be reconsidered because of the greatly increased demand for officers. In March 1943 the Admiralty ordered that

> Recommendations of ratings should not be confined to ratings in possession of some set standard of education, such as the school certificate. Intelligent men who can quickly absorb instruction and have the required character and personality are quite capable of passing successfully through H.M.S. "King Alfred", although their initial education has not been of a high standard. The essential qualities required are character, personality and powers of leadership.[14]

CWs at Sea

Having been selected, probably at the basic training school, CW candidates now had to be tested during three months at sea on active service. They met varied reactions on board ship. Nicholas Monsarrat, who had come in through the slightly easier route of the Supplementary Reserve, was rather facetious about the CWs' behaviour on board. Two of them 'strode into the stokers' mess-deck and asked cheerily: "Are there any other Cambridge chaps here?"'[15] John Whelan, then a leading seaman, was bemused when twelve CWs arrived on board. Their accents immediately attracted attention. 'Numbah twooo mess. Six of us hev to report to numbah twooo mess, the other six are going to numbah one mess.' They soon got the contempt of a gunlayer in the mess, especially when one of them washed his blue socks in a machine full of white underclothes. 'There are three kinds of officer, and you won't make none of them. ... Bear that in mind when you're an officer, and remember to wash your socks in your own water. And God help you if you comes aboard any ship I'm on!'

CW candidates might have chances to develop some of the skills they would need as officers. Employed as a captain's servant, Charles McAra found that the job 'gave me the opportunity of observing the etiquette and conventions of life at the top in a destroyer. I could see at first hand how the captain handled the ship, how he gave helm orders, how he and other officers comported themselves and one of the lessons I learned was the importance of giving orders in a calm, confident, unruffled tone of voice.'[16] In Gorley Putt's ship, 'white paper' men were sent to the navigating officer (himself a former yachtsman and graduate of the supplementary reserve) for instruction. 'He, more than any naval officer I have ever met, really did love the sea and everything about it. He watched our improving efforts at chartwork with all the infectious zeal of a born teacher.'[17]

The pressures for the CW candidate on the lower deck were immense. He had to live in a strange, crowded, uncomfortable and often dangerous environment. He had to find the exact level of relationship with the permanent members of the lower deck. Mallalieu describes an incident which is probably fictional, but crystalizes the dilemma. A man called Raikes had 'broken ship', that is gone ashore without permission. He had been seen, but not identified, by the officers. A CW called Redfern was posted on the gangway to await his return and Raikes called to him, 'Turn your back a minute, old cock, or go on your beat up the jetty a bit while I jump aboard.' Redfern refused and called to the quartermaster as Raikes jumped aboard. He was put under open arrest awaiting trial, while Redfern found himself in physical danger from his own messmates.[18]

Selection from the CWs

A substantial majority of CW candidates succeeded in getting the captain's recommendation after three months at sea. John Whelan records that ten out of eleven candidates in his ship passed, including the one who washed his socks with the white underclothes. One man failed because, as an expert in languages, he had taken on too much of the vocabulary of the lower deck, including the profuse swearing. As the gunlayer put it, 'You forgot yer plum from Gieves. You've proved such a good lower deck seaman they won't give you a commission.'[19] In the *Cardiff* in 1943, fifteen out of Brendan Maher's group passed. Two were considered unsuitable for officer rank, while another insisted in sleeping with his hammock hung down like a U, damaging his back and making him unfit for naval service.[20]

An Admiralty Selection Board, consisting ideally of a three officers including a flag officer or captain and an instructor officer, toured the home ports and met at least once every quarter in each. Its object was 'to see that a general level is maintained in the recommended candidates and to ensure, so far as possible, that they will be able to complete satisfactorily the special course …'[21]

Improvements in the CW Scheme

Some traditional officers continued to find difficulties with selecting potential officers from the lower deck. Admiral Vivian suggested that they would often find a key position on board ship, and captains would be reluctant to release them. Other ratings refused recommendations 'either out of a mistaken sense of loyalty to their ships or because they enjoyed life on the Lower Deck.' Furthermore, 'The longer a man is on the Lower deck the more difficult he finds it, as a rule, to get his brain functioning again at a speed which will allow him to compete with the intensive course at an Officer's training establishment.'[22]

It is difficult to think of a more strenuous test of character than three months on the lower deck of a wartime destroyer. The problem was not in the nature of the test itself, but in the means of assessing its results. Captains had many other duties, and they had to concentrate on the fighting efficiency of their ships. Captain Oram complained that 'the standard of selection was very irregular in the sense that candidates were put forward by virtually any CO from a thoroughly experienced officer in command of a battleship down to quite a junior officer in charge of a small vessel.'[23] Standards were very uneven and Oram found that wastage at *King Alfred* during 1941 had been as high as 33 per cent. He found three possible reasons for this:

> The Captain at *King Alfred* reasoned that the failure rate was so high because the material sent to him was not up to the minimum standard required in three main areas: firstly, many of those sent to him had not got the necessary mental capacity to absorb the basic navigational requirements for an officer; secondly, they were often too confused by the sudden and dramatic change in their lives brought about by joining the Navy to display any powers of leadership which they might possess and, thirdly, quite a large proportion of them seemed to have no desire to become officers and showed no ambition to pass out successfully from the course.[24]

Macdonald Hasting's influential article about officer recruitment in the army, which appeared in *Picture Post.*

THE PRESIDENT: *Head of the First Officer Selection Board Colonel J. V. Delahaye, D.S.O., M.C., who pioneered the new system of choosing officers in the Scottish Command. A system which is already completely displacing the old "interviewing" method throughout the Army.*

THE CANDIDATE: *He Is To Be Tested For a Commission Instead of being judged on a fifteen-minute interview, the candidate is invited to attend a three days' test. The men who decide his appointment live with him, observe his behaviour under all conditions.*

A NEW WAY TO CHOOSE OUR ARMY OFFICERS

An entirely new system for the appointment of our Army Officers is being tried out. It is one of the most progressive moves that have been made since war began. If successful it will put an end to all talk of "class-favouritism", and should lead to a high increase of efficiency.

PUT your head into the brass hat of the Adjutant-General. Imagine that you've got his job; the job of organising and making the best use of the army's man-power. Out of the raw material presented to you by the Ministry of Labour, you've got to assemble the pieces for manufacture into a fighting force.

On one side, you know precisely what sort of army you want. On the other, you can only surmise what sort of material you're going to get to make it with. Unlike the navy or air force or industry you're given no choice as to whether you'll accept a man or not. You've got to take what comes to you. Somehow, you've got to fit every piece into the machinery. And you've got to find one potential officer for every twenty men.

How will you set about it?

The first step—the rough break-up of the material to determine its immediate employment—will be relatively easy. By comparing each recruit's age, medical category and civil record with the army's needs, you should have no difficulty, in the great majority of cases, in making up your mind what's to be done with him.

Deciding which arm a man is best suited for is a concrete problem. He's got to go somewhere and the jobs to which he can be put are limited. But, having distributed your material, your real troubles are only just beginning. You've now got to pick it over to find your potential officers. How do you intend to tackle the job?

Be warned—before you begin—that you're stepping on very dangerous ground. There's nothing concrete to work on now. You're looking for abstract qualities; character, leadership, initiative, personality, dash. And you're not attacking a purely military problem. The selection of officers is a social problem too.

The First Step: A Testing Officer Meets the Candidates While they're up before the Board, the men are treated as officers. The Testing Officers treat the candidate as equals, get to know them all personally before forming an opinion.

16

So far the navy's psychologists had shown no interest in officer training:, the CW scheme seemed successful, they had their hands full setting up other schemes, and were nervous about entering such a controversial field as officer selection. Their first venture was at the behest of the captain of HMS *Collingwood*. Reports on candidates from the lower deck were prepared

> ... on the basis of tests and interviews, very soon after the entry of the men; and they were sealed and put away, no use being made of them. When eventually the Commanding Officer had decided whether a man should be passed or failed, his envelope was opened and a comparison made between the psychologist's report and the decision. It was found that in the majority of cases the psychologist's judgement had been borne out by evidence accumulated later.

A parallel test in *King Alfred* produced similar results and the psychologists began to press for better selection methods than the admiral's interview. [25]

In September 1942 Captain Oram of the Admiralty saw an article by Macdonald Hastings in the popular and influential magazine *Picture Post,* entitled *A New Way to Choose our Army Officers*. It described the system set up at the end of the previous year, in which candidates were sent to a special centre for three days and given intensive tests of initiative, intelligence and character. Well illustrated with views of candidates who looked nothing like the stereotype of a junior army officer, the article proclaimed the class-free nature of the new style of testing – 'as unprejudiced a character study as it would be possible to have.' But Oram was more interested in another virtue; that it was far more successful in weeding out those who would be likely to fail the course. 'The percentage of candidates turned down by the Board tallies exactly with the percentage of candidates failed under the old interviewing system, who were afterwards failed in their O.C.T.U [Officer Cadet Training Unit] course. ... candidates approved by the Board will, in nearly 100 per cent of cases, be passed for commissions.'[26]

In March 1943 the navy began its own version of the War Office Selection Board (WOSB) method at HMS *Glendower*. The process was spread over several weeks, and combined with training. Out of about 350 men in an average week's intake, about a hundred possibles were selected. After an interview by two officers and the psychologist these were whittled down to forty or fifty who were put into a separate division. Their privileges were restricted and they were given specially intensive training as seamen to test their ability and keenness. Components of the WOSB selection programme, such as group discussions and group and individual tasks were introduced periodically, and some candidates were deselected before the end of Part I training. The rest appeared before another selection board under the captain of the base. Some went to Lochailort for training as combined operations officers, but most went to *King Alfred*.

By this time the supply of officers was approaching a crisis. Somewhat to its surprise, the navy had been allowed nearly all the additional men it asked for at the end of 1942 and in January 1943 the Head of the CW Branch pointed out that this would create a shortage of 2000 executive officers by June.

> This is not an absolute deficit in the sense that that number of appointments will remain unfilled; part of this deficit (about 800) already exists but has been met by drawing upon the margins which are essential for manning the fleet – the margin for sickness, and reliefs, and still more important, the mar-

gin for additional appointments by means of which officers obtain training which will enable them to take up complement appointments afloat. While this process of eating into the margin can go on for some time, it cannot continue indefinitely without the appointing machinery breaking down.

It was increasingly difficult to reclaim CW candidates after they had been sent to sea, because of the widespread nature of the war. The time at sea was reduced to two months, and orders were issued to release them as soon as that was up. Some candidates went straight to *King Alfred* without sea training during this period, but the CW Branch advocated a different approach – 'a special ship solely employed in giving eight weeks' sea time to C.W. candidates.'[27]

Two old cruisers, the *Diomede*, and *Dauntless*, were chosen. The armed merchant cruiser *Corinthan* was also selected. She was of a handy size at 3100 tons and had accommodation for 150 CWs, which could be increased on conversion. In all, 750 CWs would be on board the ships at any one time for a six-week course.

Since the ships would never be fully worked up for action, they had to stay away from submarine and aircraft attack, but be near a good anchorage, in an area which offered plenty of opportunity for coastal navigation as well as gunnery practice, but was close to recreation facilities and a railway. Liverpool was too small and crowded so the Clyde found favour, until the admiral there pointed out that the Firth was already used for amphibious warfare, aircraft carrier and gunnery training, for working up ships built in the river and was also 'what must be one of the busiest mercantile ports in the world.' Eventually the Forth was chosen, despite slight risks of attack; there had not been an air raid for two years and U-boats were rarely active.

The ships sailed daily from a fixed base, except for one overnight passage per week. The candidates learned the duties of the officer of the watch and shiphandling. A short firing practice was carried out each week, and the ships returned to their anchorage for the weekend, to allow recreation for the permanent crew and interchange of courses, while the trainees were kept busy with boat work. [28]

University Entry

In the past the navy had had little connection with the universities, except in the recruitment of medical officers, instructors and chaplains. The RAF operated highly successful University Air Squadrons in which undergraduates learned to fly, and the army expanded the Officer Training Corps, but the navy recruited at an earlier age in peacetime, and did not need a presence. In the autumn of 1942 naval divisions were set up at six universities – Oxford, Cambridge, Edinburgh, Glasgow, Liverpool and Cardiff – to provide pre-entry training for undergraduates. In January 1943 the Admiralty announced that these divisions would be used as part of a course for potential officers. Candidates would be nominated by headmasters and would appear before a selection board. More than 6400 young men applied over the next two years, and 3519 were accepted. Courses started in April and October every year. At university, the men had the status of undergraduates and were only subject to naval discipline while in uniform with the naval division. They had 180 hours of instruction, including organization, seamanship, field training, navigation and signals, and it was compulsory to pass the examination in these. The rest of the time was spent in non-examinable subjects including ship and aircraft recognition, electricity, anti-submarine work and general lectures on the Royal Navy.

If successful, the trainees would go to a short course of disciplinary training at

HMS *Ganges* or *Raleigh*, then join the mainstream CW candidates on the training cruisers, followed by the course at *King Alfred*. But 30 per cent failed the course in 1943, and 65 per cent in 1945 when the demand for officers had slackened. Overall, the scheme had only limited success. The high failure rate was attributed to faulty selection processes in the early stages and 'the steady depreciation in the quality of candidates as the war progressed, due to the effect of war conditions upon standards of education and discipline both in School and in the home.'[29]

Engineer Officers

Initially the CW scheme did not apply to engineers, who required a much deeper knowledge of his subject than executive officers. According to the order of January 1940,

> In view of the high professional standard required in engineer officers and the fact that prolonged training cannot be given to ratings recommended for temporary commissions, no general scheme for the promotion of engine room or stoker ratings to temporary commissions can be approved. Any recommendations for outstanding ratings considered suitable for temporary warrants or commissions will be considered on their merits, but such ratings must have attained a standard equivalent to a University Engineering Degree (Electrical or Mechanical).[30]

Recruitment continued, mainly by means of the Special Entry scheme, but only about twenty youths were recruited per term, for a training course of eleven terms, so growth was likely to be slow. Even this was not always satisfactory. Executive, paymaster and marine cadets were selected by the same entrance examination, and often boys accepted engineering because they had not made the grade in any other part of the service. Rear-Admiral Ford commented,

> In the past the Engineering Branch has suffered by having to accept most of its officers from boys who placed engineering as a second or third choice. Few boys outside those belonging to Naval families have much or any idea of the conditions of the branch which they are joining and usually, as a generality, it may be said that the attraction is of a seagoing life in the Navy rather than those of a Naval Engineering Officer, which draw officers into the Engineering Branch.[31]

It was difficult to find qualified marine engineers from outside the service. Merchant navy engineers who had been at sea in the last five years were reserved for the merchant service. Those who had left the merchant navy and settled into shore jobs were almost all in reserved occupations. The Ministry of Aircraft Production refused to let go of any of the men even remotely connected with the vast aircraft industry.[32]

Promotions to warrant rank were accelerated, but by 1942 there was a vastly increased need for engineer officers, especially for the new frigates and for flotillas of landing craft and coastal forces. In October it was decided to open up the ranks to selected Hostilities Only ERAs and even the hastily trained motor mechanics. A selection board was set up at Portsmouth, including an engineer captain and commander. But, as Admiral Ford observed, 'Candidates for engineering commissions are peculiarly difficult people to select. Success as a commissioned officer depends so largely on his character and the way he is capable of using his technical knowledge and even more on his common sense.'

The board had to deal with men from 'varied antecedents' – from general service or the Patrol Service, or from civil life. Ford suggested that the aims of the board should be to find out

If the candidate has officer-like qualities
Has sufficient training to be able to take over an engineering appointment without further training
Is capable of being trained as an engineer officer
To recommend the type of training for which he is best suited

He considered that the board had been reasonably successful by September 1943, but recommended that tests by naval psychologists should be used in the selection. He remained unhappy about the lack of 'officer-like qualities' in the candidates. [33]

CHAPTER 14

Training Temporary Officers

The Supplementaries at *King Alfred*

HMS *King Alfred* was opened at Hove very soon after the outbreak of war. A car park with 480 spaces was converted into a mess, dormitories and classrooms. A corporation swimming pool under construction nearby had been designed to be covered over to become a hall, and it served the same function for the training base. The restaurant and dance hall became the wardroom; small rooms, intended as private bathrooms, became offices and the dressing rooms became classrooms.[1] But in retrospect it was felt that Hove was 'undoubtedly a bad selection'. An ideal site would have been remote from any town or city with a large water area for training, and a large parade ground.[2]

The first course for the gentlemen yachtsmen of the Royal Naval Volunteer Supplementary Reserve began a few weeks after the start of the war. According to one instructor, 'They came in taxis, on foot, and some even in limousines driven by liveried chauffeurs. They sported top hats, bowlers, trilbies, and golf caps, and they wore morning suits, tweeds, grey flannels, and shorts.'[3]

Uniforms remained scarce in the early days. According to Ludovic Kennedy, 'At 7.30 each morning we walked the few hundred yards to the car park, dressed (for uniforms took time to be made) in an odd assortment of sports jackets, casual trousers, Trilby hats and caps.'[4]

Early training courses at *King Alfred* were remarkably short. Nicholas Monsarrat, who went through one in the summer of 1940, dismissed it as 'learning how to salute and how to respond in a seamanlike manner to the Loyal Toast (don't stand up), and studying an ambiguous manual called *Street Fighting for Junior Officers*'.[5] Ludovic Kennedy, who preceded him at *King Alfred*, was a little more informative. 'We did extensive drills, learnt the rule of the road and the meanings of flags, practised boat handling in nearby Shoreham Harbour – and one dreadful day were taken to a nearby football field to be instructed in the one form of warfare I had joined the Navy to avoid: bayonet attack.'[6] Ewen Montagu felt that technical skill was not the most important aspect of the course.

> From the very first day of operations in the *King Alfred* the staff of that 'ship'
> began, not only to train us in the skills which we would need, navigation, sea-
> manship, gunnery and so on, but also to instil into us what was almost more
> important – the spirit of the Navy and its discipline.

Eventually '… my admiration for, and devotion to, the Navy became fixed and has persisted to the present day, in spite of ups and downs.'[7] At the very early stages it was said that 'The standard to be reached by a Sub-Lieutenant R.N.V.R. in September

1939 was the possession of a full uniform. An additional pair of trousers would almost certainly have led to accelerated promotion.'[8]

The Supplementary Reserve officers seem to have been very useful in service. Regular naval officers, though they had learned navigation at Dartmouth, had often lost interest in it and left it to the specialist Navigation Branch. Both John Fernald and Gorley Putt, albeit in works of documentary fiction, portray ex-yachtsmen in love with the subject. In *Destroyer from America* the navigator felt 'It was exciting, this business of navigation.'[9] In *Men Dressed as Seamen* the navigator, an ex-yachtsman, was 'an admirable example of the type of amateur sailor we were, as yet at a great distance, striving to emulate. He, more than any naval officer I have ever met, really did love the sea and everything about it.'[10] Yachtsmen had another advantage, compared with regular officers who had spent much of their peacetime service in battleships or cruisers, or RNR officers who had mostly worked in large ships; the RNR chief engineer of the ex-American destroyer thought to himself, 'What lucky devils these R.N.V.R. yachtsmen were, with their insides toughened by their crazy little sailing boats. He had not dared to eat for the last forty-eight hours.'[11]

The Supplementary Reserve scheme obviously could not last forever. The number of yachtsmen who were willing, fit, of suitable age and character and not already earmarked for other work was bound to be limited. Two thousand executive officers were passed through in a few months, plus 400 accountants. In January 1940 the Admiralty outlined the future use of the school at Hove.

> At present officers being sent for training consist of the gentlemen whose names appear in the list of the R.N.V.S.R., together with nominations from certain other sources such as the Joint University Recruiting Boards. The establishment will, however, be subsequently used for the training of R.N.V.R., R.N.S.R., and Hostilities Only ratings, who have been recommended for commissions.[12]

Ranks During Training

During the Supplementary Reserve courses, each candidate over the age of twenty was enrolled as a 'Probationary Temporary Acting Sub-Lieutenant.' As a lawyer, Ewen Montagu 'couldn't but admire the cautious way in which the Admiralty kept its options open – three ways of getting rid of one!'[13] Ludovic Kennedy was appointed as sub-lieutenant in 1939 until interviewed by the captain.

> He asked me how old I was.
> "Nineteen, sir," I said. "I shall be twenty in two weeks time."
> "In that case," he said, "I shall have to disrate you to midshipman. You were born two weeks too late."[14]

The former CW ratings were graded as 'cadet ratings'. They were not dressed as officers, for a uniform would cost the government about £40. Up to 30 per cent might fail the course, and men were kept in ratings' uniform until their promotion was far more certain. The only distinction was a white band round the cap, the 'purity band', which caused some embarrassment in towns where it was not known – one rumour was that it marked out men who had VD. They were given officer ranks near the end of their training at *King Alfred*. If they were over nineteen-and-a-half (twenty at the start of the war) they became sub-lieutenants, if under they were midshipmen. Most, therefore, by-passed the rank of midshipman altogether, and the numbers in that rank did not increase in proportion to the size of the navy.

The ranks of the sub-lieutenants swelled during the war, since it was the most common rank for men graduating from the course. Promotion could be quite fast from sub-lieutenant. If over twenty-five, a man needed one year's service, a Watchkeeping Certificate ('I took damn good care of that one', wrote Nicholas Monsarrat'[15]) and a captain's recommendation. If younger, he needed two-and-a-half years' service.[16] But in view of the numbers of new officers coming forward each year, there were always plenty of sub-lieutenants in the fleet. They formed the largest number of watch-keeping officers in escort vessels. Out of forty-six *River* class frigates in commission in late 1943, for example, there were fifteen midshipmen, 191 sub-lieutenants, 169 lieutenants (including medical officers) and forty-eight commanders and lieutenant-commanders.[17]

Lancing and Mowden

As well as the site at Hove, *King Alfred* used two other bases. The former public school at Lancing was taken over in 1940 and used for the first part of the course. The third site was at Mowden near Brighton, first opened in July 1941. Brendan Maher began with two weeks in Mowden in 1943 for final screening and a 'brief and informal' final interview. After that trainees went to Lancing for eight weeks, as cadet ratings. Their introduction there was rather protracted. They had to listen to 'The Captain, the Commander-in-Charge, the Training Commander's Assistant, the Junior Chaplain, the Sports Officer, the Liaison Theatrical & Amenities Officer and the

Cadet ratings at HMS *Royal Arthur* training in boat work.

Divisional Chief Petty Officer, known as the Warden, – not to mention the Chief Medical Officer', all 'giving forth' in a short space of time.[18]

At Lancing the men were put into divisions of about 120 named after famous admirals and began the course proper. Each division, under an experienced officer, was divided into four platoons, A, B, C and Y; the latter referring to 'youth, for it was made up of men who were too young to be commissioned as sub-lieutenants at the end of the course and would become midshipmen'.[19] One division entered every week during the war and the size varied. They often had nearly 200 men during the great expansion of 1943.[20]

The Staff of *King Alfred*

Captain John Pelly was in command of HMS *King Alfred* from the beginning of the war until he died in 1945. He had served in battleships during the First World War and later in the training ships *Thunderer* and *Erebus* with midshipmen, so he knew something about officer training. He had retired in 1934 after more than thirty years' service but was recalled on the outbreak of war. Ludovic Kennedy was interviewed by him and found that he had served with his father in the last war, but otherwise he seemed rather remote.[21] This is confirmed by F. S. Holt. He was 'rarely seen but made a point of interviewing each Cadet Rating personally at some stage of his training, his kindly reputation went before him.' He told him, as he apparently told many other cadets, 'Holt, the way I see it is this. We are all on the steps of a ladder, the ladder of promotion. There are many rungs; I'm on one, you're just starting to climb. Rung by rung we can both climb the ladder of promotion together.'[22] Pelly was undoubtedly the moving spirit of *King Alfred,* though unlike that other great training officer of the war, Commodore Stephenson, he rarely felt the need to intervene personally. According to his obituary in *The Times* he was 'ideally fitted by temperament for this onerous task, being gifted with a genial and strong personality and a constant thoughtfulness for the welfare of others …'[23]

In the beginning, the school was mostly run by retired officers and those unfit for sea service. In 1942 there seems to have been a change in policy, perhaps dictated by operational needs and made possible by an easing in the supply of instructors as experienced officers began to come from the sea. The divisional officers, in charge of the individual courses, tended to be appointed for six months, allowing them to see two courses through.[24] Typical of these was Commander F. A. Worsley, an RNR officer who had commanded the *Endurance* during Shackleton's famous voyage of 1916.[25] Lieutenant-Commander 'Guns' Corby, on the other hand, was a typical product of HMS *Excellent,* with strong views on discipline.

According to Norman Hampson the course fell into two parts, with instructors to match. 'The more abstract subjects, like pilotage and navigation, were taught by officers who lectured to us as though we were undergraduates. The more technical side of things – gunnery, signaling, mines and torpedoes was left to petty officers, who tended to do things by rote.'[26]

Ludovic Kennedy was one of the first to make the acquaintance of CPO Vass – 'a tubby little chief gunner's mate'.[27] In contrast to Captain Pelly, he was ubiquitous and constantly harassing the cadets. Like the captain, however, he stayed with the school for the whole of the war. Another well-known character was a chief gunner's mate from the West country, with his description of how a gun works.

> This 'ere's the trigger. You put your finger on the trigger and you squeeze 'er. Finger thinks "Oi've been squeezed, Oi 'ave," and 'e presses the little old trigger. Little old trigger thinks, "Oi've been pulled by little old finger, Oi'd better move." So 'e moves and 'e 'its little old spring."

When asked, "'Chief, I didn't quite get what the little old detonator said to the little old cartridge. Could you repeat it?'" he started the lecture from the beginning, in traditional gunner's mate fashion.[28]

Leadership and Morale at *King Alfred*

The original syllabus for *King Alfred*, laid down by Admiralty Fleet Order in January 1940, was mainly concerned with seamanship and navigation and said little about leadership, and only in traditional terms.

> (B) *Development of Officer-like Qualities*
> Voice production and ability to take charge of their own Class.
> Short Divisional Course to include :—
> Lectures on leadership
> Duties of a Divisional Officer regarding welfare and advancement of ratings.[29]

The situation was constantly in flux, and 'owing to a change in the syllabus' became something of a catch-phrase. It included seven main headings – 'Power of Command', 'Coastal Navigation', 'Pilotage', 'Naval Signalling', 'Practical Seamanship', 'Gunnery' and 'Torpedoes and Mines'.[30] In 1942 some parts were dropped, including 'extremely elementary lessons in antique technicalities and procedure for the most part relevant to big ships only'. Instead, the new syllabus was 'more rationally balanced, unfettered by unessentials, and founded on definite principles calculated to develop, in the short time available, those characteristics of alertness and versatility of mind which form an indispensable part of sound leadership'.[31]

In September 1943 Captain Pelly produced his *Officer's Aide Memoire*, a simple manual for the course and for use in service afterwards. It began with the most difficult concept, leadership, which 'is also the one attribute which cannot be learnt in the classroom or from a textbook.' Nevertheless he went on to give some guidance, mostly in a series of two- or three-line aphorisms. Leadership depended on the officer's own confidence and his bearing and example. Trainees were encouraged to develop their voices and words of command. They were told to respect the men of the lower deck, learning their names and their outside interests, and showing loyalty to them as well as expecting it from them. 'Never forget that ratings have few rights; but they definitely have got a right to good Officers.' Echoing the famous words of Lord Mountbatten, as translated into film by Noel Coward, Pelly told his cadets, 'A ship is either efficient, smart, clean and happy, or none of these things. They go hand in hand, or not at all.' He encouraged daring among his potential officers. '"Safety First" was invented to preserve the blind and ignorant amongst shore goers. It implies delay afloat and has no place, as we depend for our safety on a quick eye and rapid action.' He cited Nelson's great opponent. 'Napoleon's secret was little more than careful concentration of his thoughts, the carrying out of a mental "dummy run" whenever possible.'[32]

Cadet ratings were trained to look after the crew's welfare. John Munday took lecture notes on dental hygiene, in which Gibbs SR toothpaste was recommended; Physical and Recreational Training, extolling the virtues of the *Handbook* on that subject; and Requests and Welfare, which taught him something of the advancement of ratings.[33]

Potential officers had copies of *King's Regulations* in their possession, but Pelly drew their attention to some important points when dealing with defaulters as an officer of the watch. With a case of drunkenness they should ask,

> Is the man fit in all respects to carry on his duty? ... If, in the opinion of the
> O.O.W., the answer is *no*, and providing the man's condition is due to the
> intoxicating effect of liquor, then the man is *drunk*.

> If *yes*, then he is *sober*.

> NOTE. — There is no such thing in Naval Law as "Having Drink taken."
> The man is either Drunk or Sober.[34]

Officers needed a rudimentary knowledge of naval administration. Captain Pelly provided brief notes on letter writing, ships' business and naval stores, with a short list
of abbreviations. 'PWSS Port War Signal Station. KBO Kite Balloon Officer.'
    Just as important was the role of tradition and history in maintaining morale.

> "It is possible," said one of our lecturers, "that some of you may find your-
> selves in command of a dirty little ship dropping anchor for the night in a
> lonely little bay. I would suggest to you that it is worthwhile postponing
> your bath and your shave and seeing personally that colours are saluted at
> the proper time. St Vincent outside Toulon, at a period when men really did
> sea time, set a personal example by appearing in full dress with sword and
> decorations. Meridians are passed, weeks and years go by, but this custom
> has survived. You, too, would do well to insist on this discipline of the
> colours, even if your White Ensign is only the size of a pocket-handkerchief."

> You felt then that you were in contact with something that had roots. It gave
> you a sense of responsibility.[35]

In the wartime training courses at *King Alfred* and Lochailort, there were many myths
and rumours about officer-like qualities, mostly to do with class and subordination
rather than leadership. One common belief was that one could be failed for lighting
one's cigarette from another, rather than using a new match; though that might have
been considered commendable in view of wartime shortages. It was generally
believed that instructor officers made constant notes about small social transgres-
sions by lower-deck trainees, and that failure to use a knife and fork in the approved
manner would result in poor marks. At Lancing, as reported by several ex-cadets, two
officers staged a review in which they satirized the officers, who had been issued with
a whole orange each while the cadets only had a half – 'Half an officer, half an orange.'
They were both returned to the lower deck next day.[36]

Naval Techniques

The ability to navigate was what distinguished seaman officers from ratings, and executive officers from other branches of the service. Since most of the candidates would
eventually serve in small ships with less than half a dozen executive officers, each would
have to take his turn at navigation. It was done at three main levels. Ocean, involving
the use of sun and star sights, seems to have been somewhat neglected during the
course. Coastal navigation involved the passage along coasts and through narrow chan-
nels, which was particularly important in the days of minefields and rendezvous. Pilotage

was the conducting of the ship in and out of harbour, with the use of charts. Captain Pelly's note included 'Tidal Stream Triangles', by which a navigator could calculate the effect of a cross-current on the course of a ship, and a guide to working a sunsight for ocean navigation. Lecturers often told tales of navigational failures.

> Another "classic" was the unfolding story of a young officer who thought he had found the ideal spot to anchor his craft overnight but had quite overlooked the local rise and fall of the tide. He is awakened from his sleep below decks by a scratching sound on the boat's hull; arrives on the upper deck to find the boat high and dry with a little boy scraping off periwinkles with his penknife; quickly followed by the local populace to "see the big ship aground". The illustrator added further touches as the crowd increased, including an ice cream man keen to ply his trade, and finally a policeman to keep everyone in order.[37]

Practical exercises were not always a success.

> After we had practiced navigation on chart tables, we concluded that part of the course with a navigation exercise conducted in a large field. The field was dotted with scaled-down buoys, a miniature lighthouse, a church steeple, and a small rock or two. The whole thing looked rather like one of those putting golf courses found in amusement parks. Working in pairs, we were provided with a chart of this "ocean" and an ice cream vendor's tricycle, the top of the freezer box being fitted out as a chart table with a bearing compass, dividers, parallel rule, and binoculars. Each pair was given a task, such as "Plot course from point A to point B," these points being defined by bearings from the lighthouse or steeple. Not much was learned from this otherwise totally enjoyable and ludicrous exercise, given the facts, in addition to our ignorance, that the all-steel frame of the tricycles rendered the compasses nearly totally ineffective and that we were continually trying to avoid colliding with each other in the available space.[38]

However it was said that 'Contrary to the impression held by many outsiders, the navigation as taught in "King Alfred" really amounted to nothing more than coastal navigation, closely allied to pilotage. It consisted primarily of chart plotting exercises involving fixes, together with certain problems in connection with tides, compass errors, enemy reports, etc.'[39] Some shiphandling was learned in a canal at nearby Portslade, and by 1942 six converted motor launches were available in the River Adur at Shoreham. They were fitted with mock bridges, compasses and wheelhouses to give the impression of larger craft.[40] Signalling was regarded as 'the only part of the syllabus in which it was considered imperative to make candidates absolutely proficient.' There was training in Morse, signal flags and semaphore under officers trained in the Signal School.[41]

Charles McAra decided to do the minimum to pass the gunnery part of the course, feeling that it was biased towards big ships where he was unlikely to serve.[42] In fact, despite the presence of many products of Whale Island among the teaching staff, weapons training seems to have formed a relatively small part of the course, perhaps because officers were likely to go on to many different types of ships after graduation, with many different kinds of weapons. John Munday's notes were mainly on small arms, though he drew a depth charge under the heading of 'Torpedo Lecture'.

The Examination and Commissioning

At the end of the course the candidates were examined in all aspects of the syllabus. During 1943 there was some concern that candidates who failed narrowly in the written examination might be lost. The system allowed some flexibility, in that 'If a cadet rating fails by a small margin to obtain passing out marks in one subject but has marked officer-like abilities otherwise, he may be passed by the Board provided that his Instructor Officers and Divisional Officer can assure the Board that for some reason his examination results are not a true measure of his knowledge and that they are sure he will make a good officer.' However, no officer should be in charge of a ship at sea 'unless the Commanding Officer is satisfied that he has a thorough knowledge of the Regulations for Preventing Collisions at sea and a sufficient knowledge of Navigation and Pilotage to prevent the ship running into navigational dangers.'[43] The final examination and the announcement of the results could try the nerves of any man, for the stakes were high. Failures did not go home to consider another career, but were obliged to spend the rest of the war on the lower deck.

Officers, whether midshipmen or sub-lieutenants, now had to buy their uniforms out of a £40 grant provided by the government.

> Down to KA came the smooth, softly-spoken, reassuring naval outfitters from firms like Gieves, Moss Bros, Hope Brothers, Hector Powe, Austin Reed, all eager to measure us for two suits, number one and number three, bridge coat, cap, shirts, collars, ties, shoes, gloves, all at a total price which did not exceed the Admiralty Uniform Allowance.[44]

From the start of the war, officers had to make do with a commission bearing the King's rubber stamp, rather than one signed personally as in peacetime.[45] They spent the last two weeks as 'officers under training, learning, in effect, how to wear the uniform (and a collar and tie for the first time in months, if not years), to respond to countless salutes from ratings, and to have an officer-like bearing.'

The Success of *King Alfred*

Geoffrey Willans did not enjoy his course at *King Alfred* in 1940.

> Time was too short for anything but a smattering of naval background. We did squad drill, physical training, and trotted round in gas masks. ... but one also encountered the tradition of the Navy in a manner that was quite accidental. At times it shone like a beacon through all the other brouhaha of calling one end of the building "the bow". There was an unwilling poetry about it that was immensely stimulating.

The course was short, intensive and notoriously gruelling. When Brendan Maher was sick for a few days he had to move back to join the following week's course.[46] F. S. Holt commented, 'The whole course called for maximum concentration while at the same time being immensely practical.'[47] Furthermore, 'the great majority of Cadet-ratings suffer from over anxiety that they may fail. This is not unnatural when one considers the stakes involved:- Commissioned rank or return to the Lower deck.' As an Australian he was not always happy with British naval ways, but he did observe that 'at Lancing there was no time devoted to mere "spit and polish"'[48]

D. A. Rayner, of the pre-war RNVR, found he 'could make neither top nor tail' of the new officers of 1944. They were too young, 'terribly serious' and obsessed with form-filling. 'Responsibility sat rather heavily on shoulders not yet broad enough to bear the weight.' But he admitted that 'the fault may well have lain equally with myself, for already I was beginning to look backwards to a time when I imagined that things had been better.'[49] On the whole the course at King Alfred seems to have been well suited to the needs of the navy, and one does not encounter the standard criticism of army Officer Cadet Training Unit courses; that they produced 'the perfect private soldier' rather than a skilled leader.'[50]

Despite some faults, the course at King Alfred was one of the great successes of the war, comparable with the working-up base at Tobermory. Admiral H. R. Stark of the US Navy described it as 'Britain's greatest experiment in democracy,' while Sir P. Harris MP told the House of Commons in 1942, 'It is one of the best bits of work the Admiralty have done during the last two years.'[51] Ronald Gellatly, who passed through in 1940–41, considered it 'without doubt the most efficiently run establishment that I met during my Naval career.'[52] In all, 22,500 officers were commissioned from the school before it closed in 1945.[53]

Greenwich

After the course at King Alfred, officers were sent to the Royal Naval College at Greenwich for a kind of finishing school course. There they met Fleet Air Arm officers mostly trained by the RAF, often in Canada. H. J. C. Spencer and his colleagues, who qualified in the United States, 'had to find out how to eat peas with a fork ourselves.'[54] Norman Hanson writes,

> We attended a host of lectures, mainly on naval and general British history, naval traditions and the wartime role of warships of every category. Professor Michael Lewis, probably the most celebrated naval historian of our age, captivated us completely with his charm and consummate knowledge of his subject. We were taught unarmed combat and gaily threw one another around the spacious lawns. An instructor warned us darkly of the perils of gas and bacteriological warfare.[55]

Lewis's view, as expressed in his books, was that the true originals of the RNVR officer were men like Howard of Effingham and Sir Richard Grenville who had left their country estates to lead Elizabeth's navy against the Spanish Armada, and they had at least as distinguished a history as the regular navy – a view which proved popular with the officers under training.[56]

F. S. Holt, like all trainees, found the surrounding splendid, especially the dinners in the Painted Hall, with catering 'of a standard which matched these almost royal occasions.' The living accommodation, however, was much more spartan, with 'old-fashioned furniture unchanged since the Victorian era.' Trainees were sent on trips up and down the Thames in motor cruisers and steam yachts to improve their boathandling and pilotage skills.[57] But a post-war report found it was less useful. 'The academic slow tempo training atmosphere of Greenwich was too much of an anti-climax for the "King Alfred" Officers, the majority of whom quite openly looked upon it as a welcome rest at the conclusion of their labours, and quite naturally found themselves inclined to relax their efforts.[58]

The Special Branch

The Special Branch of the RNVR (not to be confused with Special Entry) had originally been founded in 1923, for gentlemen who could offer specialized skills – interpreters, scientists and artists employed on camouflage work were mentioned, though the latter were used much less in the Second World War than in the First. Its members wore a green stripe between the gold ones. At the start of the war the Special Branch was extended to include many officers who could not serve at sea, for one reason or another, often medical. This was not a problem in the army, for of course all officers were shore based and standards of eyesight, in particular, were lower than in the navy. In the RAF, the ground-based officer was separated by the absence of wings on his left breast. But the navy tended to feel that all officers should be able to go to sea if necessary, and those who did not were marked out, even within the ranks of the RNVR which was already distinguished from the regular navy.

There were several reasons for commissioning these men, rather than employing them as civil servants. Naval rank would put them under far greater control. In May 1940, as the Phoney War ended, the Director of Naval Intelligence (DNI) found that some of his men were tending to leave for more adventurous roles. 'I have already lost several members of my civilian staff and am in danger of losing more, as they feel that at this juncture of the war they should enter one or other of the fighting services in some capacity.' They were employed in lieu of naval officers who had gone to sea, and were liable to be sent abroad at short notice. One officer asked 'Will they feel that they are fighting because they wear a uniform?' but otherwise agreed with the proposal.

Commissions also helped in relationships with equals, and the DNI observed,

> Commissions in the Army and Air Force have been given to gentlemen holding similar appointments at the War Office and Air Ministry and my staff naturally feel that they should receive similar treatment. They feel when attending conferences on my behalf at the other Service Departments that they are at a disadvantage when everyone else is in uniform.[59]

Thirdly, naval rank could be useful when dealing with juniors, particularly on the lower deck. A transport officer at a main railway station, for example, would have far greater authority when dealing with lost or drunken seamen.

By 1941 officers were entering the Special Branch through four different routes. Men with no particular experience were recruited to supervise fixed anti-submarine defences such as minefields. Others had staff jobs, such as intelligence, for which no naval training was required. The third group was of well-qualified scientific and meteorological officers and the fourth group, the one most likely to expand, was of officers who had undergone the normal course at *King Alfred* but for some reason, usually defective eyesight, were not to be employed at sea. In November 1940 these were mostly yachtsmen of the Supplementary Reserve, but this supply was already drying up and it would mostly consist of ex-CW candidates in the future. Many of these had administrative, welfare or instructional jobs in the shore bases.

Several different parts of the branch were recognized by an Admiralty fleet order of February 1942, and distinguished by letters against their names in the Navy List. Executive officers were 'qualified for, and undertaking general duties of an executive nature on shore. These officers have the powers of an executive officer to the extent required by the appointment held, e.g. they may be officer of the watch, or of the day, in shore establishments with all the necessary powers.' They would have the letters EX.S attached to their name. Officers in charge of mines and fixed defences would have the letter M. They would be 'eligible to take command of ratings detailed for the work for which they are responsible, and also of other Special Branch or Executive Officers appointed to serve under them. They are also eligible for appointments in charge of various shore posts and establishments ...'

Other officers had no command function. Those with the letters SS were in staff posts ashore and had no naval training; those who did a short course at the Royal Naval College, Greenwich had an asterisk after the letters. Meteorological officers had the letters Met, scientific officers had Sc, specialist wireless officers had W/T and interpreters had I. Electrical officers of the RNVR belonged to the Special Branch until a separate branch was formed for them in 1940, though regular electrical officers remained in the Torpedo Branch until after the war.[60]

Cadet ratings who failed in the navigation or seamanship at *King Alfred* after 1943, but 'have some special qualifications or are of outstanding character' might be commissioned in the Special Branch instead, where they would not be employed at sea. But the selectors were warned 'to avoid any impression among cadet ratings that lack of effort will merely result in transfer to the Special Branch or prolongation of the *King Alfred* course.[61]

Allocation and Further Training

Towards the end of the course at *King Alfred,* newly commissioned executive officers were asked to specify which branch of the service they would prefer to join. Brendan Maher asked for convoy escort, then considered glamorous, but was allocated to minesweepers.[62] Eric Denton asked for coastal forces.

> I realized that if I went on a destroyer or something of that size I would be likely to see only the major ports around the British Isles, and not see quite so much of the country as I would like. If I was in Coastal Forces I would get into all sorts of smaller harbours and places where I would get a varied interest and would get a chance to see some life away from the strict rigours of the Navy.[63]

Officers were usually sent on a short course to introduce them to the type of ship they were to serve in. Geoffrey Willans went to HMS *Osprey* at Portland in the last few weeks before air raids forced it to be evacuated to the Clyde.

> Our course at Portland was a brave attempt to give us a working knowledge of anti-submarine devices within the space of three weeks. Most of it consisted of taking copious notes, but we would sometimes go to sea for practice attacks. Once again this proved for me more of a battle against sickness than submarines.[64]

Initially Ludovic Kennedy was sent to train as a balloon officer, but was not surprised or disappointed when that scheme was cancelled. In preparation for an appointment to a destroyer, he was sent to *Osprey* at Portland to learn about Asdics, with a day or two at sea in a training submarine.[65]

In August 1941 the Admiralty decided to employ an increased number of temporary officers in destroyers, and laid down how they should be trained before joining a ship – two weeks in torpedo control, three weeks in anti-submarine work and five weeks on the control systems of anti-aircraft guns. It was intended that they

> Should be trained to undertake the quarter bill duties of only one of the normal complement of Executive Lieutenants, and in addition to take charge of a watch at sea. It is not intended that they shall be fully trained for all types of executive duties, but it is hoped that many will be able to do so in due course.

Even so, they were to be carefully watched and reported on by their captains while at sea, with an estimate of when each would be able to undertake the different duties of an officer. [66]

As one of the very first RNVR officers to serve in submarines, Edward Young was taken out of *King Alfred* early and given a trial trip in a submarine. He was then sent to a destroyer at Scapa Flow to get two months of above-water experience. After that he went on a six-week course at HMS *Dolphin* near Portsmouth, to learn submarine techniques alongside regular officers.[67]

Port Edgar on the Firth of Forth was commissioned as HMS *Lochinvar* in November 1939. The only major sea training establishment on the east coast of Scotland apart from Bo'ness, it used the relatively shallow waters of the Firth to train the officers and crews of minesweepers. Part of the Hopetoun estate was taken over for living quarters and offices, while the lecture rooms and training equipment were down in the harbour. Officers were sent for a course combining practical sea experience with lectures in minesweeping, gunnery and seamanship. Twenty arrived every three weeks. They spent the first two days at sea in trawlers or paddle steamers watching crews working up, then a week of lectures on minesweeping, one on gunnery practice, another on general drill, and a fourth week on seamanship. After that they had three weeks of practical training on trawlers specially fitted with gunrooms to accommodate ten officers. Each took a turn as first lieutenant, and there were practical exercises, as described by the government pamphlet *His Majesty's Minesweepers*.

> On "Action Stations" they will range the guns on an imaginary submarine or hostile aircraft. Masked figures will race along the decks when the gas alarm is given, on fire duty or putting out collision mats. The commands "Man Overboard" and "Away Seaboats" demand the appropriate drill. Sweeps are veered out in various formations. Dan-buoys are laid and recovered, the fog-buoy streamed, the anchor weighed by hand.[68]

Brendan Maher and his colleagues had seen the pamphlet when he joined the course in 1943, and laughed at the claim that all the men were 'picked volunteers'. In the trawlers,

> We streamed sweeps, set depths, changed depths, swept occasional dummy mines set there for a purpose, gave steering orders, and navigated (not dif-

ficult to do when one is in constant sight of the Forth Bridge). We also spent a few hours in the engine room and watched the stokers as they endlessly shovelled coal into the nearly blinding glare and flare of the firebox. ... We rotated duties on these trawlers and gained a little experience doing each of the things that had to be done – except stoking.[69]

Charles McAra, who really had stated a preference for minesweepers, found the seagoing course was 'a strenuous, cheerful time, but very dirty as the trawlers were coal-burning and the washing facilities minimal'.[70]

Temporary Engineers

In October 1942, in view of the great expansion of the fleet, it was decided to expand greatly the number of engineer officer candidates from the lower deck, and to train them in separate streams, according to the type of ship and engine they would work with – landing craft, coastal forces and escort vessels, especially the new frigates. Hostilities Only ERAs, enginemen and motor mechanics of 'a reasonable standard of intelligence and promise of officer-like qualities' were to be given training courses of about six months.

The first stream was of officers for landing craft. These vessels had diesel engines which needed less work than steam. They carried no engineer officer of their own, but each flotilla or division needed an officer in overall charge. They would be trained at an established, if disputed, base at Rosneath in Scotland. Though the training of engine room ratings had moved to Northney, Rosneath remained as the main base for training landing craft engineer officers even after the Americans, who had built it, reclaimed it in 1942. During his visit in September 1943, Rear-Admiral Ford considered it to be an excellent site with good facilities for sea training in the Gareloch and Firth of Clyde. It had been built to American standards so was better equipped than British bases, with living accommodation and workshops. More facilities were needed, including a shed with a sectional engine room of a major landing craft, but the school offered 'great possibilities'.

The candidates were considered suitable for the rather specialized duties they would undertake as flotilla engineer officers, though they were 'rusty in their educational subjects', and Ford recommended that two schoolmasters be appointed. They were also lacking in officer-like qualities and had to be trained to remove their shyness in giving orders. Ford recommended a drill hall, as outdoor training was not always possible in winter in 'a very wet part of the world.'

When the course started in 1942 it was six weeks long, but that was lengthened to thirteen weeks, and Ford wanted it even longer, at seventeen weeks. The candidates had four small landing craft for training, but six more were needed to increase the range of types. The course was undersubscribed in September 1943; there were only twenty-eight trainees, though there was room for 136, and it was not anticipated that more than a hundred would be there at any one time even if the length of the course was increased. It was suggested that the newly-commissioned officers go on to Northney after completion of the course, for practical instruction in maintenance, then serve for three weeks as assistant engineer officer in a flotilla of major landing craft, before taking over a flotilla of their own.[71]

The training school for escort vessel engineer officers faced far more problems. In the first place, a site had to be found. Nothing was free in the main dockyard ports, and eventually a former teachers training college, St Marks in King's Road, Chelsea,

was taken over in the summer of 1943. It offered living as well as instructional facilities for 150 trainees but it was not entirely under the control of the navy, was very
much an improvisation and not completely suitable; in these respects it was typical
of many wartime training bases.

The second problem was with the candidates themselves. When setting up the
course the officers in charge had very little idea of what to expect, but they had
understood that they would all have had some sea time. This turned out not to be
the case, and up to a quarter on each course were men with shore-based engineering qualifications who had never been to sea. In any case it was difficult to organize
courses for men of varying backgrounds, 'ranging from that of E.R.A. or C[hief].E.R.A.
in Naval Vessels to Motor Mechanics and service in the Patrol Service,' for some had
far more theoretical knowledge than others. The lack of sea time was even more
important. Admiral Ford found that instruction in steam engines was given entirely by
blackboard and diagrams and there were no engines nearby to work with. Men who
had been to sea in steamships had no problem with this, but others needed more
contact with reality. There were suggestions to base a corvette in the Thames, to send
the men down to an old battleship at Plymouth where stokers were trained, or to
send them to the CW training squadron of cruisers at Rosyth. But Ford was emphat-
ic that candidates needed sea time, preferably at least six months in an engine room,
before starting the course. If that was not possible, then the college should run two
courses, one for those with sea experience, one for those without.

The development of 'officer-like qualities' and their relationship to engineering
skills was a perpetual problem. St Marks laid some stress on this. Ford commented,

> However good may be the methods employed in selection of these ratings
> or their theoretical knowledge there is bound to be a small proportion of
> trainees who cannot and never will make the grade as engineer officers.
> They will lack officerlike qualities or technical ability. It is considered that St
> Marks should have the right to recommend that such ratings are unsuitable
> for training and that they should immediately be reverted to their former
> occupation.

The course also had to reconcile the study of steam and internal combustion
engines. It did this by dividing candidates quite early on, to specialize in one or the
other. This was quite sensible, as the two types were very different in principle, but
Ford was not happy. 'From an appointment point of view it does of course compli-
cate the issue to have to deal with specialists rather than general service officers.'
The staff of the college wanted to train all the men in steam, then send potential
diesel engineers to a special course at Chatham. The steam knowledge would not be
wasted, as most diesel ships had auxiliary steam plants.

The staff of the course aimed to give the trainees 'sufficient knowledge to enable
them to carry out the duties of Engineer Officer in such ships as Corvettes, Frigates,
and such like small craft'. The minimum standard, it was suggested, was the Board of
Trade Second Class Certificate for merchant navy engineers. They would not be able
to sit the examination yet due to lack of sea time, but it would provide an incentive
for the future.[72]

Air Engineers
The air engineer officer was virtually unknown in any service before 1939, for aircraft

had only recently become sophisticated enough to need professional engineers to graduate standard, rather than mechanics. Even in 1939, a Fleet Air Arm consisting largely of Swordfish, Walrus and Gladiator biplanes had relatively limited needs. It was very different in 1945. the vastly expanded arm now used many of the latest high-performance aircraft, including the American Corsair and Hellcat fighters and Avenger bomber. There were 800 Air Engineer Officers in the Fleet Air Arm by the autumn of 1943, and a demand for 2000 was predicted by 1946.

At first the navy relied on supplies from the marine engineering branch and civilian colleges and industry, but these sources were beginning to dry up by late 1941. Loughborough College already had a Department of Aeronautical Engineering, and early in 1942 it began negotiations with the Admiralty about a contract to train naval officers. The first course started on 1 October, with trainees from three sources. Some were Hostilities Only ratings with school certificate qualifications in mathematics and physics; others were CW candidates who were surplus to executive branch requirements; the rest were naval airmen who had been dropped from their pilot or observer courses for reasons connected purely with flying.

Rear-Admiral Ford found that the teaching of the course was as unsatisfactory as the college's catering. 'The main aeronautical lecture room is filled with junk such as a Sunbeam motor car which made a world record and pieces of a large unfinished pressure wind tunnel.' In the final examination of the first batch of trainees, only twenty-two out of thirty-one got more than 50 per cent. Ford recommended strongly that the course be transferred to the Royal Naval Engineering College at Manadon as soon as possible, and this was done by 1945.

Meanwhile, a scheme to train officers in the universities had proved a disappointment. The first candidates left Edinburgh University in June 1943 for preliminary naval training at HMS *Gosling*, but it was found that 'all the University Short Course candidates are not commissionable'. Candidates from the fleet were still coming forward, so that remained a source of supply.

The other main aeronautical engineering college was Chelsea Aeronautical School, which continued to produce graduates. When recruited to the navy, they were sent to a course on the naval air station at St Meryn in Cornwall, also used for armament training for aircrews. This course was somewhat neglected by the Admiralty, who seem to have forgotten about its existence for a time. It took sixty officers for a maximum of six months and was intended to induct them in naval ways — discipline, 'how to conduct themselves as Fleet Air Arm officers' and the duties of an air engineering officer in a squadron, carrier or air station. As a first impression it was not successful and officers had little chance to get to know ratings and their mentality. It was suggested that much might be learned from the techniques at *King Alfred*.

A further source was from the men of the lower deck, or warrant officers in other branches, such as shipwrights and engineers, who might re-train. A course was set up at the huge RAF station at Cosford near Wolverhampton, where up to 11,000 men might be under training at once. The sailors trained alongside the RAF, though the rank of warrant officer held by many of the navy men had no precise equivalent in the RAF. The base was very well equipped, and the RAF had gone to some trouble to provide a first-class course. With the lower deck candidates, the main difficulty was that they had all been trained in their own speciality of airframe, engine, electrical or ordnance and knew little about the others. A three-month course on the other branches was recommended before starting this one. Even so, some of them were not intelligent enough to keep up. The warrant officers had no

air experience at all, but shipwrights found it easier to absorb the intensive instruction than engineers.[73]

At Manadon in 1945, the main stream of air engineer officers studied aeronautics, including aerodynamics, the dynamics off steady flight, and structures; aircraft and
automobile electrical engineering; metallurgy, fuels and lubrication; thermodynamics;
aero engines, including the study of sectioned engines in the classroom; and airframe
construction and maintenence, including 'rigging, fabric work, alighting gear, wheel
brake systems, hydraulic and vacuum systems, instruments, repairs to metal aircraft,
maintenance inspections and aircraft dismantling and assembly'.[74]

Specialist Training

Specialist courses within the Seamen Branch continued during the war. The most
important trends were towards shorter and more intensive courses, larger numbers
of trainees and the increased numbers of reserve and temporary officers who were
allowed to undertake them. Initially there was considerable prejudice at this level.
According to RNVR legend, one cruiser captain saw the wavy strips on the sleeve of
his newly-appointed gunnery officer and exclaimed, 'Good God! … No!'[75]

The Anti-Submarine Branch naturally had a considerable expansion. Only ninety-
three officers were available at the start of the war, including recalled pensioners. Seven
more were trained in the next six months, but two of the existing ones were casualties so the branch hardly expanded. By the middle of 1941 they were coming out of
HMS *Osprey* at the rate of twelve a month, and 170 were available.

Two years later 238 officers had completed the long course at *Osprey*, with thirteen more under training. Meanwhile a short course had been instituted and eighty-five
men were doing that.[76]

Naval staff courses had been suspended at the beginning of the war, but they
were later resumed, and by March 1944 the second group was on the way through.
It was now open to RNR and RNVR officers, who were given 'a thorough grounding
in the duties which a staff officer is actually called upon to perform in wartime'.[77]

Radar officers were a special case, since the branch had not existed before the
war. The earliest 'RDF' officers came from the RNVR Special Branch. Since physics
graduates were already in heavy demand for research and industry, those in other
subjects were chosen, including biology and history. In May 1940 the first batch of
Canadian physics graduates arrived in Britain to begin their radar training, and a large
proportion of ship's radar officers came from that source over the next few years. In
May 1941 British graduates began to come forward, recruited under a scheme set up
by Sir Maurice Hankey, the Secretary to the War Cabinet. Students of physics, electrical engineering or mathematics had done a six-month crash course in radio
physics. Longer radio courses began at the Signal School at Portsmouth in 1940, and
transferred to HMS *Collingwood* in 1944.[78] But there was always a shortage of suitable radar officers, and the great majority were RNVR, creating a problem for the
post-war navy.

In another radar-related development, courses for training officers in aircraft
direction began at HMS *Dryad*, formerly the school of navigation, at Southwick near
Portsmouth in 1943. The need to identify possible enemy air attacks and to direct
one's own fighters to them in sufficient numbers had become very important by this
time. The training at Southwick was slightly interrupted when it was used as the main
headquarters of the D-Day operation, but it became one of the main schools of the
post-war navy, as the School of Maritime Operations since 1974.

Medical Officers

Medical officers were perhaps the most important group who did their training out-side the navy. Naturally there was great demand for them during the war, from all the services as well as for dealing with civilian air raid casualties. The naval demand was greatly increased by the fact that each destroyer, with a crew of 130 to 250 men, car-ried its own medical officer, as did frigates in the second half of the war. In general the navy tried to keep a level of more than three doctors per thousand men, though it was not always successful during the war.

The navy had 1062 medical officers (known as surgeons) at the beginning of the war – 208 regular RN, eight-eight recalled pensioners, 288 permanent RNVR and 278 temporary RNVR. The great bulk of wartime expansion would come from the last group. Qualified doctors were taken on as Temporary Surgeon-Lieutenants, RNVR, with red cloth between their wavy stripes. The Medical Personnel Priority Committee was set up by the Cabinet in 1941 to allocate resources across the coun-try, and naval appeals to it largely failed. At the end of the year the supply of new doc-tors for the navy ceased altogether, with 1705 already in service. It resumed in the following year, and the numbers rose to more than 2000 by the end of the year. There were few women doctors in the navy, only eighteen in 1944, and they generally dealt with Wrens.

Though each doctor had, of course, gone through a full six-year degree in a med-ical school, he had not necessarily learned the techniques needed by the navy. 'There is no doubt that subjects which are of paramount importance to the Services in time of war are badly, if ever, taught in all the civil medical schools.' The schools were asked to include more of such subjects as preventive medicine, hygiene, tropical medicine and administration, but this had little effect. Nor could the navy do much to train its doctors after entry. The demand was too intense to allow it to take men away to become instructors, and recalled pensioners tended to be out of touch with modern techniques. Furthermore, there was great pressure to send trainees to the fleet. These problems, of course, were common to all parts of the navy in the early stages of the war, but in the Medical Branch they tended to get worse rather than better, mainly because the long training course could not be cut.

Pre-war naval doctors had a course of six months in naval subjects; in wartime this was cut to one or two weeks. In essence there was a system of 'apprenticeship' by which a doctor learned from a more experienced one. This worked well enough in naval hospitals, shore bases and large ships, but of course it did not help in destroy-ers and frigates which had only one doctor. In the case of shore bases, a useful inno-vation was motor transport, which allowed a single doctor to cover more than one base. It caused some resentment with the captains of the bases, who were used to the idea of having their 'own' doctor, but it worked well in practice.[79]

CHAPTER 15

Flying Training

Pilots, Observers and TAGs

Since the Fleet Air Arm (FAA) used aircraft which could be operated from ships, it employed mainly single-engined machines with a crew of three or less. It had no need for bomb aimers or flight engineers as used by the RAF. Navigators were called observers and had other duties, while the wireless operator and the air gunner were merged as the Telegraphist Air Gunner (TAG). Pilots and observers were almost invariably officers. An RAF pilot usually went on a pre-planned mission, to bomb a city, intercept an enemy raider or drop supplies or paratroops, whereas a naval pilot or observer on patrol might have immense responsibility if he sighted an enemy force. He would have to report it accurately to the fleet, and then decide whether and how to attack. Another role was spotting for artillery, where he would direct a battleship's main armament. The navy felt that 'he must have the qualities of moral fibre and self reliance normally associated with the "officer type", as much of his work will inevitably be done as a lone effort in circumstances where these qualities are all important and with only a fraction of the assistance in the way of ground organization upon which his opposite number in the R.A.F. can normally rely.'[1]

The third class of crew member, the TAG, were all on the lower deck, mostly with the rating of leading hand. The TAG had lower status than his counterpart in the RAF, for all their aircrew were sergeants or above by 1940. TAGs could eventually reach warrant rank after a long climb (though it is doubtful if many did); commissioned rank was not available to them except by retraining as a pilot or observer.

Recruitment

In its recruitment of flying personnel, the navy suffered from competition with the RAF, which had benefitted from the great pre-war expansion programmes, fostered by the myth that bombing was the way to win the next war. It made the most of the belief that it saved the nation during the Battle of Britain. During the middle years of the war, from the real beginning of the bomber offensive in early 1942 until the invasion of Europe in June 1944, Bomber Command was the only force taking the war directly to the Germans. The RAF formed the Air Training Corps early in 1941, for boys aged from sixteen to eighteen, in an effort to make them 'air-minded.' This was a great success, attracting 200,000 boys, who were inspired by the thought of a flying career to 'pore earnestly over the mathematics they so loathed at school.'[2] Though it was mainly aimed at recruitment to the RAF, it was claimed in 1942 that 14,000 cadets had expressed preferences of the Fleet Air Arm.[3]

Another problem was the rank structure of the naval air arm. RAF squadron commanders had minimal administrative duties and could concentrate on leadership in the air, so their promotion could be very quick. In the navy, officers could only rise through administrative competence. It refused to subvert the naval rank structure by accelerated promotion for the relatively small numbers of the air arm. As a result, 'Old boys of public schools, returning to their schools on visits as Midshipmen and

Sub-Lieutenants, saw their contemporaries, who had joined the R.A.F., returning as Squadron Leaders and Wing Commanders, a fact which not unnaturally had an adverse effect on recruitment for the Naval Air Arm.'[4]

The biggest advantage of the FAA was that nearly all its pilots and observers were officers, whereas the RAF relied increasingly on sergeant pilots and navigators during the war. The near certainty of a commission was useful in attracting middle-class candidates who might be unsure of their prospects of getting that far. It was less helpful with public school boys, for 'Headmasters knew well that they could get commissions for their best boys in any of the services, and that those who were keen on flying were far more likely to obtain advancement and a chance to prove their powers of leadership in the R.A.F.'[5]

H. J. C. Spencer chose to fly in the navy because 'I had always had a secret desire to be a sailor and in a different age, and with a less happy family life, I might well have run away to sea.'[6] John Kilbracken was put off when the RAF recruiting office told him he would have to wait a year, but the FAA would take him in a couple of months.[7]

Selection
Potential recruits were sent to HMS *St Vincent* for a day of medical examinations, perhaps the most testing in the services. Charles McAra found,

> The medical itself was very thorough and exhaustive, not to say exhausting. In addition to the usual probing, prodding, cough, please, there were tests on vision, hearing, sense of balance, and a test of lung capacity that consisted of blowing up a column of mercury and holding it at certain level for several seconds. The naval doctors were all brisk, friendly and in spite of the nature of their work, they remained genial.[8]

Pilots and observers needed a good standard of education. In 1942 Stan Garner was turned down because he did not have a General School Certificate and was sent to train as a telegraphist air gunner instead.[9] By the end of that year the Admiralty, concerned about recruiting figures, began education courses for intelligent young men who were otherwise qualified. But not enough suitable candidates came forward and in any case there was a surge in normal recruiting after a pamphlet on the Y Scheme was published.[10]

Shore Training
FAA training began at its main depot, Lee-on-Solent. Trainees were given yet more medical examinations. They were issued with square rig uniform and taken on as Naval Airmen 2nd Class, the equivalent of Ordinary Seamen, 'the lowest form of life in the Navy'.[11] After that they went on to HMS *St Vincent* at Gosport near Portsmouth.

Trainees soon came under the fierce discipline of Chief Petty Officer Wilmott. To Dunstan Hadley he was 'a real sailor. He chewed tobacco. He was a smallish man and a true product of HMS *Excellent* the famous gunnery training school on Whale Island.'[12] To H. J. C. Spencer he was 'a Gunners Mate, the Navy's equivalent of a sergeant major. An unremarkable figure, short and slight and with wire framed glasses. Rumour had it that he had been a postman at the start of the war. ... We were soon to learn he as a formidable character.'[13]

Apart from discipline, the course placed great emphasis on seamanship. Most trainees were anxious to get in the air and felt that this was a waste of time, but the navy had its reasons. It was important to introduce men to naval culture and customs, especially as most of them would be under the control of the RAF for the most formative months of their careers. Secondly, knowledge of seamanship was necessary for officers who might be in charge of reconnaissance aircraft, reporting enemy movements and activities. On the whole the training was felt to be worthwhile.

> Considering we were at St Vincent but something like two and a half months the subjects we studied were wide ranging. In that relatively short time we were introduced to seamanship, with some detail on knots, anchors, boat pulling in Shoreham Harbour, gunnery, target practice at icy wind swept Stokes Bay range, morse, semaphore, flag recognition, much drill and the mysteries of the progress of a new recruit's career in the Royal Navy.

> Of course we had volunteered to be naval airmen so we were lectured on airmanship, theory of flight and navigation.[14]

At the end of the course there was an examination lasting three days. According to Dunstan Hadley, 'Except for six of us we all passed. "Oh joy, oh rapture!" Those who had "dipped" were plunged into gloom. It only meant going back one month to the next course but it was the end of the world! Six more miserable naval airmen you could not find.'[15] Successful candidates were issued with their 'hook' on promotion to leading airman and went on leave before the next stage of their training.

Pilot Training

Under the agreement of 1937, the RAF was responsible for training all pilots in their basic flying skills. In 1940 it used the airfields at Luton in Bedfordshire, Elmdon in Essex, Sydenham in Oxfordshire and Netheravon in Wiltshire. These were in danger of bombing and indeed some damage was done during a raid at Luton on 30 August. After that there was a move towards more northern bases, such as Sealand in North Wales.

Each group was divided into two halves, port and starboard watches in the FAA. One would fly in the morning and have lectures in the afternoon, the other would do the opposite. In United Kingdom schools the trainees flew the Tiger Moth or the Miles Magister. The Tiger Moth, a classic biplane, was safe and easy to fly, though the open cockpit could become very cold. The monoplane Magister was 'more of a challenge and far more fun. Sleek, streamlined monoplanes, you could pretend they were Hurricanes'.[16]

Naval airmen found that RAF control was quite a relief after the rigorous discipline of St Vincent. 'Gone were the drills and divisions. Gone were the watch and watch about duties. We could go out in the evenings without hindrance unless some unusual duty or emergency arose.'[17] The navy was still anxious to maintain some control over its trainees. At RAF Sealand in 1942, there was a lieutenant-commander, a chief and two petty officers, one of whom despised all naval airmen as potential officers and layabouts.

> "Bloody naval airmen, why can't they keep the bloody place tidy. Bloody tennis, that's all they think about."

He had once found a tennis racket amongst somebody's kit and from then on we were all guilty.[18]

Trainees were issued with their flying kit, essential in those days of unheated and often open cockpits. Charles McAra was given 'Fleece lined leather boots, flying suits, helmets, goggles, white silk inner gloves and gauntlets.'[19] This did not go well with the ratings' fore and aft rig. 'The naval uniform had been designed in the reign of Queen Victoria when the only flying machines were balloons. The drop-flap front of the bell-bottoms worked at right angles to the twentieth-century zip fasteners on the flying suits. Once encased in his flying gear a man had to "wait" until he had had his flight if he did not want to repeat the lengthy formalities of getting ready for it.'[20]

Fleet Air Arm trainees are issued with their flying kit at HMS *St Vincent*.

After that the trainee went on his first flight. Very few people had traveled in civil airliners, and it was a revelation. 'A short bumpy run across the grass field and we're clear of the earth, and climbing. The hangars and buildings visibly shrunk. Turn left and right! Dive and climb! Take and feel the controls! The clock said we were up an hour and a half. It went by in a flash. It felt marvellous.'[21]

The first solo flight was the most memorable event of all. It was usually done after about ten hours of dual instruction, though some started with as little as six, and a trainee requiring twelve hours was on the verge of failure. H. J. C. Spencer discovered differences between the British and American ways of training.

The usual practice at home when a student had been cleared to solo was for the instructor to get out of the plane, say "Bless you my son", and for the student to complete one circuit and landing on his own and then retire to celebrate. It was different at Grosse Ile. After a successful up check the next flight, probably not till next day, was a full length one scheduled in the normal way, but with no instructor in the front seat. ... When the happy day for my first solo arrived I resolved to get the landing business straightened out for good. I took off from Grosse Ile and flew to one of the small satellite fields near by. I picked one where I knew the grass was long, making it easier to judge height, and softer if you got it wrong. There, with only a windsock for witness, I spent the whole period landing and taking off. I returned to Grosse Ile for my first public performance with an undamaged plane feeling cock-a-hoop.[22]

Many candidates dropped out before this stage. Charles McAra's friend failed because he tended to black out at 6000 feet. McAra himself was 'dipped' soon afterwards. The Chief Flying Instructor summoned him to his tent.

When I arrived he explained to me why he was dissatisfied with my progress, where I had gone wrong and then produced for my signature an official form which said, in effect, that I would never again attempt to fly one of His Majesty's aircraft. I signed quite gladly. Any feeling of disappointment or failure was far outweighed by a sense of relief. It meant an end to the daily exasperation of feeling inept and clumsy.[23]

Training in Canada

The RAF did much of its flying training overseas, especially to Canada where there was plenty of open land and empty skies. The FAA scheme was separate from this, though parallel. It began with No. 7 Service Flying Training School when it was necessary to evacuate it from England. A new air base was ready at Kingston, at the eastern end of Lake Ontario, by September 1940, though RAF instructors were not ready to move until early the following year. Courses began with Fleet Air pilots in the second stage of their flying training in January 1941, and the school was renumbered as No. 31 Service Flying Training School to fit in with the Canadian system.[24] Dunstan Hadley was posted there in the winter of 1942–43 and found it very cold, with the lakes frozen and the country covered in snow. He flew the Harvard, a monoplane with a retractable undercarriage, high performance and a sophisticated cockpit, 'as different from the Tiger Moth as chalk from cheese'. In 1944 a second base was set up at St Eugene in Quebec.

The Towers Scheme

In June 1941, before America entered the war, Admiral John H. Towers, the Chief of the Bureau of Aeronautics of the US Navy, offered the use of USN facilities to train British pilots. This was a radical move, in view of the strong isolationist strain in American public opinion. Originally it was agreed to take thirty naval pilots per month, plus seventy RAF seaplane pilots, whose duties would have been performed by the USN in America. They wore civilian clothes outside the base, until Pearl Harbour made them welcome to the American public. Naval trainees were sent after their course at *St Vincent*, and the first batch arrived in the USA in July 1941. There were differences between what the two services wanted from the course. American medical and other standards tended to be higher; about 36 per cent of trainees failed up to mid 1944, then 50 per cent as the US Navy raised its own standards, before falling again. In mid 1942 the scheme was altered to take fifty British naval students per month, and with operational training added as a final course. From September this was increased to sixty-six per month, and the RAF dropped out of the scheme in February 1944.

The first American base for British students was Grosse Ile, less than a mile from

Canada across the Detroit River. From early 1942 a three-month course of Primary Flying Training was carried out there. Morale was very high, despite the grating discipline of the US Navy. 'A particular problem was the "demerit" system for minor infringements of rules. Demerits were totted up and eventually led to punishment. … We had expected that in the "land of the free" they would be more, not less, easy going.' American training was efficient. 'Grosse Ile was a flow line. You went through as individuals, not in batches. Because I had been a slow learner I had been left behind by old friends and caught up by new ones.'[25]

Also from mid 1942, the three- or four-month courses of intermediate and advanced training were carried out from the great US Navy base at Pensacola in Florida. Later, students were posted there for their initial training and spent the first six weeks on theoretical work. This was different from the British syllabus, for US naval aviation had no specialist navigators, and every pilot was expected to take this in his stride.

> Officially we saw no aircraft other than in workshops, although in our spare time we hung around them like children. We studied alongside American cadets, working at their peacetime curriculum – navigation, celestial navigation, meteorology, theory of flight, fuel, oil and hydraulic systems. We attended lectures and instructional films in the auditorium and each day there was a compulsory period of two hours' physical training. Every Friday afternoon we underwent written tests on all school subjects.[26]

During operational training in the third base at Miami, pilots were taught on the well-liked Harvard before going on the Brewster Buffalo, 'probably the worst fighter produced by any allied country during the war'.

The climate of Florida was very suitable for naval flying training and in July 1943 an operational torpedo training course started at Fort Lauderdale. Early in the following year Fighter Training moved from Miami to Jacksonville. By September 1944 the Americans were taking-in a course of forty men every two weeks. At the start the Towers Scheme trained about 30 per cent of British naval pilots; by the end of 1944 that had risen to 44 per cent, and 2100 students had entered it.[27]

Graduation

At the end of the Service Flying Training School course, the pilots were awarded their flying badges, or wings, which were worn on the left sleeve above the officer's stripes, in contrast to the RAF which were worn more prominently on the left breast. In the RAF this was a grand occasion, the moment of acceptance into the elite of the service. For the navy it was much less of an issue. 'Were the wings to be presented? Were they just to be issued? If so, when? The answers were neither and never. We had to repair to an enterprising Kingston trader and buy a pair of wings.'[28] They also found out whether they were to become officers or not. Nearly all did, unless there was a compelling reason against it. At Kingston, one man who was court-martialled for unauthorized low flying was refused a commission, as were two men at Luton, both 'from very distinguished families' and 'exceptionally good pilots' who had been jailed for stealing petrol.[29]

Pilots were now allocated to training courses on the type of aircraft they would fly in service, according to their own aptitudes and the needs of the service. In the case of Dunstan Hadley's course at Kingston, four were allocated to seaplanes, thirty to fighters and forty-six to torpedo bombers.[30] Most officers went to the Royal Naval College at Greenwich for a re-introduction to naval ways by means of the 'knife and fork course,' in which they learned to be officers and gentlemen.

Observer Training

The FAA observer was the counterpart of the RAF navigator, but the observer was the equal of the pilot, and in certain circumstances he could take command of an aircraft or a squadron, whereas command was always vested in pilots in the RAF. The more able men were often chosen to be observers, and in a survey of 1942–46 they were found to the most intelligent group in the navy, apart from regular engineer and executive officers.[31] H. J. C. Spencer was told that 'really bright people' became observers.[32]

The work of the observer was closely related to that of the fleet, whether in navigation over the sea, reconnaissance or spotting for naval artillery. The navy never had much faith in the RAF's navigation, and since 1924 all observers had been naval officers. At the beginning of the war the main observers school was in the Royal Naval Air Station at Ford in Sussex. In August 1940 it was attacked by bombers, proving that it was untenable as a training base.[33]

The Admiralty considered moving to South Africa, but there was no airfield available and 'the sea conditions which prevail round the Cape are not suitable for the over-sea training of pupil observers ...'[34] It found a good and little-used aerodrome at Piarco Savana in Trinidad, well away from the war zone but close to the sea, and considerably nearer to Britain than South Africa. It was ready within a month, with provision for 140 aircraft and 100 officers, the same number of chiefs and petty officers and 730 other ratings, including 150 observer trainees.[35]

RNAS Arbroath in Scotland was opened in June 1940 as HMS *Condor* and it too was mostly used for training observers. The Admiralty's publication *Fleet Air Arm* of 1943 describes the progress of a fictitious trainee observer. Some of his colleagues were sent to Trinidad, but

> Oliver and the remainder went to a station on the east coast of Scotland known as HMS *Condor*, where his principal instruction was in reconnaissance and in navigation as a means to that end. Soon he went into the air on exercises on Swordfish and Walruses. He learnt to find his way about in the air without using landmarks, relying on his skill in plotting and air navigation. The early practices were over the land, but little by little he became accustomed to working over the sea, until he was familiar with its changing moods of wind and fog and cloud. He also had practical experience in ship recognition, and learnt to take air photographs, which were processed by specially trained Wrens.[36]

Trainee observers, still ratings, were flown on exercises by rather disgruntled, but commissioned, pilots.

> "And where would we be going today?" "If you don't mind, Sir, could we please depart over the Seaforth Hotel swimming pool on a course of 095 degrees." It was always the swimming pool: an imaginary aircraft carrier would "sail" from that point at a speed of 25 knots on a course of 030 degrees, thus bringing it close to the little port of Stonehaven after an hour, by which time we would have completed a dog leg course over the sea and

would attempt to arrive over, or "intercept" the carrier at the appropriate time and place on the coast. These attempts brooked much sarcastic comment from our pilots. "Lost again are we? And where would you suggest we go now if we're not to miss lunch?"[37]

Meteorology was part of an observer's training and its importance soon became clear.

> The early weeks were spent more in the class-room than in the air. It had never occurred to me to wonder how one set off from an aircraft carrier, flew in all directions, blown by unforeseen winds, and arrived back to whatever spot in the ocean the carrier might have sailed to in the meantime.[38]

On completing the course the observer was awarded his wings. Unlike the single wing of the RAF navigator the FAA observer had two, albeit stumpier than the pilot's.

The TAGs

Telegraphist air gunners were sent to *Royal Arthur* at Skegness for their basic training, before going on to *St Vincent*. Doug Cole volunteered because of his interests in radio and flying. He found the RAF was indifferent but a policeman suggested he try the navy recruiting office, 'whose welcome couldn't have been warmer'.[39] The usual medical tests were applied, including one for night vision for Stan Garner. 'We were blindfolded and led by a Wren into a room, where we sat and described what we thought we could see on dimly-lit screens. We liked hand-holding and groping from room to room.'[40]

At *Royal Arthur* the trainees had much foot drill and nothing specific to the FAA. At *St Vincent* they went on to 'study a variety of subjects of varying degrees of usefulness to their future role',[41] rather like the potential pilots and observers in the same establishment. On completion, trainees were sent to Worthy Down in Hampshire, or to the Royal Canadian Air Force base at Yarmouth in Nova Scotia for their flying training.

Training consisted of two parts, gunnery and radio. Since radio telephony using speech was still not considered reliable over long ranges, trainees learned morse code. At Yarmouth, the skills of CPO Milliner were legendary – 'He could change hands and light a cigarette without any apparent break in the machine-like precision of his transmission.'[42] Theoretical gunnery was learned on the ground, along with practice at stripping and maintaining guns such as the Vickers .303 used by the Swordfish and its successor the Albacore. Their first flights were usually in Ansons, which could carry a small group of men for training. The Lysander, unsuccessful as an army-cooperation machine, was used for practical gunnery training. The trainees also went up in a Swordfish, two per aircraft. Halfway through the flight the men had to change places, a hazardous process. In Britain, they flew over the range at St Merryn in Cornwall. They fired at drogues towed by other aircraft, or practiced against targets on the ground. The gunner had to learn not to shoot the tail of his own aircraft.[43] On qualification a TAG was awarded a pair of wings for his sleeve, rather like those of the observer but with a thinner rope round the anchor, and without a crown above.

Royal Naval Air Stations

On the transfer in 1939 the FAA inherited only five airfields, at Lee-on-Solent near Portsmouth, Ford in Sussex, Worthy Down in Hampshire, Eastleigh near

Southampton and Donibristle in Fife. Not all the bases were suitable – Donibristle, for example, was a small site, hemmed in by a bay on one side and the mainline railway on the other, and with a hill at one end of the runway. It became a communications unit and a maintenance base. Ford was returned to the RAF in September 1940, being too close to the action.

Since the FAA was intended to operate only ship-based aircraft, it had no need for operational aerodromes. However, it did need airfields for several purposes. in the first place for aircraft storage and long-term maintenance. Secondly, it needed them for Fleet Requirements Units, which operated communications flights and provided photo-reconnaissance and target-towing. Thirdly, it used airfields to disembark squadrons from aircraft carriers. When a carrier was in port its aircraft would be unable to fly, so they went to a shore airfield to continue training and be available for combat duties. Several airfields were taken over around the main fleet anchorages, notably in the Firth of Clyde where most carriers worked up.

Fourthly, the FAA needed bases for training. Though basic flying training was done under the auspices of the RAF and the US Navy, operational training needed far closer contact with the fleet. Even the US Navy could not provide the facilities despite Admiral Towers' efforts, for techniques differed from those of the Royal Navy. The most striking example was the use of the batsman's signals to pilots on landing on a carrier. To the Americans, raised arms meant that the pilot was too high and should go lower; to the British it meant that that he should go higher. When British pilots did train using American carriers, British batsmen were sometimes sent on board.[44] More commonly, British pilots went home to the UK to begin their deck landing training.

The FAA quickly began to build its own airfields, nearly all with ship names from birds. A large proportion of them were in isolated spots, especially in Scotland. This was partly because the RAF had already earmarked many of the sites in southern and eastern England, but also because it was important to site training bases away from enemy action. The new Royal Naval Air Stations (RNAS) differed from RAF bases in having four runways instead of three, and indeed Arbroath in Scotland and Henstridge in Somerset were the only two airfields in the United Kingdom with five. One legend is that naval pilots could not deal with crosswinds as they were used to landing on carriers that turned into the wind. A more plausible explanation is that they were built in inhospitable sites where winds were strong and variable. The runways were made of tarmac rather than concrete as used by the RAF. RNAS runways were mostly 30 yards wide instead of 50, because the FAA had no large aircraft. The standard RNAS control tower was three storeys high instead of two, with a glasshouse on top.

Simulators

Flying is one of the most costly activities known to man, so it is not surprising that the Fleet Arm used a large number of ground simulators. The most famous flight simulator of the age was the Link trainer, invented by Edwin Link in 1929 and adopted by the United States Army Air Corps five years later. It was centred on the cockpit of an aircraft, with a short fuselage and stubby wings. It was mainly intended to train pilots in instrument flying, with a hood over the cockpit, and the FAA had more than a hundred in its bases in 1943.[45] Pilots tended to consider them rather boring.

Much more exciting was the Torpedo Attack Trainer installed at nineteen bases including HMS *Jackdaw* at Crail. It was fitted in a round building with a seascape painted on the walls.

The Torpedo Attack Trainer, showing a Link trainer below, and projection system above.

Some of it with a calm sea, a blue sky and a horizon and some rough and foggy. It was illuminated to simulate various times of day. Fitted under the link and connected to it by a computer was a projector which threw on to the seascape the white silhouette of a ship. As you flew towards it the ship got bigger at a rate linked to the speed of approach. The shape of the ship varied according to the bearing of the aircraft from it. Changes of speed of the ship and avoiding action could also be simulated. The movements of the silhouette gave a very realistic illusion as the pilot flying the link, without the hood of course, made his attack. He approached – dived – made his torpedo settings ... When he had everything right he pressed the button. The computer did its sums, everything stopped and a light appeared below the ship where the torpedo had hit or in the sea ahead or astern if he had missed.[46]

The FAA had five types of simulator for use in gunnery, for either fixed forward-firing guns, or the free guns used by Swordfish TAGs. It also had a turret trainer at Arbroath, used to train gunners of the Grumman Avenger, the only first-line naval aircraft to use turrets. In the Instructional Box Type 2, 'Several 12-volt lamps with coloured filters simulate variety of lighting conditions. Turntable on which models stand is turned by windscreen wiper electric motor.' There were nine different types of aircraft radar simulator in use in 1943. They were designed round different types of radar set, whether for air interception, air to surface vessel or beam approach. For anti-submarine work, the A/S Ranging Teacher Type 46A was 'For exercise in correct release of depth charges from aircraft. Motion film represents typical attacks on surfaced submarine. Pilot presses depth-charge release and device automatically records the range.'[47]

Deck Landing

Landing on the deck of an aircraft carrier was the defining skill of a naval pilot, and one of the most difficult – taking off was considerably easier. Training for landing generally came at a late stage in a pilot's career, often after he had arrived back in Britain. Some training in the use of arrester wires was useful before the pilot went to sea, mostly on a specially-fitted runway at East Haven near Dundee. It did not always work well if the wind was not blowing along the runway as it would on a carrier, but it gave experience of being brought suddenly to a halt by the wires.[48]

HMS *Argus* of 1918, the first true aircraft carrier in the world, was stationed in the Clyde for much of the war and used for deck landing training.

> The drill was quite simple. *Argus* had six arrester wires strung across the after end of the deck. ... She had no crash barriers. Instead, standing near the island was a very brave young officer who waved a red flag if an aircraft failed to engage any of the wires with its arrester hook. The pilot was thus energetically exhorted to open the throttle and take off again, to make another circuit and another approach to the deck. We were each to do six landings, preceded by two dummy runs with the wires in the down position and with arrester hooks up.[49]

Pilots were apprehensive before their first landings, not without reason.

> In the last 200 yards to the deck, he drifted to port ever so slightly. The batsman slanted his bats to correct him, more and more energetically as Johnny failed to react. As the aircraft came in over the side of the deck and supported only by fresh air, the batsman dropped for his life – and we, standing in the nets, dropped with him. The port wheel went into the nets and the Fulmar, at about 65 knots, slewed to port and fell into the sea. As she went, we could see Johnny making the greatest and last mistake of his life; he was casting off his harness and climbing out of the cockpit. He and the Fulmar were gone.[50]

Operational Training

As well as providing planes for specialized aircraft carriers, the FAA manned the aircraft which were allocated in small flights to battleships and cruisers. In January 1940, 700 Squadron was formed by merging several other units. It had eleven Seafoxes and twelve Swordfish floatplanes, but its main strength was forty-two Supermarine Walruses. These were designed to be catapulted from the decks of ships, then to alight in the sea after the flight. A ten-week course was set up by 1942, consisting of three weeks at Donibristle in Fife for aerodrome flying and water landing, wireless instruction and practice, anti-submarine and dive-bombing attacks and air photography. At Dundee for the second three weeks, crews came together for navigation exercises and night landings. After a week in the Irish Sea learning to use ship's catapults, the crews returned to Donibristle before going on to Orkney.[51]

RNAS East Haven, near Dundee, became the centre for the training of Deck Landing Control Officers or DLCOs, the famous 'batsmen' who signalled course corrections to pilots landing on carriers. Originally it was intended that all DLCOs should be volunteers, but Lieutenant Dunstan Hadley was drafted in against his will in 1943, and disciplined when he protested. It is not surprising that volunteers were short, for DLCOs missed the joys of flying, but still faced an element of danger. They often had to flee for their lives when pilots made bad landings.[52]

A chief petty officer instructs trainee pilots in the torpedo at RNAS Crail.

The airfield at Crail in the East Neuk of Fife, HMS *Jackdaw*, was commissioned in October 1940, mainly to train pilots in the specialized art of dropping torpedoes. Unlike gunnery this could be done quite realistically, as a torpedo without a warhead was not likely to damage a target if it hit it. Torpedoes, however, were expensive and practice was done on shore as much as possible. After practice on the Torpedo Attack Trainer, the trainees flew over the Forth to drop dummies from Swordfish or Albacore aircraft. After some experience they used 'runners', which were real torpedoes without warheads, which could be recovered by drifters and used again. The paddle steamer *Glenavon* steamed at 9 knots off the Isle of May as a target. Sometimes real battleships and destroyers took part in the exercises, as when the *Nelson* and her escorts were attacked by Dunstan Hadley and his colleagues. 'Well chaps, out of nine aircraft we got one hit – on the stern, it's not good enough. Most of you dropped too far away. I warned you about its size.' Barr spoke up. 'The destroyers were in the way.' 'Of course they were, that's what they're there for, you have to get round them somehow.' However, they did better than the pilot who accidentally dropped his practice torpedo on Crail Police Station, fortunately without casualties. [53]

The airfield at Drem near North Berwick was used from 1943 to train carrier pilots in the new skills of night flying, which it seems to have done with considerable success. 'Training continued, and very high quality material was sent to us to be trained. This was now a problem. We had more instructors, course followed course, but there was nothing for the aircrew to do once they had qualified.'[54]

At the beginning of the war fighter pilot training was carried out at Eastleigh near Southampton. That was obviously too near the front line with the Fall of France, and 759 Squadron, the Fleet Fighter School, moved to HMS *Heron*, a new airfield at Yeovilton in June. This was far enough south to maintain liaison with the RAF, but far enough west to keep out of the main air battles. Training began with Blackburn Skuas and Fairey Fulmars, both unsatisfactory types in action. Hurricanes were added during 1940, as well as American types such as the Grumman Martlet, and the famous Spitfire, modified to become the Seafire. In May

1943 the School of Air Combat, 736 Squadron, was set up at Yeovilton to train more experienced fighter pilots.[55]

The first flight in a high-performance aircraft was a memorable experience.

> My first take-off in a Hurricane was like the first ride in a high-powered speed boat, noisy, shaky and out of control and, with the same colossal acceleration which almost dragged my hand off the throttle and jerked my head back against the headrest, it was so unexpected. The aircraft took charge. It shook with power as the 900 horses, only a few feet in front, wrenched round the propeller and dug into the air. It was frightening too, for the whole thing leapt into the sky well before I was ready for it and having used only a quarter of the runway.

Trainee fighter pilots then went to a small airfield near Exmouth to learn to shoot. Their target was a drogue towed by a Boulton-Paul Defiant, one of the less successful fighters of the war. The pilots were allowed to use two of the Hurricane's eight guns, and up to 100 rounds from each gun per attack.[56]

Continuing Training

Training never ended for aircrew, even when they were finally posted to operational squadrons. Carriers on operations were often too busy for training as such for most of the war, but squadrons naturally worked themselves up to high standards of readiness while patrolling the ocean for submarines, or defending a convoy or a fleet against enemy bombers.

The bases for disembarked squadrons also had a strong element of continuing training as part of their basic function. Near the great fleet base in Orkney, H. J. C. Spencer found that 'Hatston was an exciting place in 1944, very much a front line airfield with many first line squadrons passing through between operations.'[57] One diversion was to fly between the Old Man of Hoy and the land. Training facilities were good. 'We did dive-bombing practice on Sule Skerry, much to the annoyance of the rock's hundreds of thousands of gulls, shags, skuas and tern. We carried out dummy torpedo attacks on ships exercising from Scapa Flow and dummy depth-charge attacks on towed targets from the Woodwick Range. We practised air-to-air firing, navigation, homing on ASV [air to surface vessel] contacts and beacons and aerial photography.' After three months in the Flow, 835 Squadron had achieved a high standard of flying, though it was frustrated at the lack of real action.[58]

The air around Machrihanish on the Firth of Clyde became very crowded. According to Spencer,

> There were usually several squadrons at Machrihanish, due to its strategic position close to the carrier playground in the Firth of Clyde. So there was competition for the sky, particularly at night. Everyone behaved reasonably at first, each squadron having its night. The weather would take a hand. But programmes were not cancelled, just postponed. Come the first clear night everyone flew. It was an air traffic controller's nightmare, only there weren't any. No radar either. One squadron would be doing deck landing practice with its batsmen out on the runway batting in all comers. Others would be going off to the bombing ranges, or to play with HMS *Graph* [a captured U-boat used for training], or to do navigation exercises, or perhaps formation practice.'[59]

The expansion of the FAA required a great effort, because aircraft and aircrew training are very expensive. It was one field where the navy needed to use the facilities of other services, and indeed it learned much from the United States Navy. The Towers Scheme also set the pattern for post-war co-operation between allied fleets.

CHAPTER 16

The Royal Marines

The Traditions of the Marines

The Royal Marines celebrate 1664 as their date of foundation, for they claim descent from the Duke of York and Albany's Maritime Regiment of Foot, raised by the Lord High Admiral to serve alongside the sailors in the ships of the fleet. They went through many ups and downs over the next ninety years, being transferred from the control of the army to the navy and vice versa, and disbanded several times, until in 1755 they were re-formed fully under the control of the Admiralty. Though they have remained in continuous existence ever since, they have changed their role several times – they began as small arms men in action, then in the 1790s they were tried, with limited success, as the main guarantee against mutiny by the ship's company, a tradition which was maintained in the modern navy by berthing the marines between the officers and the crew. In peacetime they served as dockyard police, and when war began they formed press gangs and the nucleus of crews while seamen were found. They always provided landing parties from ships, and carried out guard duties on board ship. In 1804 the Royal Marine Artillery was formed to operate the mortars of bomb vessels, the only guns which were designed for any kind of long-range firing. Throughout the nineteenth century they took on increasing responsibility for manning the heavy guns of ships. The Royal Marine Artillery was merged with the infantry in 1923, but this served to spread the tradition of gunnery throughout the corps and it became the major role between the wars. Marines usually manned about a quarter of the armament on large ships, for example one gun turret on a battleship or cruiser, with a proportion of the secondary and anti-aircraft armament. Sometimes they were formed into battalions for service ashore, but until well into the Second World War about two thirds of marines were afloat at any given moment, and sea service was their main function. Their role

> in war and peace is to provide detachments which, whilst fully capable of manning their share of the gun armament, are specially trained to provide a striking force drawn either from the Royal Marine Divisions or from the Fleet, immediately available for use under the direction of the Naval Commander-in-Chief for amphibious operations, such as raids on enemy coast-line or bases, or the seizure and defence of temporary bases for the use of our own Fleet.[1]

The marines had a strong tradition of parade-ground discipline, which conflicted with the ethos of the seaman. As the carrier *Courageous* sank slowly in 1939, Charles Lambe noted the behaviour of the marine detachment. "'Silly buggers!" said Kiggell. "They'll stand there until someone gives them an order and if nobody does, they'll all go down with the ship, still standing at that absurd angle!" Eventually he got them to leave by shouting, "Royal Marines 'Hun! Turn for'ard – Dis-miss! Abandon ship – over the side at the double – every man-Jack of you!'"[2]

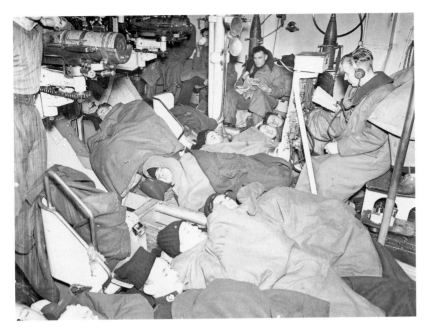

Marines resting in a gun turret in HMS *Sheffield* during a lull in action.

Ships' Detachments

As late as the winter of 1941–42, Jack Brewin found that 'service in ships was the ultimate of Royal Marines desire, the bigger the ship the more one had to be proud of and our training at Eastney had instilled this fact into us.[3] Ships' detachments, as it turned out, were not a growth area during the war. Losses were heavy among the large ships, and in the shipyards priority tended to be given to the smaller vessels, which were urgently needed, so the large ships on order were often cancelled, like the battleships of the *Lion* class or the great carriers of the *Gibraltar* class. Others would emerge too late, such as the battleship *Vanguard* and the aircraft carriers *Eagle* and *Ark Royal*. Five battleships of the *King George V* class were completed during the war, which exactly matched the three battleships and two battlecruisers lost, but several of the older ships were withdrawn from service before the end of the war. Twenty-nine cruisers were completed during the war, compared with twenty-four lost. Five fleet aircraft carriers were sunk, compared with six completed, along with four light fleet carriers; but again, some of the older ships had been reduced to reserve by the end of the war. In December 1944, only 7162 marines were serving afloat in large ships, not much more than at the beginning of the war.[4] In any case, the landing of men from a large warship was essentially a peacetime practice. It might well help on some isolated station in the British Empire, but in wartime, with enemy ships at large, a cruiser could not lightly give up the men who manned a quarter of its main armament. Nevertheless, in 1945 the battleship *Duke of York* had 350 marines of all ranks out of a total complement of 1550, and the cruiser *Gambia* had 78 marines out of 730.

Officers commanding ships' detachments had to make sure that their men were still fit for service ashore, despite restricted training facilities. The answer was a series of lectures, on such un-naval subjects such as the construction of barbed wire obstacles and track discipline – 'The best position in the world will be given away by bad track discipline. Tracks show up very clearly on a photograph, and be sure that every new track will mean something to the enemy.'[5]

New Roles

The marines' aims in amphibious warfare were quite moderate in 1932 – to raid enemy coastlines and to seize and defend naval bases. Large-scale invasion of enemy territory was not considered likely by any of the services. This contrasted with the United States Marines, originally modelled on the Royal Marines, who put consider-able energy into amphibious doctrine in the 1930s, and produced operational manuals on the subject. The US Marine Corps was already legendary to the American people as 'the first to land' in any crisis. Between the wars it demonstrated this role many times, particularly in Latin America and China. It was already quasi-independent of the navy. The Royals, in contrast, were quite self-effacing, and many parts of the public were only vaguely aware of their existence.

In 1740 the War Office had reasoned that marines were simply soldiers who did not have to march very far, and sent Chelsea Pensioners to man George Anson's squadron for an attack on the Spanish Empire. All of them died on the voyage and fif-teen years later Anson was instrumental in taking the marines under Admiralty con-trol. Standards of fitness had undoubtedly improved since then, but the marines were not regarded as an elite corps in 1939, in the same way as they became later. There was no suggestion that their standards of fitness and aggression were higher than those of the army or the navy.

One relatively new role in 1939 was the Mobile Naval Base Defence Organization (MNBDO), though such a force had been planned as early as 1921. Based on the experiences of 1914 when the Grand Fleet anchorage at Scapa Flow was unprepared, it was decided to create a force of marines to occupy and defend any forward base that might be needed, until the army was ready to operate more permanent defences. Its function was defined in 1934 as 'the rapid provision of defences for the protection of an anchorage against all probable forces of sea-borne attack other than bombardment by heavy guns'. Anti-aircraft protection was to devel-op as an important part of the defence, but initially it was only planned against rela-tively light attacks by ship-borne aircraft. The MNBDO was not expected to capture the base in the face of determined opposition, nor was it to help with the running of the base itself, in provisioning and repairing the ships.[6]

As planned at the end of 1939, the MNBDO was to consist of an anti-aircraft brigade with sixteen heavy and twelve light guns and forty-eight searchlights; a coast defence brigade with six 6-inch guns for use against cruisers, eight 2-pounder guns against torpedo boats and twelve searchlights; a signal company, a landing, transport, workshop and an administrative group; and a land defence force of one battalion of infantry.[7] The first unit, MNBDO I, was formed in the early months of the war, and MNBDO II was formed at the beginning of 1941.

While not in use, the guns of the MNBDO were deployed in the anti-aircraft defence of the homeland, initially in the estuaries and later in the less-threatened areas where their sudden withdrawal would not leave a serious gap. In December 1942 seven batteries were deployed in the mainly inland counties of Warwick, Leicester and Rutland.[8]

Despite the apparently defensive nature of the work, MNBDO I found itself in one of the toughest battles of the war. A large part of it was landed on Crete in May 1941, to defend the naval base in Suda Bay. The Germans invaded and the marines took part in much of the fighting. Out of nearly 2000 men, 1114 were casualties, including 900 taken prisoner. The unit was re-formed during 1941 and supplied troops for the war in the Far East, before disbandment in September 1944. MNBDO

II went east in 1943, but was disbanded in the following year.

As well as the 'defensive' role in connection with the naval bases, and the rather diffuse role on board ship, it was also planned to create a striking force within the Royal Marines. As First Lord of the Admiralty, Winston Churchill was determined to find a way for the navy and the marines to take the war to the enemy, despite the shortness and difficult navigation of the German North Sea coastline. He dreamed of capturing the island of Borkum, of raiding the western end of the Kiel Canal, and of an ambitious and misconceived scheme to enter the Baltic with specially armoured battleships. The Royal Marine Brigade was part of this plan. Initially it was to have three battalions, but in December 1939 this was increased to four, with 114 officers, 349 warrant officers and NCOs and 2182 marines. About 500 men would be found from the younger marines (aged nineteen and under) in the fleet, who were to be detached in parties of ten or twenty from each of the major ships. Men taking part in local defence ashore were to be replaced by the army as soon as possible, providing 277 men, and the others were to be recruited directly. Acting promotions were to be used to create the extra NCOs needed, and half the officers were to be recruited directly, including the novelist Evelyn Waugh. It was planned to have the force ready by the summer of 1940.[9]

The dichotomy in the marines' role was noted by John St John. He sought an appointment that was 'moderately interesting, and, above all, safe'. He applied to become an officer in the Royal Marines, attracted by the advertisement which mentioned the defence of mobile naval bases. 'This had a comfortable and tolerably safe ring and I have always enjoyed shipping and boats.' But on acceptance he was interviewed by a colonel who said 'It's not everyone who's chosen for this particular outfit and no wonder! It's the most exciting and hazardous in the entire armed forces.' He had, in fact, volunteered for the Royal Marine Brigade, intended to raid the enemy coast, rather than the Mobile Naval Base Defence Organization.[10]

A fourth group, the Royal Marine Engineers, was set up in March 1940. Like the MNBDO it was largely based on the experience of the last war, when a similar corps had been organized. 'When the 1939–45 war broke out it was realized that 'civil engineering and building works would have to be carried out for the Navy in places where it was extremely difficult to obtain suitable labour and where conditions would not readily allow the importation of civilian workmen from normal sources for reasons of operational security etc'. Churchill agreed that 'It would be wise to make a unit of this kind for all the contingencies of what may prove to be a long war.'[11] Initially it was planned as a force of 1000 men, recruited from those with at least two years' experience in the building trade. Recruits had an introductory course of eight weeks, including three of disciplinary training. Many specialist courses were organized, including some under the auspices of the army. The force took on new roles over the years. Apart from work at Scapa Flow, it had detachments with the MNBDOs. In 1943 a large part of the force was sent to the Far East in preparation for an offensive against Japan, in which the American Seabees or Construction Battalions, of similar function though part of the navy rather than the marines, were already proving their worth. By the end of the war the RME had a strength of just over 8000 men, but the force was not retained in peacetime.[12]

The Organization of the Marines

The corps was headed by the Adjutant General, normally with the rank of lieutenant general, though Sir Allan Bourne was promoted to full general in 1942. The post was renamed Commandant General Royal Marines in 1945. The staff of the headquarters had several officers responsible for recruitment and training, though the structure was almost as complex as that of the navy. Under the Brigadier (Administration), were staff officers responsible for the promotion and conditions of service of other ranks; another dealt with pay and allowances; and a third with war establishments, personnel estimates and war complements. In the other side of the staff, under the Brigadier, General Staff, was a senior staff officer in charge of general training policy, with assistants responsible for naval and military training policy, and courses and education.

The corps had 'grand divisions' at the three main ports, each headed by a major-general reporting to the Adjutant-General. The divisions carried most of the actual work of training in peacetime. The staff of each included a chief instructor, plus staff instructors in naval gunnery, small arms, signals, tactical training, physical training and a headmaster in charge of 'school' education. Each division also had a drafting officer who appointed marines to ships and other posts.

The Regular Officers

Regular officers were selected by the same examination and interview as Special Entry candidates for the navy, around the age of 18. They entered with the rank of second lieutenant, not as officer cadets as in the army. They did a training course of over a year, with the first four months at headquarters learning military drill, discipline and procedure, followed by five months on weapons and tactical training and seven months on seamanship and naval gunnery, with time at HMS *Excellent* and afloat in a ship. They spent nine months in theoretical military studies in the depot at Deal, then studied land artillery, electricity and searchlights at HMS *Vernon*, and finished with the study of administration and regimental duties.

The rank structure of the marines was almost identical to that of the army. An officer would be promoted to probationary lieutenant after three years' service, and was eligible to sit an examination for captain after that. These ranks were equated with naval ones, by a rather complex method. A marine lieutenant with less than four years' service ranked with a sub-lieutenant, after four years with a full lieutenant RN. A major was normally regarded as the equivalent of a lieutenant-commander, but when afloat he ranked with a full commander. Lieutenant-colonels commanded battalions or commandos; each had a major as a second-in-command, with majors or captains commanding companies, and subalterns (lieutenants and second lieutenants) in charge of platoons of about thirty men.

Training Bases

The Royal Marines obviously needed shore bases and in many cases they followed the pattern of the army, with barrack blocks, drill halls and parade grounds, armouries and rifle ranges. They had to be close to open country where the troops could exercise, but also preferred to be in towns with transport links and recreation facilities. In addition, marine bases needed some kind of interface with the sea, and close links with naval bases.

In peacetime the Royal Marines, perhaps even more than the seamen, were closely related to the home port divisions. There were large barracks at Chatham, Portsmouth and Plymouth where men lived between seagoing appointments and underwent training courses. There was also a depot at Deal in Kent, where all con-

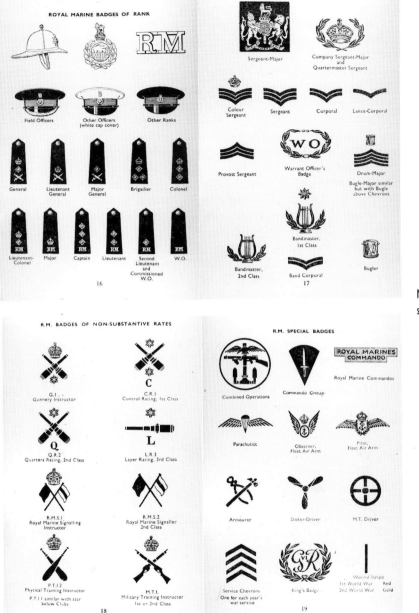

Marine substantive and non-substantive badges.

tinuous service recruits did their basic training and bandsmen learned their art. Fort Cumberland in Portsmouth was used for the development of the Mobile Naval Base Defence Organization from 1923 onwards, and some exercises in amphibious operations were carried out.

Early in 1940, as the conscript 'militiamen' came into the corps, a new camp was set up at Exton, also known as Lympstone, on the River Exe in Devon. This would eventually become the main initial training base for Hostilities Only recruits. The intake was reduced in October 1940 as the 7th and 8th Battalions were stationed there, and for a time only clerks, cooks and miscellaneous other ranks were trained there. Recruit training began again early in 1941 and 1800 men passed through in the next two months.[13] Up to 800 men arrived every month in 1942. In May 1944 it had 93 officers and 4160 men 'in various stages of training'.[14]

South Devon soon became a growth area for Royal Marine bases. A hotel in Thurleston, South Devon, was taken over in February 1941 as the main Officer Cadet Training Unit.[15] A new camp was set up Dalditch, 5 miles from Lympstone, during 1941. It started as a series of fields forming East Budleigh Common, divided into six areas with names such as Tucker, Triangle, Wheathill and Frying Pan Lines. By May there were 648 men on site, living under canvas in two of the areas, Nissen huts were constructed in each of the areas with two galleys, a 'Silent Recreation Room' and a Gymnasium. An advance party arrived in January 1942 and ten days later 660 men of the 10th Battalion moved in. Food had to be brought by road from Plymouth once a week, and water supply was arranged from a nearby reservoir. The biggest problem was with sewage disposal; because the cesspool was above the water table level, it tended to infect the drinking water.[16]

The second growth area was in North Wales, among the mountains, close to the sea and away from air raids and enemy submarines. The Royal Marines Training Group (Wales) was set up in 1942–43 in a string of villages along a 10-mile stretch of coast between Aberdovey and Barmouth. Towyn (Matapan Camp) and Barmouth (Crete Camp) were used to train landing craft crews. Peniarth (Gibraltar Camp) was also used for commando training. It had an early example of an endurance course, constructed by digging out the land round a stream and felling a tree to fall across it, so that the trainees had to go underwater to pass it. Then they ran up a muddy mountainside and fired five rounds at a target. Arthog (Iceland Camp) was for landing craft training. Llwngril (Burma Camp, or 'little Willy' to the troops) was the gunnery school and Llanegyrn was used to train assault engineers. Penally, just inland, was the Royal Marines Snipers' School.

Wartime Recruitment

The marines were little publicized in the years before the war, and the officers were 'rather smugly obsessed with their own obscurity', as Evelyn Waugh put it.[17] From a recruitment point of view, there was always the danger that they might slip between the army and the navy, and pamphlets emphasized that the marines offered the advantages of both. 'Service in the corps offers great attractions to lads having a liking for soldiering combined with service afloat.'[18] In peacetime there was a strong family tradition in the corps, with son following father, and that had some effect on wartime recruitment – many men with slight family connections seem to have opted for the marines. Also in peacetime, the marines took on recruits aged between seventeen and twenty-three, older than those for the seaman branch of the navy. The corps had a strong tradition of pro-active recruitment, and most of the staff of the Director of Naval Recruiting were in fact marines. In peacetime the corps was attractive to young men who were too late to join the navy as boys, but did not want to serve below decks as stokers.

This did not apply in wartime, when Hostilities Only men were taken on in all branches well over the age of eighteen. Instead, the marines relied on persuading young men of their virtues and advantages. In recruiting pamphlets, men were invited to specify the Royal Marines when registering their preferences. When Ted Ford went to the recruiting office he was told that he would not be able to join the navy because of colour blindness. 'I don't want the ***** Navy, I want the Marines.'[19] The uniform seemed more glamorous than that of the army, in advertising at least. Raymond Mitchell volunteered in 1940, 'after seeing a glossy poster depicting a Royal Marine, resplendent in pusser's "blues", complete with white helmet. Such men were obviously fighting "in big ships" so I put my name forward for that sort of war.' But he spent the whole war in khaki battledress, on dry land except when being transported by sea.[20] The blue uniform was rarely seen at Portsmouth by 1942, except on bandsmen and senior officers.[21]

However, shipboard marines continued to wear blue tunics during the war, albeit of inferior material and tailoring to the pre-war version. On leave this gave a great advantage over the army rank and file, who could only wear the shapeless, dust-coloured battledress. The popular association between marines and big ships continued during the war – in the highly-successful film *In Which We Serve* of 1943, Ordinary Seaman John Mills's brother-in-law wears a blue tunic on leave and asserts, 'Certainly see life in the big ships. … It's a damn sight more lively in a big cruiser than a destroyer.'

Basic Training

Royal Marines training, according to the handbook, 'must … embrace both Naval and Military subjects and include Naval Gunnery and the training of Infantry of the Line as laid down in the various army Training Manuals, modified by this Manual'. An officer had to be in possession of fifteen different books of reference, of which only two, the *Physical Exercise Tables* and the *Marine Training Manual*, were issued by the marines. The rest, including the *Field Service Pocket Book*, *Manual of Field Works*, *Manual of Sanitation* and the *Training and Manoeuvre Regulations*, were produced by the army. None were published by the navy proper.

The first part of pre-war recruit training lasted ten weeks at one of the depots. The syllabus included infantry drill, swimming, PT, general schooling, preliminary small arms training, company instruction and kit inspection. By the tenth week the recruits were considered able to mount guards on the barracks, after which they went on leave. On their return they learned boatwork, guards and fatigues and field training. After a total of forty weeks they were fully-fledged marines.[22]

Naturally this had to be abbreviated in wartime and in April 1940 two courses passed for duty on the same day, having started at different times. In May 1943 the initial course was increased from six to eight weeks.[23] Late in the war, J. E. Pollit started training as a regular at Plymouth. He was put under a corporal, who would follow the squad through all sections of training. He was assisted by a 'rear rank instructor', an acting corporal. They drilled, carried out field exercises, learned survival skills, and carried out live firing with naval guns at Penlee Point. They ended with parade ground training to fit them for overseas service.[24]

Marine Specialists

Though the marines had a far smaller proportion of specialists than the navy, selected peacetime recruits were able to train as cooks, buglers, printers, barbers, lamptrimmers, lamplighters (electricians) and dispensers, as well as horse and motor drivers, and motor driver mechanics. In wartime this was increased to include stoker drivers for landing craft. In peacetime, orderlies to officers of the rank of major and below were given a ten-week course, mainly in their operational duties ashore – map reading, verbal reporting and military organization.[25] Marines could also train as signallers or gunners, in the same way as seamen, and earn the same non-substantive ratings. The anti-aircraft rating was made available to them in 1943.[26] In peacetime, the third of the corps on shore spent a considerable amount of time in training. No less than 138 courses of varying length were on offer in April 1939 to March 1940, including thirty-four at army establishments, fifteen run by the navy, and two by the RAF. Eighty-seven were planned at the marine schools of music, land artillery, signalling, and physical and recreational training.[27]

The Technical Training Depot was at Fort Cumberland in Portsmouth, which became very crowded in wartime, and was frequently disturbed by air raids. It was divided into gunnery, searchlight and transport wings, with workshops and a tradesmen's unit which catered for sixteen different trades. It also trained a large number of driver mechanics for drafting to shore and air bases.[28]

Sometimes the marines relied directly on the army for the provision of training facilities. When the MNBDO was being set up in 1939, it was agreed that 'The War Office is to be asked to stop the intake of personnel at 4 Anti-Aircraft Training Regiments from 1st February 1940, and allot the accommodation to the M.N.B.D.O.' and a similar arrangement was to be made to train the crews of searchlights.[29] The other ranks for the Marine Brigade were also trained using War Office facilities and in January 1940 Churchill complained that 'the training of Royal Marines "hostilities only" men can only begin after March 1, when the necessary facilities can be given by the Army.'[30]

NCOs

In peace as in war, the non-commissioned officers, especially the senior ones (sergeants and above) were regarded as the backbone of the corps. Promotion in the non-commissioned officer ranks was done at 'Grand Division' level, so there were separate rosters for Chatham, Portsmouth and Plymouth. Seniority counted for a good deal in peacetime, and the corps journal, Globe and Laurel, published lists of NCOs in their order of seniority along with, just as important, the date when the enlistment of each man expired. 'Should a Colour Sergeant go to pension, three N.C.O.s have to be promoted. The Commandant studies the Sergeants' Roster and, examining the roster from the most senior downwards, selects one sergeant for promotion. In a similar manner the Corporals' and Candidates' Rosters are examined, one corporal and one candidate being selected by the Commandant for promotion.'[31]

The ranks of the non-commissioned officers were generally the same as the army. A corporal might command a section of eight to ten men on shore, or perhaps take charge of a magazine party in a ship at sea. A sergeant was the second-in-command of a platoon, while a colour-sergeant was usually either on administrative duties, perhaps as the quartermaster-sergeant of a company, or the company sergeant major, the senior NCO of the company. At this stage the comparison with the army begins to break down – an army company sergeant major was a warrant officer. A marine warrant officer, however, was the equivalent of a junior officer. He might be a warrant gunner, schoolmaster, superintending clerk, bandmaster or staff sergeant major, and in peacetime he wore an officer's uniform with Sam Browne belt but no badges. This was meaningless in wartime battledress, so a badge with the letters WO surrounded by a laurel wreath was introduced. The staff sergeant major served as the regimental sergeant major of a battalion or commando, but this caused confusion when serving alongside the army, for army warrant officers were never saluted.

In February 1940 the Admiralty defined its policy for future promotions within the ranks of the Royal Marines. Numbers of permanent NCOs in each of the divisions would be set at the level of the last peacetime Naval Estimates, 1939–40. Any promotions beyond that would be temporary, and the letters 'Ty' would be attached to the man's rank in any official paperwork, as in Corporal (Ty), to make sure there was no doubt. Even temporary promotions to the rank of sergeant and above could not be done solely on the orders of the unit commander, as the commandant of the division had to be consulted. All types of marine – regulars, recalled pensioners, reservists and HO men – would be eligible for temporary promotion on equal terms, though the divisional roster would only include regulars. At the end of the war, 'consideration' would be given to making some of the reservists' temporary promotions permanent; but 'no guarantee can be given at the present stage'.[32]

Officers under instruction by a drill sergeant, 1939. A drawing by Peter MacKarell.

By the end of the war there were three groups in each rank. Substantive Continuous Service NCOs were fully recognized in their divisional rosters. Temporary NCOs, either CS or HO, were appointed in addition to the peacetime establishment, but had a place in the permanent promotion structure. 'Ranks holding temporary promotions do not revert on ceasing to hold the appointment; as these ranks rise to the top of the substantive roster they are promoted to substantive rank (with a new date of seniority) provided that their quarterly reports have shown they are fit to hold the higher rank.' Acting temporary promotions, held by HO men only, ceased when a particular appointment ended and gave no rights for the future. NCO rank was taken very seriously in the marines. Commanding officers thinking of demoting a man were reminded that 'whereas Naval Ratings can regain their rate after a few months, R.M. N.C.O.s will take years to regain their rank if they regain it at all'.[33]

The marines had a policy of selecting potential NCOs early in their training. Recruits were invited to volunteer as recruit section commanders, at the rate of six per squad of fifty-six men. J. E. Pollet's corporal 'informed the squad that persons wishing to enter a Section Commander training class would have to have additional instruction three nights a week between tea and the evening meal and on completion of the course, which would last six weeks, there would be tests both written and oral.' He volunteered and found himself in a class of about thirty, weeded down to fifteen by the end of the week. He passed after being examined by the adjutant and 'that most fearsome of characters the Regimental Sergeant Major' and was allowed to wear a diamond on each shoulder.[34] Those who passed the course could be promoted to corporal after fifteen months' service, compared with a minimum of eighteen months for other recruits. The course's star recruit, the King's Badgeman, could be promoted after a year.[35]

Apart from specialists, the marines paid little attention to technical skill in the selection of NCOs. The qualities demanded in 1945 were power of command, leadership, initiative, zeal and energy, reliability and military bearing.[36] When assessed during and after courses, potential NCOs were put into four categories: 'definitely outstanding' and recommended for immediate promotion; 'in due course', when the man came to the top of the roster; 'not at present', until he had corrected certain faults of slackness or lack of leadership; and 'not recommended', when he had committed offences during the course, was seriously lacking in certain qualities, or had consistently poor reports.[37]

In peacetime NCOs were trained within the divisions, in command instruction, small arms and firepower, tactics and handling troops in the field, and 'interior economy'.[38] A separate NCO Training school was set up in 1940 and moved to operate alongside the officers' school at Thurlestone in 1941. Originally it was intended to take 480 candidates in eight classes of sixty in the first year, but only forty-five were available for each of the first two courses. By the time it celebrated its fourth anniversary in January 1944, it had trained 5835 junior NCOs and 105 sergeants. When it started all the candidates were continuous service men; by 1944 these made up only about 20 per cent.[39] In wartime the course lasted six weeks. There was no examination, but daily reports were compiled on each candidate and considered by a board at the end of the course.[40] The school moved to Deal later in the war where J. E. Pollet attended a course. As a diamond badge holder he had only nineteen months' seniority, but he found himself alongside less promising men who had served up to nineteen years without promotion. Because of the widespread use of temporary and acting-temporary ranks, the course also included acting sergeants who had to qualify for substantive corporals. Pollet found the course enjoyable, though men were weeded out continuously. '… at the end of each week you would see the occasional person packing his kit to return to his unit having failed during that week for one reason or another.' Even among those who completed the course, about 40 per cent failed or had their promotion deferred.[41]

Regular NCOs and warrant officers did not always mix well with HO men. Stan Blacker arrived at Matapan Camp in Wales from Dover.

> … onto the parade ground came an RSM [Regimental Sergeant Major], short and tubby like a barrel on legs, who when opening his mouth, had no face left to wash. He bawled and shouted his head off and ordered us to scrub our uniforms that day as they were dirty, but did not tell us where to dry them. It was pointless telling him that our uniforms were dirty through constantly cleaning and covering the guns at Dover with oil. It was the perfect example of what made CS [Continuous Service] and HO ranks not mix at times.

A few weeks later he was given further cause for resentment at Burma Camp nearby. He answered every question correctly during the machine-gun training session and was promised promotion to lance-corporal instructor. He was disappointed later when told that the post was reserved for a CS man.[42]

Officer Training

In October 1939 the Admiralty produced a three-part plan for the first stage of the expansion of the marine officer corps. The training of permanent service officers already in the system was to be accelerated; promotions from the ranks were to be increased; and fifty 'specially selected officers for temporary service' were to be enrolled. They would be at least nineteen-and-a-half years old and would be chosen by interview. They would be taken on as Temporary Second Lieutenants and promoted to Temporary Lieutenant after six months. They would not be available for service in ships' detachments, but would 'be trained for service in one or other special units'.[43]

This scheme was unusual for the time in that it allowed direct entry as an officer without any special qualifications. Potential army officers had to join as privates and be selected for officer training; naval officers had to do the same, unless they had some kind of sailing experience, and air force officers, by and large, were expected to be fit to fly or to offer specific engineering or administrative skills. The Royal Marines scheme was attractive to many and there were apparently 2000 applications for the fifty places, though it was not widely advertised.

John St John describes his interview with General Bourne.

> As he waved me into an armchair I spotted enough red tabs and crossed swords to suggest he was pretty important. He was in fact a major-general and adjutant-general of the entire corps of Royal Marines.
>
> … I sensed there had been a mistake, that I'd been ushered into the wrong office while the expected visitor, probably at least an under-secretary of state, was being interviewed by a recruiting sergeant in the basement. The telephone call finished, the general rapidly found my name on the list on his blotter and grinned a welcome, but then the telephone rang again. It must have rung at least five more times during the course of my interview and during the brief periods between calls there was only time to confirm the details of my education, to agree that I'd served in my school officer's training corps and passed Certificate A (Part I only), and to be asked what games I most enjoyed. Fortunately my mumbling about a "spot of mountain walking and an occasional swim" was lost in the clamour of the next telephone call.[44]

By far the most famous applicant was the novelist Evelyn Waugh. At the outbreak of the war he decided to throw himself into the struggle, but he was turned down by the Ministry of Information, the Naval Intelligence Division, the War Office and the Welsh Guards. He contemplated enlisting as a private, which would have produced some monumental culture clashes, but he was accepted as an officer by the marines, largely on the insistence of Winston Churchill. Waugh was given a medical examination and failed because of poor eyesight. This was overruled by an officer who pointed to a large advertisement across the street. 'Can you read that? … Anyway most of your work will be in the dark.' Because of his participation, the temporary officers' course which began at Chatham in December 1939 is perhaps the best-recorded of the war. Waugh wrote about it in his letters and diaries which were later published and he also fictionalized it in *Men at Arms*; his colleague John St John wrote about it, too, as did John Day and Patrick Ennor.

Fourteen men assembled in the Melville Barracks at Chatham on 10 December 1939, with similar numbers at Plymouth, Portsmouth and Deal to make up the fifty. Waugh was impressed with the courtesy and esprit de corps of the regular marine officers, but not with his fellow trainees. Only Michael Messer-Bennets, a solicitor from Plymouth, was anything like his expectations. John St John was 'a mild account-ant ... half highbrow'; Griffiths, a schoolmaster, was 'an ashen young man with a huge cavalry moustache from N Wales'; Hedley was 'a choleric-looking wine merchant of great girth'. The rest were 'pathetic youths for officers'. One of them, to Waugh's dis-taste, was 'a weedy youth with a cockney accent' who 'croons to himself & snaps his fingers'. It is still something of a mystery how such a group was chosen – perhaps a combination of Royal Marines' selection methods and modern ideas, with some Churchillian interference. According to Waugh it was 'very surprising for a force which is expected to be so tough'.[45]

During the first phase of training, the officers had to face yet another dichotomy. In the mess they were treated with great respect by senior officers – 'As soon as we arrived were surrounded by jiggering colonels and majors who stood us drinks contin-ually from 12 noon until 11 pm.[46] But on the parade ground they were under sergeants and treated like any other recruits. 'Lieutenant Wuff, press that rifle butt and keep your precious eyes to the front. To the front I said! You're not 'ere to collect daisies!'[47]

Waugh describes a typical day during this stage of training.

> Breakfast 7.30; parade 8.15; infantry drill, a tour of the quartermaster's ter-ritory learning among other things how to distinguish cat from rabbit by the number of ribs; 10.45 military law; 11.45 PT with degrading games that are designed to keep us gay and which in fact deny the natural dignity of man. Luncheon. Parade 2.30 and ID [infantry drill] till 4, after which the squad fall asleep in armchairs except for ambitious clerks who tried to ingratiate themselves with the sergeant by depriving him of his leisure with an extra drill 5–6.[48]

They also learned something of the marines' weapons, identical to those used by the army.

> Our new programme was small arms, which has meant continuous instruc-tion in the range on the mechanism of the rifle, Bren gun and anti-tank rifle, too little exercise, no fresh air, no interest – each in turn performing some mechanical trick with varying degrees of clumsiness. A charming colour-ser-geant instructor who regarded the whole thing with undisguised contempt.[49]

The course at Chatham was cut short to six weeks and the officers reassembled at Kingsdown after a week's leave, together with those who had trained at the other divisions. They also met the senior officers who would command the new brigade. Here the accommodation was much less satisfactory;

> a derelict Victorian villa surrounded by little asbestos huts which had been used in the summer as a holiday camp. One bath for sixty men, one wash-basin, the WCs all frozen up and those inside the house without seats.

Carpetless, noisy, cold. A ping-pong table makes one room uninhabitable, a radio the other. We are five in a bedroom without a coatpeg between us.[50]

Training continued at a higher level, mainly to teach the officers tactics; sand-table and tactical exercises without troops, or 'tewts'. Exercises on the snow-covered fields of Kent proved very difficult, but Waugh was proud that his suggestions often proved to be the 'staff solution'.[51] The programme was accelerated on what was originally planned and in February, rather than April, the officers moved to Bisley to take command of their troops for the first time, and to begin exercises as companies, battalions and brigades.

The Officer Cadet Training Unit

The direct-entry course was less successful than hoped. Waugh was probably not too far from the truth when his fictional Brigadier Ritchie-Hook told the officers, 'The rule of attack is "Never reinforce failure." In plain English that means: if you see some silly asses getting into a mess, don't get mixed up with 'em. ... This course has been a failure. I'm not going to reinforce it.'[52]

After that the marines began to adopt the army's policy by setting up an Officer Cadet Training Unit, or OCTU. The 8th Battalion, Royal Marines, was found to be redundant at the end of 1940, as the marine brigade was delayed in its formation and most of its men were drafted out to the MNBDO. The nucleus of officers and senior NCOs remained and in February 1941 about a hundred officers and men moved by road convoy to take over Thurlestone Hotel in an 'unusually picturesque village',[53] where according to rumour the colonel had spent his honeymoon.[54] It was in an isolated area 25 miles from Plymouth, and overlooked Bigbury Bay and the English Channel. They became the Royal Marine Officer Cadet Training Unit and the first class of cadets, HO 7, had completed their twelve-week course by mid April. By October 1942, potential cadets were sent on a preliminary course at the RM Small Arms School at Browndown near Portsmouth. By the end of the year they also did six weeks of preliminary leadership training at Deal, plus six weeks at Browndown, before going to Thurlestone.[55] The school had accommodation for 294 cadets, but it had 156 in December 1942 and only sixty-nine in May 1944, as the expansion programme wound down.[56]

Patrick Ennor, one of the original batch of trainees of 1939–40, was unhappy with the OCTU style of training.

I have always disliked the atmosphere of Cadet Training Establishments and this for serious as well as frivolous reasons. Unless the Commandant and his officers are able to keep an exceptionally close hold on everything I think there is a grave danger of far too much power and influence falling into the hands of the NCO instructors. I think the intensely competitive spirit amongst themselves which is inculcated into the cadets is the very antithesis of the team spirit which is regarded as of such importance. Certainly it is very different from the atmosphere which prevailed amongst us Second Lieutenants under instruction at Deal ... I think it is wrong that an NCO should be allowed to blackguard a cadet one day and be expected to salute him and regard him as a officer the next. I think that the end product is not a young officer but merely a super sort of private soldier. ...

In slightly less serious vein I feel that there should not be so big a gulf between those who are already officers and the potential officers. The cadets are all the time far closer to, and more under the influence of, the NCOs whom they are not required to resemble than the officers they are supposed to emulate. At the Royal marines OCTU at Thurlestone owing to the geographical layout of the premises, the Officers' Mess, the bedrooms and various offices and strategic points all seemed to be jumbled together.[57]

The Royal Marines participated in the navy's Y Scheme when it was set up in 1941. Since the marines needed relatively few technicians, they regarded the scheme as 'primarily a source of officer material'. Unfortunately standards were set too low on entry and the scheme was not a success; only about 25 per cent of entrants were commissioned. Some were sent on for further training as NCOs, but on the whole it was felt that a good deal of effort had been wasted, and expectations falsely raised.[58]

Canoeists

The Special Boat Section was set up in February 1942. It was to go to war in canoes, and its aims were beach finding and reconnaissance for amphibious operations, sabotage, landing and picking up agents, placing of flares to assist bombardments or landings, attacks on enemy shipping in harbour, and boarding of suspected vessels. Two training areas were set up in Scotland. Two officers and an NCO operated at Fort William training up to thirty-two men, and one officer and one NCO were stationed at Holy Loch on the Clyde to train thirteen men. Trainees would complete their basic training, followed by commando training. After that they would do a four-month course, during which they would do three weeks of navigation, one on map reading and six on canoe training including launching, maintenance and operating in surf; for more warlike purposes they would spend two on demolition, one on weapons, one on signalling and half a week on reporting and observing.[59] The canoeists took part on the famous raid on Bordeaux in 1942, later filmed, in a highly fictionalized version, as *Cockleshell Heroes*.

Marine Bands

Another function of the Royal Marines, since 1904, was to provide the bands for the whole of the Royal Navy. Each of the three divisions had its own band. In addition, a fleet flagship had a band of twenty-four men, a squadron flagship had seventeen men, any other capital ship, fleet aircraft carrier or large cruiser had fifteen, while a small cruiser had twelve. In battle they helped with the control of the guns. Joffre Swales and his fellow recruits were told,

at sea, your action station will be the gunnery nerve centre known as the Transmitting Station, and situated at the very bottom of the ship. There you will be positioned around a large table with glass top, below which are many moving needles and diagrams of your own and the "enemy" ship. When the enemy is sighted all visible and available information will be passed down to you from up top. You will plot these messages, sometimes known as "guff" into the clock, including your own and the enemy's speed, changes of direction relating to both ships, ballistics of the day, etc.[60]

There were 1400 boys and men in Royal Marine Band service at the beginning of the war, including 600 in the school at Deal.[61] Many naval officers would have preferred to have bands in naval uniform, as an aid to recruiting, and one observed, 'It must be a little surprising to the layman to note that the Navy is the only service not allowed its own official bands.' They advocated amateur seaman bands in the depots. This could work quite well in such places as apprentice training establishments, where the boys were likely to be there for several years; but in manning depots, the men could not be retained there without breaking drafting regulations.[62]

Boys aged fourteen to fourteen-and-a-half could join to train as marine bandsmen 'with only a slight knowledge of music'. Older boys, up to the age of eighteen, needed 'a more advanced knowledge commensurate with their age'.[63] Joffre Swales joined as an HO in 1940, after hearing of an advertisement on the radio – 'Musicians are required to serve afloat in the Royal Marines Band Service.' At Deal he found himself one of a group of thirty. '90 per cent of them were professional musicians from symphony and theatre orchestras, famous dance bands', work bands and miscellaneous ensembles. There was even a street busker, a capable violinist.'[64]

The Royal Marine School of Music was evacuated from the very exposed town of Deal. The Senior Wing went to the Norbreck Hotel, Scarborough, and the juniors to Howstrake Camp on the Isle of Man. In May 1944 there were 21 officers and 640 other ranks at the two bases, including 240 band boys.[65]

In August 1942, as the war approached its climax, the Hunter Committee reported on the future role of marine bands, to the amazement of the Director of Personal Services and the Head of the Naval Branch who commented '... it is by no means clear why this committee has put forward this document at this particular juncture in the war.'[66]

The Marines at the End of the War

After 1942 the Royal Marines began to develop in a different direction, with large parts of the corps devoted to combined operations, either as commandos or as crews of landing craft. By 1943 the aims of the Royal Marines had been re-stated.

A marine band on HMS *Rodney*, 1942–43.

1.   detachments for service in HM ships, while fully capable of manning their share of the gun armament, are specially trained to undertake such landing operations as the Naval Commander-in-Chief may find necessary to order.

2.   Units to undertake, in co-operation with other services, special amphibious operations.

3.   Units for the rapid establishment and temporary defence of Naval and Fleet Air Arm bases.[67]

Even that did not cover the full range of the marines' operations. For most of the war they manned the heavy guns firing over the Strait of Dover, operated as gunners in DEMS, and some officers served as pilots in the Fleet Air Arm, while a few NCOs transferred to become petty officer pilots. All this meant a move away from the parade ground discipline which was common before the war. Early in 1945 the Monthly Training Letter complained,

Saluting. – the point may be sublime or ridiculous; but the fact remains that there is something wrong with the saluting training in the Corps – the technique of drill or the salute itself.

Some say the beret has done it; others remember the lapse beginning well before the war. The fact [is] that only a proportion of the Corps now salutes with head properly poised and with the tip of the forefinger one inch above the right eye.[68]

By December 1944 the marines, according to the Admiralty, 'had been through many vicissitudes'. More than 7000 still carried out their traditional role as part of the crews of major warships, plus a few hundred more in Defensively Equipped Merchant Ships. Nearly 14,000 were engaged in operations in north west Europe, half in commandos and the rest in an anti-aircraft brigade at Antwerp, or with the Allied Naval Commander, Expeditionary Force, helping run captured ports. Nearly 18,000, about a quarter of the corps, were in combined operations. Almost 14,000 of these were the crews of landing craft, with others at combined operations bases, with an RM Assault Group or with two active-service battalions. Seven thousand men were attached to naval and Fleet Air Arm shore bases, mainly as motor transport drivers. There were still 743 marines at Scapa Flow, 666 repairing bomb damage in London and 335 manning the Maunsell Forts which guarded the Thames estuary against air attack. The five main bases – the three home ports plus Deal and Lympstone – had more than 10,000 men on their books, mostly base staff or men on long leave or long-term sick cases, but also with nearly 3000 trainees. In addition there were nearly 8000 men in the officers' school and the training camps in Wales, though recruiting to the marines was now frozen. The 2868 men of the anti-aircraft brigade at Antwerp were due to be replaced by the army, and two new, battle-hardened brigades of 4500 men each were to be formed from the existing resources of the corps.[69] These might have played a key part in the Pacific War, a marines' war if ever there was one, but the atom bomb intervened. The corps had survived the vicissitudes because of its amphibious nature, its great adaptability and unique esprit de corps. It had found a new and lasting role as water-borne shock troops of the British armed forces, and today all marines, except bandsmen, are commando trained.

CHAPTER 17

Combined Operations

The Setting up of the Combined Operations Organization

There had been remarkably little contact between the army and the navy during the First World War, mainly because of the nature of the conflict. Between the wars, the three services interacted mainly as rivals for government funding and popular support. There was very little central organization of defence and no minister until Chatfield was appointed for the 'Co-ordination of Defence' just before the war. Inter-service matters were dealt with at high level by the Committee for Imperial Defence, consisting of the chiefs of staff of the three services and various cabinet ministers.

Even after the Second World War started, it seemed possible to divide the conflict into three separate, self-contained areas. The army, as in 1914, would land on a friendly shore in France and when it was ready, perhaps in 1942, it would begin an offensive. The air force, if unleashed by the politicians, would launch a devastating air attack against Germany and bring it to its knees – in the meantime it would drop leaflets in the hope of damaging morale. The navy, as in 1914–18, would blockade Germany into starvation and eventually force the people to see sense and replace Hitler with a more moderate leader. All this, as with so much of British war planning, ended with the invasion of Norway and Fall of France in May and June 1940.

Churchill, on becoming Prime Minister in May 1940, also took on the role of Minister of Defence and personally supervised the work of all three services. On 17 July, eleven days after the Dunkirk evacuation was completed, Admiral of the Fleet Sir Roger Keyes was appointed to a new post as Director of Combined Operations. He was as experienced as anyone in amphibious warfare, having been at Gallipoli in 1915 and he was the hero of a famous raid on Zeebrugge in 1918, of which he never ceased to remind Churchill. He had his headquarters in Richmond Terrace in Whitehall.

Combined Operations, by definition, involved all branches of the armed forces and more than a few civilians such as merchant seamen, scientists, and factory workers. The greatest burden, however, fell on the navy. The air force bombed the enemy in his strongpoints and lines of communication, dropped paratroops to secure vital points, supplied photo reconnaissance and aerial spotting and provided air cover for the operation, but these were tasks which its aircraft and men are able to do anyway. The army provided the bulk of the personnel, but most of their training and equipment was to normal army standards, and unless there was a disaster they would soon move away from the beachheads to fight in normal army fashion. The navy, on the other hand, had to provide hundreds of ships to designs that were virtually unknown before the war and were no use for anything else. It had to man them, using hastily-trained conscripts who learned how to operate these vessels, but little else about the navy. Some 113,000 sailors were employed on amphibious operations in June 1944, and it would not have been easy to transfer any of them or their ships to other work.

Unlike other forms of operational training, amphibious warfare offered few chances to learn on the job. For the British there were only about half-a-dozen major landings during the war, culminating on D-Day in 1944. Everything had to be right when the invasion took place, but for years the soldiers and sailors involved might have seen no real action. The men of the Battle of the Atlantic were in danger for weeks at a time, but those of the amphibious forces went through many months of training, a few hours or days of intense danger, and then relative safety until the next operation took place.

Techniques had to be learned as they went along. Numerous small commando raids on the coast of Europe gave experience in landing techniques and some knowledge of the enemy-held coastline. The effects of major operations, such as the largely unopposed landing in Madagascar, the failure at Dieppe and the relatively easy successes in North Africa in 1942, taught planners about the need for headquarters ships, shore bombardment, beach groups and good communications, and to avoid strongly held enemy ports. During 1943 the landings in Sicily and mainland Italy were carried out against strong opposition. They provided essential practical experience for landing craft crews and their commanders. Successes and failures in different operations were reported on so that techniques at the training schools could be improved. Reports on the operations of signals units, for example, were sent to the school at HMS *Dundonald* for use in future operations.[1]

Training often had to be interrupted for actual operations. To mount the invasion of North Africa, Operation Torch, it was necessary to stop all combined training after the middle of August 1942 and to use landing craft crews which were not yet fully trained.[2]

Relations with the Army

Though the Fall of France caused rethinking of the role of amphibious operations, though the three services came to be dominated by Hostilities Only officers and men, the differences did not automatically decrease. The army's No. 8 Commando embarked on the Landing Ship (Large) Glenroy in December 1940, for training on the beaches of Arran, said to resemble the Mediterranean island of Pantelleria, which Keyes hoped to invade. Relations between the soldiers and sailors were appalling. The captain of the ship, a retired naval officer, was known as "booby" and "the old bugger on the roof". The junior naval officers, mostly volunteer reservists, were regarded by Evelyn Waugh as "jejune, dull, poor, self-conscious, sensitive of fancied insults, with the underdog's aptitude to harbour grievances". The army officers believed that they were first-class passengers with the navy as guard.[3] There was much to be done to create a cohesive fighting force.

Combined Operations' staff became aware that the soldier found himself in a very different world when he went on board ship.

> He wears heavy "ammunition boots" and his equipment is heavy and bulky. His equipment makes him liable to lose his balance if a ship lurches. His boots are not made for decks, many of them steel and many of them often wet. Nor do they make it easier for him to climb steep ladders or negotiate high coamings. The bulk of his equipment makes it extremely difficult to negotiate narrow gangways … Add to these difficulties pitch darkness and a desire to avoid all unnecessary noise, and one marvels that the troops manage so well, and appreciates the need of trained sailors to help and act as guides.[4]

Landing craft at Inveraray.

In the main Combined Operations base at Inveraray in 1945, trainees were told about the differences between amphibious and land assaults – 'The number of ships and craft available may limit strength and composition of the military forces. Reconnaissance limited. The lack of flexibility once units have been embarked ...' The stages of an assault were illustrated by diagrams. Different types of landing craft were illustrated with slides and their onboard accommodation was described. In a Landing Craft Infantry (Large) 'Troops are accommodated on troop decks, which are fitted with water fountains, latrines, racks for equipment, racks for rifles, limited cooking facilities, but plenty of hot water can be provided by the Royal Navy for making tea.' The vehicle deck of a Landing Ship Tank looked 'like a large garage'. The men were given lectures on how to relate to other services, particularly important for soldiers who might spend some time as guests of the Royal Navy. They were told about relative ranks in the Navy, the 'Dos and Don'ts for personnel of the Army and RAF when they are embarked in a white ensign ship' and about 'ship sense – the art of finding one's way about a ship in any circumstances'. The instructors were enjoined to 'tell a few anecdotes if possible' and allow time for questions.[5]

When Lord Mountbatten took over as head of Combined Operations in October 1941, the emphasis switched from raids on the enemy coast, to a full-scale invasion. The service became almost independent of the other three, and Mountbatten, rapidly promoted, was given a seat in the Chiefs of Staff Committee. The vocabulary which the navy had carefully instilled in its new recruits – cabins for rooms, on deck for upstairs, going ashore for leaving the base – was less than helpful in Combined Operations, and was discouraged. By 1944 many naval personnel had taken to wearing the Admiralty battledress for active service – not the dark blue version as adopted by the Fleet Air Arm, but in khaki, with naval badges, for use on invasion beaches. By that time the naval part of Combined Operations, having grown to 113 ships and 3979 landing craft and barges, manned by over 38,000 sailors in June 1943, had been identified as a private navy and in August it was re-absorbed into the rest of the fleet.[6]

The Vessels

Combined Operations soon spawned a host of new types of craft, usually known by their initials and highly confusing to the outsider. But despite the complexity combined operations vessels can be divided into categories by either size or function. Landing ships were relatively large, able to make the journey across an ocean if necessary, carrying small landing craft which they would lower or launch to take the men, vehicles, armament and supplies to the beaches. Some would carry infantry, others would transport landing craft, launching them by means of gantries or stern chutes, or using a floodable dock at the stern of the ship. The tank landing ship, however, would go right up to the beach to discharge its load of up to fifty vehicles. Major landing craft were more than 200 feet long and were able to make the complete voyage, sailing across a sea or an ocean and landing the men, stores and vehicles themselves. The Landing Craft Infantry (Large) had gangways down each side of the bow, which the men had to climb down, so were not used in the first wave of an assault. Minor landing craft, less than 200 feet long, were launched from ships to land on beaches. All had shallow draft and most had ramps in the bows for the troops and tanks to disembark on to the beach.

Within these three types there was a division by function, between those designed mainly to carry personnel, those carrying vehicles and their crews, and support craft which would go close inshore carrying guns or rockets to support the invading forces against enemy aircraft or shore artillery, or carry out other tasks such as aircraft direction. Landing Craft, Rocket, would fire salvoes on enemy positions at the moment of landing to keep their heads down. Landing Craft, Gun would go close inshore with the troops to engage enemy tanks and artillery positions. Landing Craft, Kitchen would feed landing craft crews and troops during the later stages of the operation. To add to the complexity, there was fast development in the circumstances, so each type either went through several marks, or fell by the wayside.

The Bases

Geographical considerations were perhaps more important for combined operations training bases than any others. Basic and technical training could be done almost anywhere, operational sea training needed clear areas of water, but amphibious warfare training needed that as well as suitable land areas in which to practice.

A holiday camp at Northney Island, near Portsmouth, was commissioned early in 1941 with the unimaginative title of HMS *Northney*. Landing craft crews, after their disciplinary training and induction to the navy, were taught the basic techniques. Further sites were taken over as the organization expanded. *Northney II* in Sparks' Boatyard started training landing craft stokers and engine room ratings in October 1942, and *Northney III* began training deckhands a year later. *Northney IV* was a repair base and *Northney V* was the former Sunshine Holiday Camp, used for seamen's preliminary two-weeks' training after the Mobile Naval Base Defence Organization moved out in 1942. The original camp, now *Northney I*, remained in use for training, and was the receiving base for all landing craft built from Cornwall to Essex. But the site was clearly too restricted, and too exposed to enemy bombing and reconnaissance, to become the main training station.

Inveraray, on Loch Fyne, was surveyed by a naval and an army officer in July 1940 and it was reported, 'From the naval point of view there is a suitable site for the anchorage at Kames Bay on the west side of the loch above Otter Ferry; a military camp is possible in the area of Inveraray Castle and on the park and golf course belonging to the estate.'[7] It was therefore chosen as the home of the Combined Training Centre (CTC) and commissioned as HMS *Quebec* in November 1940. According to Rear-Admiral L. E. H. Maund it was 'as far distant as possible from attack but yet within the umbrella of some fighter organization. … Here the rains might fall almost continuously, but it gave sheltered water and was, as it were, behind the defences of the Clyde.'[8] Vice-Admiral Theodore Hallet took command. The military camp was to hold 1200 men and a naval camp, initially for fifty officers, 300 ratings and the support of sixty landing craft, was hastily erected to the south-west of the town. Buoys were laid off Inveraray for a fleet of troop transports.[9]

One of the first to be trained there was Ordinary Seaman Rowland Draper.

The Majority of Inveraray's population of about 450 lived in stone houses gathered on each side of the one short main street. There was one shop, two hotels and a cafe. One house slightly larger than its neighbours sported a flagpole from which flew the white ensign; this was the admiral's house and naval headquarters. It was a peaceful scene with snow still hanging on the tops of the hills, but it was all due to change. Soon a naval camp was going to be built further down the loch, and camps to house troops which would be sent for training in combined operations.[10]

There were several useful beaches in the area. 'At the head of Loch Fyne there were sandy beaches with a rough hinterland of heath and heather; and there was an area some 2 miles long, near Strathlachan, where two companies could storm ashore firing all their weapons live, to the considerable disturbance of the MacLachlans of MacLachlan in their ancestral home of Castle Lachlan.'[11] A mock town was built at the head of Loch Fyne, with docks, houses and even traffic lights.[12]

With Inveraray becoming increasingly crowded, a new base was started in April 1941 at the southern tip of the Cowal peninsula. 'Castle Toward, opposite Rothesay, was requisitioned and an army of Nissen huts sprang up around the estate for the 6th Armoured Division to start their training.'[13] The new Combined Training Centre was commissioned as HMS *Ararat* (later renamed *Brontosaurus*). By October the base was offering a twelve-day course to armoured regiments, one arriving every week.

As part of the lend-lease agreement of March 1941, the United States Navy was allowed several bases in British waters, having failed to persuade the government of the Irish Free State to allow them to use Lough Swilly.[14] They chose Rosneath on the Gareloch in the Firth of Clyde, with the intention that it should be used for their destroyers and submarines if and when America entered the war. After Pearl Harbour in December 1941 most of the American destroyers and submarines were sent to the Pacific so Rosneath was not needed in its original form. In the meantime it was available for use by British forces. It was commissioned on 15 April 1942 as HMS *Louisbourg* after some time as an outpost of Warren at Largs and became, according to Mountbatten, 'the centre of our combined training area and all our plans were based on the assumption that we should be able to use it continuously.' Officers' accommodation was in the Ferry Inn at Rosneath and the men lived in eighteen Nissen huts, twenty-two to a hut.[15] But in July 1942 the Americans asked for it as a base for the training of Construction Battalions which would operate enemy ports after capture, and as a reception area for landing craft arriving from the United States.

Preparations for Operation Torch, the invasion of North Africa, were in train at the time and Rosneath was vital – 'it was not unlike telling a ship's captain that his bridge and engine room were being requisitioned, but he was to get on with the job all the same.'[16] Mountbatten protested, going as high as General Eisenhower, the American Commander-in-Chief. British forces were allowed to return, using it as a base for mounting operations in the Mediterranean, though they were cautious about putting down roots there.[17]

Other amphibious warfare bases in Scotland included the Tank Landing Craft Training Base at Bo'ness, HMS *Stopford*, commissioned in April 1942, which used LNER docks for its ships and the works of Bo'ness Hosiery for ratings accommodation. At Acharacle in the Ardnamurchan peninsula, Special Forces were trained at HMS *Dorlin*, situated in Dorlin House.

Army units, except those held in readiness in the Firth of Clyde for overseas operations, were mostly based in the south and east of England as a defence against invasion. For Combined Operations' training they were sent north for courses lasting from five to twenty-six days, needing fifteen trains a week at a time when the railways were hard pressed.[18]

In July 1940 General Wavell suggested a Combined Operations training centre in the Middle East, mainly to prepare army units for landings in the Mediterranean. A site at Kabrit, on the Great Bitter Lake in the middle of the Suez Canal, was chosen and began to operate in January 1941. It was highly improvised, with a houseboat as offices, a lecture room under an awning, a small pier, huts for landing-craft crews and tents for the troops. A few landing craft of different types were attached. Over the next few months similar bases were set up in North and West Africa, India and Australia.

Until late 1943 Loch Fyne remained the centre of tactical training in Britain. 'This was the only spot in all the United Kingdom where landing with the use of live ammunition was possible; and the rocky features of Barr nam Damh and Barr an Longeart bore no relation to the fat, flat pasture-lands at the back of the Normandy beaches.'[19] Five new sites for live training were found, one in the south of England, one in South Wales, and three in the north of Scotland.

A general move south began in 1943. HMS *Helder* was set up in yet another holiday camp at Brightlingsea in Essex in April 1942, to train minor landing craft crews. The evacuation of Dartmouth by the Royal Naval College allowed the site to be used as HMS *Dartmouth III* (later *Effingham*), for similar purposes. When the Fleet Air Arm left HMS *Medina* on the Isle of Wight in October 1942, it became another landing craft training base, with HMS *Manatee* at Yarmouth, also on the island. All these sites were some distance from the main cities so were largely free of bombing, but within river and estuary systems to allow training in sheltered waters.

By spring 1944 the Scottish bases had passed their peak and several training schools had been set up elsewhere. Even so, the dangers of the south coast were underlined in April when some German S-boats got among the ships of an American exercise and caused more than 600 casualties. The Clyde had launched operations against Madagascar, North Africa and Sicily when the greater distance from the objective, as compared with southern England, was insignificant. But the biggest combined operation of all time, the ultimate target of all the amphibious warfare training, was conducted at shorter range, across the English Channel. The ships for the invasion of Europe gathered in a wide range of ports, from East Anglia in the East to South Wales in the west. Force S, consisting of 28,000 soldiers and destined to form more than a fifth of the invasion force and capture Sword Beach, completed its training in Scottish waters and left for bases on the south coast of England in April 1944.

Training and Organization of Crews

Rowland Draper volunteered for 'boats' crews or something' after completing his disciplinary course and hanging around the barracks at Portsmouth waiting for a ship. He was sent to HMS *Northney* where he learned that he was to train to become part of a landing craft crew in Combined Operations.[20] Seaman entrants usually went to *Northney* for two weeks' preliminary training. In January 1943 it was proposed to turn over one of the basic training camps, such as *Ganges*, *Collingwood* or *Raleigh*, entirely over to Combined Operations training, but this was never implemented.[21]

Under a scheme proposed in August 1942, men at Rosneath would be trained in groups of six, representing the crews, including a coxswain and stoker, of a LCM. Each division would have three crews under an officer. After four weeks training some of the more promising men would be withdrawn and sent on courses as leading seamen or CW candidates. Other acting leading seamen would be drafted in from previous courses and the group would go on to train in craft at Inveraray. After two weeks some of the crews would be reduced to four-man LCA crews and the surplus men would go into a pool; the rest would remain as LCM crews.[22]

Stokers and Engineers

The engines of a minor landing craft were operated by a single 'stoker-driver', though it was accepted that the diesels were relatively easy to operate. 'There is no doubt that the actual running of an I.C. [internal combustion] engine is a comparatively simple affair and the main needs are that the starting and stopping drill should be learned correctly and the various systems operated properly.'[23] Admiral Ford was not been satisfied with conditions at Northney in 1942. 'The camp was ill-equipped for instructional purposes. Accommodation and general facilities were overcrowded … Owing to lack of instructional equipment too much time was occupied on theoretical instruction.'[24] Motor mechanics, already trained in the general principles of the engines, were given a three-week course, while stoker-drivers, each of whom would be the entire engine-room complement of a small landing craft, spent five (later seven) weeks there, living in workshop barges and working in a flotilla of fifteen landing craft. By June 1943 the stock of instructional engines had been built up and twenty lecture rooms were in use. A hundred stokers and twenty motor mechanics and ERAs were taken in every week.

By January 1943 *Northney* was turning out seventy-five stoker drivers a week after a four-week course, and Rosneath was producing twenty skilled personnel who had done a six-week course.[25] When Admiral Ford inspected *Northney* later in the year, it was mainly devoted to training marines as landing craft stoker-drivers. They were introduced to the principles of the internal combustion engine in the first week, then went on to practical work on specific types, especially starting and stopping routines. In the third week they learned about ignition, cooling and lubricating systems and about the auxiliary machinery. In the fourth week they learned mainly about administration, including the keeping of log books, and were shown films on engines and on the work of combined operations. Although much ground had to be covered by marines who had little previous experience of engines, Ford agreed that 'the instructional layout is very good, and much ingenuity has been used to make the layout simple and practical'. The second part of the course, lasting three weeks, was spent afloat running landing craft in Chichester Harbour. Ford had doubts about doing this in such sheltered waters, where the men had little chance to encounter the problems of seasickness.[26]

Minor landing craft needed more skilled engineers for maintenance, and each flotilla of twelve boats had an engineer officer, an engine room artificer and a stoker. Major landing craft each had one or two motor mechanics and up to three stokers. According to Ford they were trained by 'double-banking' or serving alongside experienced personnel. This was 'all right', but he would have preferred some kind of centralized instruction alongside this.[27]

Coxswains

Major landing craft, such as LCTs, were commanded by commissioned officers. The senior seaman rating on each, as with all ships of similar size, was the coxswain. In November 1941 it was accepted that such men, with five to eight seamen under them, should be leading seamen or above, sometimes transferred from the command of minor craft. In the minor landing craft, such as LCAs with a total crew of three and the LCMs with six men, the coxswain was in command. It was considered 'desirable' that they should be leading seamen or above, but this was not always the case.

In July 1941 Combined Operations headquarters was given authority to advance seamen to acting substantive rates on a temporary basis without reference to the depot rosters. The examination for acting temporary leading seaman (CO) included an oral test on the different types of craft and their characteristics, including 'dimensions, maximum carrying capacity, draught empty and fully laden, armour protection, speed and radius of action, maximum engine revs not to be exceeded normally and in emergency ...' There was a practical demonstration of boat handling, including going alongside, picking up a mooring, beaching and operating in surf. A candidate also had to demonstrate his knowledge of small arms.[28] In January 1943 it was noted that coxswains had little training in the use of the engines, which could be a problem if the stoker was put out of action. It was considered desirable 'that every officer and rating should be able to start, stop and keep the engines of his craft running'. A five-day course in engine work was proposed for coxswains, but 'It was pointed out that the urgent demand on instructors and engine room space to train the engineer personnel made even rudimentary training for other personnel very difficult.'[29]

Landing Techniques

Most of the training with landing ships took place in the Firth of Clyde and there was much to learn in the early days. According to Evelyn Waugh, in early 1941 'The boat training consisted of packing into ALCs [Assault Landing Craft] which the military seemed to consider an esoteric art requiring great practice, and letting the naval officers make a nonsense of the navigation.'[30] In May 1941, in the presence of Sir Roger Keyes, troops were landed on Arran from four ships. The transports anchored in line in Brodick Bay and the men were put into ordinary ships' boats. Most had no engines, so they were towed in strings by the powered boats and made the last part of the journey under oars. The whole process took hours.[31] The situation was much improved during 1941 as increasing numbers of specialized landing craft, with flat bottoms and bow ramps, came into use.

An important part of the technique was to let go the kedge (stern) anchor at the right moment, so that the craft could be hauled off the beach after the load was discharged. John Holden, an able seaman in LST 418, records,

> We were constantly wet through with rain and sea spray, doing endless landings on the beach from early morning to late evening. The worst part was if we lost our kedge anchor wire by dropping the stern anchor too soon. Apart from the skipper losing face in front of the other LSTs, it was a cold, wet job for a boat to fish for the cable with grappling hooks. The practice paid off, however, as we never lost our kedge anchor during operations in the face of the enemy.[32]

Inshore navigation was an important issue. In the case of landing ships, they had to find the 'lowering position', usually 7 miles offshore, where they would lower the landing craft, full of assault troops or tanks, from their davits for the final run to the shore. From that point the major and minor landing craft would have to work with considerable accuracy. According to the Director of Combined Training,

> The chief problem with which they will have to contend is the pilotage one, of finding the right beach within 100 yards at the right time. To train an officer or a coxswain to do this with any success requires considerably more than three weeks, in view of the instruction in Beach Pilotage, and Navigational Aids, as well as ordinary Pilotage that is involved.[33]

Specialist navigational landing craft, the LCN, provided part of the answer. They were equipped with chart tables and navigational aids, and staffed by highly-trained navigators. A Combined Operations pilotage school, HMS *James Cook*, was set up at Tighnabruaich in the Firth of Clyde in November 1942.

Group Training

Landing craft training, like all well-organized forms of training, was progressive. Men learned their individual skills as officers, coxswains, engineers, gunners and signallers and were brought together as crews. A report of November 1942 suggested that there were three needs for training landing craft crews: the general handling and navigation of the craft; the special handling during beaching; and handling in company with other craft at sea. Some officers thought this was the most difficult part of all.

> The special problems connected with beaching the Landing Craft and with the management of the troops embarked, are popularly regarded as the main

item in the training of Landing Craft crews. Actually however, they constitute the least difficult part of Naval Training. The average seaman can quickly be taught how to beach a Landing Craft and any officer of average power of command and common sense, can learn how to handle troops without difficulty. On the other hand the training needed to operate in company at sea is far and away the most difficult to provide. It calls for real experience in realistic conditions, which can only be provided by exercising in company in waters similar to those in which the force will have to operate.

Control of troops on board was less difficult when they went most of the way in landing ships, but in a cross-channel invasion this required some skill among the officers of major landing craft. They needed 'Ability to maintain discipline and an aggressive spirit both among the crews themselves and among the troops embarked, under conditions of exceptional stress through enemy action.' [34]

Unlike other parts of the service, Combined Operations' personnel did not necessarily go straight into active service, for they might wait months or years for a major landing operation. There was always a risk that training might become rusty and morale decline in the interval. Admiral Ford noted that novice stoker-drivers were 'red hot' in their keenness after training at *Northney*, but this quickly began to evaporate.[35] As individuals and small groups, the men might begin to feel that they were '"nobody's baby" and are just being moved at random like so much cattle'. One answer was to get the men into operational flotillas as soon as possible, perhaps during training itself. This provided 'ordered employment' for the men to 'build up and maintain the fighting spirit, professional progress, discipline, and hardihood.'

> When a Flotilla completes its training course at Inveraray, it should be given a number, and given 7 days at a suitable place to work up as a Flotilla. The Flotilla should continue as an entity and though it may be necessary to move personnel (other than dilution) for various commitments, this should be done on the basis of the crew, not as individuals. When they have finished that commitment, they should rejoin their flotilla.[36]

The working-up period was quite short, according to Admiral Syfret in 1944. 'The period between manning a new Major Landing Craft and that craft taking its place in an operational force, has now been reduced to six weeks, including time for working up and making coastal passages.'[37] After that they began to train in ever-larger groups, in theory at least.

> Assumed to be trained as a ship's company, we joined a flotilla of twelve craft. We practiced certain manoeuvres, mostly in moving as a flotilla and in working by signal flags, or radio-telephony. We formed, wheeled and turned, and drove on to beaches together. We should have learned the trick of taking onboard and landing tanks and vehicles, but there was no time to advance as far as that. D-Day was coming nearer, and after a few weeks training as a flotilla we moved south. At a West Coast port we joined three more flotillas and were part of 'Q' Squadron under a Lieutenant-Commander of the Royal Navy. Four days after we joined the Squadron, hardly knowing our new mates, and not having worked up with them at all.

We continued to Plymouth. That was two weeks before D-Day.[38]

Marines in Landing Craft

By 1942 the Royal Marine Division had become redundant, as had the Mobile Naval Base Defence Organization. In July 1943 the First Sea Lord, Mountbatten as Chief of Combined Operations and the Adjutant-General of the marines agreed that marines, apart from those on ships or in specialized tasks, would be trained either as commandos or as landing craft crews. It was agreed that 'there is no better disciplinary training, and that required by the Jack-of-all-trades, than that given by the Royals.'[39] The adjutant-general would be responsible for their training except when they were attached to naval training establishments for special courses. They would remain under the command of their own officers as far as possible; craft would be commanded by marines, who would also be in charge of flotillas and divisions.[40]

Initially it was planned that this would apply mainly to smaller landing craft, which were boats rather than commissioned warships. But Landing Craft Flak (Large) were intended to take anti-aircraft guns close inshore mainly to protect the troops who had already landed. They were manned mainly by Royal Marine gunners, as they would be closer to the needs of the army than naval gunners. Each ship was commanded by an RNVR lieutenant with another RNVR officer as navigator. Under them were two Royal Marine officers and forty-eight men. Was it really necessary to have them under naval command? There was much debate about this in the Admiralty in the summer of 1943. If Royal Marines were allowed to command commissioned warships it would be a 'somewhat revolutionary change' and 'a marked departure from tradition'. One officer suggested 'It will introduce yet another unusual feature in the Combined Operations Organization.' It was questioned whether this was legal under international law, but that only demanded that a commissioned officer of the state in question be in charge, and did not specify which service. In September it was agreed that Royal Marine officers would command landing craft where more than 70 per cent of the complement were marines. This included Landing Craft Flak, Gun and seven other types. They would also serve in minor landing craft embarked in a Landing Ship (Infantry), or in flotillas allocated to a Combined Operations base or disembarked from an LCI. In naval establishments with more than 300 marines, the RM officer would be in full charge of their discipline.[41]

In October 1943 it was ordered that Royal Marine officers in landing craft were to be given 'every opportunity of gaining experience in navigation and shiphandling and should be employed as Officer of the Watch at sea.' It was soon noticed that 'all R.M. Officers in Major Landing Craft are very keen on their Naval duties, and the granting of Watchkeeping Certificates would do much to reward their efforts.'[42] They began to attend the Major Landing Craft Officers' Qualifying Course, where they learned about ship administration and the duties of commanding officers, as well as seamanship and navigation.[43]

Men selected for Combined Operations were sent to the camps in North Wales after their disciplinary training, or on transfer from other duties. After a week of kitting up and tests at Towyn they went to Peniarth for six weeks' basic seamanship and infantry drill, then to Llwngwril where they were allocated to U squads to learn seamanship and gunnery, or V squads who would have an introduction to engineering. The U squads trained in boats at Barmouth for two weeks, while the potential stoker mechanics went to the naval course at Hayling Island near Portsmouth. The V squads were given psychological tests and divided into coxswains, signallers and deckhands. They, too, went to Hayling Island to learn more seamanship and elementary pilotage.[44] In August 1943 the training group in Wales had a monthly intake of around 1600 men. That month it sent 348 of them to Northney Island to train as engine room hands, 961 to HM ships *Helder* and *Effingham* to train as deckhands and 108 to HMS *Fisgard* to become signallers.[45]

Roy Nelson describes his progress in the spring of 1944.

> I was in U 20 Squad – we were allocated to either U (coxswain and deck hands) or V (stokers) squads. Our instructors were mainly RN personnel, and for 3 weeks we had basic seamanship training. Then it was on to Burma Camp for gunnery training in light ack-ack Oerlikon, pom-pom and Vickers guns. At the conclusion of our gunnery the next stop was Iceland and I recall that on transfer we marched to the next camp. Our accommodation in a row of large Victorian houses was adjacent to a jetty on the foreshore of the river. It was here that we finally got to see a landing craft, old LCPs [landing craft, personnel] being used for our handling instruction. We would be taken out by our instructor into Barmouth Bay and there practise our newly acquired seamanship and take turns at the wheel.[46]

F. C. Adams had served with the MNBDO in the Middle East and was sent to Wales early in 1944, where he was selected to train as a coxswain.

> If all our previous training was hard then what we were about to face exceeded this by far. For a start we had hardly any time to ourselves and what time we had was never really taken up, for after the daily stint we were all too tired. As soon as one period of instruction was over there would be an officer or naval Petty Officer waiting to take over. If morse code training was followed by PT then one only had a few minutes to change. Seamanship would be followed by a talk on aircraft recognition, then someone else would take us on operating the Browning machine-gun and next instruction on Ford V8 engines. It seemed that the coxswains had to know everything that concerned landing craft and the running of them.[47]

One interesting feature of the landing craft training at Iceland Camp near Barmouth was the passage under the railway bridge on the river there. Trainees quickly came to appreciate the importance of tidal streams and some of them were pushed against it by strong currents.[48]

Captain J. A. Good began a course in the Landing Craft Gun (Medium), a vessel which could carry two 17-pounder guns close inshore, along with three more CS officers and two Hostilities Only men. The trained in 25-pounder field gun drill at Eastney, then in the theory of field artillery at Llwngwril. They went to the school of artillery at Larkhill. 'Salisbury Plain had never before experienced the sight of pairs of self propelled guns driving over the ranges in echelon, crewed by Naval and Marine Officers, stopping from time to time to simulate a LCG(M) beached, and loosing off a salvo in the direction of Devizes.' He completed his training with pilotage at Whale Island, Portsmouth.[49]

By February 1944 there were nearly 9300 marines serving in landing craft.[50] Many seamen were transferred from minor to major landing craft, so marines operated more than half the assault craft in the British sectors during the invasion of Normandy.

A naval beach commando at Normandy soon after the D-Day Landings.

Beach Commandos

Naval parties to control the work on the landing beach were first formed during the Madagascar landing. The idea began to emerge after the ships sailed in March 1942, and a party was formed on each of the half-dozen ships carrying the troops. By October that year more formal groups were being organized. Mountbatten ruled out the name of 'Beach Parties', but not for the obvious reason that it would give an unwarranted impression of seaside leisure which would appeal only to dilettantes. More important, the hardened seaman regarded a 'party' as a group detailed for unpopular work, and he insisted that they be called 'Beach Commandos'. They would direct the movements of landing craft and maintain links with the much larger army units, which would defend the beach from air and sea attack and control the road movements off it. Members of the commandos would have to be 'able to endure hard work for long hours with little food' and 'live in the open for up to a week'.[51] A naval beach commando would consist of seven officers as principal and assistant beach masters, with forty-eight ratings for each army brigade front.[52] The first formal beach group, lettered C in deference to the ones which served at Madagascar, was formed at Coulport House in the Firth of Clyde in the spring of 1942. Others were formed – HMS *Armadillo* in Glenfinnart and at Inveraray until November 1943, when the lettering reached W.[53]

Beach commandos were trained at HMS *Dundonald* near Troon in Scotland. The three services worked together to ensure co-ordination. Petty officers, according to Mountbatten, needed above average 'power of command' in order to take control of disorientated parties of men from other services wandering around the beaches. For promotion they were examined in the relative ranks of the services, in beach drill and in handling the lines and anchors of craft coming ashore. They needed to know the characteristics of different types of craft, as well as the duties of such obscure acronyms as SNOL, SNOT, MLO, B Mr and ULO. They learned to use a loud hailer, and the characteristics of different types of weapons.[54]

Signals

Signalling was an important issue in the control of landings, both between the landing craft in their flotillas, and among the different services to call up air or artillery support, to warn of dangers or to alter plans. However the three services had developed their own systems of signalling over the years. Mountbatten, a wireless officer, took a special interest in this. A Combined Signal Board was set up at Inveraray in the autumn of 1940, with an officer from each of the three services. A signal school followed in November 1941, situated, like many another wartime organizations, in a collection of forty-five Nissen huts. It soon became apparent that further RAF input was needed, but there was no airfield near Inveraray. In April 1942 the school moved to Dundonald near Troon, close to the airfields at Ayr and Prestwick. It was commissioned as Dundonald II. The centrepiece was a mock-up of a headquarters ship, but personnel were also trained on landing craft in the Firth.[55]

Two types of ratings were drafted to *Dundonald* from the depots for one-month courses. Some were to remain with Combined Operations as crews of landing craft and with beach groups. Others were from general service, to learn about liaison with the new branch. Signal officers were usually newly-commissioned RNVRs, who were given a course of one month to become Combined Operations' Communications Officers or COCOs, and then went on to more specialized training in minor or major landing craft, or beach groups. Eventually 250 of them passed through the course.[56]

Pilotage Parties

In January to February 1941, as an operation was planned against the Dodecanese Islands off Greece, it was realized that the means for reconnaissance were inadequate. Existing charts and pilot books were often out of date or lacking in detail; air reconnaissance said nothing about the heights of obstacles, and could not identify them underwater; and there were no marks to identify the correct beaches. Lieutenant-Commander N. C. Wilmott began to train men in beach reconnaissance in November 1941, with the intention that they would be taken to the area by submarine and landed by canoe to make detailed surveys. HMS *James Cook*, at Tignabruaich on the Firth of Clyde, began to train Combined Operations' Beach and

Pilotage and Reconnaissance Parties, until the name was changed to Combined Operations' Pilotage Parties (COPP) for security reasons. The size of each group was limited to about ten, the number that could be reasonably carried in a submarine. Each would consist of a naval officer in charge, an army engineer officer, with two more naval officers as assistant and maintenance officer. The six ratings would include seamen to paddle and to measure the depth of water, an electrical artificer for maintenance of complex equipment, a marine commando as paddler and guard to the engineer officer and an army draughtsman.

As well as *James Cook*, a school was set up at a yacht club on Hayling Island near Portsmouth. The training was intense and highly varied. At first officers had two months on reconnaissance techniques and two more on Combined Operations subjects such as photo interpretation, beach pilotage, craft manoeuvering signals and naval and military beach work. This was found to be 'far too short and strenuous, from the medical point of view, for pupils and particularly for staff, and medical casualties resulted'. In autumn 1943 the reconnaissance training was increased to three months. It was largely done by night, with many exercises followed by analysis of the results. It was found to be impossible to train more than two units at a time, because there were eight categories of personnel in each team and training had to be individual. Ratings and army other ranks had a slightly shorter training, but had to learn a good deal of maintenance work such as joinery and sailmaking for the repair of canoes, and radio repair. Eventually ten COPPs were formed.[57]

Artillery Support

The Dieppe raid of August 1942 showed, among other things, that overwhelming artillery support was needed before, during and after a landing. The heavy guns of the navy had to stop their bombardment before the actual landings. The battleships and cruisers could stand offshore and bombard enemy positions from a distance, at a range of up to 25 miles. These were generally low-trajectory guns, so it was difficult for them to fire over ships and men. Furthermore, a 15-inch shell could not be aimed within 1000 yards of friendly forces, because of possible inaccuracies and the spread of the blast. Smaller shells, from destroyers and cruisers, could not be aimed within 500 yards.[58] Special landing craft had to be developed to go close inshore with the troops where they could engage individual targets. Landing craft were fitted with guns at Inveraray as soon as the CTC opened there, but experience showed that ever-larger ones were needed and development continued over the years. In October 1941 the captain of the cruiser HMS *Cardiff*, based at Lamlash, identified a suitable gunnery range on the shores of the Kintyre peninsula and a gunnery school was opened at Inveraray soon afterwards.[59]

Bombardment units were formed, mainly of army personnel, to direct the fire of naval guns as the army moved inshore. Naval telegraphists and signallers were attached to them, and by the time of D-Day each group included twenty-one naval telegraphists, a petty officer telegraphist and a COCO in charge. A group of three telegraphists was attached to each Forward Observer Bombardment, and seventeen signal sections had been formed by that time.[60]

Lochailort

In 1942 it was realized that many new officers would be needed to command medium-sized landing craft and to lead groups of smaller craft. The proportion of officers to ratings was much higher than in the navy as a whole; the most common types of tank landing craft, the LCTs, needed two officers and ten men each. The officers did not need all the skills of a fully-fledged naval officer, for example in ocean navigation, so a special six-week course was set up to train them – compared with three months for a normal wartime officer and six years in peacetime.

An army camp at Lochailort, between Fort William and Mallaig in west Scotland, was transferred to the Navy and thus began the 'Lochailort System', giving considerable prominence to a village which has been described as 'little more than a place-name with a telephone kiosk.'[61] The geography of the new camp was not very different from others in Scotland. At a 'respectful distance' from the house, 'Nissen huts were scattered around the parade ground with its white ensign flying. Larger huts housed the gymnasium, the main lecture and cinema hall and the mess.'[62] The camp was served by the West Highland Railway from Fort William with its two trains a day – those who dropped out of the course were put on the 1.43 to return to their units.

Initially there was some confusion about the type of entrant wanted for the course. The commodore of the Royal Naval Patrol Service was horrified when seven out of ten of the men he recommended were sent back as failures. They were men who had already had one try at officer training, failing the more regular course at *King Alfred* at a time when the demand for officers was much lower, and since then had spent much time on the lower deck. They were, according to Commodore de Pass, 'men of quality though not of great polish … experienced men of character and purpose'. They spent much of their time on the course helping out young men with no experience of the sea and were mortified to find that the young men passed while the older ones failed. The commodore suggested that this meant 'Practical seamen are not required. It was a question of education and accent.' In reply, Combined Operations' Headquarters commented tartly that 'although candidates selected for Lochailort may be above average in the Patrol Service they do not compare favourably with candidates from other sources.' However, it was agreed to modify the standards on the course, that the priority was 'leadership and practical seamanship' and the Naval Assistant to the Second Sea Lord directed that 'no candidate shall be unnecessarily rejected.'[63]

At first sight the experience of the Patrol Service ratings might seem to conflict with the welcome Lieutenant Munford gave to a new course early in 1943. 'I will warn you of one thing – I don't like failures. My last Division passed one hundred per cent – Munford's Marvels they were called. Let's see that you do likewise!' It soon became apparent that failure had several meanings and many men were weeded out before the final examination. 'But among Munford's Marvels "red lights" would generally begin to glow early on. After a fortnight three or four disappointed men might be told to catch the 1.43 train, while another one or two, unable to stand up to the physical aspects of the course, would resign of their own free will. Lieutenant Munford would have thus weeded out his doubtful finishers and be determined to bring the rest through one hundred per cent.[64]

Though Lochailort was considered less formal than *King Alfred*, officers could not neglect the social graces. 'There was a Wren petty officer in attendance to note every false move with the cutlery. Every knife filled with peas, every roll cut instead of broken, every spoonful of soup scooped from the wrong side of the plate, could count against them – or so they had been told.' Though motor boats were provided for training on the Loch, the course had a strong emphasis on drill, on physical training including boxing, and on gruelling expeditions over glens and mountains. Much of this would not be very helpful of landing craft commanders. 'Most of their time at sea would be spent standing on the bridge of an LCT or an LCI or in some minor landing craft; and the strain would not be so much physical as mental – keeping awake and alert for very long periods of duty and being able to go for long periods without rest or sleep.'[65]

At the end of the course, successful candidates were summoned to the castle for tea and cakes with the staff and given first-class rail warrants home, though they were still wearing ratings' uniform. Many of them would later undertake further training and become fully-fledged officers.

Royal Marine Commandos

The Commandos were set up in 1940, at the instigation of Churchill. Their aim was to take the war to the enemy, by means of daring raids on his now extensive coastline. The word 'commando', derived from the Boer units of the South African War of 1899 to 1902, in which Churchill had been a war correspondent. Originally it meant a new type of military unit, larger than a company but slightly smaller than a battalion, with every man ready for action and no administrative tail. Soon the name was transferred to the troops themselves, who came to be know as 'commandos', though the word also survived as a unit title. The first commandos were mainly drawn from volunteers for the army. The marines supplied some expertise and support, and Evelyn Waugh was one of those who were detached in 1940. 'You need have no misgivings about my prestige,' he wrote to his wife. 'Everyone in the army is competing feverishly to get into a commando and it is more glorious to be a subaltern here than a captain in the R.M. Brigade. It is also a great deal more enjoyable'.[66] But the Royal Marines as a whole stood aloof. As a unit which had not been seriously disrupted in the retreat to Dunkirk, the Royal Marine Division was needed for home defence during 1940. It sent forces to occupy the Faroes and Iceland, and in August it took part in an abortive expedition to Dakar, so it had no men to spare. Furthermore, the Adjutant General was determined to keep the Royal Marine Division intact.[67] This began to change late in 1942, when Mountbatten was in charge of Combined Operations.

The first marine commando was formed in St Valentine's Day 1942 from volunteers within the corps, answering a signal to ships and bases – 'For the attention of all Royal Marine trained personnel – volunteers required for special duties of a hazardous nature.' Marine J. Forbes wanted to 'escape from the tedium of depot duties' and sought 'excitement and adventure',[68] as did many others. The unit attracted men from all the divisions and ships at sea, and assembled at Deal Barracks, largely vacant since most of recruit training had moved to Devon. They were addressed as the 'Royal Marines Commando' for the first time, giving a clue about the duties involved. Medical examinations and strenuous training weeded out many of the volunteers, but others came in and by the end of March the unit was up to its strength of 446 officers and men. Early in April it moved to Scotland, not to the established army commando training base at Achnacarry between Loch Lochy and Loch Arkaig, but to HMS *Dorlin* at Acharacle. This was 20 miles over the mountains to the south west, on the sea in Kentra Bay, where landing craft were available.

A marine battalion had an establishment of over 750 men, whereas a commando needed around 450, as it had no tail and had a different organization; instead of companies of about 200 officers and men and platoons of about forty, it had six 'troops', usually lettered A, B, P, Q, X and Y in the style of gun turrets in a capital ship.

Each had three officers and about sixty men, and the commando also included a heavy weapons section and a signals company.[69] The new group, to be known as A Commando, did not adopt this at first, but modified the traditional structure.[70] On 18 May, after six weeks of training, they moved to the Isle of Wight where they continued training and were part of the local defence against invasion.

On 7 October 1942 the men of the 8th Battalion, Royal Marines, were told of their orders to convert to B Commando (later 41 Commando). Cooks and administrative staff were no longer needed, as the men would be billeted in civilian houses. According to one of its members,

> ... there was still considerable scope for shedding those men who were either unfit or unwilling to change roles voluntarily, or who should be weeded out as a matter of policy. For the vast majority, however, it would have been a major affront not to have been accepted, so there was a cliff-hanging period of expectancy until the morning of Saturday 10 October. Then the whole battalion was paraded to learn their fate man by man, all those who were 'in' were detailed off to their Troops in the new Commando.[71]

Three of the troops went to Weymouth to learn from A Commando. The rest continued at Llanion Barracks in Wales until November, when they were posted to the Isle of Wight. Early in 1943 they were sent north for the main phase of their commando training. After a 30-hour journey they de-trained and were double marched for 5 miles to their training camp at Achnacarry.

Officers already knew that they would forgo the privileges of rank. They would live in tents, with no servants to clean their uniforms, or hot water to bathe. They would follow the same syllabus as the men and carry the same loads into action. It was very different from peacetime life in the wardroom of a battleship. In contrast to the parade ground discipline of the rest of the army and marines, every man in a commando was expected to be motivated and self-reliant in any situation.

The commando training range at Achnacarry in the Scottish Highlands had been in use by the army since November 1941. It was based on a house taken over from Sir Donald Cameron, with many miles of surrounding countryside for training. It was supervised by Lieutenant-Colonel Charles E. Vaughan, a former regimental sergeant major in the Brigade of Guards, who set up an intensive and demanding programme. 'Speed marching' was a major feature of the course, as established on the march to the base. 'The speed marches progresses from a 5-miler in forty minutes, to a 7-miler in some fifty-five minutes, and eventually to a 15-miler in two-and-a-quarter hours ...'[72] There was unarmed combat with 'malignant' instructors, and several notorious tests, including the toggle bridge, made up from pieces of rope with toggles carried by each man. Trainees had to cross it, a precarious enough operation in itself, while thunderflashes and ammunition exploded underneath them. The 'death ride' consisted of a rope attached to a tree high up on one bank of the River Arkaig, with the other end on a lower tree on the opposite bank. The trainee slid down the rope on a toggle, making sure it was taut to prevent him falling in the river, where live ammunition was exploding. The 'Tarzan course', as its name suggests, consisted of rope swings, single rope bridges and grapping nets. The course concluded with a Night Opposed Landing Exercise, in which live ammunition was used by instructors who were trained for shoot to miss – but accidents did happen.[73]

Six more commandos were formed in August 1942, mainly by converting Royal Marine Battalions; a ninth (48 Commando) was formed at Deal in March 1944. Combined Operations was one of the great successes of the war, opening new fields of military endeavour and breaking down permanently the barriers between the services. Though it languished for ten years after the war, it then became one of the two or three principal activities of the Royal Navy.

CHAPTER 18

The Wrens

Foundation

The Women's Royal Naval Service had first been formed in 1917, when the idea of women in military uniform was new and radical. The army formed the Women's Army Auxiliary Corps in January, and the navy started the Women's Royal Naval Service in November that year and adopted the initials WRNS, which became a very early example of an acronym, as the Wrens. It was a fortunate choice, which gave it as strong an identity as any women's service in the world. At its peak the service included 7000 women. The service was disbanded immediately at the end of the First World War, but it had 'left its mark so indelibly on its members'.[1] Many of them kept in touch with one another throughout the inter-war years.

Between the wars, women were half liberated from their grievances of the Edwardian era. They gained the vote in two stages, and had it on equal terms with men by 1928. Some women had entered the professions as doctors and lawyers and others served in the more traditional role as teachers. Some from the lower middle classes worked as clerks and typists. Working class women had long been employed in factory work, especially in the textile industry in the north of England, and in catering and domestic service. There were few opportunities for a career.

In 1939 the government began to make plans, beginning where they had left off in 1918, and recruitment of women was immediately accepted as policy. An advertisement was placed in the newspapers.

> WOMEN'S SERVICE IN THE ROYAL NAVY
>
> A number of women (initially about 1500) will be wanted to take the place of Naval and Marine ranks and ratings in Naval Establishments upon secretarial, clerical, accounting, shorthand and typewriting duties; and domestic duties as cooks, stewardesses, waitresses and messengers.[2]

About ten women applied for each place.

Mrs Vera Laughton Mathews was appointed as director of the revived service. She was the daughter of the great nineteenth-century naval historian, Sir John Laughton. In her youth she had been a suffragette, but she served as an officer in the first Wrens from 1917. Between the wars she married, worked as a journalist and served as a Commissioner of the Girl Guides. She became chairman [sic] of the St Joan's Social and Political Alliance in 1932 and represented it in the League of Nations. As well as her experience inside and outside the naval establishment, she had great energy. Her momentum during numerous visits to naval bases earned her the nickname 'Tugboat Annie'. She stayed in the same job for the whole of the war and was able to grow with it, whereas men tended to change job every two years or so to gain experience of active service.

Her letter of appointment described her duties.

You will be responsible to the Board of Admiralty for the recruitment, efficiency, welfare and discipline of the Women's Royal Naval Service, and your duties will include all matters concerning the entry, promotion, accommodation, medical attendance, pay, allowances, traveling expenses, leave of absence and retirement or discharge of members of the service.[3]

Terms of Service

Mr A. S. LeMaitre, head of the Civil Establishments Branch at the Admiralty in 1939, first suggested that the term 'Wren' could also be used as a rating title, so non-commissioned women became Wrens, Leading Wrens and Chief Wrens. The rating of Petty Officer Wren was established soon after the start of the war, so that women's ratings corresponded to men's. They wore the same badges, of anchor, crossed anchor and three brass buttons.

There was a great deal of scepticism about the revival of the Wrens within the navy. It was placed under the CE, or Civil Establishment, Branch, implying that they were civilian workers rather than members of the service. Initially wrens were expected to be 'immobile', that is they would be signed on to serve at a particular naval port, travelling to work daily from the family home. The 'mobile' wren was introduced tentatively, when a semi-official list was drawn up in headquarters; it was legitimized just before the war. Though the emphasis swung towards the mobile Wren over the years, the immobiles survived. 'Mike' Crossley enjoyed their presence while training as a fighter pilot at Yeovilton.

> The 'immobile' part of their title was intended to remind the naval appointment authorities ... that these particular Wrens were not volunteers for any job but only the one which was near their home. They therefore lived at home in splendour, knowing they could not be posted to Singapore, Colombo or Scapa Flow. Their mums were keen that they should meet a good cross-section of Fleet Air Arm officers. There were therefore plenty of party invitations for us. We played tennis and croquet outdoors and various other games indoors.[4]

Wrens were paid less than male sailors, as was common in all walks of life at the time. Vera Laughton Mathews came to accept the rationale of this.

> ... there were men in shore bases doing precisely the same work as women and no better, even men precluded by health from going to sea, yet in the main, men in the armed forces were recruited to a life of hardship and danger and sacrifice beyond all comparison of what was demanded of women.[5]

Wrens were originally recruited under contract as civilians, but by June 1940 the army and air force became concerned about wastage in their own women's services – the Auxiliary Territorial Services (ATS) and the Women's Auxiliary Air Force (WAAF) – particularly among women who acquired secret information and then walked out. The Home Policy Committee of the cabinet told them to sort out the problem among themselves. Meanwhile, it was suggested that the women's position might be difficult under international law. The Admiralty consulted its own legal adviser and those of the Foreign Office and Treasury and was assured that there was no problem under the Hague and Geneva Conventions. But the army and air force went to the cabinet and convinced it that the ATS and WAAF needed full military status, which was announced in April 1941. The navy felt no need for this; for only 37 out of 11,000 Wrens deserted between December 1940 and March 1941.

The Director, WRNS, still believed that they should be brought under the Naval Discipline Act. They replaced men who were under the act and worked alongside others; it would be good for morale to be recognized as part of the navy; it would be undesirable to bring charges against one in a civilian court; some of their duties were quasi-combatant; and, she argued coyly, 'A Naval and W.R.N.S. rating may be guilty of the same offence jointly (e.g. improperly absent from duty) and should be subject to the same punishment.'

This did not convince the Second Sea Lord, Sir Charles Little, who produced a detailed argument as he left office in June 1941. The home commanders-in-chief were strongly opposed to any change in a system which seemed to be working, except for the admiral at Plymouth who felt it would be necessary when 'the present high standard of morale and discipline deteriorates'. There were already enough punishments for recalcitrant Wrens, including discharge, disrating, suspension, stoppage of leave and deductions from pay. To imprison women by court martial would be 'repugnant to many minds'. The Admiralty accepted this and Wrens remained free of the Naval Discipline Act until 1977.[6]

Serving under the CE Branch was proving difficult, for they tended to regard Wrens as civilians, and did not see the need for accommodation and uniforms. In 1941 it was decided to transfer the administration to the CW Branch for officers, and the Naval Branch for ratings, treating them in the same way as male naval personnel.

Recruiting

The WRNS of the First World War had worn a uniform based on the square rig of the seaman, with a 'fore-and-aft' style uniform for officers and petty officers. This time the officers' uniform came first. In 1918 Vera Laughton Mathews had been reprimanded for wearing her top button undone, but this became standard in 1939, as being 'easier to the average woman's figure'.[7] It first appeared at a parade in Hyde Park in July 1939. The cap in particular was a great success. 'Whoever designed it was a genius. It suited nearly everyone I ever saw in it,' wrote Angela Mack.[8] The ratings' uniform of 1918 was no longer considered suitable, and the use of the sailor's collar was 'unpopular in the ports',[9] so a version of the officers' uniform was adopted, though it took some time for supplies to come through. The hat was based on that of 1918, which in turn was derived from a fashionable style of yachting cap of the period. Poor materials had to be used in 1939 and the 'pudding basin' hat was floppy and unattractive.[10] 'The brim of mine flopped too far down, so as soon as I was allowed home on a 48-hour leave I got one of my brothers to thread a wire through the hem of the rim.'[11] Early in 1942 it was replaced by a version of the seaman's cap, which immediately became popular.

As with male ratings, the uniform was a definite benefit in recruiting. The khaki of the Army's ATS uniform was not popular, and one Leeds housewife wrote, 'the colour of the stockings frightens some of them off …'[12] The blue-grey of the WAAF was slightly more popular, but the cut, like the ATS uniform, was military and unflattering.

In contrast to the WRNS the army's ATS was dogged with problems. It had a title that was weak and meaningless. It was set up before the war under the lord lieutenants of the counties and its first officers were generally chosen for their social

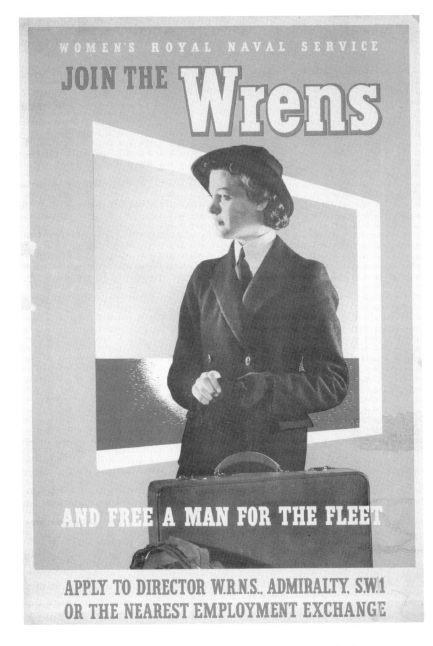

A Wrens recruiting poster. The demure images is perhaps intended to reassure parents.

status in the district. When war started it soon got a reputation for incompetence. Its first two directors were removed, apparently as the result of failures. Most important of all, it had a poor moral reputation, with accusations of drunkenness and immorality among its members. It improved over the years, but in 1941 an MP claimed that 'the ATS is not the sort of service that a nice girl goes into.'[13]

Many women saw the classic Wrens poster, 'Join the WRNS and Free a Man for the Fleet.' A five-minute recruiting film was produced by the Ministry of Information early in 1942, but it had limited success in the cinemas. Picturegoers felt that there was 'too much teleprinting', that it was too good to be true – 'Surely the girls must have uncongenial tasks as well' – that the settings were over-luxurious and that the

girls were 'a picked team of beauties' and 'only acting a part in the kitchen'.[14]
The recruiting policy was described in 1942.

> The W.R.N.S. recruiting policy has hitherto had the effect of controlling
> intake of recruits to provide a steady replacement of [male] personnel in
> shore establishments and to fill expansion vacancies as they have arisen. The
> regulation of recruitment in this way has had a number of advantages of
> which the main ones are:-
>
> An even monthly intake has been possible.
> Accommodation requirements have been met as the need has arisen.
> The withdrawal of women from useful civil employment before they could
> be put to work in the Service has been avoided.
> The problems arising from having keen volunteers waiting around with
> nothing to do have been practically non-existent ...[15]

By August 1942 Wrens were in great demand in the naval bases. The
Commander-in-Chief, Portsmouth, claimed to be 1300 short of immediate
needs, and would eventually want a further 1500. Throughout the navy, 12,000
more Wrens were needed by the end of the year. Conscription for women started late in 1941, for the three women's services and civil defence, while women
in vital jobs in industry were not reserved. The act applied to women between
eighteen and fifty, though only those between nineteen and thirty-one were
actually called by proclamation.[16] The service did not need to take conscripts as
such, for volunteering for the WRNS was the most popular of the options open
to potential conscripts, though the Ministry of Labour policy was not helpful.
Women were only drafted to the Wrens if they had previous experience of the
service, of cooking and domestic work or of boatwork, had knowledge of
German, had relatives in the navy or had filled in the application form before
becoming liable for conscription. There were only seven centres where women
could join, in the naval ports and in London, Liverpool, Manchester and Rosyth.
Medically facilities were only available in a few centres, on certain days of the
month. The taking up of references also slowed the process, and the service
needed these to maintain a high standard of entrants, since it had no redress
against desertion. The ministry sent out contradictory signals about recruitment
– 'It is impossible for the general public to grasp two apparently irreconcilable
lines of policy. National Service girls are told by Local [Ministry of Labour]
Offices that the W.R.N.S. do not need them, unless they have certain reasons or
qualifications for being allowed to join that Service. On the other hand, the
Service is trying to make known the fact that the W.R.N.S. do need recruits for
practically all their categories.'

As well as persuading the Ministry of Labour to change its practices, it was
decided to set up new recruiting centres at Birmingham, Leeds, Belfast, Glasgow,
Cardiff, Aberdeen and Newcastle. More active recruitment was undertaken, largely
aimed at women not liable for conscription, including those over thirty-one and
married women without children. Husbands who might discourage their wives from
joining were also to be targeted. To find the younger recruit, Girl Guide groups were
visited.[17]

Nancy Spain had served with Air Raid Precautions, but 'My life continued to be eccentric and colourful but it ceased to be artificial. I felt that total warfare demanded a further responsibility of me. I wanted to work really hard. So I joined the W.R.N.S.'[18] By 1942 the Wrens had moved away from the original upper-middle-class recruitment. Stephanie Batstone describes the members of her course.

> Into the melting pot we all went – conscripts, volunteers, engaged, married, widowed, single, Zara from Brazil, Rita from Balham. Cathy from Anglesey, Marianne from Barclays Bank in Aberdeen, Joy from Sainsbury's cold meat counter in Birmingham, Clodagh from milking her father's cows near Kinsale in County Cork, Maureen from being a hotel chambermaid in Dublin, with the bright lights and butter and German embassy, Joan from helping her mother run a boarding school in Skegness, Judy straight from school, Pauline from an estate agents in Wood Green, Celia from the Prudential in Exeter, Vivienne a second-year nurse at Leeds General Infirmary, Patricia from a repertory company in Belfast, Betty who thought life was fun, Irene who wore glasses.[19]

For all that, the daughters of several famous admirals were to be found serving in the ranks. Mountbatten's daughter, Patricia, got her 'hook' as a Leading Wren and she asked 'Ma'am, is this because I'm good or because of Daddy?' Sir Dudley Pound, the First Sea Lord until his death in 1943, was outraged when he was unable to telephone his daughter in the depot. And Vera Laughton Mathews' own daughter became a Leading Wren.[20]

Training Bases
Because of the use of immobile Wrens, training bases were needed in all parts of the country where naval bases coincided with large centres of population. In 1943 there were schools near Plymouth, King's School, Rochester, for the Chatham Command, Portsmouth, Dunfermline for Rosyth, Loch Lomond for the Clyde, and Liverpool. There were no training schools at other major commands such as Orkney and Shetland, because the local populations could not provide enough recruits to make it worthwhile, and immobile Wrens were far rarer in such areas. There was also a school for Wren telegraphists at Soberton Towers in Hampshire.[21] The first depot in London was at Westfield College, Hampstead, followed by one on the Finchley Road in north London. The main depot at Mill Hill was opened by the First Lord of the Admiralty in May 1942.

Until 1942, mobile Wrens were trained in the place where they joined. London recruits were trained in the Central Training and Drafting Depot at Hampstead, the others in the naval bases. The local WRNS superintendents were responsible for filling vacancies in their areas with either mobile or immobile ratings. This policy, it was noted, had certain disadvantages. '... there was a variation in standards of training between ports. Confusion arose in drafting and in training when a port was unable to supply sufficient personnel of any particular branch a demand was made on Headquarters, and where this could not be met immediately Headquarters arranged entry and training; frequently entries to fill the same billet were made by the port depot without warning; the result was that frequently two batches of entries were made and trained for the same commitment.'

It was decided to centralize training of mobiles in the London area, though 'Every endeavour will be made to continue the present policy of sending back to a port

Wrens learning to type under a Chief Wren.

personnel who had been recruited at that port and whose services were particularly desired.' All recruits would go to the depot at Mill Hill, for disciplinary training during which time 'all will be required to take their share in cooking and cleaning.' Domestic and administrative trainees, drivers, radio mechanics and cinema operators would go to further training in the London area after seven days; those who were to go to other services or civilian establishments for training, such as armourers, plotters, radar operators and telephone operators would have fourteen days before moving on.[22]

Initial Training

Initial training for Wrens was very brief – just two weeks. An officer of the Mill Hill Depot described it in 1944. 'They have lectures from us on Naval procedure and tradition, how to tell ranks and badges, how they will be expected to behave in different establishments, how to draw their pay and apply for leave and things like that. Then they attend lectures given by naval officers in specialized subjects, and interviews to see whether they qualify for joining certain categories.'[23] In the early stages, women were often drafted directly into their jobs without any training at all.

A sceptical official asked Vera Laughton Mathews if marching would make the women type better. The Director was clear about her answer.

A march is different. One loses the sense of individuality. There are no longer single human beings but one unit, one soul, one aim. And marching oneself one forgets one's own small life and becomes merged in something bigger, a great comradeship, 'shoulder to shoulder and friend to friend'.[24]

It is no surprise, then, that marching figured largely in the first two weeks of training. During this period, tiny amounts of seniority seemed all-important. One woman, not yet in uniform, was asked during a royal visit, 'Have you just joined the service?' 'Oh no, Ma'am, I'm a second weeker.'[25]

The women were on probation as 'pro-Wrens'; they could leave at any time, or be dismissed if they were found to be unsuitable. In some bases they continued to wear their own clothes. In others they were issued with a uniform which was evidently designed to test their determination. It was described by Stephanie Batstone.

> Bluettes would have looked at home in a penal settlement. They were designed expressly to make you pack in the whole daft idea and go home before your probationary fortnight was over. They were boiled out blue overall dresses of a kind of sponge cloth, buttoning up to the neck. Worn without slips, they rucked up in front, sticking to our stockings as we walked. The only thing missing was the arrows.[26]

At last the real uniforms were issued.

> Two skirts and two jackets, a tiddley one and an everyday one; two pairs of 'blackouts', i.e. knickers, navy artificial silk down to the knee; two pairs of black lisle stockings; two pairs of shoes, a greatcoat, a tie. Six collars, two sizes too large because they would shrink in the laundry. Six shirts, the right size because they wouldn't. Between the back stud and the front stud there was always a bulge of collar over shirt. The collars did shrink, but before they were down to shirt size they got so worn that they rubbed our necks even when we put candle grease on. The hat, the crowning glory! A taffeta hat ribbon with the letters 'H.M.S.' worked in gold on it. And, because we would work outdoors, two pairs of thick navy woollen blackouts, two pairs of bellbottoms, a seaman's jersey, and woollen socks and gloves.[27]

Wrens are instructed in sausage-making.

Roles

Originally Wrens were confined to domestic and clerical duties. In 1941 the Commander-in-Chief at the Nore pointed out that women had so far only been employed on 'duties conventionally applicable to women', and suggested that they might be trained for many more jobs.[28] After that, the Wrens began to train in technical work such as signalling and maintenance.

Early on, a few Wrens were allowed to serve as wireless operators, receiving and decoding messages. Because of the technical nature of the work, the secrecy, and the need to give them equal pay with the civilian Shore Wireless Service who worked alongside them, they were rated as chief petty officers. Early in 1941, after favourable reports on these women, it was agreed to employ Wrens on transmitting duties as well, on similar terms to naval wireless telegraphists. Though the work was at least as skilled, and involved transmitting as well as receiving and a considerable knowledge of procedure, the CPO rate was no longer available to them. Women with a knowledge of Morse Code were invited to apply for a six-months' training course; those who held the Postmaster General's certificate in radio telegraphy would only have to train for four months. By 1943 they were fully accepted in the navy. 'WRNS ratings qualifications in wireless telegraphy have been proved to be of the same standard on leaving training establishments as ordinary telegraphists and are employed accordingly.' But the Chief Officer of Wrens at Dover complained that they were at a disadvantage compared with other branches. '... having attained a high standard in a training establishment, upon reaching a port they are put on to elementary routine work only, as it is apparently necessary for all important operational work to be undertaken by Royal Navy telegraphists.'[29]

By early 1942 there were nearly 7000 women serving in the traditional roles as stewardesses and cooks. More than 5000 more were clerical workers as supply assistants, shorthand typists, Writers (General) and Writers (Pay). More than 3800 worked in a less stereotyped role in naval communications. In addition, many new and ground-breaking categories had been added during the previous year. Many of the Wrens duties were connected with the entry of new ratings, and with assisting in training at several levels. Among the new trades introduced in 1941 were Recruiting Assistant, Night Vision Tester, Cinema Operator and Exercise Corrector. There were Aircraft Checkers and Fitters, Radio Mechanics, Range Wardens and Machinists, all doing jobs that would have been unthinkable before the war.[30]

Though women could obviously not be employed in the main seaman non-substantive role as gunners, the Torpedo Branch was largely concerned with maintenance and was therefore opened to them during 1942. In shore bases they could relieve seaman torpedomen and wiremen in maintenance duties. They were given one week in the depot at Mill Hill, then four weeks in a Government Training Centre at Hounslow in Middlesex, followed by a month or six weeks at the torpedo school HMS *Vernon*. The Head of the Naval Branch objected to the use of the initials ST, meaning Seaman Torpedoman and suggested Wren (T), but he was overruled.[31]

Despite the obvious discomforts of working in the open, Stephanie Batstone was determined to train as a visual signaller. She approached the petty officer in the recruiting office.

> I said, "I want to be a visual signaller."
> "Sorry," she said. "I'm afraid that category is closed and there's a waiting list. I doubt if we shall recruit any more. At the moment the only categories

open are Writers and Cooks, Can you do shorthand and typing?"
"No." I said.
"What a pity," she said. "Well, just fill in the form and where it says 'catego-
ry' put 'cook'. I'm sure you like cooking, don't you?"
"No," I said. "I hate it."

She got round the problem by putting 'visual signaller' on the form anyway, and was
called for an eye test three weeks later.[32]
   After training,

> We sat the final exam, with practical tests in semaphore, ten inch and Aldis,
> and papers in V/S procedure, coding practice, and V/S general. When the
> results came out Chief was so relieved he hired a taxi and took eight of us
> out to a dinner in Manchester. We had saved his reputation.[33]

There was no great role for Wrens in the Engineering Branch. Running repairs were
done by the ship's own engineers, while major overhauls were done by civilian
workers. Nor could women serve in aircraft carriers, but in any case much of naval
aviation was shore-based. By September 1940 the Admiralty was thinking of employing women as storekeepers in naval air stations and asked Flag Officer Naval Air
Stations (FONAS) to suggest possible roles. He replied that they could be trained
locally in the different stations, mostly in 'ordinary hum-drum routine work such as
dopers, battery chargers, plug cleaners and fabric workers'. This was impracticable
as it would have led to widely varying standards, but in November FONAS suggested training them in the semi-skilled grades of air mechanic, and even in the more
skilled grades of air fitter. The idea languished until July 1942, when the Admiralty
agreed in principle to train them as air mechanics, and approached the Air Ministry
about facilities. There was some hesitation about using too many women, who would
not be able to take part in local defence in the event of invasion; but it was agreed
to go ahead with 'the replacement of men on a "head for head" basis, plus 10 per
cent extra Wrens to compensate for them being "the weaker sex"'. But by October
FONAS now wanted only 130 Wren air mechanics without preliminary training, for
work in 'servicing and lesser maintenance'. The rest would have to be properly
trained. After that, Wrens could make up a quarter of the airframe and engine air
mechanics at air stations, and a third of electrical and ordnance mechanics.
   RAF accommodation was found to be unsuitable, and the service seemed reluctant to help, so the navy set up its own programme. Wren electrical and ordnance
mechanics were trained alongside the air artificer apprentices at Newcastle-under-
Lyme, with more ordnance mechanics at HMS *Excellent*. Plans were made for airframe
and engine mechanics at the Fleet Air Arm depot at Lee-on-Solent, and up to 1450
Wren air mechanics (WAMs) were now needed.
   In January 1943 a high-level meeting was held in a Ministry of Supply camp at
Millmeece 13 miles south of Newcastle. 'The camp appeared very suitable in every
respect and of adequate size to accept the full training commitment.' Adapting the
Fleet Air Arm policy of naming shore bases after types of birds, it was commissioned
on 15 April 1943 as HMS *Fledgling*. Training of airframe and engine fitters started on
3 May and electrical fitters two weeks later; fifteen women were entered for each
category every week. Ordnance training remained at Newcastle. After a visit to the
camp, Rear-Admiral Ford had the highest praise for the results.

A member of a Wren boat crew jumps ashore.

Since early September trainees have been flowing regularly off course. The efficiency of the instruction and the unbounded enthusiasm of both trainees and instructional staff, together with the high standard of trainees selected, are indicated in the extremely good passing out results, the average pass-ing-out marks for all four trades being about 62 per cent; the wastage over all four trades being only 12.4 per cent, which includes all withdrawals for medical reasons etc. Reports from Naval Air Stations show that these girls are producing astonishing results. Their energy and intelligence put the men to shame, as does the fact that on an average they "qualify to sign" in a month, while the average man takes three months. Naval Air Stations are clamouring for more and it will be disastrous if, due to the manning situa-tion, the training of these women must cease ...

Women could not be sent to sea and that was an advantage in the circumstances, for they would be able to stay on in a base as the men were drafted out, forming a stable and permanent staff. Though they did not have the skill with tools that most boys learned, they had 'deftness and lightness of touch' instead and they were far better at remembering their training. One problem was that many of them were good enough to be commissioned. If that happened they would be put into general service where their training would be wasted. Ford recommended that they should be kept on to assist the air engineer officers at naval air stations, or return to *Fledgling* as instructors.[34]

Even menial tasks could be made to seem important. Eileen Bigland noted the women's work in a submarine depot ship.

In a cabin where the sun streamed through the porthole I found the Book Correctors – Wrens for whom I held great respect as I couldn't see much exhilaration in sitting hour after hour making amendments to Admiralty Fleet Orders. They, however, took a different view. … Tame as this task might appear beside that of the girls who hoisted themselves so lightly over the boom into the little tossing boats, it was equally vital to the safe conduct of His Majesty's ships and to the men who sailed in them. Next month or the month after the books being so carefully prepared might be in submarines in the Atlantic, the Mediterranean, the North Sea.[35]

Wrens at Sea

Wrens were first tried as crews of harbour craft in October 1941, at the instigation of Admiral Sir Charles Forbes at Plymouth. It was a success and the policy soon became general. Each crew was all-woman, with a Leading Wren or Petty Officer Coxswain, a stoker and one or more deckhands. They transported senior officers, carried mail and operated patrols. One of the more demanding jobs was to take parties of seamen on leave or 'liberty' from ships at anchor.

> The last trip at midnight was the worst. It was blowing pretty hard, and we had to take eighty men out and many of them were not sober. Before we had even started four of them went over the side. Luckily it was moonlight so we had no difficulty in fishing for them with a boathook. I just saved a fifth from going over by catching him by his gas mask. … None of them ever get fighting drunk. You have just got to treat them like a lot of small boys.[36]

Boats' crews for the Firth of Clyde area were trained in the submarine depot ship HMS *Forth*, moored in the Holy Loch, under a Wren petty officer coxswain. They were proud of their ability to climb out along the boat boom from the side of the ship, then down rope ladders to the boats. Some of the early Wrens were former yachtswomen, but they soon 'affected toughness' to mingle with the seamen.

Another duty which involved going afloat was the Naval Control of Shipping. Wren boarding officers went out to arriving merchant ships with their instructions after training at Southend or Liverpool in 'Routeing (chart work and elementary navigation), Convoy (preparation of orders and convoy conferences), Secretarial (naval control of shipping officer requirements), Confidential books and Signal Work'. According to one officer, a boarding officer should have already been in a boat's crew to learn seamanship; to have 'a complete lack of sense of modesty' as she was likely to find sailors in all states of undress on boarding; to be able to resist continuous offers of drinks; and to be 'elastic and acrobatic' enough to climb ladders and planks.[37]

In the Navy Estimates of 1943 the question of whether to send the Wrens to sea for longer periods came up for debate and the First Lord was briefed by the Director.

> D.W.R.N.S. points out the impracticability of employing "mixed" crews. The additional refittings that are constantly being developed for use afloat make a double demand upon the limited space and weight permissible in warships, both by reason of the fittings themselves and the extra personnel to work them. It is becoming increasingly difficult to fit an adequate comple-

ment into existing ships, and it is impossible to spare space and weight for separate female accommodation.

To "man" a warship wholly by a female crew would be impossible owing to lack of expertise.

The employment of W.R.N.S. in harbour craft is possible, and is done in some places; and an extension of this employment is being considered as the need arises.[38]

During the actual debate, the Civil Lord agreed that women could be employed at sea in certain cases. One of the women to benefit from this was Angela Mack, now an officer. She was sent Liverpool to join the great liner *Mauretania* as a signals officer, and a number of women served in such roles where they could be accommodated separately without too much disruption.[39]

The Selection and Status of Officers
The early WRNS officers were selected, often personally by Vera Laughton Mathews and her deputy, Angela Goodenough. The Director inspected the Wrens at Lympne early in the war and found that one ordinary Wren had taken the initiative in organizing the issue of clothing. She was immediately identified as officer material and eventually became a Chief Officer. In another case, the third officer in charge seemed rather inadequate, but her Chief Wren was found to be the moving spirit; she was immediately put up for an officer. Fast promotion was possible in the circumstances, because of the rapid expansion and because there could be no rules about seniority; no one had more than a few months in any case.[40]

By the middle of December 1939, the WRNS had 233 officers. Angela Goodenough, the Deputy Director, was the unmarried daughter of an Indian army officer, and cousin of one of the best-known admirals of the First World War. There were superintendents at Devonport, Chatham, Portsmouth and Rosyth, and another in charge of the officers' training course at Greenwich, but only Mrs Welby at Devonport had naval connections, as the widow and daughter of naval officers. A third of the nine chief officers were naval, as were eight of the twenty-six first officers. The naval content was strongest in the lowest grade, second officer; out of 191, more than a third were wives or widows of naval officers and thirty-one were daughters. Churchill was pleased that this high naval content brought in people who already had experience of the service, but it was not an unmixed blessing.[41] Naval officers' wives tended to wear 'invisible stripes' reflecting their husbands' ranks, and this did not always fit in with the WRNS rank structure.

After the initial phase, all WRNS officers came via the lower deck, if that is an appropriate term in the circumstances. Angela Mack was almost thwarted in her promotion prospects in the first instance, by a lieutenant who commented, 'We have just got the Wrens trained to do the work properly, and I won't have you taking them away.' But she came before the selection board at Queen Anne's Mansions in London.

The Captain had an eyeglass which reminded me of a joke of my father's about a colonel who could throw up his monocle and catch it in his eye. I waited for this monocle to fall at some reply of mine. They all asked questions in turn, some in a kind tone, others crisply and in no-nonsense fashion. I answered as best as I could. I was still breathing. Of course I don't remember a single question, but I do remember being encouraged to talk about a job I had done for a friend of my father's, which consisted of assembling ships' models for the Admiralty Inspector and subsequently posting them to training establishments for aircraft recognition. A pleasant thought is that there is no video of that interview and I don't have to sit through it again. But I was in.[42]

Training of Officers

Vera Laughton Mathews suggested that the buildings of the Royal Naval College at Greenwich should be used for the training of WRNS officers, and was delighted when this was agreed. It was vacant at the time, for the various naval activities – the War Course, Staff Course, Specialist courses in gunnery, torpedo and navigation and sub-lieutenants' courses, had either been suspended or had been evacuated due to threat of bombing. The college was almost empty when the first group of thirty officers began a three-week course in the Queen Anne Block.[43] Superintendent French was in charge for most of the war, and was noted for her ability to produce accurate, perceptive reports on the thousands of women who passed through.[44] According to Angela Mack she was 'stately, slim and kindly, with rolls of little grey curls on each side of her face. She was quietly authoritative but also friendly. ... She managed to calm the nervous and to draw out of everyone their best. She had no rough corners.'[45]

In October 1941 the course at Greenwich was restored to three weeks, after being two weeks' long for a time. Trainees spent forty minutes in foot drill every morning, and rounded off the day with half an hour of PT or games in the afternoon. In between, they listened to a series of high-powered lecturers. The superintendent of the training course welcomed them, and they would also hear from the deputy director of the service, the superintendents of the divisions at Chatham and Portsmouth, and the Director herself on 'What the W.R.N.S. expects of its Officers.' Professor Michael Lewis lectured on 'The Evolution of the Naval Officer' and Admiral Sir William Goodenough would talk on discipline. Commander Drake of the RNR would attempt an introduction to navigation in two-and-half hours, but most of the time would be devoted to subjects such as naval law and administration.[46] During the war there were up to 200 women cadets at Greenwich at any moment, and eventually 8587 officers passed through the college.[47]

Role in the Training Bases

In the early stages of the organization, women in the male training bases concentrated on catering, stores and accountancy, but many new areas were added during the war. There were several trades which were almost exclusively used in the training bases, such as cinema operators. Air Synthetic Trainers spent three or four months learning air navigation to work with the Fleet Air Arm's Link trainers. There were Bomb Range Markers and Torpedo Recorders. A Cine Gun Assessor trained for four to six weeks to work with dome trainers and other simulators.

> Passes length of 16mm film through special projector in order to assess accuracy of special projector in order to assess accuracy of gunner's aim during firing practice shoots. Plots aim of guns as recorded by film strips,

and makes out charts. May have specialized in assessing rocket projectile runs. Does not process films or load cine cameras.[48]

Eileen Bigland watched Wrens at work in a 'tattical [sic] trainer.'

> The school itself was a largish shed, around the walls of which were little curtained compartments not unlike bathing tents. In these sat the destroyer Captains with charts before them. On the floor, over which Wrens crawled at speed, was drawn another, immense chart and here the game was played according to instructions issued to the Wrens by the Naval Officer in charge.

> The destroyer Captains in their little compartments plotted to outwit enemy attack. The Wrens on the floor counter-plotted, making chalk marks with rapidity, while others of their number flicked back the curtains in order to see how the Captains were getting on. It was an astonishing sight and, game or no game, it taught many valuable lessons.[49]

The Experience

For some women no doubt, service in the Wrens was merely the exchange of one kind of drudgery for another – from the kitchen of a hotel or house to a naval base, for example. But for nearly all of those who decided to recount their service, it was a life-broadening experience. The Wrens built up a unique spirit during the war, stronger than the equivalent organizations in the army and navy. Partly this was due to naval tradition. The army as a body has little tradition of its own – most of it is delegated to the individual regiments and corps, but no woman could belong to any of them, as distinct from being attached. She could only be in the ATS, a separate corps, with no tradition or history so far. The RAF was a very new service, while the Royal Navy had traditions as strong as almost any service in the world, and Wrens were allowed to feel part of that, as far as circumstances allowed. The WRNS was the only women's service to survive with its name unchanged after the war, until it was merged in the Royal Navy in 1993.

CHAPTER 19

Relations with the Merchant Navy

Cultural Differences

The Royal Navy officer tended to regard the merchant navy captain as the equivalent of a bus driver, expert at getting his ship economically and safely from place to place, but knowing nothing of the military and social skills of a naval officer. The merchant seamen, on the other hand, saw naval officers as dilettantes, with enormous crews to do the simplest task, and often diverted away from the real tasks of a seaman into the study of tactics, guns, torpedoes or signals.

After the First World War the merchant service was renamed the 'Merchant Navy' in recognition of its services in the U-boat war and a standard uniform was approved by Order-in-Council. A merchant navy master, who held the courtesy title of captain and might command any ship however small, was given four gold rings. This was the same as a Royal Navy post-captain, who would command at least a cruiser, with a crew of 200 to 900 men; though there was no suggestion that the merchant navy ranks were equivalent to naval ranks. The rank of post-captain in the Royal Navy was permanent, held by the officer in any post, afloat or ashore. The four stripes of a merchant navy captain did not just signify that he had passed the examination for his master's ticket, but that he was actually in command of a ship, or at least had held such a command.

Even in wartime, merchant ships were manned by the shipping companies rather than the Admiralty. Merchant seamen were exempt from conscription, and generally received much higher wages than Royal Navy men. Discipline tended to be much less restrictive than in the Royal Navy. A boy could join at the age of sixteen and for all these reasons the merchant navy, despite a higher casualty rate than any of the armed services, never had any difficulty in attracting men. On average there were about 145,000 men in the merchant navy during the war, and more than 50,000 became casualties.[1]

The Merchant Training Ships

In 1875 there were fifteen static ships in ports around the British coast with room for nearly 4000 boys. Some trained ordinary boys for the lower deck, but others, largely run by local authorities, were of the 'reformatory' type. Lord Brassey the shipowner, had serious doubts. 'Desirable as it is to make an effort to reclaim the unfortunate children of the pauper or criminal classes, it must be admitted that, in introducing boys of this class in large numbers into the Merchant Service we incur a serious risk.' By the 1930s there was only one 'reformatory' training ship, the Cornwall in the Thames at Gravesend; 80 per cent of its boys eventually entered the merchant; the Royal Navy never accepted boys from reformatory ships.[2]

At the other end of the scale were the ships and schools which produced officers for the merchant service, with a few for the Royal Navy. In 1859 a group of Liverpool merchants set up a ship in the Mersey, to train potential merchant service officers and the Admiralty, keen to encourage higher standards among potential reserve officers, loaned HMS *Conway* for the purpose. Two years later HMS *Worcester* was lent to set up a school at Gravesend. Along with a shore-based school at Pangbourne well up the River Thames, and the training ship *Mercury*, which also sent boys to the lower deck of the Royal Navy, these schools provided the top level of merchant navy training until after the Second World War.

Fees were high for these training ships. On average, just over a hundred men a year entered the merchant navy from 1928–32, compared with about 650 a year trained by apprenticeship alone, and about a hundred who rose from the lower deck.[3] The training ship boys tended to gravitate towards the more prestigious posts. P&O, best known for passenger ships to India, sponsored a prize for a Worcester cadet, and the winner was entitled to 'preference for employment in that company's service'. Other companies such as British India Steam Navigation, Furness Withy, Houlder Brothers and Elder Dempster were associated with the *Worcester*.[4]

Training ships maintained links with the Royal Navy and its reserves. Addressing the annual distribution of prizes of HMS *Worcester* in 1929, Admiral Sir Sydney Fremantle drew attention to many ex-training ship boys who had distinguished themselves as RNR officers in the last war, and hoped that many of the present cadets would 'prepare yourselves by joining the Royal Naval Reserve to do whatever sea service the country may require of you in time of war.'[5] Two of the cadets became RNR midshipman each year during their training, and one was selected each year to enter the Royal Navy proper as a Special Entry midshipman.

During the early stages of the Second World War there was little recognition of the merchant training ships, because they fell between the Ministry of Labour and the Ministry of Shipping. Admiral James at Portsmouth campaigned on behalf of the *Mercury*, which was in danger of being 'unable to keep their instructors, clothing and food', and eventually persuaded Churchill to do something.[6]

RNR Officers

The Royal Naval Reserve was neglected between the wars. Though it had risen to 67,000 officers and men in the First World War, it was down to about 9000 in the 1930s. In July 1938 there were only 1608 active officers. For merchant navy officers, service in the Royal Naval Reserve bestowed a certain social cachet. Some shipowners, especially in the long-distance passenger trades, encouraged their officers to join. As well as increasing their status with the passengers, it allowed certain ships (eighty-five in 1938) to fly the blue instead of the red ensign from the stern, emphasizing a connection with the crown. For the rating it gave a little extra money, often earned during unemployment or in an inactive season. In wartime they were likely to be called up to serve with the navy, often with reduced pay.

Most officers joined the RNR with the rank of probationary midshipman between the ages of sixteen and nineteen after at least one year's service in a 'first class British merchant ship'. They did six months' training with the navy to learn about 'discipline, gunnery, torpedo, seamanship, signals, handling of boats, anti-gas training and such like', as well as 'acquiring the spirit, traditions and customs of the Navy'. Older men from twenty to twenty-two, holding second mates' certificates, could enter as probationary sub-lieutenants and become acting sub-lieutenants after three months' training. A few could enter direct as probationary lieutenants between twenty-one and twenty-seven, if they held first mates' or masters' certificate. After eight years as a full lieutenant an officer was advanced to lieutenant-commander, as in the regular navy, provided they had obtained a master's certificate.[7]

Promotion in the RNR always lagged behind that of the regular RN. The honorary rank of commodore was established in 1933, but only six officers could hold it in peace. In 1938 there were only eighty-eight officers above the rank of lieutenant-commander. Even in wartime few new avenues were opened up. The number of commodores was vastly expanded, but mostly for retired RN officers. There was still no rank above commodore open to ex-merchant seamen. The RNR was not likely to expand in wartime through individual recruitment, as potential recruits were needed in the merchant service, and usually preferred the higher rates of pay and conditions they were more used to. Its only means of expansion was through merchant ships taken into the navy.

Between the wars the navy felt no need for a large reserve of engineers, and there were only thirty-five engineer officers in 1938, mostly lieutenant-commanders of considerable seniority, plus fourteen warrant officers. Nor was the navy keen to recruit administrative officers of the Paymaster Branch to the RNR. Such officers were too deeply imbued in merchant ship ways, and it was better to train them direct from the shore via the RNVR. Nevertheless, merchant navy pursers were quite keen to join, and there were 224 officers in the Paymaster Branch of the RNR in 1938.

The greatest achievement of the RNR was to provide a supply of experienced seamen officers at a time when they were desperately needed. In June 1941, as the Battle of the Atlantic became serious and amateurs of the RNVR were still barely trusted at sea, RNR officers captained sixty-seven out of eighty-one *Flower* class corvettes in commission.[8]

RNR Skippers

The rank of Skipper RNR was for qualified skippers of fishing boats, who would aid the fleet with transport, patrol and minesweeping in time of war. It was a warrant rank, as the class prejudices of the time would not have allowed the men of the fishing fleet to mingle freely with naval officers. Large numbers served in the First World War, often in boom defence in the naval ports, but numbers were small after the war, with less than 300 officers in all three grades of skipper. They served in a separate part of the RN, the Patrol Service, and were not regarded as the best possible recruits. A later report suggested

> The R.N.R. Patrol Service failed before the war to attract the best type of fishing skipper; it was, in fact, largely the unsatisfactory skipper who could not get permanent employment in the fishing industry who turned to the R.N.R. so that he could do his training period when unemployed. In view of the very high earnings of the best skippers in civil life, and the financial loss which they would suffer when performing R.N.R. training, the Admiralty can never hope to attract many of the best of these men into the R.N.R.

Skippers were recruited from men between twenty-three and thirty-five who had commanded a fishing boat for at least a year. They did fourteen days' naval training in minesweeping, station keeping and signals for each of their first three years, and fourteen days every second year after that. After eight to twelve years each officer was eligible for promotion to chief skipper, and up to 8 per cent could be selected as skipper lieutenant. In 1944 the rank of Skipper, lieutenant-commander was introduced for lieutenants of eight years' service.[9]

Large numbers of Temporary Boom Skippers were recruited early in the war, but the more traditional role in minesweeping was in decline.

> There was little increase during the war in the numbers of minesweeping officers of the R.N.R. Skipper class ... The reason lay partly in the reluctance to deprive the fishing industry of all the most knowledgeable trawler and drifter-men, and partly in the realization, born of war experience, that the average Skipper could not contend with the intricacies of influence sweeping. The necessity for meticulous station keeping, navigational accuracy and constant vigilance ran counter to his ingrained habits. The temporary reserve officer of the other classes, usually better educated, more amenable to training and bringing to the task a fresh, enthusiastic and unbiased mind, proved far more efficient and reliable.

RNR skippers made up 43 per cent of minesweeping officers at the beginning of the war and 6 per cent at the end. The balance was largely made up by the RNVR, who made up 63 per cent at the end.[10]

RNR Ratings

As with officers, RNR ratings were divided into two groups – General Service and the Patrol Service, recruited from fishermen. The highest rating in the Patrol Service was second hand, a man who had served as mate in a fishing boat and had a Board of Trade certificate as such. He was rated just above a petty officer and was second-in-command of a naval trawler in wartime. There were leading seamen and seamen, while the man in charge of the engines in a naval trawler was known as the Engineman and was equivalent to an ERA. He was assisted by one or more stokers, who really did shovel coal in many trawlers. On the eve of war the Admiralty in July 1939 took up eighty-six trawlers and planned for a force of 200 minesweeping trawlers and 100 anti-submarine trawlers, but there were not enough men for them – 215 second hands, 213 leading seamen, 492 seamen, the same number of enginemen and 626 stokers, a deficiency of nearly 500 men in the case of the seamen and enginemen. The situation became even worse soon afterwards, when a force of 200 anti-submarine trawlers was planned.[11] In wartime the Patrol Service was greatly expanded by taking in Hostilities Only men.

Convoy Commodores

The 1938 the Admiralty realized that it could not find shore employment for all the retired captains and flag officers who might be available in time of war and looked at ways of 'utilizing the services of these officers, whose experience and standing are of considerable value to the Naval service, in other capacities'.[12] The answer was to employ them as commodores in charge of the merchant ships of a convoy. The first fifty-three were appointed in September, with the rank of Commodore 2nd Class, the highest available in the Royal Naval Reserve. For the majority this was a slight rise in rank from captain; for many others it was a considerable drop, for several had served as full admiral, three grades higher.

A year later, after war had begun, a course was set up in the Admiralty under Commander Davis of the Trade Division. Up to fourteen officers could be trained at once, in a very intense course lasting two or three days. Sir Frederick Dreyer describes his training in September 1939. It included,

> The organization for forming convoys at various ports and the orders, man-uals, and signal books issued for the conduct of convoys at sea, including their defence by ships and aircraft of the Royal Navy and of Coastal Command. The course also dealt with the installation of weapons, life-sav-ing rafts, and bridge protection, the supply of signalling gear, smoke-making apparatus, the fitting of communications from bridges to engine rooms, the training of guns' crews in merchant ships, and other matters.

In all more than 150 officers were to serve as commodores of ocean convoys dur-ing the war, with 150 as commodores of coastal and Mediterranean convoys. The ocean convoy commodores were senior, and included several quite famous admirals such as Sir Frederick Dreyer and Sir Reginald Plunkett-Ernle-Erle-Drax. A few had been captains in the RNR before the war, many were captains in the Royal Navy, and others were retired rear-, vice- and full admirals. The coastal convoy commodores had been much less prestigious in their previous lives. Some had been mere lieu-tenant-commanders in the RNR, most were retired commanders or captains.

DEMS Gunners

Even before the war, the Admiralty was aware that merchant ships needed means to defend themselves, whether sailing alone or in convoy. Initially the main threat was believed to be from enemy surface raiders and surfaced submarines which might use their guns to conserve torpedoes, so a large part of the training was in low-angle guns, rather than anti-aircraft weapons. The Admiralty chose the title 'Defensively Equipped Merchant Ships' (DEMS) perhaps because the title 'Defensively Armed Merchant Ships' was less suitable as an acronym, perhaps because it still retained a hint of aggression. There were several elements in a merchant ship's gun crews: fully trained naval or military gunners commanded and aimed the guns; partly-trained merchant navy men aimed light guns and carried out less skilled tasks on larger ones, and untrained merchant navy sailors passed ammunition. The idea of using RNR gunners in merchant ships was rejected. They would be paid less when called up into the navy, but would still serve alongside merchant seamen, which would cause much resentment.[13] In June 1938 the Admiralty drew up syllabi for refresher courses for recalled reservists and pensioners of the Gunnery Branch. A pensioner seaman gunner, for example, would have a five-day course at HMS *Excellent*, includ-ing fire control, standard methods of passing orders and the use of various fire con-trol instruments.[14]

Training for merchant navy officers and men began in eight major ports in July 1938, and a year later 1400 officers had been trained in fire control, with 180 a month passing through. Two seaman gunners were to be trained for each ship in a course lasting ten working days, though merchant seamen often found it difficult to remain in port for the whole course, Paddy Henderson of Glasgow, among others, pointed out that nearly all their seamen and stewards were Indians, or Lascars, and it was taken for granted that they should not be trained as gunners. The Admiralty could only suggest that they should 'employ two more white seamen, qualified as Merchant Seaman Gunners, in their ships in wartime'.[15]

A few days before the outbreak of war the Admiralty outlined its policy on the provision of service personnel in merchant ships. Ships carrying 6-inch and 5.5-inch guns were to have two naval ratings, one as gunlayer, while those with 4.7-inch guns or less would have only a single gunlayer. No extra ratings would be allowed for extra guns borne. The term 'DEMS ratings' was introduced officially and from 1941 the letters were borne as part of the non-substantive badge. They were borne on the books of HMS *President III*, the depot ship for London, but based in merchant shipping ports as appropriate. They could come from the Royal Navy, Royal Marines, RFR, RNR or RNVR. When afloat they would not be employed in ordinary ship work.[16]

In February 1940 the army was asked to provide 500 light machine guns and 1000 men and it agreed, partly to give them some experience in anti-aircraft gunnery while the 'phoney war' was still in effect in France. This commitment grew steadily over the years and in May 1941 they were formed into the Maritime Royal Artillery. They were given an anchor shoulder patch and the Admiralty took steps to allow them to use naval canteens. Three regiments were trained in machine guns and a fourth in the highly efficient 40 mm Bofors gun, 300 of which were supplied from army stocks. The numbers peaked at 14,200 men in September 1942, after which some were transferred back to normal military duties.[17]

Admiral Dreyer inspecting gunnery training at HMS *Glendower*.

The need for DEMS gunners outstripped the supply from recalled reservists, and from January 1941 the basic training camp in Wales, HMS *Glendower*, was largely devoted to training Hostilities Only men for service in merchant ships. They did five weeks of basic disciplinary training, followed by two-and-a-half weeks each on advanced seamanship and gunnery, then three weeks on specialized DEMS training, to make a total of thirteen weeks. The final part was increased to four weeks in August 1941 to allow instruction in certain types of weapon including the 20 mm Oerlikon gun, and in look-out duties.

Admiral Sir Frederick Dreyer, a leading gunnery officer before the war and more recently a convoy commodore, was appointed Inspector of Merchant Navy Gunnery in February 1941. He inspected *Glendower* in July when 2300 potential DEMS gunners were under instruction. He reported 'I am greatly impressed with the fine appearance and marching of these men. They are obviously imbued with a very fine spirit and great attention has been paid to inculcating them in the traditions of the Royal Navy.' The gunnery school was well equipped with 'a covered drill battery, class rooms, rifle and machine gun range, and two 4" B.L. [breech-loading] guns for simple full calibre firing'. The standard of instruction was 'very high and I was gratified to see how well the Instructors took charge of their classes and the very good methods of teaching which are carried out'. After completing the course at *Glendower* the men went on to further training at HMS *Wellesley* in Liverpool.[18]

Dreyer also initiated a two-day course for merchant navy personnel in brief gaps between voyages, which was announced in June 1941. Two merchant navy personnel were to be trained for each machine gun manned by them, and two more to under-study the DEMS ratings on the larger guns on each ship. Up to ten men were to be trained per crew, and the master of a ship could attend the course as a supernu-merary if he wished. The courses were to be held in a dozen major ports, and in four-teen specialized centres in places where merchant ships were likely to find them-selves in wartime, including small ports such as Mallaig in Scotland, and Manchester at the end of the Ship Canal.[19]

Dreyer encouraged the development and use of the Dome Teacher, which he regarded as a 'wonderful invention'. He also supported a very simple but effective device, invented by Lieutenant Matthew Cope. A single-barrel shotgun was mounted on a post, without sights, to give trainees the feel of aiming a pivotted machine gun, very different from a gun which moves from the shoulder. It also developed the 'will to fire' among trainees – it taught each man 'to make up his mind quickly to shoot at a fast target in a short time'. Dreyer also produced a pamplet, 'Notes on Close-Range Bombing Attacks on Merchant Ships', to supplement the official handbook *Notes on Gunnery for Defensively Equipped Merchant Ships*, first printed in 1939.

The two-day course started with a preliminary lecture, the *Eyeshooting* film, a machine-gun demonstration and an eyeshooting lecture. In the afternoon the men trained in the Dome Teacher and did drill with machine-guns. On the second day they fired ten shots at clay pigeons with the shotgun then did various exercises with machine-guns, culminating with shots at a target towed by an aircraft. Each range, according to Dreyer, was 'like a very orderly village fair'. More than 100,000 men passed through the two-day courses during the war, including some who did it more than once.[20]

In service the DEMS gunners, 'dressed in the uniform of the day', formed a strik-ing contrast with the merchant navy crew in their 'miscellaneous garments', though things became much more relaxed at sea. DEMS gunners carried civilian clothes to avoid being interned as combatants in neutral ports, and in the early stages of the war the Netherlands insisted in searching some ships to find hidden uniforms, so only an armband was carried. The great fault of the naval training is that it did not teach men to hold their fire until the aircraft was within range. According to Captain Stephen Bone, 'only a few of our D.E.M.S. gunners had done more than loose off a round or two at a towed sleeve-target. Upon sighting the four planes of the enemy they soon came roaring in on their runs, we opened fire too soon and in conse-quence the Oerlikon drums were empty of shell when the two aircraft on our port beam closed within effective range'. It was the job of the CPO gunner on this ship to 'restrain the gunner's untimely enthusiasm'.[21]

In October 1943 the Admiralty outlined its policy for manning guns on merchant ships. There were three scales – normal, double manning in areas particularly susceptible to air attack, and special rates for some ships such as 'monster' liners. Most ocean-going ships would now carry 20 mm Oerlikon guns, though some still had to make do with machine guns. Large liners would have a DEMS gunnery officer in charge, medium-sized vessels would have a petty officer or leading seaman in charge (or sergeant in the case of the Maritime Regiment) while small coasters would 'have to be content with an Able Seaman in charge'. Every low-angle gun would have its layer, and a layer would also be provided for each anti-aircraft gun, if one was available – otherwise a seaman gunner would have to do it.[22]

Merchant Seamen under Royal Navy Command

Traditionally merchant seamen under Royal Navy command were signed on a T124 agreement, on a form provided by the Transport Board. The idea of converting merchant ships into warships, in the form of armed merchant cruisers, had long been appealing. It was argued that fast ocean liners would be short of work in a major war, and had the speed and range to operate on the ocean. Most were designed to be fitted with guns in some form, and they could be useful in certain areas. Though they were not intended to face enemy warships, they could help blockade Germany by patrolling the seas between Scotland and Iceland, and could help with convoy escort. More than fifty merchant ships were taken over in 1939, complete with crews, and fitted with guns.

Early in 1940 the Admiralty assured the merchant seamen concerned that they were not liable to be shot if they were captured. The Geneva Convention specified that warships, including armed merchant cruisers, should be under the direct authority of the state concerned; that they should fly the flag of warships; that they should be commanded by a commissioned officer; that the crew should be under the rules of military discipline, and that they should be shown as warships in the Navy List. There was no rule that seamen had to wear uniform. 'There is accordingly no foundation whatever for the view that men on T.124 Agreement or variants, serving in commissioned Auxiliary War Vessels, may be regarded as civilians illegally engaged in combatant activities, because they are not provided with naval uniform.'[23]

In its original form the T124 agreement only covered an individual seaman in a particular ship. During 1940 the Admiralty found that this could be inconvenient and introduced the T124X agreement, which meant that a man could be transferred from one ship to another, and that his services could be retained 'for the period of the present emergency'. They would be 'Naval Auxiliary Members of the Armed Forces', and not required to register for conscription. All seamen employed by the navy would be transferred to T124X in the course of time.[24]

The role of the armed merchant cruiser began to decline after 1941. The *Rawalpindi* and *Jervis Bay* were sunk by regular German warships, putting their role under question. The American entry to the war created a demand for these ships as fast troop carriers, while the supply of purpose-built warships was increasing. By the end of 1942 it was proposed to retain only thirteen in service, mostly in the fringe areas of the South Atlantic, West Africa and the Indian Ocean.[25]

Meanwhile other needs had arisen. In 1943 the Admiralty introduced another form of the agreement, for the crews of rescue tugs, as Royal Navy seamen had no experience of this kind of work. A merchant aircraft carrier (MAC) was commanded and manned by merchant navy crews, with Fleet Air Arm aircrew and mechanics. From 1943, nineteen of these ships were converted by removing the superstructure and adding a flight deck. They continued their role as merchant ships, carrying grain or oil in addition to the aircraft. The operator of the first one, *Empire Macalpine*, commented,

> The crew of the vessel was roughly fifty each merchant navy and fleet air
> arm, and these were under different codes of discipline and were paid at
> very considerably different rates. Also the accommodation provided was of
> the usual types for the two services – the merchant navy men having con-
> siderably the better part of the bargain. None of these problems provided
> any real difficulty in practice.[26]

This was largely borne out by John Kilbracken, who flew a Swordfish from *Empire
Macalpine*. The Royal Navy men were enrolled as merchant seamen by signing the
ship's articles. The informality of the merchant navy proved popular. The Fleet Air Arm
officers adopted merchant navy language, calling the wardroom the saloon and lounge,
the ship a boat, a great solecism in the Royal Navy. Some aircrews had the words
'Merchant Navy' painted on their aircraft, in place of 'Royal Navy'. MACs escorted 217
convoys across the Atlantic, and only one was successfully attacked.[27]

Escort carriers were larger. They were designed to operate entirely as small aircraft carriers, and in the first instance it was planned that they, too, should be mer-
chant-navy manned, with FAA aircrews and servicing crews. This was indeed done
with the first ships, *Activity* and *Pretoria Castle*, which were merchant conversions, but
the next ships, *Nairana* and *Vindex*, did not have enough room.

> The large complement of these ships precluded merchant navy standards of
> accommodation being provided for the special agreement personnel. By
> maintaining RN standards throughout however, it was possible to accom-
> modate all personnel in 2nd deck and above …[28]

Later escort carriers were American built and had accomodation to American naval
standards.

HMS *Gordon*

In general, the navy left the merchant service to train its own men, either afloat or
ashore. However, in February 1940 it began to look at ways of helping its manning position, especially since a temporary shortage had been caused by taking up men on T124
agreements. Men who volunteered for the navy but were surplus to requirements were
to be allowed, at the interview stage, to accept training for the merchant navy instead,
rather than go into the army. In March the Second Sea Lord held a meeting with the
Ministry of Shipping and representative of various departments visited the Sea School
at Gravesend on the Thames. They found that there was sleeping accommodation for
240 trainees and ten instructors, but the dining hall could only hold 170. There was 'one
large classroom which could take two classes, a good-sized gymnasium with roller shutters, by means of which two rooms can be created, a wireless-telegraphy classroom'.
There was a forecourt with 'a complete set of Merchant ship hatch-coaming, hatches,
tarpaulins, battens and wedges, a steam winch and cargo derrick, a life boat on davits
which can be turned in and out.'

The *Triton* was to be allocated as a training ship, and the visitors concluded that
apart from cleaning and painting and new black-out arrangements, the premises were
'ready for almost instant occupation'. Even so it was January 1941 before the school
was commissioned as HMS *Gordon*.

Trainee merchant seamen learn steering at HMS *Gordon*.

The trainees were slightly below naval standard, and a few were illiterate, but in general they were very keen. They covered the full age range of conscripts from eighteen to forty-one. According to the commander of the school they were generally from the 'labouring class' and the 'well-educated man' was 'the rare exception'. It was planned to run the school on 'semi-Naval lines' under naval discipline, and for a

Learning lifeboat work, an essential skill for wartime merchant seamen.

time the introduction to merchant navy ways caused difficulty. It was hoped that at least six of the first twelve instructors would be chief petty officers RNR, but in the event only two were available, so regular RN petty officers had to adapt, 'as methods on board ship, and even terms, vary considerably in the two services'.

The trainees were divided into classes of twenty-five, and the twelve-week course began with an introduction by the commanding officer, who warned that duty-free tobacco was a great privilege which should not be abused. The men were issued with single-breasted blue jackets, two pairs of trousers, a peaked cap and working gear such as sea-boots, a sou'wester and oilskins. They learned about signals, knots and splices and did a week of boat-rowing on the nearby canal before embarking for three weeks in the *Triton*. After that they learned about compasses and steering both on shore and afloat, the lifeboats, and the use of hatches and winches in handling cargo. Up to twelve classes might be passing through at once, which caused some difficulties with the single classroom, though more were added in 1941. There was an examination at the end of the course and in 1942 it was suggested that failures might be retrained as firemen, the merchant navy equivalent of stoker. This was rejected, such transfers would 'create the impression that the Fireman Branch is on a lower grade than the Seaman Branch'. By the time the school was closed in January 1944 it had trained 4000 men.[29]

CHAPTER 20

Operational Training and Working Up

Drafting and Commissioning

After completing their disciplinary and technical training, seamen might spend an indefinite amount of time in the naval barracks awaiting a posting. They might be sent as individual replacements for casualties or promotions, or they might be drafted as a whole crew for a new ship. Tristan Jones described how they were assembled on the barrack square at Chatham.

> Soon the different ships' drafts were in some semblance of order, drawn up in ranks three deep, each man with his kit-bag and hammock set alongside of him, and his gasmask over his left shoulder. There was no band – no bull-shit. The order to "shoulder kit-bags and hammocks" was given. "Left turn! Quick march!" and we were off.[1]

They marched out of the barracks to traditional cries of 'Any more for the skylark?' and 'You'll be sorree!' So far they knew nothing of the ship they were going to, but they might guess from the size of the draft. When Albert H. Jones found himself part of a group of 500 men at Plymouth, rumours suggested a battleship; in fact it was the new aircraft carrier *Illustrious*.[2]

The captain and first lieutenant were probably the first to arrive at the shipyard, followed by the other officers and the key petty officers. The tour of the ship was an essential first step for new joiners, such as Nicholas Monsarrat in the *Campanula* in August 1940.

> M. and I toured the ship together, green as grass. Neither of us had seen a corvette before … Ours was afloat, almost finished, and jammed with workmen; the chief noise was supplied by some last-minute riveting going on on the after gun platform, but there were several minor performers of note among the welders, caulkers, joiners, carpenters and plain crash-and-bangers employed on board. We were an hour on our tour, mostly climbing over obstacles and avoiding paintwork, but examining every discoverable corner and going over the ground from bridge to magazine and forepeak to tiller-flat.[3]

The first lieutenant, or 'number one' was the key figure over the next few weeks. He was the senior seaman officer after the captain and would take command of the ship in his absence, but his main job was to organize the crew in appropriate hammock spaces and messes and to allocate them duties for every conceivable routine or emergency. The 'Watch and Quarter Bill … labelled every soul aboard the ship to his manifold duties for there must be no confusion in the minds of anyone as to what part he played in a night or day action, or whilst at cruising stations, entering or leaving harbour, at anchor, or secured alongside dock'. Since most of the crew had not yet arrived, the first lieutenant had to draw the bill up from the men's formal qualifications, as indicated by their substantive and non-substantive rates. 'Commissioning cards' were made out, one for each man, with his duties written down, to be handed out when the bulk of the crew arrived.

> At 8.30 a.m. the crew would board her officially for the first time and there must be no confusion. Nothing would destroy the ratings' confidence in the ship's Number One more swiftly than to allow a slap-happy boarding of a warship … or to have improperly assigned bewildered ratings wandering below, not knowing where to go, what to do … truly a bad beginning for a destroyer.

The men were mustered on the dockside and divided into parties according to their roles on board.

> Right Coxswain! Leaving their kits on the jetty, group one will proceed up the gangway, each receiving his commissioning card and will then enter the after-hatch where he will pick up his berth hammock from the Leading Supply Assistant and proceed to his allotted berth. After making up his berth he will return for his kit and stow same. Subsequent groups are to follow until all are aboard. Is that clear?[4]

The crew stood to attention as the captain's orders were read out.

> The Lords Commissioners of the Admiralty having directed that His Majesty's Ship *Braithwaite* is to be commissioned, you are to proceed to commission that vessel and to cause the utmost dispatch to be used, so far as the same may depend on you, in preparing her for War accordingly.

The captain formally took responsibility for the ship, though she still flew the builder's flag until she had completed her sea trials. F. S. Holt was present as an ordinary seaman when the destroyer *Panther* was taken over in the Clyde in 1941. She carried out 'a multitude of manoeuvres, in which we all had some part to play; however the significance of many of them was not understood by me at the time'. The most dramatic was the full speed trials off Arran.

> The final test was the most impressive; when steaming at "full speed ahead", the order was given for "full speed astern". "Panther" shuddered and quivered like a wounded animal as she came to a stop, then quickly gathered speed going astern until a huge wall of water came over the stern … and swept along the upper deck. We quickly understood why we were required to stay below decks for that particular test.[5]

The trials complete, the captain signed for the ship, the builder's flag was hauled down and the white ensign was hoisted at the stern.

As the ship left the yard, everyone on board was painfully aware of the inexperience of the great bulk of the officers and crew. Commander D.A. Rayner commissioned the corvette *Verbena* in 1940 with only two sub-lieutenants and a midshipman RNVR, and no qualified first lieutenant.[6] When D. S. Goodbrand joined the destroyer *Obdurate* in 1943, the captain addressed the crew: 'Most of you have never been to sea before, therefore you are a liability, not an asset, to this ship. Eighty per cent of you are as green as grass.'[7] Normally the ship's orders at this stage were to proceed to a working-up base where some attempt would be made to rectify this.

Location of Bases

As with Combined Operations and the Fleet Air Arm, a large proportion of working-up and operational-training bases were sited in Scotland. Scapa was used for big ships and fleet destroyers, which were able to exercise there with the Home Fleet.

HMS *Western Isles*, the main working up base for escort vessels, was originally planned as a joint operation with the French at Quiberon Bay on the Atlantic coast of France, but events soon overtook that. The harbour at Tobermory on the island of Mull is one of the safest in Britain, sheltered from almost all winds. Since the ships would arrive complete with crews and most of their stores, the lack of a rail link was not important. The base began to operate in July 1940. By the spring of 1943 it was overstretched, and there was a plan to form a satellite base at Loch Lataich on the south of the island near Iona, where ships on exercise often anchored. This, however, was a much poorer harbour, protected from the sea but not the winds. Later in the year space became available at Stornaway in Lewis, and HMS *Mentor* was commissioned there in December 1943, as an independent command.[8]

In the early stages of the war submarine training was carried out from Portsmouth and Portland on the south coast of England, and in the Forth from Rosyth, where several flotillas were based. In May 1940 it was decided to concentrate on Rosyth and the 3rd and 10th Flotillas moved there from Harwich and Blyth. On 18 June it was ordered that torpedo trials should be moved entirely to the range at Loch Long and it was recognized that as Portsmouth was 'unsuitable as a base for sea training or the Commanding Officers' qualifying course'. It was proposed that this should be carried out in the Campbeltown area. On 21 June the *Cyclops* left Rosyth for the Firth of Clyde, to begin a naval presence that was to last for the rest of the century. Vice-Admiral (submarines) chose the Holy Loch as her anchorage in preference to the site in Rothesay Bay. She was to be the headquarters of the Seventh Flotilla, and to provide submarines for anti-submarine and Combined Operations training, which were being set up in the area. More submarines moved into the area over the next few weeks, along with the small depot ship *White Bear*. At the end of August the *Forth* was ordered to go to the Holy Loch, while the *Cyclops* would move to Rothesay.

The Firth of Clyde became very crowded during the war, as Rear-Admiral Hill pointed out in 1943. Training activities included,

> Aircraft carriers, both fleet and escort, continually working up and exercising.
> H.M.S *Cardiff* carrying out gunnery school firing.
> R.D.F. training flotilla at work.
> The target and picking up vessels working with aircraft from Machrihanish and the R.A.F. stations at Turnberry and Castle Kennedy.

New construction ships on trials or working up.
Various other HM. Ships not included in the above working up and
exercising.
Through the centre of this area runs the main searched channel to what
must be one of the busiest mercantile ports in the world.[9]

Port Edgar, on the Firth of Forth under the shadow of the famous bridge had been
built as an artificial harbour in the last century, but failed because it needed constant
dredging. In 1917 it was taken over as a destroyer base for the Battle Cruiser Fleet,
and later for the Grand Fleet. Between the wars it was occasionally used for the
training of boy seamen. As HMS *Lochinvar* it became the main base for minesweeper
training in 1939, for the Firth of Forth, unlike the Clyde, offered reasonably shallow
water in which to practice.

The main training base for the small, fast craft of Coastal Forces was set up at
Fort William and commissioned as HMS *St Christopher* in October 1940. A base at
Ardrishaig on Loch Fyne, HMS *Seahawk*, was commissioned in January 1941 for
working inshore anti-submarine vessels.

The working up base at Bermuda, HMS *Malabar*, opened late in 1942, mainly for
ships such as destroyer escorts which had been built in the USA for the British navy.
It shared the site with an American 'Shake-Down Group' fulfilling a similar function,
and with the Royal Dockyard.

Big Ships

The working-up time of a ship was roughly proportional to her size. In 1943 a new
battleship was expected to take eight to nine weeks, a cruiser or destroyer six
weeks, a frigate three to four weeks and a corvette two weeks.[10] Battleships and
cruisers were largely self-contained, with enough specialist officers and petty officers
to work up from their own resources. Fleet destroyers usually went to Scapa Flow
where they could practice with the Home Fleet in relatively safe waters.

It was suggested that a fleet aircraft carrier needed only six weeks to work up,
though presumably this meant the ship itself, without the squadrons of aircraft. For
an aircraft carrier in the later stages of the war, the process might be spread
through time and space. When HMS *Implacable* was commissioned early in 1945,
she did her trials in the Clyde, then went round to Rosyth on the Forth, where a
dry dock was available to treat her bottom. It was planned that she should return
to the Clyde to carry out a full-power trial, then fly on her first squadrons. Then
she would sail east, stopping at Alexandria for two weeks to carry out extensive
flying and gunnery training. This was abandoned because of the tactical situation, for
U-boats were active in the Clyde area, and because three carriers were already
working up at Alexandria on the way to the Far East. It was decided that she should
embark the personnel and stores of two squadrons at Rosyth before sailing, then
the two-seat fighters of 1771 squadron would fly on before the ship left the Forth.
The stores and non-flying personnel of two more squadrons would embark at
Scapa, three more squadrons of aircraft would fly on and carry out a few exercises, then she would sail, without calling at the Clyde. She would stop at Ceylon on
the way east, to complete her working up.[11]

Tobermory

Vice-Admiral Sir Gilbert Stephenson RN (retired) was chosen to command the main

A Canadian Navy cartoon of Vice-Admiral Stephenson at *Western Isles.*

working up base for escort vessels. He had been a torpedo specialist and during the First World War he commanded a group of small craft off Crete, making the acquaintance of the RNVR for the first time. In the peace he served as Director of Anti-Submarine Warfare before retiring in 1928. At the outbreak of war he was recalled as a commodore RNR, the highest rank available to a retired officer.

The first *Western Isles* was a former Isle of Man ferry of 1420 tons, converted in the Glasgow shipyard of Barclay Curle in 1940. In 1941 she was replaced by a slightly larger ship, formerly the Dutch *Batavier IV*. Sometimes it was suggested that a shore base would have been more appropriate than a training ship, against which it was argued that

> the fact that the ship is moored amongst the flotilla wearing the broad pendant of the Commodore has an important bearing on the success of the base. The psychological value of being afloat cannot be over-estimated. … Power boats transport classes back and forward and many pulling boats – whalers and skiffs – are seen approaching the gangways, all under they eyes of the Commodore and his staff officers, who are on the look-out for slackness in observing the rig of the day, or for the errors of the inexperienced oarsman or coxswain. Human nature being what it is, it is safe to say that the first impression gained on arrival at Tobermory would be considerably lessened if the introductory interview took place in a shore establishment instead of the flag ship.[12]

Many stories were told about Stevenson. Richard Baker provides the 'authorized version' of a celebrated incident. The Commodore came on board a corvette one winter's morning.

> Without any preliminaries he flung his gold-braided cap on the deck and said abruptly to the Quartermaster – "That is a small unexploded bomb dropped by an enemy plane. What are you going to do about it?" The sailor,

who had evidently heard about these unconventional tests of initiative, promptly took a step forward and kicked the cap into the sea. Everyone waited for a great roar of protest from the Commodore. But not at all. He warmly commended the lad on his presence of mind, and then, pointing to the submerged cap said: "That's a man overboard! Jump in and save him!"[13]

Sometimes Stephenson was outwitted, almost to his delight.

Once, when he was putting a trawler through its paces, he said to a Leading Seaman, a member of a gun crew: "You're dead, lie down." The rating obeyed but, after a few minutes, the Commodore noticed he was on his feet at his usual station and, in his usual fierce manner, exclaimed: "I said you're dead!" The rating's reply was: "Dead or alive my place is at this gun." The Commodore's reaction? "Full marks."[14]

His eye for detail was often noted.

… the commodore concerned himself with everything and everybody and nothing was too small to escape his notice — he even questioned me thoroughly over a reported shortage of soap. On his rounds of inspection he noticed that rats were getting at some of the stores and told me to get rid of some of these pests. I did my best with wire netting and poison, but rats are cunning creatures and still the odd one managed to get in. This did not satisfy him and I remember his remark to this day: "Walker, are you going to beat the rats or allow the rats to beat you?"

Officers had to be constantly wary of his tricks. One corvette captain was disconcerted when a new first lieutenant arrived on board his ship. 'I was disturbed by a rather casual knock at my cabin door and before I could reply, in rushed a very young RNVR officer who placed his cap on my table, sat down (without invitation) and lit a cigarette! … Taking care to avoid a cardiac arrest I just shouted "Get off my ship immediately and return to whoever sent you to learn manners, I have no wish ever to meet you again."' Fortunately the captain had been to *Western Isles* before and knew what to do. 'Had I fallen for the Commodore's ruse it would have been Lieutenant Commander N. B. J. Stapleton, RD, RNR who would have been removed from his command and posted to *Western Isles* for additional training and possibly appointed to some unknown second-rate shore establishment.'[15]

The Syllabus at *Western Isles*
Though the personality of the commodore might have appeared to dominate the base, there was in fact a training syllabus, in its fifth edition by February 1944. Ideally, the newly-commissioned frigate or corvette would arrive at 1630 and the commodore would meet the captain to explain the objects of *Western Isles*. This was more harrowing than the syllabus implied. Three motor launches arrived at Tobermory in March 1943 and according to Lieutenant-Commander C. A. Head, the commodore's barge sped over to them.

The barge, very close now, seemed to disappear. Its engine cut. Where was it? Suddenly, over the flare of the bows of 559, in the centre, appeared a be-

Sailors from the French frigate *La Surprise* improvise a derrick at Tobermory.

whiskered face, visible from the bridge but invisible to the Ordinary Seaman leaning on a broom, … He hauled himself up, straddled the guardrails, slapped the Ordinary Seaman on the back, picked up the broom he had dropped, and, holding it out in front of him like a boarding pike, charged at the bridge.[16]

On the first full day a staff officer would come on board to discuss the fighting organization of the ship, while the *Western Isles* gunnery officer would inspect the armament, followed by inspections by the engineer, electrical and radar officers attached to the base. Towards the end of the morning the men would see the film *Escort Teams at Work,* followed by a short address by the commodore. He told one captain, 'You take it for granted that everyone knows nothing about his job and start from rock bottom.'[17]

That afternoon the crew would split into departments. The signallers would be kept busy by incessant exercises. Radar teams, including unqualified ratings, would have theoretical instruction, with practical work in a radar-raining yacht later. Submarine Detector ratings and officers would see a film on attack procedures and then go on the Attack Teacher. Gunners would carry out drill on the ship's own guns, plus practice on the Dome Teacher and showings of the *Eyeshooting* film. Seamen would practice boat drill, look out duties by day and night, and study seamanship under the boatswain of *Western Isles*. Foot drill ashore, known as 'Field Training', would bring up to half the crew together at a time. There were demonstrations of pyrotechnics, rifle practices and inspections of the ship's stores.

At last on the sixth day, the ship would go to sea, carrying anti-submarine and gunnery officers from *Western Isles,* with a radar instructor rating. She would chase a motor launch acting as a surfaced U-boat, and carry out sub-calibre firing of her main armament. In the afternoon she would begin anti-submarine practices with a real boat, the 'clockwork mouse' and then anchor in Loch Lataich, in the south of Mull. Next morning she would do more anti-submarine practice, then sea exercises such as taking a ship in tow, before returning to Tobermory to do two more days of departmental exercises; on the ninth day there was a 'make and mend' or half-holiday 'at the commanding officer's discretion'.

The second sea trip would begin at 0815 on the tenth day, with another surface chase, followed by eight rounds of full-calibre firing. In the afternoon there were more exercises with the 'clockwork mouse'. This continued for two more days, before return to Tobermory on the twelfth day. The next day was a long one, starting at 0830 with buzzer exercises for signallers, rocket flare drill for gunners and boat work for seamen. The ship sailed early in the afternoon and did an anti-aircraft firing practice with a towed target, followed by a second full-calibre practice with the main guns. After dark there was a night-firing exercise.

The fourteenth and fifteenth days of the course offered no let up. Over the last few days the Group Communications Exercise, to test the ship's communication and plotting organization, had been discussed and planned in several periods. It took place on the morning of day fourteen and involved all the ship's executive officers, signallers, radar and anti-submarine operators and plotters. A time-ball dropped by *Western Isles* started the exercise and several ships anchored in Tobermory Bay would take part. The ships had already been briefed on the convoy they were supposed to be escorting, the state of the weather and the tactical situation. Signals flashed from *Western Isles*, sending ships on mock chases of submarines identified by radar or asdic; if the latter, they opened a pack of prepared asdic traces and followed the information given by them. They might be detailed to pick up survivors, which would take them out of the exercise for fifteen minutes and no more. They might be credited with sinking a submarine by gunfire. After two hours the officers and senior ratings would go on board *Western Isles* with their logs and plots, and compare them with the master plot prepared by the instructors, followed by a discussion on the lessons learnt.

Finally on the sixteenth day the ship was cleaned for a last inspection and the commodore came on board for a debrief. This could be a nerve-wracking moment for officers, for it was well known that Stephenson was harder on them than on the crew.

> It appeared that numerous items in the course of Tobermory training had gone wrong with that particular ship; there was a long list of failings, from omitting to receive signals to taking up the wrong station. The commodore continued, breathless. Once or twice the Captain attempted to interrupt, only to be shut up. I stood back a few paces, feeling extremely sorry for the man. However the Commodore eventually came to the end, exhausted at such expenditure of "steam". He turned to go down the gangway and only then could the Captain of the frigate get out the words: "I am afraid, sir, you have come to the wrong ship!" And so he had.[18]

The time at Tobermory varied according to the size of the ship – twelve days for a coastal trawler, fourteen for a *Flower* class corvette, twenty for a destroyer and twenty-one for a sloop. A frigate spent twenty days and, compared with a corvette, it had extra training in gunnery, harbour drills and boatwork, damage control and field training.[19]

Stephenson earned his nickname the Terror of Tobermory but 1132 ships were trained under his command.

Bermuda

The base at Bermuda was far less successful. While Captain Holloway of the US Shakedown Base was regarded as 'ideally suited to this assignment', Captain H. A. Simpson of HMS *Malabar*, though 'keen and efficient', had no active experience of the Battle of the Atlantic (as distinct from his service in *Western Isles*). *Malabar* was poorly equipped, with only one 'clockwork mouse' submarine compared with the Americans' six. It needed four anti-submarine aircraft to practice co-operation. It was poorly staffed and needed an engineer officer to teach damage control, a qualified signal officer, and a RAF officer to teach co-operation with Coastal Command aircraft. The latest operational instructions for different types of equipment were not always sent out in time. There was no headquarters ship and shore facilities did not fill the gap. It was expected to work up 130 destroyer escorts from September 1943, at a rate of at least twenty ships per month.[20] Captain E. H. Godwin was appointed to the command in the place of Captain Simpson.

Stornaway

Captain D. M. Cann commissioned the Stornaway base in October 1943. He did not have the sense of drama of Stephenson, but he seems to have been highly competent. If his orders and instructions are anything to go by, he was more thoughtful about the procedures. He outlined his principles in 1944. 'The thought in the mind of all instructors must be "We are here to help and advise these ships", not "We've got you now and you jolly well do as you're told." He gave a list of priorities.

> Fighting organization is the first item.
> All instruction must be progressive.
> All radar instruction should be completed before the ship proceeds to sea.
> All gunnery instruction, except for Stores and Accounts, Shallow Diving Apparatus, Range and possibly one session of Field Training should be completed satisfactorily before proceeding for the Sea Gunnery Programme.
> The majority of A/S Attack Teacher and D.C. Training should be done before commencing A/S Exercises. A.T.W. [Ahead-throwing weapon] Training should be completed by this time to enable full value to be obtained from a second day's A.T.W. Attacks.
> Remaining subjects may be fitted in as convenient. It is desirable to keep a few harbour subjects in hand in case the sea programme has to be cancelled. In the case of a smaller ship, fewer subjects are required but it is not possible to programme so many subjects at one time. The total time required is therefore much the same in either case.

Captain Cann made some effort to study techniques at other bases, such as Tobermory and the coastal forces base HMS *Sea Hawk*, and produced his own syllabus which he regarded as 'flexible'. In most respects it was not radically different from the one at Tobermory. [21]

Pre-Commissioning Training

In 1943 the sloop *Starling* trained her gun crews with a method which by-passed the school at Tobermory. The gunnery and two gunners' mates were sent to the Devonport gunnery school along with the crews of the 4-inch guns, the control parties, the gunnery radar operators and the crews of the anti-aircraft Oerlikon guns.

They soon found that the school was too busy to pay much attention to them, and that most of the training equipment was in use. They were forced to rely on their own instructors. The got half a day on 4-inch guns and then organized their own sessions on subjects such as aircraft recognition and fire-fighting. The control ratings, in particular, had 'an uphill job' as there was nothing for them to train on. The radar ratings were found to be 'shockingly trained'. None of them knew how to turn the set on, and there was no instruction; they would have 'profited more by a week's leave'. There was a clash within the gun teams. Some were old hands from HMS *Stork* who had evolved their own drill. 'The complicated full drill book detail was like Greek to them' and they were confused by any new instruction. The rest were new ordinary seamen, keen but lacking action experience.

The ship commissioned at Londonderry, but spent the first two weeks alongside. After that gunnery practices of various types were carried out at sea, and 'Most of the faults were eradicated by the time the last firing took place, but only by much "blood and sweat."' The ship's first cruise was uneventful and gave some time for working up; on the second she forced *U-202* to the surface and sank her by gunfire. 'The psychological effect was enormous. Guns' crews had confidence not only in their gun drill and competence, but also that guns were still, after all, of use in an A/S ship.'[22] Despite her unpromising start, the *Starling* went on to become the most successful ship in Western Approaches under Captain F. J. Walker.

Escort Group Training

A further stage in anti-submarine training, involving several ships of an escort group, was added in the second half of the war. Since there had been few realistic anti-submarine exercises before the war, each group had to evolve its own screen arrangements for convoys, its own tactics, and its own terms to describe them. When convoys were handed over from one group to another in mid-ocean, or a ship was transferred to another group, there was a great deal of confusion. In August 1941, for example, two groups united in defence of convoy SL81. It was not possible to put one group on each side of the convoy so that they could 'employ their own group tactics in the allotted area', so one group, without its normal leader, was somewhat underused. 'It is probable ... that many of them missed the old leader's voice and may on occasion have waited for an executive order which never came.'[23]

The first attempt to remedy this was in November 1942, when extensive shore exercises were carried out in the Tactical School at Liverpool, allowing an analysis of techniques used by individual group commanders, after which Captain Gilbert Roberts compiled a common series of orders.[24] Meanwhile Captain A. J. Baker-Creswell, in command of an escort group based in the Clyde, made contact with the submarines based there and gave his group half a day's practice before sailing with each convoy. Late in 1942, at the instigation of the First Sea Lord, he was given the chance to organize a group training school. He chose the yacht *Philante*, formerly belonging to the millionaire, Sir Thomas Sopwith, as his flagship, and she was sent to Hull to be fitted out with staff offices. He settled for a submarine and two motor torpedo boats to simulate U-boats at night. He was to operate from Londonderry, where a naval base had been improvised from nothing since the start of the war, and he would be in constant touch with ships on active service. This was not entirely successful. The river channel was badly marked and ships under training often went aground; Baker-Cresswell had to lead them in and out in an MTB, doing his own navigation. He felt he was not getting enough co-operation from Captain Stewart at

Londonderry, and the course moved to Larne for a time.[25]

Group training was not wholeheartedly supported at all levels, for many destroyer captains felt no need for further lessons. Captain F. J. Walker, the star U-boat killer of the war, was prepared to lecture in courses but not to undergo one himself.[26] Sir Max Horton, the Commander-in-Chief of Western Approaches, had never been out on an ocean convoy, was persuaded by Baker-Cresswell to come for a night and day exercise in 1943.

An exercise of August 1943 was intended to train a hunting group, to patrol the Bay of Biscay for submarines on passage to and from their bases. The three ships of the escort group would start with a day of firing and radar practices, with a 'creeper' attack on a submarine. On the second day they would go to sea for a full-scale exercise in hunting down a submarine. According to the scenario, an area 100 miles wide was constantly patrolled by aircraft, and one of these would signal contact with a U-boat about 20 miles away. The hunting group would turn and try to home in by radio direction finding, with help of the aircraft radar. The submarine would dive, and the group would hunt it using one of three methods. The object of a Square Search was to 'restrict the movements of a U-boat which has been dived for some time while waiting for it to surface to recharge, rather than to obtain asdic contact before the time arrives'. If this was impossible because of the large area involved, then a Sector Search would be used, in which each escort would search a particular area. In an Inward Spiral Search, the escorts would gradually close in on a chosen position, on the analogy of 'the cutting of a cornfield, and the killing of rabbits therein when the centre of the field as yet uncut becomes small'.[27]

Another exercise was observed by a naval operational research team in July 1944. They involved the investigation of high-speed evasive tactics by the submarine during attacks by Hedgehog ahead-throwing weapons, and the conference at the end of the day was regarded as very useful, though the observer lamented that no notes and statistics were compiled.[28] The group training course was highly successful, though it suffered from too many changes of command – Baker-Cresswell himself was drafted out against his will in 1943.

Continuity Training

Though escort vessels in the Battle of the Atlantic were in constant danger while escorting convoys, they might go sometime without any contact with the enemy. In 1943, for example the frigate HMS *Itchen* escorted eight successive convoys without incident. It was important to maintain skills in weapons and sensors, and for that reason the shore bases were well equipped to train crews.

Londonderry developed as the largest escort base, with space for up to seventy-five ships to berth alongside. The base was equipped with an anti-submarine tactical school, two anti-submarine Attack Teachers, a Depth Charge, Hedgehog and a Squid Driller, gunnery, signal, and direction finding schools and a mock-up of a U-boat interior to aid boarding parties to prevent scuttling and capture vital equipment. On arriving back from a convoy, half of each crew would be sent on leave during boiler cleaning, including all but one of the submarine detector ratings. After they returned the second half went on leave and almost all the anti-submarine team was available to train on the anti-submarine equipment. The whole crew was united two or three days before the ship was due to resume operations, and went out for intensive training off Londonderry.[29] Peter Gretton, one of the most successful escort group commanders of the war, describes the process.

Before leaving on each escort duty, two or three days and nights were spent exercising off the entrance to the River Foyle, working with submarines, firing at targets and carrying out the multitude of jobs which might fall to a convoy escort. In fact, the men sometimes complained that they felt more tired after the pre-convoy exercises than after the convoy itself!

Gretton considered that this training was a vital factor in British success against the U-boat. 'I personally believe that the difference in standards of training between British escorts and German submarines was important …' [30]

Damage Control

Sailors in the basic training schools learned how to row with a view to survival in a lifeboat, and a good deal about anti-gas precautions which in the event were never needed, but they were not taught systematically how to prevent their ship sinking. This had been considered by a committee in 1937, which found two main gaps in procedure. The use of venting in the case of internal explosion was not appreciated, and officers were too obsessed with keeping the ship on an even keel by means of counter-flooding after damage. Apart from that, 'the general standard is high.' The committee was convinced that 'in time of war, our organization and training … should generally ensure that the correct defensive measures are taken.'[31] This was not borne out by combat experience and the navy's damage control procedures were certainly underdeveloped in the early stages of the war. The *Ark Royal*, the most famous British aircraft carrier, was sunk on 14 November 1941, when a single torpedo caused a severe list but no fatal damage in itself. Counter-flooding should have righted the ship, but some watertight doors had been left open. There were design faults in the ship; the steam and electric power systems were put out of action, and there were not enough diesel generators to pump the water out. She sank after more than twelve hours.[32]

Some training was given in fire-fighting, and a rating of stoker-fire fighter was created, mainly for service in shore bases. Admiral Ford found that they were the rejects of the Stoker Branch, which was already low in priorities; they were 'ill-disciplined and dirty, … disgruntled with the navy' and 'unteachable'.[33]

The first suggestions for systematic training in damage control proper were made in the Autumn of 1942, but the idea was rejected by Captain Oram. 'While sympathizing with the objects of the proposal, the manning situation is now such as to render the provision [of] whole time instructors impracticable.' The idea was revived in May 1943, by the Deputy Controller of the Navy. A school was set up in the basement of a requisitioned house in west London, then others in the four main naval ports, including Rosyth. In each, a Nissen hut was fitted with a lecture room and a large floodable tank. There were five-day courses for petty officers, and they would be expected to train the men under them. Damage control would be included in all examinations for a higher rate.[34]

There was a separate section in the new *Seaman's Manual* of 1943, which was soon reprinted on its own. It advised sailors to get to know their way around their ship. 'It may well be that during battle you may be in the same position as a blind person – the lights may have failed or there may be dense smoke from fires and you can see nothing.' In the case of flooding, they were told that the main aim was to confine it to as small an area as possible, and that watertight doors and hatch coamings should be treated as 'aids to preserving your ship and yourself, which they are, and

The use of the pump in a damaged ship.

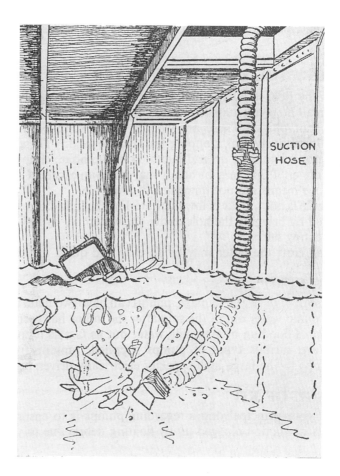

SUCTION HOSE

not just as obstacles which hamper your movements'. When using pumps, they were instructed to prevent the intake being choked, and this meant the correct stowage of personal gear before the action. They were given lists of the main types of fire extinguisher and their uses, and warned against neglecting anti-flash gear in warm climates – 'In battle this thoughtless practice may prove fatal.'[35]

Submarine Training

Submarines were never so central in British strategy in this period as they were to Germany, or indeed to the post-war British navy. The submarine service was quite small, with only 9090 ratings in September 1944,[36] though it was growing with the launching of new boats – 3226 men were allocated to fifty new submarines built in 1943. One of the difficulties of the service was that when a submarine was lost the crew was almost certainly lost with it.[37]

Potential submarine ratings were in theory volunteers who had completed their disciplinary and technical training, though it seems that some were drafted in without being asked. They started with six weeks theoretical training in the Portsmouth depot, HMS *Dolphin*, during which, according to Arthur Dickison, 'We never set foot in a submarine.' Instead they spent two weeks being drilled in escape procedure, and the use of the Davis Escape Apparatus in a mock submarine compartment at the bottom of a tank. 'The experience of that water slowly rising up my body made the hairs stand up on the back of my neck and when it touched my chin I was not far off pan-

The British crew in the captured U-boat HMS *Graph* having a break in the mess.

icking. One of my fellow trainees did. When the water was at chin height the pressure was equalized and the instructor opened the hatch at the top of the chamber. In turn, we ducked under a canvas tube and floated up to the surface, 100 feet above. On subsequent runs most of us achieved more confidence but sadly there were two of the class who could not get it right.'[38] On average about 12 per cent failed the course, often at this stage.[39]

The class then went to the submarine base at Blyth in Northumberland for two months' practical training in an old seagoing submarine. Then they went to the Seventh Submarine Flotilla based in HMS *Cyclops* off Rothesay in the Firth of Clyde, where they trained in old boats left over from the First World War.

The *Cyclops* was quite large at 11,300 tons, and this allowed room for training facilities such as an Attack Teacher. 'The purpose of the Seventh Submarine Flotilla was twofold: to give sea training to new submarine officers and ratings, and at the same time to provide live targets for destroyers and other escort craft. Many of the boats in this flotilla were dispersed at the various bases where anti-submarine forces had their training. So we spent the next few winter months up and down the rugged and beautiful coastline of Western Scotland, dividing our time between Rothesay, Campbeltown, Ardrishaig and Tobermory.'[40]

Potential submarine commanders set out from *Cyclops* on practical courses, known as 'Perishers'. One theory suggests that this was simply a corruption of the 'Periscope' Course, another that they were so-called because failure would bar the candidate from any further appointments in the submarine service. Edward Young describes his experiences in 1943. After two weeks shore training at Gosport near Portsmouth he was billeted in a local hotel but had to catch a boat to the *Cyclops* every morning before breakfast. He describes his first mock attack.

> I swept [the periscope] rapidly across the green shores of Bute, ... swung past the entrances to Loch Fyne and Kilbrannan Sound, and continued along the steep shores of Arran, which rose nearly three thousand feet to the imposing summit of Goat Fell. The only ship in sight apart from the target

was an outward-bound merchantman steaming down the main channel of the Firth of Clyde. Completing the circle I came back once more to the target, still going away to the eastward. … Waiting for the *White Bear* to turn, I felt horribly uncertain of myself. … In as calm a voice as I could muster, I gave the order, "attack team close up."'

After three hard weeks he was sent to Scapa to practice with modern warships and conducted a mock attack on the battleship *King George V*. He passed, as did all but one of his course, and was appointed to command an old submarine operating as a 'clockwork mouse' from Rothesay.[41]

The final stage was the working up of a boat with its operational crew, also done in the Firth of Clyde. In 1942 Arthur P. Dickinson of HM Submarine *Safari* found that 'The two months based at HMS FORTH were hectic. We were in and out of the Holy Loch and into the Clyde estuary on trials and exercise to bring the boat and her crew up to operational standard.'[42] In 1944 Arthur Hezlett took the *Trenchant* through her working up and trials. Guns were fired at sleeve targets towed by aircraft, and sub-calibre firing was carried out against surface targets. One of the biggest tasks was practising torpedo attacks.

Practice in making attacks was done in three stages. In every submarine base and depot ship there was a Submarine Attack Teacher in which, with model ships and a rotating 'submarine' with a short periscope, attacks could be simulated. The second stage was to make dummy attacks at sea in the submarine, using ships as targets. The third stage was the same as the second but practice torpedoes were fitted with dummy heads set to run under the target. The complexity of these exercises could be varied from an attack when the target steered a straight course at moderate speed to others when the target zig-zagged or used high speed. Finally exercises could be carried out with escorts round the target. In *Trenchant* we carried out some of all of these exercises during a period of some three weeks.[43]

Coastal Forces

Coastal forces were another new development during the Second World War. They included the Motor Torpedo Boats or MTBs, Motor Gun Boats (MGBs), Motor Launches (MLs), Harbour Defence Motor Launches (HDMLs), Motor Minesweepers (MMs) and many other miscellaneous types. The MTBs were amongst the most glamorous and publicized types in the Navy. They were constantly in contact with the enemy in the English Channel and North Sea, often fighting with the German equivalent, S-boats (also known to the Allies as E-Boats). HDMLs and MMs had much more mundane but often equally dangerous duties. More than any other part of the service, it was the preserve of the temporary wartime RNVR officer.

HMS *St Christopher* had nineteen MLs, eight MTBs and nine MGBs at its peak. These were moored to trots in Loch Linnhe, accessible by open boat from Fort William. The training boats had skeleton crews of instructors, with the other berths filled by trainees of the different branches and skills – officers, gunners, torpedomen, mechanics, radio operators and so on. Boats usually went down the loch towards Oban for several days at a time, though it was felt by some that the enclosed waters of the Firth of Lorne did not give a full range of sea-going experience. About 50,000 men passed through *St Christopher* during the war.

HMS *Seahawk*'s role was to train coastal forces crews in anti-submarine warfare. It had three MLs, two Motor Anti-Submarine Boats and an HDML, but no MTBs because they were not intended for a anti-submarine work. It also had two midget submarines or X-craft as 'clockwork mice', plus the services of boats from the Seventh Submarine Flotilla when needed.[44]

For the 600 ten-man Harbour Defence Motor Launches built during the war, the course lasted three weeks. Judging by the syllabus it kept quite civilized hours; work finished by about 5.00 p.m. on most days, unless there was a sea exercise. It carried on during Saturday morning, as was common in all walks of life in those days, but exercises might continue all day if required. During the week there was the usual mixture of foot drill (for men below petty officer), films on anti-aircraft and anti-submarine warfare, a general drill to check the effectiveness of the quarter bill, and exercises in the anti-submarine Attack Teacher. There were night manoeuvres on certain evenings and if enough boats were available they practiced forming an endless chain round an anti-submarine defence. Since the school was in the confined area of Loch Fyne it was not possible to practice anti-aircraft gunnery, but a midget submarine was available for asdic practice. Coxswains were given instruction in victualling procedures, and cooks who were found to be below average were sent to work under a petty officer of the Patrol Service.[45]

Coastal Forces gave a certain amount of training to their motor mechanics after the courses at Royal Naval Training Units. HMS *Attack* at Portland, formerly the asdic training school, offered a course of eight to ten weeks in a flotilla of MTBs, MGBs and motor launches, in order to familiarize the men with the types of engine they would work with. They also had to be acclimatized to the sea, and in preparation for this they spent the last two weeks at Portland training afloat. 'During this period they get their sea legs, are seasick and learn how to handle their engine.'[46]

Minesweeping

As well as officers, minesweeper ratings were trained at *Lochinvar* on the Forth. At the height of the war, fifty arrived each week to begin a three-week course. 'Like the officers, they spend two days at sea and acquire practical experience in the manual working of the sweeps, in splicing the wire hawsers, in steering the trawler, and in those deck duties which the Navy describes by the expressive term "pulley-hauley." Ashore, Petty Officers give them general instruction in trawler gunnery, rifle practice, deck work and general seamanship, so that they may take their places as efficient members of any minesweeping ship, whether she be trawler, drifter, dan-layer, or fleet sweeper.[47]

The other task at *Lochinvar* was the working-up of newly commissioned ships and their crews. 'The process of working-up consisted of taking a newly commissioned ship, usually fresh from the builder's yard and sea trials, and in fourteen days turning it into a unit sufficiently efficient to work with the fleet at sea, or in the case of trawlers to go immediately into operations around our coast. So far as it was possible we would work up the Fleet sweepers together and the trawlers together, because the two did not work together very well.'[48]

After the working up, the ships went off to join their operational fleets and flotillas in various parts of the world. The crew of each was, in theory at least, welded together as a unit, in which all men, from different ranks and branches of the service, would work together as a team for a common end. Despite the haste of the training, they were regarded as ready to fight the enemy on and under the sea, in the air and occasionally on land. Many of them would witness the great events of history –

the Dunkirk evacuation, the sinking of the *Bismarck*, the Battle of the Atlantic, the Normandy landings – through a fog of exhaustion, seasickness or terror. Of the million men and women who went to war with the Royal Navy, 14,663 would be wounded and 7,401 would become prisoners of war. About one in twenty of them – 50,758 – would not return.[49]

CHAPTER 21

An Assessment

How can we assess the performance of the navy's wartime training programme? In the final analysis the navy was successful, even in the eyes of the most penetrating critics of British strategy. '[The British] had, for all their blundering, fought well – perhaps better than they had ever done previously – and against heavy odds. The Royal Navy in particular had improved upon its performance in the First World War and it would be churlish to deny to the service the praise it rightly deserved.'[1] But was it successful because of or despite its training techniques?

The navy had little respect for the teaching profession, perhaps because of the educational background of many officers – they were torn away from the ordinary education system in their early teens, often sent to naval crammers where they did not see teaching at its best, then on to the highly specialized world of Dartmouth. In pure educational terms, the navy would probably not come out very well from an inspection. It made little effort to recruit and deploy qualified teachers, and relied too much on untrained instructors. It took too long to set up training programmes for instructors.

Operational Performance

It is quite easy to find examples of disasters caused by poor doctrine among the senior officers. The carriers *Glorious* and *Courageous* were lost early in the war because of misunderstandings about their role in action. The *Hood* was lost because of her poor armour protection, the *Ark Royal* because of poor damage control. The *Prince of Wales* and *Repulse* were unescorted in an area dominated by enemy air power. More generally, the navy rapidly made up for its overconfidence in asdic before the war, and did its best to develop techniques of naval air power. A more fundamental problem was the failure to adopt a tachymetric system for aiming anti-aircraft guns, a problem which was not rectified by the end of the war. Naval defeats can usually be attributed to specific causes, but one rarely finds captains attributing failure to poorly trained or inexperienced crews. Exceptions included the tendency for anti-aircraft gunners to fire too soon; the loss of the battleship *Barham* in 1941, attributed to poor group training in the anti-submarine escort;[2] and the failure of the new anti-submarine weapon, Hedgehog, in 1943, because it was beyond the skills of hastily-trained operators.[3]

The importance of thorough training was highlighted during the most complex joint operation of all time – the D-Day landings. These took place between two periods of bad weather, in far worse conditions than planned. The British forces in Gold, Juno and Sword beaches were not without their difficulties. 'Soldiers and sailors had been well practised in the drill for getting the small craft away from their parent ships, but when loaded each weighed over thirteen tons and great skill was needed to release them smartly and safely into the short steep seas. These shallow craft are lively and wet and the fact that all were got away without a single mishap was proof not only of skilled seamanship but good training, good organization and good discipline.' But the passage to the shore was not so straightforward on Juno Beach.

> Only on one sector of the divisional front did the D.D. tanks beach ahead
> of the infantry and at once engage the defences; on all other Canadian sec-
> tors the tanks arrived after the infantry. Most of the craft which carried the
> engineers' tanks were delayed through having got into the wrong swept
> channel during the passage, and the leading infantry were a little late too.
> ... The larger landing craft had therefore to drive on-shore in spite of
> obstructions and the smaller craft to worm their way through if they
> could.

A quarter of the craft on Juno Beach were lost or damaged in landing or withdrawal.[4]

In the American sector, things were far worse. The Utah Force landed on the
wrong beach by mistake, which proved a blessing as it was less heavily defended than
the correct one. But on Omaha Beach there was near disaster, caused initially by failures among the landing craft crews.

> ... units became scattered on the final approach. Since the men had been
> briefed only for their particular areas, they were confused by the changed
> picture ... Debarking in water sometimes up to their necks, the troops on
> some sectors of the beach were met with a hail of bullets that drove some
> to seek shelter under the surf, others to scramble over the sides of their
> craft. ... the first wave should have landed nine companies evenly spaced
> along the beach. Because of enemy fire and mislandings, however, the right
> wing all but disintegrated; two companies bunched in front of Les Moulins,
> and the remainder of the landings (elements of four companies) clustered
> in the Colleville sector. One company was carried so far east that it landed
> an hour and a half late.[5]

The American commander attributed these problems to the fact that the landing
crews were inadequately trained, that they had received 'only a few days instruction'
and that 'they did not arrive in the theatre soon enough'.[6]

Comparison with the Past

It would be possible to write a history of British naval disasters during the wars with
France from 1689–1815, solely in terms of failures to man the fleet. In each of the
wars of the long eighteenth century it took two or three years to build the navy up
to its full operational strength, though the ships were available from the reserve fleet
as soon as they were manned. After that, fleet numbers tended to reach a plateau;
wartime shipbuilding served to replace losses but actual expansion was quite slow.
All these wars ended in some kind of British victory at sea, but that was only possible after the fleet had been fully mobilized, which usually took at least two years.

The navy's problems in the age of sail were partly caused by the brutal and inefficient system of impressment. It encouraged seamen to find any way possible to
avoid the navy, and almost certainly put many young men off the idea of a seafaring
career. But the lack of any training system was just as much at fault. It took a long
time to find the seamen, not just because they were hiding, but also because many of
them were on long voyages to America, the West Indies and India. All this meant that

the British naval build up was always a slow one. Hundreds of ships were kept in reserve in peacetime, and any one could be made ready for sea in about three weeks; but only if crews were available to man them.

The situation was reversed in the Second World War. Naval strength was no longer limited by British shipbuilding and ships captured from the enemy; the resources of the United States produced hundreds of escort vessels, carriers and landing craft. The numbers of men in the navy continued to expand throughout the war but it was a national, rather than a naval manpower crisis which slowed this expansion down. In contrast to the sailing navy, the twentieth-century fleet was highly successful in absorbing non-sailors into its ranks.

Morale

The navy benefitted from high national morale in wartime. The vast majority of recruits could understand the need to fight the war – not perhaps in detail or with any sophistication, but with conviction and passion. In the case of technical instruction, in anti-aircraft gunnery or submarine detection for example, the need for the training was clear to everyone – failure to learn the techniques could result in the loss of a ship or a convoy. At the time, the British public saw the navy as the most reliable of the services. The square collar and bell bottoms of the sailor remained the symbol of resourcefulness, leadership and success.

The navy's most subtle advantage was its own history, its will to win and its refusal to accept defeat, something which went very deep in naval culture. Could one imagine a British officer in the situation of Captain Langsdorff of the *Graf Spee* in 1939? He first showed excessive bravado in taking on three British cruisers, against Hitler's orders. Then he scuttled his ship rather than face three British cruisers, of inferior gunpower, waiting outside, fooled by false intelligence suggesting the British force was much stronger. This was clearly not a question of personal fear, as Langsdorff committed suicide immediately, but of confidence. In another example, the U-boats had to be withdrawn from the Battle of the Atlantic for a time in 1943, partly because of the failure of their captains to press home attacks. The first generation of highly successful commanders had been lost, the new ones had not the determination to carry them through adversity, ultimately because of a lack of a deep naval tradition in Germany. In general the U-boat captains and crews were incredibly brave, but at this moment their nerve failed. It is difficult to imagine a British admiral having to issue an order like the one Admiral Donitz signalled in May 1943.

> If there is anyone who thinks that combatting convoys is no longer possible, he is a weakling and no true U-boat captain. The Battle of the Atlantic is getting harder but it is the determining element in the waging of the war.[7]

The German armed forces were justly famed for their discipline and determination, but in these cases it seems to have failed them, perhaps because officers had less training in how to operate alone, without the infrastructure of military command around them.

British captains, ever since the days of Sir Richard Grenville of the *Revenge* in 1591, had always been expected to take their ships into action alone against impossible odds, and it was maintained by Captain Kennedy of the *Rawalpindi* and Captain Fegen of the *Jervis Bay* in 1940. Nor was this just a matter of culture among the officers. No self-respecting member of the lower deck would want to come home with his ship or himself in disgrace, even at the cost of his life. Ratings had no specific training in naval history, but the expectation of success permeated down to them, and was reinforced by their own pride and bravado.

Morale under Stress

Unlike other services, the Royal Navy had no system of rotating its men and ships in dangerous situations. In trench warfare the army only needed a proportion of its men in the line at once, unless a major attack was planned, and the others could rest some way behind the lines. The air force took bomber crews off operations after a fixed number of missions, while fighter pilots were rested after a specific time. The US Navy also developed policies for taking ships out of operational areas for periods of rest, but the Royal Navy was too hard-pressed throughout the war to attempt this. If men were rested it was because of the operational needs of the navy, or the mechanical needs of the ship. Boiler cleaning or dry docking often gave a chance for part of the crew to go on leave. But there was no systematic thought on this, and D. A. Rayner spent five years in continuous operations in escort vessels and eventually lost his nerve.[8] In the air, John Godley lost his self-confidence after more than a thousand hours on active service.[9] Captain F. J. Walker, the most successful U-boat hunter of the Atlantic campaign, died in 1944 of cerebral thrombosis brought on by 'overstrain, overwork and war weariness'.[10] Stress on the individual and the organization continued to grow throughout the war.

Apart from defeat in battle, a major breakdown of discipline is probably the worst problem that can confront a navy. Certainly there was nothing to compare with the revolts at Kronstadt and Wilhelmshaven at the end of the First World War, which inspired revolutions in Russia and Germany respectively; or even with Invergordon, which remained entirely peaceful but forced Britain off the Gold Standard in 1931. Yet discontent was not far beneath the surface of the navy by 1945. Several cases found their way into courts martial. In 1942, the chief engineer of the seaward defence vessel *Helvig* refused to obey the captain's orders. In 1944 marines had to be called out to control the crew of the headquarters ship *Lothian*. In July 1945 the men of the destroyer *Relentless* refused to fall in to do work in the afternoon.[11] There were other examples of disobedience where the issue was settled locally and the case never came to any kind of court. Tristan Jones mentions that the crew of the destroyer *Obstinate* refused duty in 1942 in 'the nearest thing I ever saw to fullscale mutiny on board one of His Majesty's ships'. Roderick Macdonald describes how the men of the destroyer *Fortune* refused duty in what was undoubtedly 'Mutiny as defined in the Naval Discipline Act' until the first lieutenant went round the messdecks and read extracts of the act to them. There was a mutiny among landing craft crews around Ipswich before D-Day, in which a chaplain was sent to mediate. A. H. Cherry described a mutiny among the crew of the destroyer *Braithwaite*, in which the marines from another ship were used as a threat.[12] Since these cases only came to light by chance, there can be little doubt that many more were unrecorded.

By 1944 there was concern at the Admiralty. In March, Sir Algernon Willis, the Second Sea Lord, remarked that 'We have seldom got through a major war without some breakdown of morale varying from serious mutiny down to vociferous expressions of dissension and dissatisfaction.' One official foresaw a wider problem – ' the real risk that there is of indiscipline because of social upheavals that may be expected in the country as a whole'. A document on the subject, 'Notes on Dealing with Mutiny or Massed Disobedience', was sent out to senior officers in June. It advised captains to avoid the development of any grievance if at all possible. When mutiny became likely, they were to separate the loyal men from the disloyal; to address the men if that was felt to be appropriate, often from the direction least expected so that the ringleaders could not hide at the back; they were to 'indicate unmistakably that they intend to retain or regain control and to uphold discipline'. If the situation developed further they were to set up a defensible citadel, to have patrols armed with guns or cudgels and to prevent illicit signals between ships; shooting to kill, however, was only to be resorted to 'as a last extremity'.

The paper provoked controversy among the admirals. The causes of revolt, according to the first draft, were likely to be 'War weariness and a strong desire to return to home life' and 'a realization that the men of the Fleet are not likely to be released in the same proportions as men in the other Services, because a large part of the Fleet will have to be moved to the East'. This part was edited out of the 2000 copies sent to captains, but incorporated in a letter to flag officers. Even then it caused some disquiet. Admiral Sir Max Horton, Commander-in-Chief of Western Approaches, took exception to the tone of the document. 'I feel that if they are generally distributed in their present form and at the present time there is a grave danger that they will not achieve their object and may indeed help to bring about the contingencies which they are designed to prevent.' Their effect on reserve officers 'with relatively short experience of the traditional methods and principles of naval discipline and leadership' was 'likely to be very unsettling and to produce in them a state of anxiety and distrust which must inevitably arouse similar reactions in their men'. Furthermore, Horton saw the individual rather than general mutiny as the real problem, and as one which could be contained. 'It is my firm conviction that no ordinary ship's company will resort to mass indiscipline unless they are labouring under grievances which a reasonable investigation will prove well founded.'[13]

An examination of actual mutinies suggests that Horton was probably closer to the truth than Willis. The *Helvig* affair was the result of merchant navy officers being taken into the navy without proper training, and the unreasonable behaviour of the captain. The *Lothian* mutiny was attributed to the lack of leadership by the captain and the 'unfortunate manner' of the first lieutenant. In *Relentless* it was caused by the 'extreme youth and inexperience' of the officers and an old problem, the 'failure of the leading hands of the messes to stop the talk on the messdecks as soon as it started'. With Jones in the *Obstinate*, it was a protest against the orders to withdraw the escort from convoy PQ17, leading to one of the great disasters of the war. In the Fortune, the poor leadership of an inadequate captain led to the growth of discontent and demoralization. Among the landing craft at Ipswich, the officer concerned referred to 'the scum on the lower deck', suggesting a lack of leadership on his part. In the case of the *Braithwaite*, Cherry attributes it to the weakness of the coxswain, though he himself was quickly replaced as first lieutenant.

Each of these cases can be attributed to a failure in leadership somewhere along the line, from the Admiralty itself in the case of PQ17, to the much put-upon leading hands of the *Relentless*. They certainly show signs of an organization under extreme stress, where many officers and ratings were promoted beyond their ability, where good leaders were in short supply. It is difficult to attribute any of them directly to wartime training programmes. The captain of the *Fortune* was a peacetime officer, promoted further than he might have been because of the war. The *Helvig* case was specifically caused by the lack of training. Only the *Braithwaite* suggests any general fault in the navy, for Cherry writes that by November 1943, when the mutiny happened, senior officers recognized that the navy was 'scraping the bottom of the barrel' for personnel.[14]

No signs of a general mutiny can be traced in practice, and Willis was wrong in his fears, while the 'social upheavals … in the country as a whole' never materialized, perhaps because the Labour government of July 1945 began to tackle some of the potential causes. Perhaps an even longer war, largely against Japan, would have caused much more serious problems, but the atom bomb removed that prospect.

Comparison with the Army

Several important failings were noticed in the British army during the war, and most of them could be traced back to faults in doctrine and training.[15] There was too much drill and therefore too little initiative at the lower levels; operational experiences, for example in the desert war, were not fed back to troops training at home; there was far too little co-ordination between the different arms of service in battle conditions. How far did these faults apply to the navy?

Certainly the navy used foot drill to train men in obedience, though it was perhaps less central to naval training than to the army. The genial petty officers and leading seamen did not 'break' the recruits in the way that army sergeants traditionally did. Since the navy depended on ships rather than individual men, the problem was rather different. Initiative was certainly demanded of captains and admirals, and the lack of it in the First World War had caused serious errors.[16] This was not a problem in the second war, partly because inter-war training had greatly increased and developed the initiative of captains. It was even more important for the hundreds of commanders of coastal forces, submarines and corvettes or for aircrew officers than for the captains of a great battlefleet, who were usually in company with the admiral.

On board the individual ship, short-term initiative was needed for engine room watchkeepers, lookouts, radar and sonar operators, and particularly by anti-aircraft gunners who had to decide whether to fire on approaching aircraft. A deeper kind was needed by the senior men of the various specialist departments, who had no-one else to rely on in case of difficulty – for example, the senior medical officer or rating who had to deal with shocking casualties on his own. It was needed by the senior engineer of each ship, from the engineer-commander of a battleship to the stoker of a small landing craft. The people concerned developed self-confidence which made them respected and relatively independent within the hierarchy of the ship.

Army initiative tended to fail most obviously in the chaos of battle, where command structures broke down and nothing went according to plan. At sea, the nearest equivalent was when a ship was damaged and perhaps on the verge of sinking. Fighting fires or blocking leaks might well depend on the man on the spot, whatever his rank or rating. This was a case where the navy was less than successful. Its damage control procedures were underdeveloped until late in the war, and training only started quite late.

Unlike the army, the bulk of the navy was constantly engaged from the start of the war to the end. The mechanism for sending information back to the training schools was a little slow to develop, and it was 1942 before enough officers and petty officers with active service experience were available in the schools. Combined Operations was a special case here, as experience was gained through several major operations, rather than continuously; but efforts were made to diffuse the lessons.

The breakdown between the different arms of the service was also less of a problem in the navy. The army was a collection of regiments and corps, which lived, trained and operated separately except in manoeuvres or in battle. The regimental tradition was of overriding importance, especially in the infantry and cavalry, and transfers of men (or ideas) were strongly resisted. In that sense, the navy had the advantage of coherence. The different branches, such as seamen, engineers or marines, trained separately but came together when they joined a ship. There was always rivalry between the branches, but everyone knew that each had its vital role in running and fighting the ship. At a higher level, different types of ship were trained to operate together in peacetime, and a balanced fleet would include battleships, cruisers, destroyers, aircraft carriers, escort vessels and minesweepers, each with its role in a major battle. Peacetime officers and men served in turn in different types of ships and had a broad experience of the navy as a whole.

Oddly enough, this was partly reversed in wartime. There was no time to give temporary officers a balanced career, and in any case strategic needs had changed. There were several different campaigns going on at the same time, largely independent of one another. Crews of deep-sea escort vessels knew nothing of amphibious warfare. Submarines had little to do with battleships, coastal forces did not co-operate with aircraft carriers. At the same time, there were many cases where co-operation was essential, especially in the larger operations such as the chase of the *Bismarck*, Arctic convoys and the D-Day landings. In general the navy was more successful than the army in this war, partly because its training and doctrine were more adaptable, and more closely related to actual practice.

Comparison with Other Navies

Of all the navies of the Second World War, only the British and Americans produced anything like a 'balanced' fleet. Apart from the shortage of surface vessels, the Germans never put an aircraft carrier to sea. The Japanese were of course strong in naval aviation, but they failed to grasp the value of the submarine in raiding enemy supply lines, or to protect their own lines. The Italians, though individually brave, were too committed to keeping their 'fleet in being' by hiding in port, a tactic which proved useless when ships were sunk by torpedo attack at Taranto. They, too, did very little to develop carrier aviation. All the enemy powers were essentially military societies, in which conscription was normal and service to the state overrode the feelings of the individual, so they do not compare easily with Britain, the United States and the Commonwealth countries.

Among the allied powers, the French had only a single, unsatisfactory aircraft carrier in this period, and in any case they were not in the war long enough to prove themselves. Of the other short-lived allies, the Polish, Norwegian, Denmark, Belgian and Greek navies were essentially coast defence forces and only Denmark and Greece had ships as large as cruisers. The Netherlands, once a great naval power, had a coast defence force at home and a substantial force of cruisers and destroyers to defend their possessions in the East Indies. China had a few light cruisers and destroyers, and a flotilla of gunboats to attempt internal control on the great rivers. The Soviet Fleet concentrated on coastal warfare in the Baltic, with a certain amount of effort in protecting the Arctic convoys against submarine, surface ship and air attack. The dominion navies – Canada, Australia, New Zealand and South Africa – were all heavily dependent, in their own ways, on the Royal Navy, and tended to find specialist functions within the Commonwealth force.

Before the war the Royal Australian Navy concentrated on cruisers, as being effective vessels in the vast distances of the Pacific. In September 1939 they had six (of which three were lost in the war) along with five destroyers and two sloops under construction. The naval force began in 1939 with 5440 men and rose to nearly 37,000, plus 2600 members of the Women's Royal Australian Naval Service – a sevenfold expansion, comparable to the British effort. Basic training of ratings was carried out at the Flinders naval depot, with specialist schools in other parts of the country. In a nation which lives by the sea, has a legendary beach culture and had a definite enemy in the shape of Japan, naval affairs were considered important. The Royal Australian Navy Volunteer Reserve was quite strong at the beginning of the war, and some officers were sent to Britain to work with the Royal Navy. Up to 1942, numbers of yachtsmen were trained in a scheme similar to the Supplementary Reserve in Britain. By the end of the war the RAN had four cruisers, eleven destroyers, three landing ships, eight sloops and frigates and nearly 300 escorts, motor launches and other vessels.[17]

Like Australia, New Zealand favoured the cruiser before the war and provided half the crews of HMNZ ships *Leander* and *Achilles* – the latter soon gained fame at the Battle of the River Plate. Twelve-year engagements were unpopular in the pre-war navy, but in wartime men were recruited for hostilities only, including yachtsmen who were sent to Britain for training and to serve with the Royal Navy. A training establishment was set up for ratings at Auckland in 1941, and Hostilities Only men were recruited at the rate of 600 per year in the early stages. New Zealand also produced more than 1000 aircrew for the Fleet Air Arm. At its peak, the Royal New Zealand Navy had 10,649 men and women in July 1945.[18] South Africa was less committed to the naval war and had less of an independent naval force.

Canada, a rather un-military country where most of the major centres of population, apart from Vancouver, are some distance from the open sea, supported a remarkable expansion of naval forces during the war. There were only 2000 regular officers and ratings in the Royal Canadian Navy in 1939, plus 3000 reservists. This increased nearly twenty-fold to a high point of 92,000 men and women in 1945. It was a considerable achievement, even though it relied heavily on British resources for instructors, methods and facilities. The Canadians produced a very specialized navy, concentrating on escort vessels for the Battle of the Atlantic. Two escort carriers were commissioned during the war, but a Canadian light fleet carrier did not materialize until after it. Two cruisers were added in 1944–45 as the Battle of the Atlantic began to wind down, but otherwise the RCN consisted of ships of destroyer size and less.

The Canadians usually trained their own officers and ratings, in schools at Halifax on the east coast and Esquimault in the west at the beginning of the war. After that basic training was devolved to about twenty volunteer reserve divisions throughout the country, where many of the men were billeted out – a practice that the Royal Navy would not have countenanced at that stage of training. As the major convoy base at Halifax became increasingly crowded, a purpose-built training centre was opened at Deep Brook in the Bay of Fundy, where the world's highest tidal range restricted boatwork.[19]

The expansion programme was hastier and less well planned than the American one, which increased the numerical strength of the navy in a similar proportion. It took some time to get fully-manned ships to sea, for many of the experienced personnel were needed for training. When they did, they were found to be very inefficient. One British captain complained, 'The appearance of many of these travesties of warships was unbelievably dirty and unseamanlike.'[20] There were disasters to convoys under Canadian escort in September and November 1942. During the crucial stage of the Battle of the Atlantic, in late 1942 and early '43, Canadian escorts had to be withdrawn for additional training at Tobermory and Londonderry, after which the situation was much improved.[21] Baker-Cresswell, the Captain at Londonderry, found that they were 'very bad at first but were very co-operative and learnt quickly'.[22]

British naval officers attributed these faults entirely to lack of training and too fast an expansion. These were certainly important factors, though in fact the position is more complex. The Canadians were probably mistaken in trying too early to have a quasi-independent fleet, rather than using a British cadre aboard each ship; but the British were at fault, too, in treating the Canadians as 'colonials' who were not susceptible to discipline, and in putting their ships at the end of the queue for the latest radar, asdic and weapons. By the later stages the Royal Canadian Navy was much more efficient and provided nearly half the escorts in the Atlantic battle.

The US Navy

Unlike other navies, the British and the Americans both maintained a traditional battlefleet alongside substantial carrier aviation. They took full part in anti-submarine warfare, minesweeping and coastal warfare and operated submarines, with great strategic success in the case of America. Jointly or separately they mounted numerous amphibious landings, including the greatest military operation in history.

The United States Navy had certain advantages at the beginning of the war. It was backed by the largest industrial economy in the world, still with a good deal of slack in its system. It had made a good deal of progress in naval aviation and amphibious operations between the wars. It had the chance to learn from British techniques during two years of war, though it did not take the opportunity in the case of anti-submarine warfare. Even Pearl Harbour was not the disaster it might have been – it removed a large part of the battlefleet from the scene, and forced the most conservative admirals to accept it was no longer the key weapon in naval conflict. All naval aircraft, including shore-based ones, were under naval control, avoiding the problems the Royal Navy had at the beginning of the war.

Though the strategic situation was urgent after Pearl Harbour, it was never as desperate as for Britain in 1940–41, so more resources could be devoted to training, allowing luxuries such as an eight-week working-up period for ships.[23] America was never under serious threat of invasion or bombing, so there was no need to remove bases and their equipment in great haste, as the Royal Navy had to do in 1940. Though U-boats operated off the East Coast during 1942, there were millions of square miles of sea and inland waterways where seamen could learn their trade.

Its people generally had a high standard of education and were well-fed and healthy, despite the ravages of the depression. The main educational requirement for a commission was a college education rather than a secondary education as in Britain.[24] Unlike the Royal Navy, the Americans had been operating a Reserve Officer Training Corps programme in selected universities for some time, so had greater contact with potential recruits.

The US Navy had more tradition of finding its men outside the seafaring population. Ever since its expansion programme at the turn of the century, it had operated recruiting stations in inland towns, and training bases round the country, including one on the Great Lakes. Since most of the recruits had no seafaring experience, training was thorough and systematic. Men tended to sign on for short engagements, so the navy had to make some effort to keep them in the service once they had learned the trade. This included improving conditions on board ship, which soon became far better than those for the British lower deck. The US Navy of around 1900 had no illusions about the role of the seaman – he was 'seven-tenths a soldier and mechanic' according to one captain.[25]

At the centre of the American training effort was the Bureau of Naval Personnel, or BuPers. Unlike the First Sea Lord's office at the Admiralty, it had direct control of naval training stations, except the more specialized ones. It did attract some of the most promising officers and Chester W. Nimitz, future Commander-in-Chief in the Pacific, was chief of its predecessor, the Bureau of Navigation, until a week after Pearl Harbour. It was able to produce a far more coherent training programme than the British one.[26]

Though it was not without its own class distinctions, the US Navy avoided some of the taboos of the British. Regular officers were recruited later in life than Dartmouth candidates. The USN was far more positive about giving commissions to warrant and petty officers, and more than 60,000 officers, 20 per cent of new wartime commissions, came from that source.[27]

A direct comparison between the US Navy's expansion and the British one is not straightforward, for the roles varied. American Naval Aviation included the functions of RAF Coastal Command, while the US Marines, who numbered nearly half a million in 1945, had rather wider responsibilities than their British equivalents. The US Coast Guard had duties which overlapped with several British organizations, including lifeboats, customs, quasi-naval patrols, river police and the weather service, and the force of 170,000 men and women was under naval control in wartime. The American SeaBees or Construction Battalions were far larger than their nearest British equivalents, the Royal Marine Engineers. The whole force, including marines and coastguard, expanded from 203,000 to 4,064,000 in four years; the US Navy proper, including aviation and Seabees, went from 161,000 to 3,408,000 in the same period.[28] Either way a twenty-fold expansion, without a major breakdown in logistics or morale, was a great achievement.

The Efficiency of the Training

The final question is about the efficiency of the Royal Navy's training. Were considerable resources wasted in teaching men and women irrelevant skills and filling them with useless information? Did training inevitably lag behind reality, because it was often conducted by instructors out of touch with operational conditions? Certainly Mr Ammon, MP for Camberwell, thought so. '… a lot of time is spent in such things as making hitches and splices – things which are not of much use in the modern Navy.'[29] No training system in history has ever been totally immune from these faults, and some features of the naval system are clearly doubtful. The controversy over foot drill has already been touched on, but it is not easy to resolve. The majority of people at the time – administrators, instructors and trainees – seem to have felt that it was worthwhile, but modern ideas tend to suggest that it was irrelevant, and perhaps even destructive of real leadership and initiative.

The relatively weak central authority of the Royal Navy's training programmes caused duplication and wastage. This was a fault endemic in British defence organization at the time, and it would have been necessary to go very deep to correct it. On more detailed matters, the system of personnel selection seems to have worked well, both in choosing the best candidates and avoiding square pegs in round holes. It is slightly disturbing to find that Commodore Stephenson of HMS *Western Isles* felt it necessary to assume 'that everyone knows nothing about his job', even though they had already completed disciplinary and technical training. But perhaps it was just that they needed to learn the lessons again in an operational context.

When assessing the success of the training programmes, it is necessary to look at the circumstances in which they were conducted. Certainly there were many difficulties – unexpected speed of expansion, over-stretching of industrial and personnel base, lack of instructors with experience of modern conditions, imminent danger of invasion and constant need to take account of enemy bombers and submarines.

On the other hand, the Royal Navy had certain clear advantages. It was always able to keep up a certain voluntary element in its recruiting, unlike the army. There were always enough men for the navy to pick and choose its recruits to a certain extent, and it never had to take the dregs of society. The navy and marines won over some very disparate and often unlikely people to its culture. Left-wingers such as James Callaghan and J. P. W. Mallalieu, came out with a lasting regard for the navy; Evelyn Waugh, gives a strong impression of the virtues of the marines in *Men at Arms*; natural rebels like Tristan Jones and George Melly came to respect all that was best in naval life.

Could courses have been shorter? There were more than 77,000 men and women in basic training courses at the peak in February 1944, plus 5500 rating instructors[30] – about twice the size of the present-day Royal Navy. Did the temporary shortening of certain courses have any effect in mid-war? Was there too much concentration on theory, which was familiar to the instructors but filled out courses and kept men away from active service? Again it is impossible to give clear answers. Practical training was obviously essential, but a background in theory might never be needed by an individual seaman when he was confronted with an unusual problem. At the back of all naval technical training was the knowledge that the man might some day find himself in the middle of the ocean in a corvette or destroyer, the only man able to operate or repair a piece of equipment on which the safety of the ship might depend. This was an issue at the peak of its importance in 1939–45. In previous campaigns, ships had carried far less experimental and specialized equipment. In later years, supplies of expertise and spare parts would be available by aircraft and helicopter. But in this war, a radar technician or engine room artificer might find himself the centre round which the safety of the ship revolved.

The navy of the Second World War, in contrast to the Grand Fleet of 1914–18, managed to blend the discipline and determination of the regular force with the enthusiasm, intelligence, initiative and ingenuity of the RNVR and Hostilties Only men. One of its unheralded successes was in bridging the 'gulf of mutual incomprehension' between the 'two cultures', to use C. P. Snow's phrase of 1959.[31] Perhaps it is true to say that any naval officer needs some blend of the artist and the scientist – that he has to be a mathematician as he navigates, some kind of engineer to understand the workings of his ship, and a psychologist to lead his crew and to get into the mind of his enemy. He might need diplomacy on an isolated station, or organizational skills, and he always needed power of command and leadership.

The navy succeeded in taking men and women from a liberal arts background and turning them into technicians – the poet Roy Fuller was quite successful as a radar mechanic, history graduates were trained as radar officers. One Wren radio mechanic, formerly a beautician, told a journalist, 'I love it! I never want to go back to my own job, I want to be a radio mech. for always.'[32] Perhaps these lessons could have been learned in post-war Britain, where the liberal arts eventually came to dominate culture and anyone with technological knowledge or interest was written off as an 'anorak' or a 'boffin', while British industry continued its long decline.

The navy's faults were also apparent, in clinging to the old rank and long-service structure. The naval establishment was remarkably ready to take on ideas, recruit and promote new personnel and develop new techniques. But in all this sea of innovation and improvisation, it insisted on preserving the old navy within the much larger wartime one.

After the War

Most of this training effort disappeared very quickly from national consciousness. A few books dealing with lower deck life were published during and just after the war, all by middle-class sailors who had been thrown into a hitherto unrevealed culture. Of these, Mallalieu's *Very Ordinary Seaman* and Davis's *The Stone Frigate* dealt largely with training establishments. Apart from that, fiction said very little about naval training. In the meantime, on both sides of the Atlantic, army, marine and air force training formed a staple diet of novel, film, play and television series for many years after the war, in styles ranging from tragedy to low comedy. One could mention Arnold Wesker's *Chips with Everything*, David Lodge's *Ginger You're Barmy*, the films *The Way Ahead*, *Carry on Sergeant*, *Private's Progress*, *Biloxi Blues* and *Full Metal Jacket*, the sitcom *Get Some In* and the stage farce *Reluctant Heroes* to get some idea of the range. But the navy was strangely unrepresented in this mixture. The most famous fictional account of the wartime navy, Monsarrat's *The Cruel Sea*, strangely understates the role and effectiveness of naval training early in the war. Not all these films were flattering to the services concerned, so the navy was perhaps thankful not to be mentioned.

Like writers and film producers, many of the senior officers of the navy tried to forget the wartime training programme as soon as they could. Even the experience of one of the Royal Navy's most important campaigns of all time seemed in danger of oblivion at one point, as the RNR and RNVR officers who had fought it left the service. 'I know nothing about the Battle of the Atlantic! I was never involved in it! My war experience was in completely different theatres!' said Admiral Oliver in 1948.[33] Amphibious warfare also almost disappeared for a while. In 1947 the First Sea Lord scotched proposals for a large Combined Operations force on the grounds that 'there can be no strategic mobility unless control of sea communications has been assured by the exercise of sea power.'[34] The age of Dartmouth entry was changed from thirteen to sixteen in 1948, against the will of the naval officers, but twelve years remained the standard length of engagement for the lower deck. Conscription was restored soon after the war, but little used by the navy, while the army and RAF were dominated by the need to train conscripts for short periods of service.

Some of the more obvious wartime lessons were consolidated. A separate Electrical Branch was formed in 1947, the Wrens were established permanently, a training squadron was set up at Portland using some of the experience of Tobermory, and the new engineering college at Manadon finally opened.[35]

By the mid 1950s the pace of change increased. American naval dominance had to be accepted, the threat of nuclear war had to be contained and the empire, a large part of the *raison d'etre* for the Royal Navy in Victorian times, came to an end. Ashore, full employment and the end of conscription in 1961 meant that the services had to compete on equal terms with civilian employers. In the late 1950s, special duties' officers were commissioned in large numbers from the lower deck and the upper yardsman scheme became more prominent, altering the nature of the wardroom. The coloured cloth which had distinguished engineers and accountants was abolished and their career paths made more equal with the executives, in theory at least. The port divisions were eliminated in favour of centralized drafting. The standard engagement was now nine years instead of twelve, and that was progressively reduced over the next decades, until two-year engagements became accepted. In 1962, as a reversal of the attitudes fifteen years earlier, 'amphibious warfare was now the acknowledged role of the Royal Navy. There was no mention of other kinds of operations.'[36] The navy was given responsibility for the nuclear deterrent, in the form of Polaris submarines. The anti-submarine role revived as the Soviet Union placed emphasis on its fleet of nuclear submarines. The navy moved progressively into missiles and electronics, and the Gunnery Branch, once the most powerful part of the navy, was defunct by 1980. Since the mid 1950s, officers have been recruited from the age of 18 and upwards, but university graduate entry has come to dominate the wardrooms of the fleet, while short-service commissions, first introduced for the Fleet Air Arm, are now quite normal.

'Stripey' is a far rarer figure than in 1939. Seamen sign on for shorter periods and only a minority stay long enough to qualify for three badges. Those who do tend to be more ambitious than their grandfathers and expect to be petty officers or at least leading hands by that time. Good-conduct stripes are seen far less often. Sailors wear civilian clothes when off duty and mostly the 'wooly-pully' for working dress, without the stripes.

It was a navy trained and organized in this way which went to war in the South Atlantic in 1982. Most of its officers and seamen had joined as young adults. They were not conscripts, but they had signed on for relatively short periods, so many of them were no more experienced than the sailors of 1939–45 when they first saw action. Britain was no longer a seafaring nation, in the sense that it had been in 1945. It imported and exported a far greater volume of goods than ever before, but increasingly in foreign ships, and the British merchant navy was in the middle of its most spectacular decline. The British people still took their holidays by the seaside, but it was as likely to be at Tenerife or Benidorm as Skegness or Ayr. They travelled by air rather than sea, unless they took their cars with them. Though the Cold War was approaching a climax, the navy was smaller than in the inter-war years – 73,000 men and women compared with a low point of just under 90,000 in 1932–33. It was just about to begin another series of severe cuts.

The navy made some mistakes in the Falklands Conflict, and suffered losses, mainly because no one at any level had predicted such a war. The Royal Navy of 1982 had been designed to fight an anti-submarine war in the North Atlantic, as a relatively small part of a huge alliance. In fact it fought an amphibious war 8000 miles from home, in which the main danger was land-based air power. It lacked airborne early warning, it was short of close-range anti-aircraft weapons and its damage control techniques were inadequate. But it was flexible enough to adapt, and much of the reason can be found in the traumatic experiences of 1939–45.

The grand themes of British history – empire, industry, class and warfare – are all reflected in the Royal Navy. The navy was a prime instrument in creating and above all in protecting the British Empire, and at the end of the Second World War it was building up for an ultimately unsuccessful attempt to restore its prestige in the Far East. Britain's industrial economy provided the Royal Navy with its ships, armaments and engines; its effort was faltering by the 1940s, and the navy became heavily reliant on American production. The navy reflected and often exacerbated the class divisions of the age. During the war it went some way towards what was called at the time 'democratization', which might be more accurately described as meritocracy. Yet the privileges of officers, the gap between officers and ratings, the anomalous position of the warrant officer and the restrictions on long-service ratings continued to reflect Victorian society.

The navy's role in warfare is self-evident. Its two greatest achievements in the Second World War, with incalculable effect on world history, were in winning the Battle of the Atlantic and in providing the bulk of the forces to put the allied armies ashore in Normandy. By maintaining and exploiting the vital link between Europe and North America, the Royal Navy allowed the resources of the United States to enter Europe.

It was not material advantage that led the navy to success. It was numerically inferior to its combined enemies in many theatres and areas. Its battleships were old or built to compromise designs, and were inferior to those of Germany, Japan and the United States. The Fleet Air Arm's greatest triumphs were won with aircraft which were obsolete by any normal standards. The most common type of ship in the Battle of the Atlantic was the corvette, designed for a different kind of war and barely adequate for the job. Rather it was the spirit of the navy, the combination of ancient tradition and modern innovation, of the discipline and determination of the 'real' navy with the initiative and broad experience of the Hostilities Only men and RNVRs. According to one of the navy's severest critics, 'Adversity had rescued the Navy from the arrogant complacency bequeathed by the Victorian era, and which had marred its performance in the Great War; had awoken it from the conservatism and torpor of the inter-war years; and had restored it to the bold, hardy, resourceful and highly professional service that it was in Nelson's time.'[37]

Much of this can be traced back to the recruitment and training programmes. There were defects and inequalities in the system, but on the whole it was successful in attracting the right kind of recruit, finding him the right job at the right level, training him to be both a sailor and a technician, and in maintaining his morale though long years of extreme danger and hardship.

Notes

Chapter 1

1 J. L. S. Coulter (ed.) *Medical History of the Second World War, The Royal Naval Medical Services,* vol. 1, Administration, London, 1954, p. 34
2 PRO ADM 1/1884
3 B. Lavery (ed.), *Shipboard Life and Organisation,* Navy Records Society, 1998, p. 45
4 Sir Nicholas Nicolas, *The Dispatches and Letters of Lord Nelson,* reprinted London, 1998, Vol. VII, p. 91
5 Charles Owen, *No More Heroes,* London, 1975, p. 131
6 Stephen W. Roskill, *Naval Policy Between the Wars,* vol. 2, London, 1976, pp. 191–2
7 *Hansard,* vol. 357, col. 1980
8 John Davis, *The Stone Frigate,* London, 1947, p. 162
9 Hannen Swaffer, *What Would Nelson Do?,* London, 1946, p. 89
10 Tristan Jones, *Heart of Oak,* 1984, reprinted Shrewsbury, 1997, pp. 29, 44–5
11 *The Royal Navy as a Career,* 1937 edition, p. 12b
12 PRO ADM 181/133
13 *The Royal Navy as a Career,* p 26
14 PRO ADM 1/12133
15 PRO ADM 167/95
16 While the navy believed that aircraft operations should be geared to assisting ships' guns to sink the enemy vessels, the RAF held the view that aircraft alone could do the job.
17 N.M.M. KEL/109
18 Roskill, *Naval Policy,* Vol. 2, p. 190
19 *Ibid.,* p. 99
20 G. D. Franklin, *A Breakdown in Communication: Britain's Over Estimation of Asdic's Capabilities in the 1930s, Mariners Mirror* Vol. 84, pp. 204–14

21 Roskill, *Naval Policy,* vol. 2, p. 171
22 Roskill, *Naval Policy,* vol. 2, pp. 445, 458
23 *Brasseys Naval Annual,* 1938, p. 121
24 Coulter, *The Royal Naval Medical Service,* Vol. 1, p. 34
25 Vera Laughton Mathews, *Blue Tapestry,* London, 1949, p. 277. *Hansard,* Vol. 378, col. 1093

Chapter 2

1 *Brassey's Naval Annual,* 1906, p. 1
2 *Brasseys Naval Annual,* 1919, pp. 215, 225
3 *Brassey's Naval Annual,* 1939, pp. 65, 66, 69
4 H. K. Oram, *The Rogue's Yarn,* London, 1993, p. 230
5 PRO DEFE 2/804
6 Sir Roderick Macdonald, *The Figurehead,* Bishop Auckland, 1993, pp. 76, 196
7 PRO ADM 1/16551
8 *Ibid.*
9 *Ibid.*
10 PRO ADM 1/10088
11 H. K. Oram, *The Rogue's Yarn,* London, 1993, p. 228
12 'Scheme of Complement for Captain Class Frigates', Christopher Green, *Mariners Mirror,* February 2000, pp. 85–7
13 PRO ADM 205/51
14 *Hansard,* vol. 357, cols 1923–4
15 PRO T161/1083, 161/1042
16 PRO T 161/1042
17 Parker, H. M. D. , *Manpower: A Study of Wartime Policy and Administration,* London, 1957, p. 103
18 *Ibid.,* p. 162
19 Michael Howard, *Grand Strategy,* Vol. IV, August 1942–September 1943, London, 1972, p. 5
20 *Ibid.,* p. 6
21 *Ibid.,* p. 7

22 PRO ADM 1/12133
23 PRO CAB 66/43
24 PRO ADM 205/33
25 CAFO 1793/1943
26 PRO ADM 116/5345
27 W. S. Churchill, *The Second World War,* Vol. V, *Closing the Ring,* London, 1952, p. 595
28 PRO ADM 116/5345
29 W. S. Churchill, *The Second World War,* Vol VI, *Triumph and Tragedy,* London, 1954, pp. 614–5
30 PRO ADM 116/5346

Chapter 3

1 G. Granville Slack and M. M. Wells, *Liability for National Service,* second edition, London, 1943, p. 6
2 PRO ADM 167/103
3 Slack and Wells, *Liability* p. 500
4 *Ibid.,* p. 105
5 PRO ADM 1/10088
6 M. Gilbert, ed, *The Churchill War Papers,* London, 1993, p. 204
7 PRO LAB 6/150
8 Jessica Mitford, *Hons and Rebels,* reprinted London, 1982, p. 218
9 Davis, *Stone Frigate,* London, 1947, p. 14
10 Mass Observation Archive, Report nos 886–7
11 PRO INF 1/293
12 Mass Observation Report, no. 886, *op. cit.*
13 Parker, *Manpower* pp. 488–89
14 PRO ADM 1/12133
15 Brendan A. Maher, *A Passage to Sword Beach,* Shrewsbury, 1996, pp. 10–11
16 George Melly, *Rum, Bum and Concertina,* London, 1977, p. 3
17 John W. Davies, *Jack, the Sailor with the Blue Eyes,* Bishop Auckland, 1995, p. 6
18 J. P. W. Mallalieu, *On Larkhill,* London, 1983, p. 202

[19] Ken Kimberley, *Heavo, Heavo, Lash up and Stow*, Kettering, 1999, p. 10

[20] PRO ADM 1/12144

[21] Coulter, *Royal Naval Medical Services 1*, p. 27

[22] PRO ADM 1/12114

[23] Coulter, *Royal Naval Medical Services 1*, p. 26

[24] Ibid, p. 452

[25] Ibid, p. 454

[26] Mallalieu, *Larkhill, op. cit.*, p. 202

[27] Coulter, *Royal Naval Medical Services 1*, p. 32

[28] PRO ADM 1/21955

[29] Davies, *Stone Frigate*, p. 6

[30] PRO ADM 1//21955

[31] *Ibid.*, pp. 4, 5

[32] PRO ADM 1/12114

[33] PRO ADM 1/12133

[34] PRO ADM 1/12114

[35] PRO ADM 1/12133

[36] PRO ADM 1/16326

[37] Coulter, *Royal Naval Medical Services 1*, p. 33

[38] *Pocket Manual*, 1937, p. 3

[39] PRP ADM 1/12114

[40] PRO ADM 1/12133

[41] Vernon, Phillip E., and John B. Parry, *Personnel Selection in the British Forces*, London, 1949, pp. 137, 139

[42] Admiralty, Naval Training Department, *History of the Y Scheme*, London, 1946, p. 1

[43] Maher, *Sword Beach*, p. 13

[44] Admiralty, *The Navy and the Y Scheme*, London, 1944, p. 7

[45] Naval Training, *Y Scheme*, Appendix A

[46] PRO ADM 1/16644

[47] *Ibid., passim*

Chapter 4

[1] Paul Fussell, *Wartime, Understanding and Behaviour in the Second World War*, Oxford, 1989, p. 84

[2] Christopher Lloyd (ed.), *The Health of Seamen*, Navy Records Society, vol. CVII, 1965, p. 265

[3] Geoffrey Willans, *One Eye on the Clock*, London, 1943, p. 13

[4] Quoted in Bridget Cherry and Nikolaus Pevsner, *The Buildings of England, London 2: South*, London, 1983, p. 262

[5] Davis, *Stone Frigate*, p. 24

[6] Melly, *Rum, Bum and Concertina*, pp. 5–6

[7] PRO ADM 1/17685

[8] PRO ADM 1/12114

[9] Ian Brown et al, *20th Century Defences in Britain*, York, 1995, pp. 114–18

[10] PRO ADM 1/10745

[11] PRO T161/1083

[12] L. E. H. Maund, *Assault from the Sea*, London, 1949, pp. 75

[13] PRO ADM 1/17685

[14] PRO ADM 116/3680

[15] Mathews, *Blue Tapestry*, p. 162

[16] Jones, *Heart of Oak*, p. 39

[17] PRO ADM 1/17981

[18] PRO ADM 1/12114

[19] Melly, *Rum, Bum and Concertina*, p. 20

[20] Sir William Butlin, *The Billy Butlin Story*, London, 1982, pp. 118, 125–6

[21] Hansard, vol. 357, col. 1375

[22] Butlin, *Billy Butlin Story*, p. 132

[23] Melly, *Rum, Bum and Concertina*, p. 6

[24] John L. Brown, *Diary of a Matelot, 1942–45*, Lowesmoor, Worcester, 1991, pp. 7–8

[25] Derek Hamilton Warner, *A Steward's Life in the Royal Navy*, Ilfracombe, 1990, pp. 7–8

[26] Butlin, *Billy Butlin Story*, pp. 130, 133–34

[27] Imperial War Museum manuscripts, 92/27/1

[28] PRO ADM 1/12114

[29] Fred Kellet, *A Flower for the Sea, a Fish for the Sky*, Carlisle, 1995, p. 5

[30] David Jefferson, *Coastal Forces at War*, Yeovil, 1996, p. 68

[31] A. H. Cherry, *Yankee RN*, London, 1951, p. 148

[32] John Whelan, *Home is the Sailor*, London, 1957, p. 172

[33] PRO T161/1083

[34] Ludovic Kennedy, *On My Way to the Club*, London, 1990, p. 92

[35] Peter Young, *Assault from the Sea*, London, 1989, p. 75

[36] PRO ADM 1/17685

[37] John Gifford, *The Buildings of Scotland, Highlands and Islands*, London, 1992, p. 247

[38] Paul Lund and Harry Ludlam, *The War of the Landing Craft*, London, 1976, p. 90

[39] PRO ADM 1/12114

[40] PRO ADM 1/17685

[41] Charles McAra, *Mainly in Minesweepers*, London, 1991, p. 52

[42] Whelan, *Home is the Sailor*, p. 175

[43] Cherry, *Yankee RN*, p. 141

[44] Brown, *Diary of a Matelot*, p. 13

[45] PRO ADM 1/17685

[46] Raymond Mitchell, *They Did What was Asked of Them*, Poole, 1996, p. 25

[47] PRO ADM 1/14152

[48] CAFO 1728/1943

[49] PRO ADM 1/16044

Chapter 5

[1] Davies, *Jack the Sailor*, p. 7

[2] Davis, *Stone Frigate*, p. 15

[3] Davies, *Jack the Sailor*, p. 8

[4] Kimberley, *Heavo*, p. 14

[5] *Ibid.*, p. 14

[6] Jones, *Heart of Oak*, p. 22

[7] Imperial War Museum Manuscripts 83/5/1

[8] Kimberley, *Heavo*, p. 17

[9] Davis, *Stone Frigate*, p. 39

[10] S. Gorley Putt, *Men Dressed as Seamen*, London, 1943, pp. 34–5

[11] James Callaghan, *Time and Chance*, London, 1987, p. 58

[12] Jones, *Heart of Oak*, p. 19

[13] Swaffer, *What Would Nelson Do?*,

p 93

14 Melly, *Rum, Bum and Concertina*, p. 57

15 Robert Burgess and Roland Blackburn, *We Joined the Navy*, London, 1943, p. 7

16 Kellet, *Flower*, p. 11

17 Quoted in Martin Stannard, *Evelyn Waugh*, Vol. II, *No Abiding City*, London, 1993, p. 13

18 Davis, *Stone Frigate*, p. 122

19 J. P. W. Mallalieu, *Very Ordinary Seaman*, pp. 18–19

20 *Not What You'd Call a War*, p. 3

21 Eric Denton, *My Six Wartime Years in the Royal Navy*, London, 1999 p. 17

22 Kellet, *Flower*, p. 29

23 Trevor Royle, *The Best Years of their Lives*, London, 1986, pp. 277–78

24 Coulter, *The Royal Naval Medical Services 1*, p. 51

25 AFO 2738/42

26 Denton, *Six Wartime Years*, p. 20

27 *Not Really what You'd Call a War*, p. 7

28 Albert H. Jones, *No Easy Choices*, Upton on Severn, 1999, pp. 22–3

29 Imperial War Museum manuscripts, 83/45/2

30 PRO ADM 2324/181

31 PRO ADM 1/15575

32 Mallalieu, *Very Ordinary Seaman*, p. 34

33 Maher, *Sword Beach*, p. 17

34 Mathews, *Blue Tapestry*, p. 179

35 F. S. Holt, *A Banker All at Sea*, Newtown (Australia), 1983, p. 29

36 *Royal Navy as a Career*, 1937 edition, p. 4

37 J. Lennox Kerr and David James, *Wavy Navy, by Some Who Served*, London, 1950, p. 194

38 Denton, *Six Wartime Years*, p. 52

Chapter 6

1 PRO ADM 1/8768/120

2 Charles Lambe, *War in a Stringbag*, London, 1977, p. 27

3 *Brassey's Naval Annual*, 1939, p. 170

4 *Kings Regulations and Admiralty Instructions*, Article 406, clause 1, p. 151

5 116/2888

6 Reproduced in Andrew Mollo, ed., *Uniforms and Insignia of the Navies of World War II*, p. 36

7 *Gunnery Pocket Book*, BR 224/45, 1945, pp. 1, 3

8 Davies, *Jack, the Sailor*, p. 21

9 ADM 1/17685

10 ADM 1/21955

11 PRO LAB 29/249

12 PRO PREM 4/55/3

13 PRO ADM 1/16774

14 PRO ADM 1/16774

15 PRO LAB 29/249

16 AFO 524/41

17 Coulter, *Royal Naval Medical Services 1*, pp. 31–3

18 PRO ADM 1/13702

19 Derek Howes, ed., *Radar at Sea, The Royal Navy in World War 2*, London, 1993, pp. 244–7

20 PRO ADM 1/17685

21 PRO ADM 1/21855

22 PRO ADM 1/16326

23 AFO 3976/40

24 PRO ADM 1/15685

25 Angus Cunninghame Graham, *Random Naval Recollections*, Gartocharn, 1979, p. 267

26 Swaffer, *What Would Nelson Do?*, p. 26

27 NMM, BGR/M/3

28 *Brassey's Naval Annual*, 1939, p. 173

29 PRO ADM 1/15685

30 PRO ADM 116/5346

31 PROADM 1/17685

32 *H M Frigate*, op. cit., p. 7

33 *Navy List*, June 1944

34 PRO ADM 1/15685

35 Peter Scott, *The Battle of the Narrow Seas*, London, 1945, pp. 9–10

36 *Navy List*, April 1945, pp. 2866–74

37 PRO ADM 1/15685

38 Edward Young, *One of Our Submarines*, London, 1952, p. 28

39 J. Lennox Kerr and Wilfred Granville, *The RNVR, a Record of Achievement*, London, 1957, p. 187

40 PRO ADM 116/5346

41 CAFO 137/1942

42 *Navy List*, April 1945, pp. 2576–77

43 H. K. Oram, *The Rogue's Yarn*, London, 1993 p. 229

44 PRO ADM 116/5346

45 Oram, *Rogue's Yarn*, p. 229

Chapter 7

1 PRO ADM 1/16774

2 PRO ADM 1/11361

3 PRO ADM 1/16774

4 *King's Regulations and Admiralty Instructions*, 1939 edition, article 316

5 Oram, *Rogue's Yarn*, p. 233

6 PRO ADM 205/33

7 PRO ADM 1/17685

8 Holt, Banker, *All at Sea*, p. 32

9 Roy Fuller, *Vamp Till Ready*, London, 1982, pp. 160, 165

10 Tom Hayward and Keith Ashton, *The Royal Navy, Rum Rumour and a Pinch of Salt*, Glasgow, 1985, p. 80

11 Whelan, *Home Is the Sailor*, pp. 176–80, 191

12 PRO ADM 298/461

13 PRO ADM 1/15575

14 Fuller, *Vamp Till Ready*, p. 140

15 PRO ADM 1/11361

16 PRO ADM 1/11361

17 Brown, *Diary of a Matelot*, pp. 14–5

18 *Information and Instructions for the Guidance of all V/S Instructors*, in the NMM pamphlet collection

19 PRO ADM 1/11361

20 PRO ADM 1/18959

21 PRO ADM 1/17685

22 *British Machine Tool Engineering*,

January–June 1945, p. 11
23 McAra, *Mainly in Minesweepers*, p. 17
24 PRO ADM 1/11361
25 Davies, *Stone Frigate*, pp. 99, 129–39
26 Jones, *Heart of Oak*, p. 23
27 Quoted in B. Lavery, ed., *Shipboard Life and Organisation*, p. 366
28 Ernle Chatfield, *The Navy and Defence*, London, 1942, p. 73
29 Admiralty, *Royal Naval Handbook of Field Training*, London, 1920, p. 19
30 Richard Baker, *The Terror of Tobermory*, London, 1972, p. 123
31 PRO ADM 205/12
32 *Naval Review*, November 1954, pp. 452–5
33 *Ibid.*, January 1955, pp. 80–83, 128–29
34 Admiralty, *Monthly Anti-Submarine Reports*, October 1944, p. 15
35 Kimberley, *Heavo*, p. 18. Brown, *Diary of a Matelot*, p. 9, Davies, *Jack the Sailor*, p. 16, Fuller, *Vamp Till Ready*, London, 1982, p.142
36 Joseph H. Wellings, ed. Hattendorf, *On His Majesty's Service*, Newport, 1983 p. 184
37 Admiralty, *Manual of Seamanship*, Vol I, London, 1937, reprinted 1940, *passim*
38 Davis, *Stone Frigate*, p. 127
39 Fuller, *Vamp Till Ready*, p. 148, *Manual*, p. 165
40 PRO ADM 1/16601
41 United States Navy, Bureau of Naval Personnel, *Naval Orientation*, 1945, pp. 444–5
42 PRO ADM 1/18959
43 Davis, *Stone Frigate*, p. 128
44 Davies, *Jack the Sailor*, pp. 243–4

Chapter 8
1 PRO ADM 116/3598
2 PRO ADM 116/5023
3 PRO ADM 116/5023

4 *Ibid.*
5 *Ibid.*
6 PRO ADM 116/4721
7 PRO ADM 116/5023
8 PRO ADM 298/641
9 CAFO 1027/43
10 Melly, *Rum, Bum and Concertina*, pp. 9–10
11 PRO ADM 116/4721
12 Illustrated in Peter Padfield, *Guns at Sea*, London, 1973, pp. 139, 148, 214, 228–9
13 PRO ADM 1/18969
14 IWM Documents 84/45/2
15 PRO ADM 1/18969
16 PRO ADM 116/5023
17 PRO ADM 116/5023
18 F. C. Dreyer, *The Sea Heritage*, London, 1955, p. 380
19 PRO ADM 1/18969
20 John Wells, *Whaley — The Story of HMS Excellent*, Portsmouth, 1980, pp. 113, 134
21 PRO ADM 205/12
22 PRO ADM 1/18969
23 Willem Hackmann, *Seek and Strike*, London, 1984, p. 188
24 PRO ADM 186/142
25 PRO ADM 1/17573
26 PRO ADM 1/18969
27 PRO ADM 199/1728
28 PRO ADM 204/1661
29 PRO ADM 1/11361
30 PRO ADM 298/461
31 Kellet, *Flower*, p. 16
32 PRO ADM 1/11361
33 Cherry, Yankee RN
34 PRO ADM 1/11361
35 PRO ADM 1/17685
36 PRO ADM 1/17685

Chapter 9
1 PRO ADM 1/16774
2 Captain J. N. Pelly, *An Officer's Aide Memoire*, HMS *King Alfred*, September 1943, copy in the NMM pamphlet collection, p. 23
3 *Ibid.*, p. 104
4 *Ibid.*, p. 2

5 *Ibid.*, pp. 143–4
6 IWM Documents, PP/MCR/306
7 *Gunnery Pocket Book*, p. 189–90
8 *Ibid.*, p. 162
9 *Ibid.*, p. 190
10 Tim Hamilton, *Identification Friend or Foe*, London, 1994, p. 86
11 BR 150, *Manual of Aircraft Recognition*, 1942, amended 1944, pp. 9, 16
12 AFO 2530/39
13 *Ibid.*
14 PRO ADM 1/15575
15 Vernon and Parry, *Personnel Selection*, p. 211
16 PRO ADM 1/17575
17 PRO ADM 220/109
18 Admiralty, *Monthly Anti-Submarine Reports*, CB 04050, July 1941, p. 52, July 1943, p. 33
19 PRO ADM 1/11361
20 Cherry, *Yankee RN*, p. 143
21 PRO ADM 1/11361
22 Macdonald, *Figurehead*, p. 43
23 *King's Regulations*, 1938 p. xi
24 PRO ADM 1/11980
25 Davies, *Stone Frigate*, p. 7
26 IWM Documents, 83/45/2
27 *Information and Instruction for the Guidance of all V/S Instructors*, type written copy in the NMM pamphlet collection, pp. 1, 3, 4, 6, 8, 9
28 IWM Documents, 92/27/1
29 PRO ADM 1/18969
30 AFO 2532/39
31 AFO 6256/42
32 *Monthly Anti-Submarine Report*, March 1941, pp. 35–6
33 CAFO 1815/42
34 PRO ADM 1/14677
35 CAFO 1815/42
36 IWM Documents, 92/27/1
37 *Monthly Anti-Submarine Reports*, April 1942, p. 44
38 PRO ADM 1/16774
39 PRO ADM 1/16774
40 John Davies, *Lower Deck*, London, 1945, marginal note in the author's copy

41 PRO ADM 1/14677

42 PRO LAB 29/249

43 PRO ADM 1/14110

44 Fuller, *Vamp Till Ready*, p. 142–3

45 PRO LAB 29/249

46 AFO 2214/42

Chapter 10

1 BR 91, 1936, *Training of Artificer Apprentices*, p. 17

2 PRO ADM 1/17685

3 *British Machine Tool Engineering*, January–June 1945, p. 26

4 PRO ADM 1/17685

5 *Ibid.*

6 1/17685

7 CAFO 2531/39

8 PRO ADM 1/17685

9 *Ibid.*

10 Jones, *Heart of Oak*, p. 195

11 PRO ADM 1/17865

12 IWM Documents, 95/23/1

13 *British Machine Tool Engineering*, pp. 1–13

14 PRO ADM 1/17685

15 *Ibid.*

16 *Royal Navy as a Career*, p. 22

17 Winston Churchill, *The Second World War*, Vol. I, *The Gathering Storm*, London, 1948, p. 688

18 Royal Institution of Naval Architects, *Selected Papers on British Warship Design*, London, 1983, p. 124

19 BR 91, 1936

20 PRO LAB 29/249

21 *Ibid.*

22 *Ibid.*

23 PRO ADM 1/12638

24 PRO ADM 116/5346

25 PRO ADM 1/17685

26 PRO ADM 1/17685

27 PRO ADM 1/12638

28 PRO LAB 29/249

29 PRO ADM 116/5346

30 PRO LAB 29/249

31 Melly, *Rum, Bum and Concertina*, p. 28

32 Alan Brundett, *Two Years in Ceylon – The Diary of a Naval Secretariat Member*, Lewes, 1996, pp. 44–67

33 PRO ADM 1/10966

34 *Manual for Officers' Stewards*, BR 97, p. 137

35 Derek Hamilton Warner, *A Steward's Life in the Royal Navy*, Ilfracombe, 1990, pp. 13–4

36 PRO LAB 29/249

37 Gregory Clark, *Doc – 100 Year History of the Sick Berth Branch*, London, 1984, pp. 149, 155

38 PRO LAB 29/249

39 Coulter, *Royal Naval Medical Services 1*, pp. 151–5

Chapter 11

1 *Royal Navy as a Career*, p. 4

2 Navy Records Society, Vol. CVI, *The Papers of Admiral Sir John Fisher*, ed. P. K. Kemp, Vol. II, 1964, pp. 127–8

3 *Committee on Manning, op. cit.*, p. 18

4 *Queen's Regulations and Admiralty Instructions*, 1862 edition, pp. 81, 120, 121

5 Pelly, *An Officer's Aide Memoire*, p. 20

6 Pelly, *An Officer's Aide Memoire*, p. 15

7 PRO ADM 1/10930

8 *King's Regulations and Admiralty Instructions*, 1938 edition, p. 112

9 NMM BGY/M/3

10 *Royal Navy as a Career*, p 4.

11 Nicholas Monsarrat, *Three Corvettes*, reprinted London, 2000, p. 188

12 Davies, *Jack The Sailor*, p. 264

13 Roy Fuller, *Home and Dry*, London, 1984, pp. 28–29

14 *King's Regulations and Admiralty Instructions*, 1943 edition, appendix, p. 154

15 AFO 498/40

16 Welling, *On His Majesty's Service*, p. 67

17 Pelly, *An Officer's Aide Memoir*, p. 15

18 Melly, *Rum, Bum and Concertina*, p. 7

19 D. A. Rayner, *Escort – The Battle of the Atlantic*, London, 1955, p. 66

20 Monsarrat, *Three Corvettes*, pp. 187–8

21 Cherry, *Yankee RN*, p. 385

22 PRO ADM 1/10930

23 PRO ADM 1/10917

24 PRO ADM 1/10334

25 AFO 400/40

26 CAFO 149/41

27 PRO ADM 1/14725

28 PRO ADM 1/14722

29 PRO ADM 1/14722

30 PRO ADM 1/12133

31 CAFO 173/43

32 AFO 2530/29

33 CAFO 2051/40

34 AFO 4496/42

35 CAFO 1793/43

36 BR 77, *Machinery Handbook*, 1941, p. iv

37 AFO 6257/42

38 PRO ADM 1/17685

39 AFO 1197/40

40 PRO ADM 1/14734

41 Sidney Greenwood, *Stoker Greenwood's Navy*, Tunbridge Wells, 1983, p. 58

42 Whelan, *Home is the Sailor*, pp. 170–1

43 Davis, *The Stone Frigate*, p. 70

44 Whelan, *Home is the Sailor*, p. 178

45 PRO LAB 29/249, p. 31

46 AFO 5128/42

47 Nicholas Monsarrat, *HM Frigate*, London, 1946, p. 14

48 Richard McKenna, *The Left-Handed Monkey Wrench*, Annapolis, 1984, pp. 194–5

49 Quoted in *Navy Uniforms, Insignia and Warships*, produced by WE Inc., Greenwich, Conn., 1968, p. 120, not in the edition by Andrew Mollo, *Uniforms and Insignia of the*

Navies of World War II, London, 1991
50 *Naval Orientation*, p. 41, fig. 7
51 *King's Regulations*, 1943 ed., appendix, p. 158, article 415
52 PRO ADM 1/14722, quoted above

Chapter 12
1 PRO ADM 1/11616
2 PRO ADM 1/17904, 1/11616
3 PRO ADM 1/11616
4 PRO ADM 1/20505
5 PRO ADM 1/17904
6 Rodney Agar and Murray Johnstone, eds, *Hold Fast the Heritage*, Fontwell, 1994, p. 18
7 *Ibid.*, pp. 15–16
8 PRO ADM 116/4569
9 Agar and Johnstone, *Hold Fast the Heritage*, p. 19
10 PRO ADM 178/187
11 PRO ADM 1/16640
12 PRO ADM 1/17904
13 PRO ADM 1/20505
14 PRO ADM 178/210
15 *Brassey's Naval Annual*, 1937, p. 17
16 PRO ADM 178/210
17 Churchill, *The Gathering Storm*, pp. 692–93
18 P. G. La Niece, *Not a Nine to Five Job*, Yalding, 1992, p. 8
19 PRO ADM 116/3926
20 PRO ADM 178/187
21 *Brassey's Naval and Shipping Annual*, 1934, p. 18
22 MacDonald, *Figurehead*, p. 193
23 *King's Regulations and Admiralty Instructions*, 1943 edition, pp. 62–3
24 MacDonald, *Figurehead*, p. 199
25 *Hansard* vol. 378, col. 1090
26 *King's Regulations*, 1943 edition, appendix, p. 81
27 PRO ADM 1/17685
28 PRO ADM 1/17685
29 PRO ADM 181/133
30 AFO 276/40
31 *King's Regulations*, 1943 edition,

appendix, p 86
32 AFO 277/1940
33 PRO ADM 1/17944
34 AFO 882/1941
35 PRO ADM 181/133
36 Dunstan Hadley, *Barracuda Pilot*, Shrewsbury, 1992, p. 12
37 Melly, *Rum, Bum and Concertina*, p. 8
38 PRO ADM 1/17944
39 *An Officer's Aide Memoire*, p. 14
40 MacDonald, *Figurehead*, p. 195
41 Wellings, *On His Majesty's Service*, p. 66
42 PRO ADM 1/12114
43 *Brassey's Naval and Shipping Annual*, 1932, p. 17
44 *Brassey's Naval and Shipping Annual*, 1934, p. 22
45 *Brassey's Naval Annual*, 1936, p. 17, 1937, p 19, 1939, p. x
46 *Hansard*, vol. 350, col. 1441
47 PRO ADM 1/17944
48 *Hansard*, vol. 387, col. 598

Chapter 13
1 PRO ADM 1/9778
2 PRO ADM 1/9778
3 Churchill, *The Gathering Storm*, p. 689
4 PRO ADM 178/210 for Special Entry. There was a slightly different wording for the Supplementary Reserve.
5 Rayner, *Escort*, p. 27
6 PRO ADM 116/3509
7 Ewen Montagu, *Beyond Top Secret U*, London, 1977, p. 16
8 PRO ADM 116/3509
9 Kennedy, *On My Way*, pp. 93–4
10 PRO ADM 1/12133
11 AFO 4136/1939
12 AFO 276/1940
13 *Hansard*, vol. 378, cols 1088–89
14 AFO 1163/1943
15 Nicholas Monsarrat, HM *Corvette*, in *Three Corvettes*, London, 1975, p. 49
16 McAra, *Mainly in Minesweepers*,

p. 49
17 Putt, *Men Dressed as Seamen*, p. 84
18 *Ibid.*, p. 110
19 Whelan, *Home is the Sailor*, pp. 146–7
20 Maher, *Sword Beach*, p. 24
21 AFO 276/1940
22 PRO ADM 1/18959
23 Oram, *Rogue's Yarn*, p. 230
24 *Ibid.*, 233
25 PRO ADM 1/21955, p. 9
26 Reproduced in Tom Hopkinson, ed., *Picture Post 1938-50*, Harmondsworth, 1970, pp. 122–26
27 PRO ADM 1/13988
28 PRO ADM 1/13408
29 *Naval Training*, Y *Scheme*, pp. 8–12
30 AFO 276/40
31 PRO ADM 1/17685
32 *Ibid.*
33 *Ibid.*

Chapter 14
1 Judy Middleton, *HMS King Alfred, 1939–1945*, Brighton, 1986
2 PRO ADM 1/18959
3 Kerr and Granville, *The RNVR*, p. 151
4 Kennedy, *On My Way*, p. 93
5 Nicholas Monsarrat, *Life is a Four Letter Word*, vol. II, *Breaking Out*, London, 1970, p. 6
6 Kennedy, *On My Way*, p. 93
7 Montagu, *Beyond Top Secret U*, op. cit., pp. 17, 19
8 Kerr and Granville, *The RNVR*, p. 151
9 John Fernald, *Destroyer from America*, London, 1942, p. 22.
10 Putt, *Men Dressed as Seamen*, p. 85
11 Fernald, *Destroyer From America*, p. 25
12 AFO 94/1940
13 Montagu, *Beyond Top Secret U*, p. 17
14 Kennedy, *On My Way to the Club*,

p. 92

15 Monsarrat, *Breaking Out, op. cit.*, p. 19

16 AFO 97/1940

17 *Navy List*, October 1943

18 PRO ADM 1/18959

19 Maher, *Sword Beach*, p. 27

20 Middleton, *HMS King Alfred*, p. 31

21 Kennedy, *On My Way*, p. 92

22 Holt, *Banker All at Sea*, pp. 108–9

23 Quoted in Middleton, *HMS King Alfred*, p. 51

24 *Ibid.*, p. 17

25 *Ibid.*, p. 52

26 Norman Hampson, *Not Really What You'd Call a War*, Caithness, 2001, p. 29

27 Kennedy, *On My Way*, p. 93

28 Maher, *Sword Beach*, p. 29

29 AFO 276/40

30 Holt, *Banker All at Sea*, p. 103

31 PRO ADM 1/18959

32 Pelly, *An Officer's Aide Memoire*, pp. 6, 7, 10, 12, 16

33 NMM BGY/M/3

34 Pelly, *An Officer's Aide Memoire*, pp. 19, 20

35 Willans, *One Eye on the Clock*, pp. 13–14

36 Middleton, *HMS King Alfred*, pp. 26–7

37 Holt, *Banker All at Sea*, p. 104

38 Maher, *Sword Beach*, pp. 28–9

39 PRO ADM 1/18959

40 Middelton, *HMS King Alfred*, p. 41

41 PRO ADM 1/18959

42 McAra, *Mainly in Minesweepers*, p. 52

43 PRO ADM 1/14015

44 McAra, *Mainly in Minesweepers*, p. 54

45 PRO ADM 1/10370

46 Maher, *Sword Beach*, p. 30

47 Holt, *Banker All at Sea*, p. 103

48 *Ibid.*, p. 103

49 Rayner, *Escort*, pp. 218–9

50 David French, *Raising Churchill's Army*, Oxford, 2000, p. 75

51 *Hansard*, vol. 378, p. 1090

52 Middleton, *HMS King Alfred*, p. 21

53 *Ibid.*, p. 1

54 H. J. C. Spencer, *Ordinary Naval Airmen*, Tunbridge Wells, 1992, p. 45

55 Norman Hanson, *Carrier Pilot*, Cambridge, 1979, p. 60

56 Hadley, *Barracuda Pilot*, p. 77

57 Holt, *Banker All at Sea*, pp. 113–19

58 PRO ADM 1/18959

59 PRO ADM 1/10946

60 PRO ADM 1/10946

61 PRO ADM 1/14015

62 Maher, *Sword Beach*, pp. 33–4

63 Denton, *Six Wartime Year*, p. 61

64 Willans, *One Eye on the Clock*, p. 18

65 Kennedy, *On My Way*, p. 104

66 CAFO 1615/41

67 Young, *One of our Submarines*, pp. 18, 26, 28

68 Ministry of Information, *His Majesty's Minesweepers*, London, 1943, pp. 30–33

69 Maher, *Sword Beach*, pp. 35, 45

70 McAra, *Mainly in Minesweepers*, p. 57

71 PRO ADM 1/17685

72 PRO ADM 1/17685

73 PRO ADM 1/17685

74 *British Machine Tool Engineering*, January–June 1945, pp. 54–6

75 Kerr and Granville, *The RNVR*, p. 176

76 Admiralty, Anti-submarine Division, *Monthly Anti-Submarine Reports*, July 1941, p. 52, July 1943, p. 33

77 *Hansard*, vol.397, col. 1909

78 Derek Howse, ed., *Radar at Sea*, London, 1993, pp. 112–3

79 Coulter, *Royal Naval Medical Services 1*, pp. 8–20

Chapter 15

1 Naval Training, *Y Scheme*, p. 13

2 Quoted in Angus Calder, *The Peoples War*, St Albans, 1982, p. 398

3 PRO ADM 1/16644

4 Naval Training, *Y Scheme*, p. 14

5 *Ibid.*, p. 14

6 Spencer, *Ordinary Naval Airmen*, p. 5

7 John Kilbracken, *Bring Back My Stringbag*, reprinted 1996, London, p. 10

8 McAra, *Mainly in Minesweepers*, p. 3

9 Leo Sayer and Vernon Ball, *TAG on a Stringbag*, Borth, Dyfed, 1994, p. 1

10 PRO ADM 1/16644

11 Hadley, *Barracuda Pilot*, p. 12

12 *Ibid.*, p. 22

13 Spencer, *Ordinary Naval Airmen*, p. 10

14 George E. Sadler, *Swordfish Patrol*, Wrexham, 1996, p. 11

15 Hadley, *Barracuda Pilot*, p. 27

16 *Ibid.*, p. 5

17 Sadler, *Swordfish Patrol*, p. 13

18 Hadley, *Barracuda Pilot*, p. 30

19 McAra, *Mainly in Minesweepers*, p. 21

20 Hadley, *Barracuda Pilot*, p. 31

21 Spencer, *Ordinary Naval Airmen*, p. 32

22 *Ibid.*, pp. 33–4

23 McAra, *Mainly in Minesweepers*, p. 25

24 W. A. B. Douglas, *Official History of the Royal Canadian Air Force*, Vol. II, *The Creation of a National Air Force*, Toronto, 1986, p. 235

25 Spencer, *Ordinary Naval Airmen*, *op. cit.*, pp. 28, 37

26 Hanson, *Carrier Pilot*, p. 26

27 PRO ADM 1/17286

28 Sadler, *Swordfish Patrol*, p. 23

29 Hadley, *Barracuda Pilot*, pp. 69–70, Kilbracken, *Bring Back my Stringbag*, pp. 19–20

30 Hadley, *Barracuda Pilot*, p. 74

31 Vernon and Parry, *Personnel Selection*, p. 211

32 Spencer, *Ordinary Naval Airmen*, *op. cit.*, p. 6

33 Winston G. Ramsey, ed., *The Blitz Then and Now*, vol. 1, London, 1986, pp. 211, 215
34 PRO ADM 116/4176
35 *Ibid.*
36 Admiralty, *Fleet Air Arm,* London, 1943, p. 26
37 Gordon Wallace, *Carrier Observer*, Shrewsbury, 1993, p. 23
38 *Ibid.*, p. 22
39 Sayer and Ball, *TAG on a Stringbag, op. cit.*, pp. 24–5
40 *Ibid.*, p. 5
41 *Ibid.*, p. 5
42 *Ibid.*, p. 9
43 *Ibid.*, p. 8
44 Spencer, *Ordinary Naval Airmen, op. cit.*, p. 106
45 PRO ADM 1/18969
46 Hadley, *Barracuda Pilot, op. cit.*, p. 86
47 PRO ADM 1/18969
48 PRO ADM 1/13567
49 Hanson, *Carrier Pilot, op. cit.*, p. 66
50 *Ibid.*
51 Ray Sturtivant and Theo Balance, *The Squadrons of the Fleet Air Arm,* Tonbridge, 1994, p. 15
52 *Barracuda Pilot, op. cit.*, pp. 170–3
53 *Ibid.*, p. 85
54 John Hoare, *Tumult in the Clouds*, London, 1976, pp. 170–1
55 P. M. Rippon and Graham Mottram, *Yeovilton, The History of the Royal Naval Air Station,* Yeovil, 1995, *passim*
56 R 'Mike' Crosley, *They Gave me a Seafire*, Shrewsbury, 1986, pp. 44, 50
57 *Ordinary Naval Airmen, op. cit.*, p. 146
58 E. E. Baringer, *Alone on a Wide, Wide Sea*, London, 1995, pp. 40, 42
59 Spencer, *Ordinary Naval Airmen, op. cit.*, p. 136

Chapter 16
1 PRO ADM 193/19
2 Charles Lamb, *War in a Stringbag,*

London, 1977, pp. 27–8
3 Jack Brewin, *LCF (L) 5* – typescript in the Royal Marines Museum, p. 2
4 PRO ADM 116/5346
5 Anon, *Training a Royal Marine Detachment Afloat*, 1945, copy in Royal Marines Museum
6 PRO ADM 234/129
7 PRO ADM 1/10770
8 PRO DEFE 2/984
9 PRO ADM 1/10334
10 John St John, *To the War with Waugh*, London, 1973, pp. 1–3
11 Martin Gilbert, ed., *The Churchill War Papers, Vol. I, At the Admiralty, September 1939 – May 1940*, London, 1993, p. 594
12 PRO ADM 1/19260
13 PRO ADM 202/439
14 PRO DEFE 2/984
15 James D. Ladd, *The Royal Marines, 1919–1980, an Authorised History*, London, 1980, pp. 423–26
16 PRO ADM 202/118, Ladd, p. 424
17 Mark Amory, ed., *The Letters of Evelyn Waugh*, London, 1980, p. 453
18 Admiralty, *The Royal Navy as a Career*, 1937, p. 29
19 Ted Ford, *The Nearly Man*, Wolverhampton, 1997, p. 11
20 Mitchell, *They Did What Was Asked*, p. 16
21 Ford, *Nearly Man*, p. 16
22 PRO ADM 193/19
23 Ladd, *Royal Marines, 1919–1980*, pp. 424, 140
24 J. E. Pollit, *Marine to Mayor*, Exeter, n.d., c. 1989, pp. 19, 28, 30, 33
25 PRO ADM 193/19
26 AFO 4936/43, 5326/43
27 *Royal Marine Orders*, copy in the Royal Marines Museum, item 24
28 PRO ADM 202/301
29 PRO ADM 1/10770
30 Gilbert, *Churchill War Papers: At the Admiralty*, p 604
31 *Royal Marine Pocket Book*, 1945, p.

87
32 CAFO 401/1940
33 *Royal Marine Pocket Book*, pp. 89–91
34 Pollit, *Marine to Mayor*, pp. 23, 25, 26
35 *Royal Marine Pocket Book*, p. 84
36 *Ibid.*, p. 85
37 *Ibid.*, pp. 85–6
38 *Ibid.*, p. 88
39 *Globe and Laurel*, February 1944, p. 35
40 *Royal Marine Pocket Book*, pp. 88–9
41 Pollit, *Marine to Mayor*, pp. 40–1
42 Anthony J. Perrett, *Royal Marines in Wales*, Portsmouth, 1992, pp. 113–14
42 PRO ADM 1/20545
44 St John, *To the War with Waugh*, pp. 2–3
45 Michael Davie, ed., *The Diaries of Evelyn Waugh*, London, 1976, pp. 452–3. Waugh, *Letters*, p. 130
46 Waugh, *Letters*, p. 129
47 St John, *To War With Waugh*, p. 6
48 Waugh, *Diaries*, p. 459
49 *Ibid.*, p. 460
50 *Ibid.*, p. 461
51 Waugh, *Letters*, p. 136
52 Evelyn Waugh, *Men at Arms*, London, 1964, p. 118
53 Nikolaus Pevsner, *The Buildings of England, South Devon*, Harmondsworth, 1952, p. 282
54 Mitchell, *They Did What Was Asked*, p. 17–18
55 Ladd, *Royal Marines, 1919–1980*, p. 425
56 PRO ADM 202/439, DEFE 2/984
57 *Sheet Anchor, Vol. XVII, summer 1992. np
58 *Naval Training, Y Scheme*, pp. 16–17
59 PRO DEFE 2/927
60 Joffre Swales, *The Life and Music of RMB X1522*, Haverfordwest, 1993, pp. 43–4
61 PRO ADM 1/11911

62 PRO ADM 1/11911

63 *The Royal Navy as a Career, op. cit.*, p. 31, *The Royal Navy Today*, London, 1942, p. 121

64 Swales, *Life and Music of RMB X1522*, pp. 41, 42

65 PRO ADM DEFE 2/984

66 PRO ADM 1/11911

67 Quoted in Ladd, *Royal Marines, 1919–1980*, p. 8

68 *Globe and Laurel*, February 1945

69 PRO ADM 116/5346

Chapter 17

1 PRO DEFE 2/1068

2 Amphibious Warfare Headquarters, *The History of the Combined Operations Organisation, 1940–45*, London, 1956, p. 97

3 Waugh, *Diaries*

4 Kenneth Edwards, *Operation Neptune*, London, 1946, p. 85

5 PRO DEFE 2/1319

6 Phillip Ziegler, *Mountbatten*, London, 1985, p. 206

7 PRO DEFE 2/815

8 Maund, *Assault from the Sea*, p. 75

9 PRO DEFE 2/815

10 Lund and Ludlam, *War of the Landing Craft*, pp. 15–16

11 Bernard Fergusson, *The Watery Maze*, London, 1961, p. 324

12 Lund and Ludlam, *War of the Landing Craft*, p. 51

13 Maund, *Assault from the Sea*, p. 109

14 PRO DEFE 2/900

15 Fergusson, *Watery Maze*, p. 228

16 *History of the Combined Operations Organisation*, p. 96

17 Samuel Elliot Morrison, *History of United States Naval Operations in World War Two*, Vol XI, *The Invasion of France and Germany*, Oxford, 1957, p. 58

18 PRO DEFE 2/900

19 Fergusson, *Watery Maze, op. cit.*, p. 324

20 Lund and Ludlam, *War of the Landing Craft*, p. 14

21 PRO DEFE 2/898

22 PRO DEFE 2/1430

23 PRO ADM 1/17685

24 PRO ADM 1/17685

25 PRO DEFE 2/1429

26 PRO ADM 1/17685

27 PRO ADM 1/17685

28 PRO ADM 1/14725

29 PRO DEFE 2/1429, 2/898

30 Waugh, *Diaries*, p. 492

31 Lund and Ludlam, *War of the Landing Craft*, pp. 22–3

32 Brian Macdermott, *Ships without Names*, London, 1992, p. 28

33 PRO DEFE 2/898

34 PRO DEFE 2/898

35 PRO ADM 1/17685

36 PRO DEFE 2/1430

37 PRO ADM 116/4956

38 Kerr and James, *Wavy Navy*, p. 224

39 PRO DEFE 2/898

40 PRO DEFE 1/984

41 PRO ADM 1/15087, 1/14045

42 PRO ADM 202/448

43 PRO ADM 202/448

44 Ladd, *Royal Marines, 1919–1980*, p. 174

45 PRO ADM 202/128

46 Anthony J. Perrett, *Royal Marines in Wales*, Portsmouth, 1992, pp. 116–7

47 *Ibid.*, p. 82

48 *Ibid.*, pp. 84, 117

49 J. A. Good, typescript in the Royal Marines Museum, pp. 8–10

50 PRO ADM 1/15685

51 PRO DEFE 2/929

52 *History of the Combined Operations Organisation*, p. 141

53 PRO DEFE 2/987

54 PRO ADM 1/14725

55 *History of the Combined Operations Organisation*, pp. 134–5

56 PRO DEFE 2/1068

57 PRO DEFE 2/987

58 PRO DEFE 2/1319

59 *History of the Combined Operations Organisation*, p. 125

60 PRO DEFE 2/1068

61 Gifford, *Buildings of Scotland*, p. 225

62 Lund and Ludlam, *War of the Landing Craft*, p. 82

63 PRO ADM 1/14003

64 Lund and Ludlam, *War of the Landing Craft*, p. 86

65 *Ibid.*, p. 82, 91

66 Waugh, *Letters*, p. 145

67 Ladd, *Royal Marines, 1919–1980*, p. 147

68 J. C. Beadle, *The Light Blue Lanyard, Fifty Years with 40 Commando*, Worcester, 1992, p. 2

69 Ladd, *Royal Marines, 1919–1980*, pp. 345, 352

70 Beadle, *Light Blue Lanyard*, p. 8

71 Mitchell, *They did What Was Asked*, p. 20

72 *Ibid.*, p. 23

73 Tony Mackenzie, *44 (RM) Commando*, Brighton, 1996, p. 8

Chapter 18

1 Mathews, *Blue Tapestry*, p. 31

2 *Ibid.*, p. 51

3 *Ibid.*, p. 56

4 R. 'Mike' Crossley, *They Gave me a Seafire*, Shrewsbury, 2001, pp. 48–9

5 Mathews, *Blue Tapestry*, p. 81

6 PRO ADM 1/1114

7 Mathews, *Blue Tapestry*, pp. 67–8

8 Angela Mack, *Dancing on the Waves*, Little Hatherden, 2000, p. 55

9 Mathews, *Blue Tapestry*, pp. 86–7

10 *Ibid.*, p. 123

11 Mack, *Dancing on the Waves*, p. 21

12 *Wartime Women*, ed. Dorothy Sheridan, London, 1990, p. 151

13 Roy Terry, *Women in Khaki*, London, 1988, pp. 125, 131–2

14 PRO INF 1/293

15 PRO ADM 1/12680

16 G. Granville Slack and M. M.

Wells, *Liability for National Service*, second edition, London, 1943, pp. 75–8
[17] PRO ADM 1/12680
[18] Nancy Spain, *Thank You, Nelson*, London, 1945, p. 9
[19] IWM Documents, 86/61/1
[20] Mathews, *Blue Tapestry*, pp, 191–2
[21] AFO 1728/43
[22] PRO ADM 1/14687
[23] Eileen Bigland, *The Story of the WRNS*, London, 1946, p. 20
[24] Mathews, *Blue Tapestry*, p. 146
[25] *Ibid.*
[26] IWM Documents, 86/61/1
[27] Stephanie Batstone, *Wren's Eye View*, Tunbridge Wells, 1994, p. 24
[28] Mathews, *Blue Tapestry*, p. 136
[29] PRO ADM 1/14672
[30] PRO ADM 1/12114
[31] PRO ADM 1/15617
[32] IWM Documents, 86/61/1
[33] IWM Documents, 86/61/1
[34] PRO ADM 1/17685
[35] Bigland, *Story of the WRNS*, p. 50
[36] Quoted in *Ibid.*, p. 202
[37] *Ibid.*, p. 174–5
[38] PRO ADM 1/12133
[39] Mack, *Dancing on the Waves*, pp. 68–9
[40] Mathews, *Blue Tapestry*, pp. 95, 193
[41] *Hansard*, vol. 357, col. 1222
[42] Mack, *Dancing on the Waves*, p. 45
[43] PRO ADM 1/14038
[44] Mathews, *Blue Tapestry*, p. 163
[45] Mack, *Dancing on the Waves*, p. 48
[46] PRO ADM 1/13981
[47] Mathews, *Blue Tapestry*, p. 168
[48] PRO LAB 29/250
[49] Bigland, *Story of the WRNS*, p. 95

Chapter 19
[1] Hope, p. 383
[2] Millington, pp. 122–3, 146
[3] Millington, p. 165

[4] 1929 programme
[5] 1929 prog pp. 10–11
[6] Portsmouth Papers, 18–19, 92
[7] Brassey's, 1936, pp. 82–3
[8] Navy List
[9] AFOs 2018/40, 6396/44
[10] Waters, p. 186
[11] PRO ADM 1/9936
[12] PRO ADM 116/4313
[13] PRO ADM 1/18883
[14] PRO ADM 116/3960
[15] PRO ADM 1/11604
[16] AFO 2512/39
[17] PRO WO 32/10913, AFO 4048/41
[18] PRO ADM 205/12
[19] CAFO 1728/43
[20] Dreyer, *The Sea Heritage*, pp. 375, 378, 380–4, 387
[21] *Merchantmen Rearmed*, pp. 142, 172, 175
[22] CAFO 2313/43
[23] AFO 1186/40
[24] AFO 3606/40
[25] PRO ADM 1/15854
[26] *British Warship Design*, p. 55
[27] Kilbracken, *Bring Back my Stringbag*, pp 113–29
[28] D. K. Brown, *British Warships*, p. 88
[29] PRO ADM 116/4942

Chapter 20
[1] Jones, *Heart of Oak*, p. 84
[2] Jones, *No Easy Choices*, p. 28
[3] Monsarrat, *Three Corvettes*, p. 14
[4] Cherry, *Yankee RN*, pp. 366–7
[5] Holt, *Banker All at Sea*, p. 50
[6] Rayner, *Escort*, pp. 64–6
[7] Davies, *Jack the Sailor*, pp. 168–9
[8] PRO ADM 1/13255
[9] PRO ADM 1/13408
[10] PRO ADM 1/15931
[11] PRO ADM 1/18614
[12] Admiralty, *Monthly Anti-Submarine Reports*, October 1944, p. 18
[13] Richard Baker, *The Terror of Tobermory*, reprinted Edinburgh 1999, p. ix

[14] Baker, *Terror of Tobermory*, p. 112
[15] Naval Review, p. 329
[16] Baker, *Terror of Tobermory*, p. 104
[17] *Monthly Anti-Submarine Reports*, October 1944, p. 16
[18] Baker, *Terror of Tobermory*, p. 115
[19] *Monthly Anti Submarine Reports*, October 1944, p. 17
[20] PRO ADM 1/12252
[21] PRO ADM 199/1729
[22] NMM GUN/23
[23] *Monthly Anti-Submarine Reports*, July [sic] 1941, p. 27
[24] Rayner, *Escort*, pp 158–9
[25] NMM MS93/008, letter from Baker-Cresswell to Admiral Sir Peter Gretton, 1981
[26] Terence Robertson, *Walker RN*, London, 1956, pp. 142–3
[27] PRO ADM 1/13744
[28] PRO ADM 219/142
[29] PRO ADM 239/248
[30] Cresswell, *Crisis Convoy*, p 171. Gretton, p. 37,
[31] PRO ADM 186/558
[32] Norman Friedman, *British Carrier Aviation*, London, 1988, pp. 125–7
[33] PRO ADM 1/17685
[34] PRO ADM 1/15577
[35] Admiralty, *Seaman's Manual*, 1943, pp. 104–14
[36] PRO ADM 116/5346
[37] PRO ADM 205/28
[38] Arthur P. Dickison, *Crash Dive*, Stroud, 1999, pp. ix–x
[39] PRO ADM 205/28
[40] Young, *One of Our Submarines*, p. 43
[41] *Ibid.*, pp. 115–7
[42] Dickison, *Crash Dive*, p. xii
[43] *HMS Trenchant*, op. cit., p. 32
[44] From David Jefferson, *Coastal Forces at War*, Yeovil, 1996
[45] PRO ADM 199/1729
[46] PRO ADM 1/17685
[47] Ministry of Information, *His Majesty's Minesweepers*, London, 1943, p. 34
[48] Paul Lund and Harry Ludlam,

Out Sweeps!, London, 1978, p. 124
[49] Central Statistical Office, *Fighting with Figures*, reprinted London, 1995, p. 13, Table 14

Chapter 21
[1] Paul Kennedy, *The Rise and Fall of British Naval Mastery*, third edition, London, 1991, p. 380
[2] Roskill, *War at Sea*, vol. 1, p. 534
[3] PRO ADM 116/5001
[4] L. F. Ellis et al, *History of the Second World War, Victory in the West*, Vol. I, London, 1962, pp. 164–5, 179
[5] Quoted in *Ibid.*, pp. 191–2
[6] *Ibid.*, p. 191
[7] Quoted in Correlli Barnett, *Engage the Enemy More Closely*, London 2000, p. 610
[8] D. A. Rayner, *Escort Group Commander*, London, 1955, pp. 232–3
[9] Kilbracken, *Bring Back my Stringbag*, pp. 216–31
[10] Robertson, *Walker RN*, p. 207
[11] PRO ADM 1/12020, 178/237, 178/238
[12] Jones, *Heart of Oak*, p. 230,

Macdonald, *The Figurehead*, pp. 141–3, private information to the author, Cherry, *Yankee RN*, pp. 384–95
[13] PRO ADM 1/22967
[14] Cherry, *Yankee RN*, p. 391
[15] French
[16] Andrew Gordon, *The Rules of the Game*, passim
[17] Frances Margaret McGuire, *The Royal Australian Navy*, Melbourne, 1948, pp. 85, 91, 92, 339
[18] S. D. Waters, *The Royal New Zealand Navy*, Wellington, 1956.
[19] Gilbert Norman Tucker, *The Naval Service of Canada*, Ottawa, 1952, vol. II, pp. 275–83
[20] Donald Macintyre, *U-Boat Killer*, London, 1956, p. 78
[21] Marc Milner, *North Atlantic Run*, London and Toronto, 1995, pp. 159
[22] NMM, MS 93/008
[23] Julius Augustus Furer, *Administration of the Navy Department in World War II*, Washington, 1959, pp. 334–5
[24] *Ibid.*, p. 273
[25] Frederick S. Harrod, *Manning the New Navy, the Development of a Modern Naval Enlisted Force,*

1899–1940, Westport, Connecticut, 1978, pp. 80–2, 5–6, 77
[26] Furer, *Administration of the Navy Department in World War II*, pp. 262–5
[27] *Ibid.*, pp. 277, 307–9
[28] Samuel Eliot Morison, *History of United States Naval Operations in World War II*, vol. 15, *Supplement and General Index*, Boston, 1962, pp. 116–7
[29] *Hansard*, vol. 378, col. 1087
[30] PRO ADM — 1/15685
[31] *Oxford Dictionary of Quotations*, Oxford, 1996, p. 654
[32] Bigland, *Story of the WRNS*, p. 31
[33] Navy Records Society, vol. 137, *The Defeat of the Enemy Attack on Shipping*, ed. Eric Grove, 1997, NRS, p. xvi
[34] *Vanguard to Trident, op. cit.*, p. 180
[35] John Wells, *The Royal Navy – An Illustrated Social History*, Stroud, 1994, p. 276
[36] *Vanguard to Trident, op. cit.*, p. 253
[37] Barnett, *Engage the Enemy More Closely*, p. 881

Abbreviations

AA	Anti-aircraft
AB	Able-bodied (Seaman)
AFO	Admiralty Fleet Order
ATS	Auxiliary Territorial Service
CE	Civil Establishments
COCO	Combined Operations' Communications Officers
COPP	Combined Operations' Pilotage Parties
CS	Continuous Service
CTC	Combined Training Centre
CW	Commission and Warrant (Branch)
DNI	Director of Naval Intelligence
DNR	Director of Naval Recruiting
DPS	Director of Personnel Services
ERA	Engineer Room Artificers
FAA	Fleet Air Arm
HF/DF	High Frequency/Direction Finding
HO	Hostilities Only
HSD	Higher Submarine Detector
MAC	Merchant Aircraft Carrier
MNBDO	Mobile Naval Base Defence Organization
N	Naval (Branch)
NCO	Non-commissioned Officer
NQ	Not Qualified
OCTU	Officer Cadet Training Unit
PRO	Public Records Office
RDF	Radio Direction Finding
RNAS	Royal Naval Air Service
RNR	Royal Naval Reserve
RNTU	Royal Naval Training Units
RNVR	Royal Naval Volunteer Reserve
RSM	Regimental Sergeant Major
SBA	Sick Berth Attendants
SD	Submarine Detection
ST	Seaman Torpedomen
TAG	Telegraphist Air Gunners
WAAF	Women's Auxiliary Air Force
WAM	Wren Air Mechanics
WOSB	War Officer Selection Board
WO	Warrant Officer
WRNS	Women's Royal Naval Service
W/T	Wireless/Telegraphy

Bibliography

Personal Memoirs

Mark Amory (ed.) *The Letters of Evelyn Waugh* (London, 1980)

E. E. Baringer, *Alone on a Wide, Wide Sea* (London, 1995)

Stephanie Bastone, *Wren's Eye View* (Tunbridge Wells, 1994)

J. C. Beadle, *The Light Blue Lanyard, Fifty Years with 40 Commando* (Worcester, 1992)

John L. Bown, *Diary of a Matelot, 1942–45* (Lowesmoor, Worcester, 1991)

Alan Brundett, *Two Years in Ceylon – The Diary of a Naval Secretariat Member* (Lewes, 1996)

Robert Burgess and Roland Blackburn, *We Joined the Navy* (London, 1943)

James Callaghan, *Time and Chance* (London, 1987)

Ernle Chatfield, *The Navy and Defence* (London, 1942)

A. H. Cherry, *Yankee RN* (London, 1951)

W. S. Churchill, *The Second World War, Vol V, Closing the Ring* (London, 1952)

W. S. Churchill, *The Second World War, Vol VI, Triumph and Tragedy* (London, 1954)

W. S. Churchill, *The Second World War, Vol I, The Gathering Storm* (London, 1948)

R. 'Mike' Crosley, *They Gave me a Seafire* (Shrewsbury, 1986)

Angus Cunninghame Graham, *Random Naval Recollections* (Gartocharn, 1979)

John Davis, *The Stone Frigate* (London, 1947)

John W. Davies, *Jack, the Sailor with the Blue Eyes* (Bishop Auckland, 1995)

Eric Denton, *My Six Wartime Years in the Royal Navy* (London, 1999)

F. C. Dreyer, *The Sea Heritage* (London, 1955)

John Fernald, *Destroyer from America* (London, 1942)

Ted Ford, *The Nearly Man* (Wolverhampton, 1997)

Roy Fuller, *Home and Dry* (London, 1984)

Roy Fuller, *Vamp Till Ready* (London, 1982)

S. Gorley Putt, *Men Dressed and Seamen* (London, 1943)

Sidney Greenwood, *Stoker Greenwood's Navy* (Tunbridge Wells, 1983)

Albert H. Jones, *No Easy Choices* (Upton on Severn, 1999)

Tristan Jones, *Heart of Oak* (1984, reprinted Shrewsbury, 1997)

Fred Kellet, *A Flower for the Sea, a Fish for the Sky* (Carlisle, 1995)

John Kilbracken, *Bring Back My Stringbag* (reprinted London, 1996)

Ken Kimberley, *Heavo, Heavo, Lash up and Stow* (Kettering, 1999)

Dunstan Hadley, *Barracuda Pilot* (Shrewsbury, 1992)

Derek Hamilton Warner, *A Steward's Life in the Royal Navy* (Ilfracombe, 1990)

Tom Hayward and Keith Ashton, *The Royal Navy, Rum Rumour and a Pinch of Salt* (Glasgow, 1985)

F. S. Holt, *A Banker All at Sea* (Newtown, Australia, 1983)

Ludovic Kennedy, *On My Way up to the Club* (London, 1990)

Charles Lamb, *War in a Stringbag* (London, 1977)

Vera Laughton Mathews, *Blue Tapestry* (London, 1949)

Sir Roderick Macdonald, *The Figurehead* (Bishop Auckland, 1993)

Brendan A. Maher, *A Passage to Sword Beach* (Shrewsbury, 1996)

J. P. W. Mallalieu, *On Larkhill* (London, 1983)

Charles McAra, *Mainly in Minesweepers* (London, 1991)

Richard McKenna, *The Left-Handed Monkey Wrench* (Annapolis, 1984)

George Melly, *Rum, Bum and Concertina* (London 1977)

Jessica Mitford, *Hons and Rebels* (reprinted London, 1982)

Nicholas Monsarrat, *Three Corvettes* (reprinted London, 2000)

Ewen Montagu, *Beyond Top Secret U* (London, 1977)

H. K. Okram, *The Rogue's Yarn* (London, 1933)

Charles Owen, *No More Heroes* (London, 1975)

J. E. Pollit, *Marine to Mayor* (Exeter, nd, c. 1989)

H. J. C. Spencer, *Ordinary Naval Airmen* (Tunbridge Wells, 1992)

Joffre Swales, *The Life and Music of RMB X 1522* (Haverfordwest, 1993)

Joseph H. Wellings, Hattendorf (ed.), *On His Majesty's Service* (Newport, 1983)

John Whelan, *Home is the Sailor* (London, 1957)

Geoffrey Willans, *One Eye on the Clock* (London, 1943)

Edward Young, *One of Our Submarines* (London, 1952)

Contemporary Official Documents

Admiralty, *Monthly Anti-Submarine Reports* (October, 1944)

Admiralty, *Manual of Seamanship, Vol I* (London, 1937, reprinted 1940, *passim*)

Admiralty, Naval Training Department, *History of the Y Scheme* (London, 1946)

Admiralty, *Royal Naval Handbook of Field Training* (London, 1920)

Admiralty, *The Navy and the Y Scheme* (London, 1944)

Gunnery Pocket Book, BR224/45 (1945)

Information and Instructions for the Guidance of all V/S Instructors (NMM pamphlet collection)

King's Regulations and Admiralty Instructions (1938 edition)

Kings Regulations and Admiralty Instructions (1939 edition)

King's Regulations and Admiralty Instructions (1943 edition)

Manual for Officers' Stewards, BR 97

Navy List (April, 1945)

Captain J. N. Pelly, *An Officer's Aide Memoire, HMS King Alfred* (NMM pamphlet collection, September 1943)

Queen's Regulations and Admiralty Instructions (1862 edition)

The Royal Navy as a Career (1937 edition)

Training of Artificer Apprentices, BR 91 (1936)

United States Navy, Bureau of Naval Personnel, *Naval Orientation* (1945)

Official Histories

Amphibious Warfare Headquarters, *The History of the Combined Operations Organisations, 1940–45* (London, 1956)

Central Statistical Office, *Fighting with Figures* (London, 1995)

J. L. S. Coulter (ed.), *Medical History of the Second World War, The Royal Naval Medical Services, Vol I, Administration* (London, 1954)

W.A.B Douglas, *Official History of the Royal Canadian Air Force, Vol II, The Creation of a National Air*

Michael Howard, *Grand Strategy, Vol IV, August 1942–September 1943* (London, 1972)

Force (Toronto, 1986)

Ministry of Information, *His Majesty's Minesweepers* (London, 1943)

Samuel Elliot Morrison, *History of United States Naval Operations in World War Two, Vol XI, The Invasion of France and Germany* (Oxford, 1957)

H. M. D. Parker, *Manpower: A Study of Wartime Policy and Administration* (London, 1957)

World War Two Histories

Richard Baker, *The Terror of Tobermory* (second edition, Edinburgh, 2002)

David Jefferson, *Coastal Forces at War* (Yeovil, 1996)

Derek Howes (ed.), *Radar at Sea, The Royal Navy in World War Two* (London, 1993)

J. Lennox Kerr and Wilfred Granville, *The R.N.V.R., a Record of Achievement* (London, 1957)

J. Lennox Kerr and David James, *Wavy Navy, by Some Who Served* (London, 1950)

Paul Lund and Harry Ludlam, *The War of the Landing Craft* (London, 1976)

L. E. H. Maund, *Assault from the Sea* (London, 1949)

Raymond Mitchell, *They Did What was Asked of Them* (Poole, 1996)

Roy Terry, *Women in Khaki* (London, 1988)

Peter Young, *Assault from the Sea* (London, 1989)

Other Naval Histories

Rodney Agar and Murray Johnstone (eds), *Hold Fast the Heritage* (Fontwell, 1994)

Eileen Bigland, *The Story of the W.R.N.S.* (London, 1946)

Gregory Clark, *Doc – 100 Year History of the Sick Berth Branch* (London, 1984)

Norman Friedman, *British Carrier Aviation* (London, 1988)

Willem Hackmann, *Seek and Strike* (London, 1984)

P. K. Kemp (ed.), *Navy Records Society, Vol CVI, The Papers of Admiral Sir John Fisher* (Vol. II, 1964)

James D. Ladd, *The Royal Marines, 1919 – 1980, an Authorised History* (London, 1980)

Brian Lavery (ed.), *Shipboard Life and Organisation* (Navy Records Society, 1998)

Paul Lund and Harry Ludlam, *Out Sweeps!* (London, 1978)

Andrew Mollo (ed.), *Uniforms and Insignia of the Navies of World War II*

Sir Nicholas Nicolas, *The Dispatches and Letters of Lord Nelson* (reprinted London, 1998)

Anthony J. Perrett, *Royal Marines in Wales* (Portsmouth, 1992)

Nikolaus Pevsner, *The Buildings of England, South Devon* (Harmondsworth, 1952)

Stephen W. Roskill, *Naval Policy Between the Wars, Vol II* (London, 1976)

John Wells, *Whaley – The Story of HMS Excellent* (Portsmouth, 1980)

Articles

British Machine Tool Engineering (January–June 1945)

G. D. Franklin, *A Breakdown in Communications: Britain's Over Estimation of Asdic's Capabilities in the 1930's* (*Mariners Mirror*, Vol. 84)

Christopher Green, *Scheme of Complement for Captain*

Class Frigates (Mariners Mirror, February 2000)

Royal Institution of Naval Architects, *Selected Papers on British Warship Design* (London, 1983)

Other

Brassey's Naval Annual, 1906

Brassey's Naval Annual, 1919

Brassey's Naval Annual, 1939

Ian Brown et al, *20th Century Defences in Britain* (York, 1995)

John Gifford, *The Buildings of Scotland, Highlands and Islands* (London, 1992)

M. Gilbert (ed.), *The Churchill War Papers* (London, 1993)

G. Granville Slack and M. M. Wells, *Liability for National Service* (second edition, London, 1943)

Mass Observation Archive Report, no. 886–7, University of Sussex, 1941

Trevor Royle, *The Best Years of Their Lives* (London, 1986)

Evelyn Waugh, *No Abiding City,* Vol. II, (London, 1993)

Picture Credits

Page 11 Royal Naval Museum
Page 15 © Crown Copyright 2004. Published by permission of the Controller of Her Majesty's Stationery Office (www.ukho.gov.uk)
Page 16 Royal Air Force Museum [5672-12]
Page 17 Royal Naval Museum
Page 19 Getty Images/Hulton Archive
Page 32 Royal Naval Museum
Page 35 (top and bottom) With kind permission from Silver Link Publishing Ltd. © Ken Kimberley
Page 40 Imperial War Museum [A29904]
Page 50 Mirrorpix
Page 53 With kind permission from Silver Link Publishing Ltd. © Ken Kimberley
Page 56 Royal Naval Museum
Page 66 Royal Naval Museum
Page 75 Imperial War Museum [A2237]
Page 76 Royal Naval Museum
Page 79 (top and bottom) © Crown Copyright 2004. Published by permission of the Controller of Her Majesty's Stationery Office (www.ukho.gov.uk)
Page 88 © Crown Copyright 2004. Published by permission of the Controller of Her Majesty's Stationery Office (www.ukho.gov.uk)
Page 89 © Crown Copyright 2004. Published by permission of the Controller of Her Majesty's Stationery Office (www.ukho.gov.uk)
Page 94 © Crown Copyright 2004. Published by permission of the Controller of Her Majesty's Stationery Office (www.ukho.gov.uk)
Page 96 © Crown Copyright 2004. Published by permission of the Controller of Her Majesty's Stationery Office (www.ukho.gov.uk)
Page 98 (top and bottom) © Crown Copyright 2004. Published by per-

mission of the Controller of Her Majesty's Stationery Office (www.ukho.gov.uk)
Page 101 Mirrorpix
Page 115 © Crown Copyright 2004. Published by permission of the Controller of Her Majesty's Stationery Office (www.ukho.gov.uk)
Page 121 Mirrorpix
Page © Crown Copyright 2004. Published by permission of the Controller of Her Majesty's Stationery Office (www.ukho.gov.uk)
Page 132 [Copyright holder not found]
Page 135 Imperial War Museum [A24576]
Page 136 Imperial War Museum [A24562]
Page 142 Royal Naval Museum
Page 150 © Crown Copyright 2004. Published by permission of the Controller of Her Majesty's Stationery Office (www.ukho.gov.uk)
Page 154 Getty Images/Hulton Archive
Page 161 Imperial War Museum [A9145]
Page 179 Imperial War Museum [A18367]
Page 185 Imperial War Museum [A18248]
Page 187 Imperial War Museum [A3165]
Page 193 (top and bottom) Royal Marines Museum
Page 197 Peter MacKarell
Page 203 Imperial War Museum [AD15470]
Page 227 Royal Naval Museum
Page 230 Imperial War Museum [A5063]
Page 231 Imperial War Museum [A3205]
Page 244 Imperial War Museum [A5242]
Page 248 (top) Imperial War

Museum [A9144]
Page 250 © Crown Copyright 2004. Published by permission of the Controller of Her Majesty's Stationery Office (www.ukho.gov.uk)
Page 252 © Crown Copyright 2004. Published by permission of the Controller of Her Majesty's Stationery Office (www.ukho.gov.uk)
Page 258 © Crown Copyright 2004. Published by permission of the Controller of Her Majesty's Stationery Office (www.ukho.gov.uk)

The following are NMM photographic references.

Pictures may be ordered from the Picture Library, National Maritime Museum, Greenwich, London, SE10 9NF (tel. 020 8312 6600).
All © National Maritime Museum, London.

Frontispiece: AD26510
Page 8 58/3267
Page 25 Paddy Mounter
Page 62 Paddy Mounter
Page 70 Paddy Mounter
Page 86 PU9715; 90 P23008
Page 104 Paddy Mounter
Page 111 PZ0539
Page 138 N11780
Page 140 PT3023
Page 145 PT2893
Page 189 AD6879
Page 217 AD24092
Page 234 AD26510
Page 259 AD9888

Index